Numeracy and Accounting

A Business Education Council Course
National Level

Contributing authors:
Ron Jones, BA(Econ.)
Frank Owen, BSc(Econ.), AMBIM
Joe Townsley, B.Com, FCA
Frank Wood, BSc(Econ.), FCA

LONGMAN
London and New York

First Published 1979
Second Impression March 1983
Third Impression June 1984
Fourth Impression July 1985

Set in 10 pt Times series
Produced by Longman Group (FE) Ltd
Printed in Hong Kong

Preface

This book has been prepared for the Business Education Council (B.E.C.) common core module Numeracy and Accounting at the National Award Level.

The approach adopted by B.E.C. favours an integrated approach to course teaching. It is a requirement of their courses that students should be involved in cross modular assignments of various kinds. Within this context the module syllabus for Numeracy and Accounting requires that students be taught basic numerical skills involving for example arithmetic algebra and statistics, and at the same time be introduced to the framework and techniques of accounting.

In this book we have relied on our combined experience of teaching the subjects for many years in reinforcing our belief that the basic elements of numeracy and those of accounting need to be taught in clear and discrete units. There is no theoretical reason for or practical advantage in doing other than this. However commonsense would predicate phasing the teaching in such a way that for example students who start the course without adequate numerate skills must first remedy this deficiency before commencing Accounting. Similarly at more advanced stages the order in which topics are dealt with needs to be carefully scheduled.

The book has thus in effect been prepared in two sections. Chapters two to sixteen cover Accounting topics which are dealt with in logical order. Chapters seventeen to thirty one similarly cover the Numeracy section. At all points of contact, examples and illustrations have been introduced to emphasise intra modular links. However the two sections must be permitted to develop their subject matter in a logical and consistent manner, for the material they contain. The intra modular elements are secondary to a proper academic development of the subjects. Their place is to reinforce learning rather than interfere with it and this we hope to have achieved.

TO THE STUDENT

This book contains a number of exercises after each chapter. About half of them have answers at the back of the book. You will not be helping yourself at all if you merely copy out the answers which have been provided. You will merely be deceiving yourself — and nobody else.

Contents

Chapter 1

Numeracy and Accounting

Learning Objectives:

At the end of your study of this chapter you should:

1. **know something about the meaning and use of Numeracy and Accounting,**
2. **be aware of various ways that historic social and economic development has influenced accounting,**
3. **be aware that accounting and numerate information is intended for different groups of users.**

What is Numeracy?

Numeracy is a word which describes an ability to count and reckon in numbers. This ability is the foundation of modern life based on technology science and commerce. If you think of what would disappear if people were not able to calculate, measure, add or subtract then in fact all our homes, places of work, clothing and food as we know them would disappear. There would be no music or television. Numbers in themselves would not of course provide these things on their own. They are simply tools which are used by men to convert things from their natural state into a form which is more convenient for man's use, by weighing, measuring and calculating their properties.

Numeracy in fact describes the ability to use numbers in a way that is proper and useful. There is little point in being able to add up if you cannot apply this ability to add up a bill which you owe, or to count the number of eggs you are selling if you are a farmer. If you cannot do this you are likely to be cheated out of your possessions.

This module links together the teaching of skills which you need to have with numbers, with accounting which is one of the applications in business where skill with numbers is important. You can think of this in terms of sport. Basic skills required are general physical fitness, muscular development, coordination, balance and so on. The basic skills need to be developed in particularly specialised ways if for instance you want to play soccer, where emphasis will be needed on ball playing ability. The skills on their own however are not sufficient, they can only be applied if the person concerned fits into the team and understands the tactics of the game.

So it is with numeracy. An ability to use numbers is an essential skill. For business purposes special aspects of numeracy need to be emphasised like ball-playing for soccer. Finally your basic numerate skills need to be applied to the team requirements of the organisation and its business. Accounting is one important aspect of a business which needs the skills of numeracy.

NUMERACY IS AN ABILITY TO USE NUMBERS ACCURATELY AND IN THE PROPER MANNER FOR THE REQUIRED PURPOSE.

What is accounting?

Accounting is concerned to give people information of an economic type about businesses or organisations. Economic information basically means that it is information capable of being measured in money terms. For example the amount a business spent last year on wages is economic information. Telling people that all the employees were very happy is not economic information because there is no precise way of measuring happiness in money units.

Because information of a non economic sort is often very useful accounting reports are frequently issued with supplements containing more general material. This helps to overcome the limitation of accounting being expressed in purely economic data.

The information included in accounting statements is of two sorts. Firstly there is information about the resources used. For most organisations the resources cover a very wide range of items. On the one hand there will be things with a very long life such as land and buildings and at the other extreme small items like elastic bands and ball point pens. It would be possible to list thousands of individual items that a large business includes in its resources. Accounting will also list the obligations an organisation incurs in obtaining its resources. For example if someone lends £5000 cash to a business accounting is concerned to record both the new cash resource and quite separately the obligation to repay the lender.

The second type of information in accounting statements is concerned with the organisation's performance. This is basically a measurement of the changes that have taken place between two points in time. For accounting measurement one year is the normal time span. For commercial and industrial organisations the changes are expressed in a statement which shows whether the business has made a profit or loss. The profit or loss figure is a very important measure of success. Virtually everybody who has anything to do with a firm will want to know how profitable it is. Investors, employees and government are all concerned with this accounting index of performance.

Accounting is still useful for organisations which do not operate for profit. Organisations of this type such as the National Health Service still need to measure their resources and to assess performance over time.

ACCOUNTING COMMUNICATES INFORMATION OF AN ECONOMIC NATURE WITH PARTICULAR REFERENCE TO THE RESOURCES AND THE PERFORMANCE OF AN ORGANISATION.

How has accounting developed?

Accounting methods have changed over many hundreds of years to reflect the nature of the organisations being accounted for. A small farmer in the reign of Elizabeth I would have little need for accounts as he could probably remember all his resources because he lived amongst them. He could also assess his performance from year to year by inspection of his herd and crops and with reference to his memory. It is also likely that he could neither read, write, nor calculate with numbers. The steward who managed the estates of a large landowner was in a different position. The landowner would expect the steward to be able to account to him both for all the resources of the estate and the performance in managing resources over time. This type of situation demands a proper method of accounting because the estates could be large and the transactions many. Also the landlord might be absent over long periods. Proper accounts were essential then as now to provide a check on honest management. Stewardship is just as important for the manager of a large modern corporation who acts on behalf of absent owners.

The other situation which gave rise to a need for proper accounts was trading ventures where more than one man was sharing in the profits or losses of the business. Indeed the basic framework of modern accounting started in fifteenth century Italy. The merchants of Venice and the other Italian states would charter a vessel between them which they would send to the East to buy spices and other scarce commodities. The risks of such ventures were high but the rewards were correspondingly great. Human nature then as now tends to be suspicious of fraud where large amounts of money are involved. Therefore a system of accounting which fairly recorded and reported the economic results of the business had to be devised. The system of recording events known as 'Double entry' has stood the test of time for five hundred years although the ways in which it is applied have changed a great deal.

The Industrial Revolution and the changes it led to in the organisation of society gave rise to the next major development in accounting. It was the need to collect large amounts of capital to build large units such as railways in the 1830's which led to the development of the modern concept of the limited liability company. The main feature of this type of organisation is that many people can invest an amount of money in a company by buying 'shares'. Although some shareholders may be managers of the firm particularly in small firms, the majority will not, especially in large companies. Whilst a senior manager has access to whatever information is available, a shareholder does not. The reason for this is that it is considered likely to be harmful to a business if detailed information on its affairs were available to its competitors. If shareholders could obtain any information they wanted, then competitors would only have to buy a few shares to obtain what information they needed. The conflict of interest here is vital for accounting. On the one hand the owner of shares must have enough information to ensure that the management carry out their function honestly and efficiently; on the other hand the company will need to preserve some confidential information.

4

The company law enactments which have been passed by Parliament throughout a century or more have reflected changes in society's attitudes and the experience gained with time. Accounting requirements for companies have grown substantially both in quantity and in sophistication.

ACCOUNTING DEVELOPED AS A RECORD OF STEWARDSHIP FOR EXAMPLE WHERE AN OWNER EMPLOYED SOMEONE ELSE TO MANAGE HIS PROPERTY. WHERE A NUMBER OF PEOPLE COMBINE TOGETHER IN A BUSINESS VENTURE THE NEED FOR ACCOUNTING INFORMATION IS ESPECIALLY IMPORTANT. THIS NEED IS OF GREAT IMPORTANCE FOR MODERN COMPANIES.

Who is Accounting information for?

Traditionally we are accustomed to preserving information about our personal wealth and income as private rather than public knowledge. There is nothing to stop us telling anybody what we like about our own affairs but nothing in the UK requires private individuals to make public disclosure of their wealth or income. This is not true however in our dealings with the government. They are entitled to ask us for information they require about all our wealth and income in order to tax us. Many small businesses prepare accounts largely for the benefit of the tax authorities.

The position of limited companies and their shareholders has already been mentioned. The accounts of limited companies are required by law and are basically prepared for the shareholders in their capacity as owners but with specific provisions to safeguard the creditors of the business. However as time has passed more and more people have become involved in the need to obtain accounting information. Limited Companies have become the most popular form of organisation in commerce and industry. Some companies are very small family concerns; others have become huge organisations operating internationally. Increasingly there has been recognition that there may be greater need for special disclosure particularly from the very large firms, who wield considerable economic power and employ important resources both of labour and capital.

In addition to stewardship information therefore there is a general movement towards disclosure of information specifically for employees, government and the public at large. The sort of Accounting which is aimed at providing information to people outside management is called Financial Accounting.

So far all the emphasis has been given to describing accounts which a company is required by law to produce for those outside who do not have managements' access to inside information. In a large and complex modern business it poses quite a problem simply to provide management with enough of the right information to manage the business properly. As we said earlier a small farmer can probably remember most of what he needs to manage the operations of his farm. Very soon however if the business grows this becomes impossible and proper records need to be kept so that proper decisions can be taken. This type of accounting which is for use inside the business is called Management Accounting.

ACCOUNTING WHICH IS FOR THOSE OUTSIDE THE BUSINESS IS CALLED FINANCIAL ACCOUNTING. ACCOUNTING WHICH IS PREPARED TO HELP MANAGERS RUN THEIR BUSINESS EFFICIENTLY IS CALLED MANAGEMENT ACCOUNTING.

Assignment Exercises

Assignment Exercises followed by the letter x do NOT have answers shown at the back of the book.

1.1x Complete the following sentences by listing the missing words on a piece of paper:-
   (a) Numeracy is an ability to use ____ accurately and in the proper manner for the required ____.
   (b) Accounting is concerned to give people information of an ____ type.
   (c) Economic information means information that is capable of measurement in ____.
   (d) The ____ of a business includes items with long lives and short lives.
   (e) The main aspect of performance measured by accounting statements results in a statement of change showing either a ____ or ____.

1.2 Complete the following references by listing the missing words on a piece of paper:-
   (a) Accounts are required as a check on managers by the legal owners. This type of accounting is described as ____ accounting.
   (b) Joint Proprietors of a business need accounts in order to ____ the economic results of the venture between them.
   (c) In ____ the owners of shares in a business may be quite distinct from the managers.
   (d) If shareholders could obtain all available information about a business this might help ____ and harm the interests of the business.
   (e) Recent developments in accounting have moved towards greater disclosure. In addition to shareholders there are movements to make more information available to ____, ____, and ____.

1.3　In the following statements write down whether you think they are true or false.

(a) Accounting for those outside the business is called Financial Accounting.

(b) Management Accounting primarily provides information to shareholders.

(c) A shareholding in a limited company gives the owner a right to manage the business.

(d) Many small businesses prepare accounts largely for the benefit of the tax authorities.

(e) Only senior managers may be shareholders in limited companies.

(f) Only profit making organisations need to measure their resources and performance.

(g) Accounting is concerned with information that is capable of money measurement.

(h) Numeracy is simply another word to describe accounting.

1.4x　Imagine that a close relative has recently died and left you as proprietor of a retail newsagents business. In the will you are asked to retain the services of the manager who has run the business for the past few years. Think about the things that a newsagent does and make a list of the things that ought to be checked in order to make sure that the business is run honestly and well.

1.5x　Think about your favourite professional football team and estimate some of the accounting information about it. How much has the club paid for players? How much are the players worth if sold on transfer? What are the attendances like at games, and what therefore all the receipts from the crowd likely to be?

What are other expenses such as wages likely to be?

When you have done this list the ways the club management might use the information.

Chapter 2

The Accounting Equation

Learning Objectives:

At the end of your study of this chapter you should understand:

1. the meaning in accounting use of Capital, Assets and Liabilities,
2. the basic way in which an accounting Balance Sheet is constructed.

The whole of financial accounting is based on the accounting equation. We can state this equation in very simple terms, for the basic idea underlying all financial accounting is very logical and very simple. You will appreciate that for a firm to exist it will need resources, and that the resources will have had to be supplied to the firm by someone. These resources are known as Assets, and quite obviously some of them will have been supplied by the owner of the business. The total of the amount of resources supplied by him is known as capital. If we assume that in fact the only resources supplied have been from the owner, then the following equation would be correct.

$$\text{Capital} = \text{Assets}$$

However, normally some of the assets will have been supplied by someone other than the owner. The indebtedness of the firm for these resources is known as liabilities. In such a case we can now express the equation as

$$\text{Capital} + \text{Liabilities} = \text{Assets}$$

The totals of each of the two sides of the equation equal each other. You can see that on one side of the equation are the resources possessed whilst the other side shows the sources from which the resources were obtained. This means that the equality of the totals of the two sides will always hold true, it will not matter how many transactions are entered into, nor matter how long the firm exists, the totals of the two sides will always be the same as each other.

Assets consists of such things as property of all kinds, machinery, motor vehicles, office equipment, warehouse & shop fittings, stocks of goods, benefits such as debts owing by customers, money in a bank account and cash in hand. That is not a full list, but it covers most things and will be enough for you to know at the moment.

Liabilities will consist of such items as goods and services supplied to the firm, also for any loans made to the firm.

Capital is also often known as the owner's equity or net worth.

Once we start to put figures into the accounting equation we usually call it a Balance Sheet. At this point you may wonder why it has that name, but if you will bear with us for the time being we can easily explain that in chapter 7. It is not the first accounting record to be made, but it is the most convenient place to start to look at accounting.

Balance Sheets and the effect of business transactions

(a) *The Introduction of Capital*

Let us now look at a man, R. Andrews, starting up a new business. On 1 July 19-5 he puts £10,000 into a bank account for the business. The balance sheet would be drawn up as follows:

R. ANDREWS
Balance Sheet as at 1 July 19-5

	£	Assets	£
Capital	10,000	Cash at Bank	10,000
	10,000		10,000

(b) *Purchase of an asset by cheque*

On 2 July 19-5 Andrews buys equipment for £4,000, paying for it by cheque. This means the cash at bank will be reduced, and a new asset, equipment will appear.

R. ANDREWS
Balance Sheet as at 2 July 19-5

	£	Assets	£
Capital	10,000	Equipment	4,000
		Cash at Bank	6,000
	10,000		10,000

(c) *The purchase of an asset and the incurring of a liability*

On 7 July 19-5 Andrews buys some goods for £2,000 for resale from T. Morgan, agreeing to pay for them within the next 4 weeks. The effect of this is that a new asset, stock of goods, is acquired, at the same time a liability for the goods is created. A person to whom we owe money for goods is known in accounting language as a creditor.

R. ANDREWS
Balance Sheet as at 7 July 19-5

Capital and Liabilities	£	*Assets*	£
Capital	10,000	Equipment	4,000
Creditor	2,000	Stock of Goods	2,000
		Cash at Bank	6,000
	12,000		12,000

(d) *Sale of an asset on credit*

On 15 July 19-5 goods which had cost £500 were sold to S. Ford for the same amount. The sale was on credit, which means that Ford took the goods on this day, but he will pay for them at a future date. In accounting language a person who owes money to the firm is known as a debtor. With this transaction there is a reduction in one asset, stock of goods, and the creation of a new asset, debtor.

R. ANDREWS
Balance Sheet as at 15 July 19-5

Capital and Liabilities	£	Assets	£
Capital	10,000	Equipment	4,000
Creditor	2,000	Stock of Goods	1,500
		Debtor	500
		Cash at Bank	6,000
	12,000		12,000

(e) *Sale of an asset, payment being made immediately*

On 20 July 19-5 goods which had cost £200 were sold to J. Firth for the same amount, Firth paying for them immediately by cheque. In this case one asset stock of goods, is reduced, whilst another asset, bank, is increased.

R. ANDREWS
Balance Sheet as at 20 July 19-5

Capital and Liabilities	£	Assets	£
Capital	10,000	Equipment	4,000
Creditor	2,000	Stock of Goods	1,300
		Debtor	500
		Cash at Bank	6,200
	12,000		12,000

(f) *Collection of an asset*

On 24 July 19-5, S. Ford, who owed Andrews £500, makes a part payment of £300 by cheque. This reduces one asset, debtor, and increases another asset, bank.

R. ANDREWS
Balance Sheet at at 24 July 19-5

Capital and Liabilities	£	Assets	£
Capital	10,000	Equipment	4,000
Creditor	2,000	Stock of Goods	1,300
		Debtor	200
		Cash at Bank	6,500
	12,000		12,000

(g) *Payment of a liability*

On 27 July 19-5 Andrews pays a cheque of £1,500 in part payment of the amount owing to the creditor. The asset of bank is thereby reduced, and the liability of creditor is also reduced.

R. ANDREWS
Balance Sheet as at 27 July 19-5

Capital and Liabilities	£	Assets	£
Capital	10,000	Equipment	4,000
Creditor	500	Stock of Goods	1,300
		Debtor	200
		Cash at Bank	5,000
	10,500		10,500

You can see that each transaction, (a) to (g) inclusive, has affected two items. Sometimes it has changed two assets by increasing one and reducing another. At other times it will have a different reaction.

A table showing a typical transaction with all of the possible changes in the composition of assets, capital and liabilities is now given.

Examples of Transactions

1.	Owner pays more capital into the bank	Increase Asset (Bank)	Increase Capital
2.	Buys goods on credit	Increase Asset (Stock of Goods)	Increase Liability (Creditors)
3.	Buys goods by cheque	Increase Asset (Stock of Goods)	Reduces Asset (Bank)
4.	Pay creditor by cheque	Reduce Asset (Bank)	Reduce Liability (Creditors)
5.	Owner takes money from the business bank account for his personal use	Reduces Asset (Bank)	Reduces Capital
6.	Owner pays creditor with his private money outside the firm	Reduces Liability (Creditors)	Increases Capital

You can see that the equality of the total of Assets with the total of Capital and Liabilities has always been maintained. We can show the examples just given, 1 to 6, in the form of a table.

Transaction No.	Assets	Liabilities and Capital	Effect on balance sheet totals
1	+	+	Each side added to equally
2	+	+	Each side added to equally
3	+ −		A plus and a minus, both on the assets side, cancelling out each other
4	−	−	Each side has an equal reduction
5	−	−	Each side has an equal reduction
6		+ −	A plus and a minus, both on the same side, cancelling out each other

Assignment Exercises

Note: Assignments with the suffixed letter 'x' do *not* have answers shown at the back of the book.

2.1 Complete the gaps in the following table:

	Assets £	Liabilities £	Capital £
(a)	16,800	2,300	?
(b)	?	20,500	14,700
(c)	165,450	?	30,150
(d)	?	17,200	44,850
(e)	222,000	147,000	?

2.2x Complete the gaps in the following table:

	Assets £	Liabilities £	Capital £
(a)	?	14,320	12,940
(b)	165,400	?	45,000
(c)	198,000	79,500	?
(d)	85,600	?	17,800
(e)	?	145,600	77,000

2.3 You are to list the following items under separate headings of liabilities and assets:

Office Equipment
Cash in Hand
Buildings
Shop Fittings
Creditors for goods

2.4x List the following items under the separate headings of assets and liabilities:

Loan from J. Clarke
Motor Vehicles
Machinery
Debtors
Owing to bank
Premises
Stock of goods

2.5 You are required to complete the columns to show the effect of the following transactions:

Effect upon
Assets   Liabilities

(a) A debtor pays us £560 in cash
(b) Bought goods on credit £760
(c) Sold goods on credit £900
(d) Bought motor van paying £4,000 by cheque
(e) A debtor pays us £920 by cheque
(f) L. Wilson lends us £2,000 by cheque
(g) The proprietor puts another £10,000 into the firm's bank
(h) Goods sold by us on credit returned to us £55
(i) Bought motor van on credit £4,500
(j) Bought goods for cash £70

2.6x Complete the columns to show the effect of the following transactions:

Effect upon
Assets   Liabilities

(a) We paid a creditor £350 by cheque
(b) We return goods costing £15 to a supplier whose bill had not been paid
(c) A debtor pays us £550 by cheque
(d) We repay by cheque £200 part of money originally lent to us by J. Carr
(e) Bought shop premises by cheque £20,000
(f) Goods sold by us on credit now returned to us £44
(g) The owner takes out £200 cash for his personal use
(h) Bought goods paying by cash £100
(i) Bought office equipment on credit £2,500
(j) Proprietor pays a creditor £600 from private money outside the firm

2.7 Draw up A. Manchester's balance sheet from the following:

	£
Capital	23,750
Debtors	4,950
Motor Vehicles	5,700
Creditors	2,450
Fixtures	5,500
Stock of goods	8,800
Cash at bank	1,250

2.8x You are to draw up J. York's balance sheet from the details now listed:

	£
Loan from T. Leeds	2,900
Cash at Bank	1,640
Stock of Goods	5,420
Cash in Hand	140
Creditors	1,360
Debtors	2,450
Motor Van	5,000
Shop Fittings	2,850

The figure of capital has to be ascertained by you.

2.9 T. Chorley starts a business. Before he actually starts to sell anything he has bought, Fixtures £2,000, Motor Vehicle £5,000 and a stock of goods £3,500. Although he has paid in full for the fixtures and the motor vehicle, he still owes £1,400 for some of the goods. J. Preston had lent him £3,000. Chorley, after the above has £2,800 in the business bank account and £100 cash in hand. You are required to calculate his capital.

2.10x M. Wigan started up a new business with capital of £10,000. Before he actually sold anything he bought Office Equipment £2,850 and Shop Fixtures of £3,600. He had also bought goods costing £8,000, but he had not yet paid in full for them. He had borrowed £2,000 from C. Fleetwood. His business bank account, after the above transactions had £850 in it, and he had £50 cash in hand. You are to ascertain the money still owing by him for goods.

2.11 P. Portsmouth has the following items in his balance sheet as on 30 April 19-4: Capital £18,900; Loan from T. Andover £2,000; Creditors £1,600; Fixtures £3,500; Motor Vehicle £4,200; Stock of Goods £4,950; Debtors £3,280; Cash at Bank £6,450; Cash in Hand £120.

During the first week of May 19-4 Portsmouth:-
(i)   Paid a creditor £700 by cheque.
(ii) Bought extra stock of goods £770 on credit.
(iii) One of the debtors paid us £280 in cash.
(iv) Paid a creditor £80 in cash.
(v)   Bought extra fixtures by cheque £1,000.

You are to draw up a balance sheet as on 7 May 19-4 after the above transactions have been completed.

2.12x F. Hampshire has the following balance sheet as at 31 October 19-3:

Capital and Liabilities		Assets	
Capital	35,060	Buildings	11,000
Loan from C. Bognor	3,800	Machinery	6,380
Creditors	2,970	Motor Vehicle	5,120
		Stock of Goods	8,000
		Debtors	6,310
		Cash at Bank	4,680
		Cash in Hand	340
	£41,830		£41,830

14

The following transactions occur in the first week of November:
(i) Repaid part of Bognor's loan by cheque £1,600.
(ii) A debtor paid us in cash £150.
(iii) Bought extra stock of goods on credit £3,450.
(iv) Bought machinery paying by cheque £770.
(v) Paid a creditor by cheque £420.
(vi) A debtor paid us by cheque £1,260.

Draw up a balance sheet as at 7 November 19-3 after the transactions have been completed.

Chapter 3

The Double Entry System

Learning Objectives:

At the end of your study of this chapter you should:

1. **understand how the accounting equation is used in a system known as double entry,**

2. **be able to enter simple items into the double entry system.**

In the previous chapter you have seen that each transaction has affected two items, be they assets, capital or liabilities. Consequently, if accounting is to show the full effect of a transaction, it cannot do so if it shows the effect on one item only, it is vital that the effect on both items is shown. To satisfy this need the double entry system was devised to show this twofold effect. The name double entry was given to the method because it involves entering the transaction twice, once to show the effect on one item, and a second entry to show the effect upon the other item.

You were shown the effects of different transactions in chapter two, by seeing a new balance sheet drawn up after each transaction had been concluded. But if you think about it, would such a balance sheet tell you *everything* that you would want to know? Well, for a start, it would tell you how much money was owing to the business, but it wouldn't tell you who actually owed the money, nor would it say how long it has been owing. Similarly with creditors, it would only give a total figure and nothing else, and similar remarks could be made about the other assets and liabilities. It was easy to draw up a fresh balance sheet after each entry, because there were only a few entries. If there had been hundreds of transactions each day then the task would become more or less impossible. In fact, because of the work involved, balance sheets are drawn up only periodically; certainly once a year as a minimum, but sometimes half-yearly, quarterly or monthly.

The double entry system divides the pages into two halves. The left-hand side is called the "debit" side and the right-hand side is the "credit" side. These are accounting terms, and you would be well advised not to confuse them with normal language use of the words "debit" and "credit", as they are not comparable. For the capital, each asset, and each liability an account (meaning 'a history of') is opened. There will accordingly be an Equipment Account (being the history of the equipment), a Motor Van account (being the history of the motor vans) and so on. Each account should be on a separate page, the title of the account being written across the top of the account at the centre.

You might have guessed already that the two sides of the page represent the two sides of the accounting equation, and you would have been correct. The debit side is taken for assets, and the credit side for capital and liabilities. The original reason for the choice of the debit side for assets, and the credit side for capital and liabilities, is not now known. It simply happened to be the choice made by the Venetian merchants over 500 years ago who were the first business men to use double entry.

Assets therefore appear in an account on the left hand side, but in a balance sheet they appear on the right hand side. Capital and liabilities appear in their respective accounts on the right hand side, but in a balance sheet on the left hand side. Certainly for students it would be easier for learning purposes if assets in both the balance sheets and in accounts kept to the same side, similarly with liabilities. This is true in many countries in the world, but Britain does the opposite.

If we wanted to enter an addition to an asset in its account we would simply make the entry on the debit side of the account. This then leads to what should be done for a reduction in an asset. You will eventually realise that a lot of things in accounting are done simply because it is easier to do it in that way, less time is used up and the accounting system will accordingly cost less to operate. It isn't always easy for a student at an early stage to see that using a particular method is easier. This usually stems from the fact that in exercises in a book only a few items need entering, but in a real business this can amount to thousands of items. What seems to be just as easy for a few items does not necessarily appear to be as easy when there are a few thousand items. Well, we can now tell you that a reduction in an asset could be shown on the debit side and deducted from the other items already on that side. Alternatively, suppose that a reduction was shown instead by an entry in the credit side, then which would be the easiest? We can tell you that the Venetian merchants, correctly so for ease of operation, chose to show the reduction of an asset as an entry on the credit side of the asset account. It is really a different arithmetical way of showing subtractions. Instead of showing a subtraction as a deduction on the line underneath on the same side of the page, it is instead shown as an item on the opposite side of the page.

For Capital and Liability accounts, being the opposite side of the accounting equation, the opposite applies. For them, an increase in an item is shown by an entry on the credit side of the account, a reduction being shown on the debit side.

The rules can be summarised:

	Entry in the account
To increase an asset	Debit the asset account
To increase a liability	Credit the liability account
To increase the capital	Credit the capital account
To reduce an asset	Credit the asset account
To reduce a liability	Debit the liability account
To reduce the capital	Debit the capital account

If this is shown in the pages for accounts, it will appear as:

Any Asset Account

Increases	Reduces
+	−

Any Liability Account

Reduces	Increases
−	+

Capital Account

Reduces	Increases
−	+

Now we can see how transactions are entered in the accounts:

1. The proprietor starts the firm with £5,000 in cash on 1 May 19-4.

Effect	*Action required*
(a) Increases the asset of cash in the firm	Debit the cash account
(b) Increases the capital	Credit the capital account

These will be entered as follows:

Cash

19-4	£
May 1	5,000

Capital

	19-4	£
	May 1	5,000

You can see that the date of the transaction, and the amount, has been entered in each account. All that remains for us to do is to enter a description of each entry alongside the amount. The way that this is done is by entering a cross reference to the title of the other account in which the double entry is completed. You can see that the double entry to the item in the cash account has been completed by an entry in the capital account, consequently the word 'Capital' will appear in the cash account. Similarly, as the double entry to the item in the capital account is completed by an entry in the cash account the word 'Cash' will be shown in the capital account. The accounts, when finally completed, will therefore appear as:

Cash

19-4	£
May 1 Capital	5,000

Capital

	19-4	£
	May 1 Cash	5,000

We can now try to enter a few more transactions completing everything immediately.

2. Office Equipment bought on credit from Better Offices Ltd £390 on May 2 19-4.

Effect	*Action required*
(a) Increases the asset of office equipment	Debit Office Equipment account
(b) Increase in the liability of the firm to Better Offices Ltd	Credit Better Offices account

Office Equipment

19-4	£
May 2 Better Offices Ltd	390

Better Offices Ltd

	19-4	£
	May 2 Office Equipment	390

3. Shop Fittings are bought for £880 cash on May 3 19-4

Effect	*Action required*
(a) Reduces the asset of cash	Credit the cash account
(b) Increases the asset of shop fittings	Debit the shop fittings account

Cash

	19-4	£
	May 3 Shop Fittings	880

Shop Fittings

19-4	£
May 3 Cash	880

4. Paid the amount to Better Offices Ltd in cash on May 21 19-4.

Effect	*Action required*
(a) Reduces the asset of cash	Credit the cash account
(b) Reduces the liability of the firm to Better Offices Ltd	Debit Better Offices Ltd account

Cash

	19-4	£
	May 21 Better Offices Ltd	390

Better Offices Ltd.

19-4	£
May 21 Cash	390

If we now take the transactions 1 to 4 together, the accounting records will now appear as:

Cash

19-4	£	19-4	£
May 1 Capital	5,000	May 3 Shop Fittings	880
		May 21 Better Offices Ltd	390

Office Equipment

19-4	£
May 2 Better Offices Ltd	390

Better Offices Ltd

19-4	£	19-4	£
May 21 Cash	390	May 2 Office Equipment	390

Shop Fittings

19-4	£
May 3 Cash	880

Capital

	19-4	£
	May 1 Cash	5,000

A Worked Example

19-3	Transactions	Effect	Action
June 1	Started in business as a baker, putting £10,000 into a business bank account	Increases asset of bank Increases capital of proprietor	Debit bank account Credit capital account
June 2	Bought baking equipment on credit from Quicker Bakes Ltd £6,000.	Increases asset of baking equipment. Increases liability to Quicker Bakes Ltd.	Debit baking equipment account. Credit Quicker Bakes Ltd. account
June 3	Withdrew £500 cash from the bank and put it in the cash till	Reduces asset of bank. Increases asset of cash.	Credit bank account. Debit cash account.
June 4	Bought shop fittings paying in cash £440.	Increases asset of shop fittings. Reduces asset of cash.	Debit shop fittings account. Credit cash account.
June 6	Returned some of baking equipment value £50 to Quicker Bakes Ltd.	Reduces asset of baking equipment. Reduces liability to Quicker Bakes Ltd.	Credit baking equipment account. Debit Quicker Bakes Ltd.
June 12	Some of baking equipment unsuitable. Sold on credit to J. Hill for £30.	Reduces asset of baking equipment. Increases asset of money owing from J. Hill.	Credit baking equipment account. Debit J. Hill account.

June 20	Bought more baking equipment paying by cheque £800.	Reduces asset of bank. Increases asset of baking equipment.	Credit bank account. Debit baking equipment account.
June 26	Paid the amount of £5,950 to Quicker Bakes Ltd by cheque.	Reduces asset of bank. Reduces liability to Quicker Bakes Ltd.	Credit bank account. Debit Quicker Bakes Ltd account.
June 30	J. Hill pays us the amount owing, £30, by cheque.	Increases asset of bank. Reduces asset of money owing by J. Hill.	Debit bank account. Credit J. Hill account.

This can be shown in account form as follows:

Bank

19-3		£	19-3		£
June 1	Capital	10,000	June 3	Cash	500
June 30	J. Hill	30	June 20	Baking Equipment	800
			June 26	Quicker Bakes Ltd.	5,950

Cash

19-3		£	19-3		£
June 3	Bank	500	June 4	Shop Fittings	440

Capital

			19-3		£
			June 1	Bank	10,000

Baking Equipment

19-3		£	19-3		£
June 2	Quicker Bakes Ltd.	6,000	June 6	Quicker Bakes Ltd.	50
June 20	Bank	800	June 12	J. Hill	30

Shop Fittings

19-3		£
June 4	Cash	440

Quicker Bakes Ltd.

19-3		£	19-3		£
June 6	Baking Equipment	50	June 2	Baking Equipment	6,000
June 26	Bank	5,950			

J. Hill

19-3		£	19-3		£
June 12	Baking Equipment	30	June 30	Bank	30

Assignment Exercises

Note: Assignments with the suffix x do *not* have answers at the back of the book.

3.1   You are to complete the following table, showing which accounts are to be debited and which to be credited.

	Account to be debited	Account to be credited
(i) Bought office equipment by cheque.	O/Equip	Bank
(ii) Bought motor vehicle on credit from Sussex Garages Ltd.		
(iii) J. Harwich gave us a loan in cash.		
(iv) A debtor P. Redhead paid us by cheque.		
(v) We paid a creditor J. Powell in cash.		
(vi) Paid a creditor, L. Monks by cheque.		
(vii) Sold office equipment for cash.		

3.2x   Complete the following table:

	Account to be debited	Account to be credited
(i) Bought office machinery on credit from D. Orpington Ltd.		
(ii) The proprietor paid a creditor, C. Jones, from his private monies outside the firm.		
(iii) A debtor, N. Fox, paid us in cash.		
(iv) Repaid part of loan from P. Exeter by cheque.		
(v) Returned some of office machinery to D. Orpington Ltd.		
(vi) A debtor, N. London, pays us by cheque.		
(vii) Bought motor van by cash.		

3.3   You are to write up the asset, liability and capital accounts in the records of H. Sidmouth from the following:

19-6

August 1	Opened up in business with £10,000 in the bank.
August 3	Bought office equipment £1,900 on credit from F. Kent & Co.
August 5	Bought a motor van £4,600 paying by cheque.
August 9	Paid F. Kent & Co. the money owing to them by cheque £1,900.
August 12	Bought more office equipment on credit, this time from J. Surrey Ltd. £740.
August 14	Received a loan of £2,000 by cheque from C. Cheshire & Son.
August 16	Returned some of faulty office equipment costing £48 to J. Surrey Ltd.
August 20	Sold some of office equipment — found not to be suitable — to T. Somerset for £70 on credit.
August 30	Received the amount due from T. Somerset in cash.

3.4x Enter the following transactions in the books of T. Luke:

19-7

June 1   Started business by putting £10,000 into a bank account for the business.

June 3   Bought fixtures on credit from J. Matthews £770.

June 4   J. Mark lent the business £500 in cash.

June 7   Bought motor van paying by cheque £3,600.

June 8   Took £300 out of the cash till and paid it into the bank.

June 12   Bought extra fixtures for cash £120.

June 14   Returned some of fixtures to J. Matthews £60.

June 18   Paid cheque £710 to J. Matthews.

June 25   Repaid part of J. Mark's loan by cheque £200.

June 30   Bought machinery on credit from A. John £850.

3.5 Write up the necessary accounts to record the following in the books of J. Jackson:

19-4

May 1   Started business with £4,000 in cash.

May 2   Paid £3,700 of the opening cash into the bank.

May 4   Bought works machinery on credit from J. Hart Ltd. £2,200.

May 6   Bought office equipment paying by cash £280.

May 8   K. Devonshire lent £1,000 paying the money by cheque.

May 10   Bought office equipment on credit from Mini-Computers Ltd. for £1,200.

May 15   Took £200 out of the bank and put it into the cash till.

May 20   Paid money owing to J. Hart Ltd. by cheque.

May 23   J. Jackson puts a further £500 cash into the business.

May 28   Paid part of money owing to Mini-Computers Ltd. by cash £600.

May 29   Sold some of the works machinery for cash £70.

May 31   Bought motor van on credit from High Lane Garages £3,200.

3.6x Write up the accounts to record the following transactions for the business of D. Morecambe:

19-6

March 1   Started business with £10,000 in the bank and £1,000 in cash.

March 2   Bought shop fittings on credit £1,200 from L. Winner Ltd.

March 4   Bought office equipment £650 paying in cash.

March 6   P. Arnold lent the business £4,000 by cheque.

March 8   Some of the office equipment costing £80 unsuitable. Sold at cost price on credit to V. Bingham.

March 10   Bought office equipment on credit for £1,450 from Better-Forms Ltd.

March 12   V. Bingham paid us £80 in cash.

March 15   Paid L. Winner Ltd. £1,200 by cheque.

March 16   Paid part of amount owing to Better-Forms Ltd by cheque £800.

March 18   P. Arnold lent the business a further £300 in cash.

March 19   Took £600 out of the cash till and paid it into the bank.

March 21   Returned office equipment costing £190 to Better Forms Ltd.

March 24   Repaid part of money lent by P. Arnold by cheque £1,000.

March 30   Morecambe put a further £2,000 capital into the firm in cash.

March 31   Paid Better-Forms Ltd. £460 in cash.

March 31   Bought a motor-van paying by cash £1,500.

Chapter 4

The Asset of Stock

Learning Objectives:

At the end of your study of this chapter you should:

1. **understand clearly the use of the words 'Sales' and 'Purchases' in accounting,**
2. **be able to handle transactions both for cash and on credit.**

Sometimes goods are sold at exactly the same price at that which they were bought, but this is obviously not the usual case. Normally they are sold at a figure higher than the cost price, in this case the difference is the profit. Sometimes however they are sold below cost price, the difference being a loss.

If all sales were at cost price then it would be possible to have a stock account, the goods bought being shown on the debit side as they represent increases in the asset. The goods sold, being a reduction in the asset, would be shown as a credit. The difference between the two sides would represent the cost of the goods unsold at that date, if wastages, thefts, breakages etc. of stock are ignored.

However, most sales are not at cost price, and therefore the sales figures includes elements of profit or loss. This means that the difference between the two sides would not represent the stock of goods. Such a stock account would accordingly not serve a useful purpose.

The Stock Account is therefore divided into four accounts, each one showing a movement of stock. These are:

1. Increases in stock. This can happen for one of two reasons.
   (a) By the purchase of goods.
   (b) By the return into the firm of goods previously sold. There are quite a few reasons for such returns. The goods may have been faulty, or of the wrong type, and so on.

To distinguish between the two aspects of the increase of stocks of goods two accounts are opened. These are:

   (i) Purchases Account — purchases of goods are entered in this account.
   (ii) Returns Inwards Account — goods being returned in to the firm are entered here. The alternative name for this account is the Sales Returns Account.

2. Reductions in the stock of goods. If wastages and breakages of stock are ignored this can be due for one of two reasons.

(a) By the sale of goods.

(b) Goods bought previously by the firm now being returned back by the firm to the supplier.

To distinguish between the two aspects of the reduction of stock of goods two accounts are opened. These are:

(i) Sales Account — sales of goods are entered here.

(ii) Returns Outwards Account — goods being returned by the firm to the supplier are entered here. The alternative name for this account is the Purchases Returns Account.

We can now look at some illustrations of the recording of movements of stock.

Purchases of Stock on Credit

May 1st 19-5. Goods costing £750 are bought on credit from J. Ashworth. We should first of all consider what the two-fold effect of the transactions are, so that the book-keeping entries can be ascertained.

1. The asset of stock is increased. An increase in an asset needs a debit entry in an account. The account concerned is a stock account which should show the particular movement of stock, and as it is a 'Purchases' movement the account concerned must be the Purchases Account.

2. An increase in a liability. We can see that this is the liability of the firm to J. Ashworth in respect of the goods bought but for which payment has not yet been made. An increase in a liability needs a credit entry, so that this aspect of the transaction is recorded by a credit entry being made in J. Ashworth's account.

	Purchases	
19-5	£	
May 1 J. Ashworth	750	

J. Ashworth		
	19-5	£
	May 1 Purchases	750

Purchases of Stock by Cash

May 2nd 19-5. Goods costing £45 are bought, cash being paid for them immediately.

1. The asset of stock is increased, for which a debit entry is needed. The movement of stock is that of purchases, so that the entry will be made in a Purchases Account.

2. The asset of cash is reduced. This calls for a credit entry, and the asset is that of cash, so that the Cash Account needs crediting.

Cash

		19-5	£
		May 2 Purchases	45

Purchases

19-5	£
May 2 Cash	45

Sales of Stock on Credit

May 3rd 19-5. Sold goods on credit £900 to B. Wilson.

1. The asset of stock is reduced. This will need a credit entry to show a reduction in an asset. The movement of stock is that of 'Sales' so the account credited is the Sales Account.

Sales

		19-5	£
		May 3 B. Wilson	900

B. Wilson

19-5	£
May 3 Sales	900

Sales of Stock for Cash

May 5th 19-5. Sold goods for £90, cash being received immediately.

1. The asset of stock is reduced. Such a transaction needs a credit entry and the movement of stock is that of 'Sales'. This means that the entry needed is a credit in the Sales Account.

2. The asset of cash is increased. An increase in an asset needs a debit entry, the asset is that of cash, and so the debit entry is in the Cash Account.

Sales

		19-5	£
		May 5 Cash	90

Cash

19-5	£
May 5 Sales	90

Return inwards

May 8th 19-5. Goods previously sold to M. Bond for £46 are now returned by him.

1. The asset of stock is increased by the goods returned. This will need a debit entry in an asset account. The movement of stock is that of 'Returns Inwards' and therefore the entry needed is a debit in a 'Returns Inwards' account.

2. A reduction in an asset. The debt previously owing by M. Bond is now reduced, and to record this a credit is needed in the account of M. Bond.

Returns Inwards

19-5		£
May 8	M. Bond	46

M. Bond

	19-5		£
	May 8	Returns Inwards	46

Return Outwards

May 12th 19-5. Goods previously bought from M. Mullins for £70 are now returned to him.

1. The asset of stock is reduced. A credit entry is therefore needed in an asset account, and as the movement of stock is that of 'Returns Outwards' the entry is a credit in a 'Returns Outwards' account.

2. A reduction in a liability. The amount previously owing to M. Mullins is now reduced, and to show this a debit is needed in the account of M. Mullins.

Returns Outwards

	19-5		£
	May 12	M. Mullins	70

M. Mullins

19-5		£
May 12	Returns Outwards	70

We can now look at a fully worked example.

19-5

August 1	Bought goods on credit £480 from J. Oliver Ltd.
August 3	Goods sold for cash £220.
August 5	Sold goods on credit to B. Perkins for £175.
August 8	Bought goods on credit £145 from K. Walsh & Son.
August 11	Goods bought for cash £130.
August 16	Sold goods on credit to F. Mathis for £496.
August 21	Bought goods on credit £370 from J. Oliver Ltd.
August 24	Returned goods £25 to K. Walsh & Son.
August 29	B. Perkins returned goods to us £44.
August 30	F. Mathis paid the amount owing by him £496 in cash.
August 31	Paid cash to J. Oliver Ltd. £480

(handwritten annotations: DR Stock / CR J. Oliver; CR Sales, DR cash A/c; CR Sales, DR B.P; DR Stock; DR Purch, CR Cash; DR R/Inw CR M.P.)

Purchases

19-5		£
Aug. 1	J. Oliver Ltd.	480
Aug. 8	K. Walsh & Son	145
Aug. 11	Cash	130
Aug. 21	J. Oliver Ltd.	370

Sales

			19-5		£
			Aug. 3	Cash	220
			Aug. 5	B. Perkins	175
			Aug. 16	F. Mathis	496

Returns Outwards

			19-5		£
			Aug. 24	K. Walsh & Son	25

Returns Inwards

19-5		£			
Aug. 29	B. Perkins	44			

J. Oliver Ltd.

19-5		£	19-5		£
Aug. 28	Cash	480	Aug. 1	Purchases	480
			Aug. 21	Purchases	370

K. Walsh & Son

19-5		£	19-5		£
Aug. 25	Returns Outwards	25	Aug. 8	Purchases	145

B. Perkins

19-5		£	19-5		£
Aug. 5	Sales	175	Aug. 29	Returns Inwards	44

F. Mathis

19-5		£	19-5		£
Aug. 16	Sales	496	Aug. 30	Cash	496

Cash

19-5		£	19-5		£
Aug. 3	Sales	220	Aug. 3	Purchases	130
Aug. 30	F. Mathis	496	Aug. 31	J. Oliver Ltd	480

Definitions of 'Sales' and 'Purchases'

It is important not to confuse the ordinary language usage of the words 'Sales' and 'Purchases' with their meanings in accounting.

'Purchases' in accounting is restricted in its meaning to the purchase of those goods which the firm buys with the prime intention of selling. Sometimes the goods are added to, altered, or are used in the manufacture of something else, but the important part is the element of resale. To a firm that deals in calculators for example, calculators constitute purchases. When something else is bought by such a firm, such as a motor car, such an item cannot be called purchases, although in ordinary language it may be said that a motor car has been purchased. The prime intention of buying the motor car by the firm was for usage and not for resale. In the case of a garage trading in motor cars then when a car was bought it would be purchases, as it would be for the prime intention of resale.

In the same way, 'Sales' means the sale of those goods in which the firm normally deals and were bought with the prime intention of resale. The word 'Sales' must not be given to the disposal of other items.

If these meanings were not kept to then the various forms of stock account would contain something other than goods sold or for resale. We will see later than this would bring in a great deal of confusion when calculating the profits made by a firm.

Cash and Credit Transactions: A comparison

We can now compare the difference between the records needed for cash and credit transactions.

The complete cycle for purchases paid for immediately needs the following entries:

1. Credit the cash account.
2. Debit the purchases account.

However, the complete cycle for the purchase of goods on credit can be broken down into two parts. First, the purchase of goods, second, the payment for them.

The first part on purchase is:

1. Debit the purchases account.
2. Credit the supplier's account.

While the second part is:

1. Debit the supplier's account.
2. Credit the cash account.

Examining these you can see exactly what the difference is between recording cash purchases and credit purchases. With the cash purchase no record is kept of the supplier's account. This is because cash passes immediately and consequently there is no need to keep a check on indebtedness to a supplier. In the case of purchases on credit the records should show the identity of the supplier, and the amount owing, until payment is made.

If you will look at cash sales and credit sales records you will notice a similar difference.

Assignment Exercises

4.1 The following table is to be completed, showing which accounts are to be debited and which are to be credited:

*Account to   Account to
be debited   be credited*

(a) Goods sold on credit to P. Barnes.

(b) Goods bought on credit from J. Corrigan.

(c) Motor van bought on credit from M.C. Ltd.

(d) Goods sold for cash.

(e) Bought office fixtures paying by cheque.

(f) Goods bought, paying by cheque immediately.

(g) Creditor, D. Watson, was paid in cash.

(h) Goods returned to P. Power.

(i) Goods sold on credit to W. Donachie.

(j) Office machinery returned to A. Hartford Ltd.

4.2x Complete the following table:

*Account to   Account to
be debited   be credited*

(a) Goods bought on credit from T. Morgan.

(b) Goods returned to us by J. Thomas.

(c) Machinery returned to L. Jones Ltd.

(d) Goods bought for cash.

(e) Motor van bought on credit from D. Davies Ltd.

(f) Goods returned by us to I. Pugh.

(g) D. Picton paid his account by cheque.

(h) Goods bought by cheque.

(i) We paid creditor, B. Howells, by cheque.

(j) Goods sold on credit to J. Mansell.

4.3 Write up the following in the books:

19-5

January 1 Bought goods on credit from H. Kelly £228.

January 4 Sold goods for cash £95.

January 5 Sold goods on credit to P. Murphy £77.

January 6 Bought goods for cash £28.

January 11 Sold goods on credit to T. O'Connor £63.

January 18 We returned goods to H. Kelly £14.

January 26 Bought goods on credit from J. McShane £190.

January 31 Sold goods on credit to P. Brogan £55.

4.4x   Enter up the following items in the requisite accounts:

19-6

March 1	Started in business with £10,000 in the bank.
March 2	Bought goods on credit from D. Bradman £856.
March 3	Cash Sales £237.
March 5	Bought goods for cash £72.
March 8	Sold goods on credit to G. Boycott £258.
March 12	Returned goods to D. Bradman £76.
March 16	Bought goods on credit from L. Hutton £295.
March 18	Sold goods to A. Greig £154.
March 26	Paid D. Bradman's account by cheque £780.
March 31	G. Boycott paid us his account by cheque £258.

4.5   You are to enter the following in the accounts:

19-7

April 1	Started business with £9,000 in the bank and £500 in cash.
April 2	R. Redford lent us £5,000, giving us a cheque.
April 3	Bought goods on credit from P. Lorre £806.
April 4	Bought fixtures paying by cheque £750.
April 6	Bought goods for cash £150.
April 8	We returned goods to P. Lorre £36.
April 10	Sold goods on credit to S. Greenstreet £236.
April 12	Paid P. Lorre by cheque £770.
April 14	Bought goods on credit from G. Fitzgerald £420.
April 15	Sold goods for cash £110.
April 17	Sold goods on credit to H. Bogart Ltd. £308.
April 21	Bought fixtures on credit from G. Raft & Son £306.
April 24	Greenstreet returned goods to us £46.
April 28	Some of the fixtures were returned to G. Raft & Son £28.
April 30	Bogart Ltd. returned goods to us £30.

4.6x   Enter in the necessary accounts:

19-6

October 1	Started in business with £5,000 in the bank.
October 2	Bought goods on credit from: E. Baker £290; A. Cunningham £1,560.
October 3	Bought goods paying by cheque immediately £155.
October 4	Sold goods for cash £370.
October 5	Sold goods on credit to: H. Pollard £550; J. Jones Ltd. £295.
October 6	Bought office fixtures on credit from A. MacLennan £750.
October 7	We returned goods to A. Cunningham £120.
October 8	Bought motor van paying by cheque £2,360.
October 10	Sold goods on credit to J. Spencer Ltd. £477.
October 12	Paid A. Cunningham's account by cheque £1,440.
October 16	H. Pollard returned goods to us £40.

October 18 Sold goods for cash £110.

October 21 Some of office fixtures unsuitable: returned £55 worth to A. MacLennan getting full allowance, and sold some others for cash £40.

October 23 Bought goods on credit from: E. Baker £60; G. Hall Ltd. £510.

October 26 J. Jones Ltd. returned goods to us £32.

October 28 Bought office fixtures for cash £90.

October 31 We returned goods to E. Baker £14.

Chapter 5

Double Entry System for Expenses and Revenues

Learning Objectives:

At the end of your study of this chapter you should:

1. **understand what is meant by Revenue, Expense and Profit in accounting,**

2. **be able to distinguish and record Revenue and Expense transactions.**

The accounting content of this book so far has been concerned with the need to record changes in capital, assets, and liabilities. However you have not yet been shown how to record changes in the capital brought about by profits earned by the business. The word 'profit' here means the excess of revenues over expenses for a particular period. Revenues consist of the monetary value of goods and services that have been delivered to customers. Expenses comprise the monetary value of the assets used up in obtaining those revenues.

We can examine the effect of profit upon capital by means of an example.

On January 1st 19-6 the assets and liabilities of a firm are:

Assets: Machinery £10,000, Motor Vans £6,000, Stock £4,000, Debtors £2,000, Cash at Bank £1,000.

Liabilities: Creditors £3,000.

To find capital we use the formula: Assets — Liabilities = Capital.

£10,000 + £6,000 + £4,000 + £2,000 + £1,000 − £3,000 = £20,000

Then during January the whole of the stock is sold for £6,500 cash. On January 31st 19-6 the assets and liabilities have become:

Assets: Machinery £10,000, Motor Vans £6,000, Stock Nil, Debtors £2,000, Cash at Bank £7,500.

Liabilities: Creditors £3,000.

Using the formula Assets − Liabilities = Capital.

£10,000 + £6,000 + £2,000 + £7,500 − £3,000 = £22,500

We can see therefore that profit from the sale of stock affects the capital as follows:

Old Capital	+	Profit	=	New Capital
£20,000	+	£2,500	=	£22,500

If a loss had been incurred this would have reduced the capital. It can be shown as:

$$\text{Old Capital} \quad - \quad \text{Loss} \quad = \quad \text{New Capital}$$

You can see therefore that to alter the capital account we will have to be able to calculate profits and losses. It is only feasible to calculate profits at intervals, at least annually, but sometimes quarterly, monthly or even weekly. This obviously means that accounts will be needed to collect together all of the expenses and revenues until the periodic calculation of profits is made.

All of the expenses could be charged to one account only with the title 'Expenses Account'. You can see that it would be far more informative and useful if full details of each of the different expenses are shown in Profit and Loss calculations. Similar considerations also apply to revenues. Consequently a separate account is opened for each different kind of. expense and revenue. Illustrations of these could be:

Wages Account	Packaging Expenses Account
Rent Account	Stationery Account
Rates Account	Lighting and Heating Account
Motor Expenses Account	Postage and Telephone Account
Rent Receivable Account	Commissions Received Account

The choice as to which accounts will be opened for expenses and revenues, and what titles will be given to them, is solely at the discretion of the firm. For examples postages and telephone expenses could be put together in one account if desired instead of having separately a "Postage Account" and a "Telephone Account". The account could be called "Postage and Telephone Account", "Communications Account" or any other appropriate name. For small amounts of a type which appear infrequently an account called either "Sundry Expenses Account" or "General Expenses Account" is used.

Whether to Debit or to Credit

We can now look at how to decide on which side of the records revenues and expenses should be recorded. Assets involve expenditure by the firm, and they are recorded on the debit side of the books. As expenses also involve expenditure we will also record these on the debit side of the books. On reflection you can see that assets consist of expenditure of money by a firm for which something still remains, whilst expenses consist of expenditure of money which has been used up in the running of the business, and for which there is no benefit remaining at the date of the balance sheet. The difference between assets and expenses is therefore purely one of whether or not any benefits remain unused at the balance sheet date.

Revenues are the opposite of expenses and consequently appear on the opposite side of the records to expenses, that is they will appear on the credit side.

Effect of Transactions:

We can now look at a few examples demonstrating the double entry required.

1. Motor Expenses of £42 are paid by cash. The two-fold effect is:

    (a) The asset of cash is reduced. To record this a credit is needed in the Cash Account £42.

    (b) The total of motor expenses is increased. As expenses are shown as debits what is needed is a debit in the Motor Expenses Account £42.

2. Postage stamps costing £90 are paid for by cheque.

    The two-fold effect is:

    (a) The asset of bank is reduced. To record this a credit is needed in the Bank Account £90.

    (b) The total of postage expenses is increased. As expenses are shown as debits then what is needed is a debit in the Postages Account £90.

3. £200 cash is received for rent of part of warehouse used by another firm. *Revenue*

    (a) The asset of cash is increased. This calls for a debit in the cash account £200.

    (b) The revenue of rent received is increased. Revenue is recorded by means of a credit entry, therefore to do this we enter a credit in the Rent Received Account £200.

Now we can look at a few more examples. This will be shown in the form of a table:

19-6		Increase	Action	Reduction	Action
May 1	Paid rates by cheque £180.	Expense of rates.	Debit rates account.	Asset of bank.	Credit bank account.
May 5	Paid wages by cash £440.	Expense of wages.	Debit wages account.	Asset of cash.	Credit cash account.
May 8	Paid advertising by cheque £210.	Expense of advertising.	Debit advertising account.	Asset of bank.	Credit bank account.
May 12	Paid motor expenses by cash £55.	Expense of motor expenses.	Debit motor expenses account.	Asset of cash.	Credit cash account.
May 14	Received rent in cash £150.	Asset of cash.	Debit cash account.		
		Revenue of rent.	Credit rent received account.		
May 16	Received commission by cheque £190.	Asset of bank.	Debit bank account.		
		Revenue of commission received.	Credit commission received account.		

These can be shown in normal account form as:

Cash

19-6		£	19-6		£
May 14	Rent Received	150	May 5	Wages	440
			May 12	Motor Expenses	55

Bank

19-6		£	19-6		£
May 16	Commission Received	190	May 1	Rates	180
			May 8	Advertising	210

Rates

19-6		£
May 1	Bank	180

Wages

19-6		£
May 5	Cash	440

Advertising

19-6		£
May 8	Bank	210

Motor Expenses

19-6		£
May 12	Cash	55

Rent Received

	19-6		£
	May 14	Cash	150

Commission Received

	19-6		£
	May 16	Bank	190

Obviously the proprietor will want to take cash out of the business for his private use from time to time. These withdrawals are known as 'Drawings'. You will be able to see that, as they reduce the claim of the proprietor against the resources of the business, the effect of drawings is to reduce the amount of Capital. If you will look again at the basic accounting formula you will see that a reduction in capital needs a debit entry in the Capital Account. For convenience, you will be able to see later why it is more convenient, the accounting custom has developed by debiting a 'Drawings Account' as an interim measure. It should therefore be obvious to you that drawings is a shorter way of saying 'withdrawals of capital'.

We will now look at an example.

19-7

June 1   Proprietor takes £100 cash out of the business for his private use.

Effect	*Action*
1. Cash is reduced by £100.	Credit the Cash Account £100.
2. Capital is reduced by £100.	Debit the Drawings Account £100.

Cash

	19-7	£
	June 1 Drawings	100

Drawings

19-7	£	
June 1 Cash	100	

Classification of Accounts

It used to be the case that accounts were classified as either being Personal or Impersonal accounts. Personal accounts were those concerned with people, i.e. debtors and creditors. Impersonal accounts were also divided into Real and Nominal accounts. Real accounts are those in which property is recorded, such as buildings, machinery, fixtures or stock. Nominal accounts referred to revenue and expenses. Although this terminology is now going out of use, you may still come across it quite often.

Assignment Exercises

5.1   Complete the following table:

	Account to be debited	Account to be credited
(a) Paid rent by cash		
(b) Paid for goods by cash		
(c) Received by cheque a refund of rates already paid		
(d) Paid general expenses by cheque		
(e) Received commissions in cash		
(f) Goods returned by us to T. Jones		
(g) Goods sold for cash		
(h) Bought office fixtures by cheque		
(i) Paid wages in cash		
(j) Took cash out of business for private use		

5.2x The following table should be completed:

Account to Account to
be debited be credited

(a) Sold surplus stationery receiving proceeds in cash

(b) Paid salaries by cheque

(c) Rent received for premises sub-let, by cheque

(d) Goods returned to us by B. Streisand

(e) Commission received by us previously in error, we now refund this by cheque

(f) Bought machinery by cheque

(g) Paid lighting expenses in cash

(h) Insurance rebate received by cheque

(i) Buildings bought by cheque

(j) Building repairs paid in cash

5.3 Enter the following transactions in the books of J. Dempsey:

19-4

October 1 Started business with £5,000 in the bank.

October 2 Bought goods on credit from J. Louis & Son £1,360.

October 3 Paid for stationery by cheque £44.

October 4 Cash Sales £280.

October 5 Paid wages in cash £192.

October 6 Paid rates by cheque £330.

October 8 Goods sold on credit to S. R. Robinson £295; J. Conte £440.

October 10 Paid lighting and heating expenses by cash £80.

October 12 Bought fixtures on credit from M. Ali £1,950.

October 14 Bought motor van paying by cheque £2,160.

October 20 Received commission in cash £70.

October 22 Paid for motor expenses in cash £61.

October 24 Paid rent by cheque £100.

October 31 Goods returned to J. Louis & Son £30.

5.4x The following items need entering in the books of R. Monkhouse:

19-6

May 1 Started business with £10,000 in the bank and £800 in cash.

May 2 Bought office equipment from A. Mullard on credit £820.

May 3 Paid rent in cash £450.

May 4 Goods bought on credit from K. Dodd £1,050; E. Wise £295.

May 5 Bought stationery paying by cheque £36.

May 6 Goods sold on credit to E. Morecambe & Son £300; L. Dawson Ltd. £950.

May 8 Rent should have been £400. Accordingly a refund of £50 by cheque is now received.

May 10	Bought motor lorry on credit from S. Powell & Co. £5,160.
May 12	Cash Sales £292.
May 14	Goods returned to us by K. Dodd £270.
May 16	Paid motor expenses by cheque £87.
May 18	Paid salaries by cheque £440.
May 19	E. Morecambe & Son paid us by cheque £300.
May 24	Received commissions in cash £120.
May 29	Cash taken by Monkhouse for his own use £100.
May 31	Paid account by A. Mullard by cheque £820.

5.5 Write up the following in the books of G. Ford:

19-8

November 1	Started business with £25,000 in the bank.
November 2	Took £500 out of the bank and put it into the cash till.
November 3	Goods bought on credit from F. Roosevelt & Co. £1,960; C. Coolidge £720.
November 4	Paid rent by cheque £340.
November 5	Goods bought by cash £190.
November 6	Bought office fixtures on credit from G. Washington Ltd. £590.
November 7	Paid travelling expenses in cash £48.
November 8	Goods sold on credit to H. Hoover £620; W. Wilson £490.
November 10	Paid wages in cash £220.
November 12	Bought motor van on credit from H. Truman £2,350.
November 14	We returned goods to C. Coolidge £140.
November 16	Part of premises sub-let. We receive rent in cash £120.
November 18	Goods sold on credit to W. Wilson £70; L. Johnson £370.
November 20	Goods returned to us by H. Hoover £40; W. Wilson £30.
November 22	I. Eisenhower lent us £2,000 by cheque.
November 24	Received refund of part travelling expenses by cheque £16.
November 26	Ford withdrew £50 for his own use in cash.
November 28	We paid Coolidge amount owing by cheque £580.
November 30	G. Washington Ltd. was paid by us by cheque £590.

5.6x Enter the following transactions in the accounts of M. Foot:

19-8

December 1	Business started with £20,000 in the bank.
December 2	Goods bought on credit from M. Thatcher £2,160; E. Powell & Son £720.
December 4	Office Fixtures bought on credit from J. Callaghan & Co. £420.
December 5	Paid salaries by cheque £680.
December 6	Cash Sales £385.
December 7	Goods sold on credit to K. Joseph Ltd. £375; S. Williams £590; W. Churchill £810.

December 8	Bought Stationery paying by cheque £55.
December 9	Paid rates in cash £320.
December 10	J. Prior lent us £400 in cash.
December 13	Goods bought on credit from G. Brown & Co. £1,240; H. MacMillan £192.
December 16	Received commission earned by cheque £270.
December 19	Paid rent by cheque £480.
December 22	M. Foot paid in £1,000 cash from his private resources.
December 23	Paid motor hire expenses by cheque £85.
December 24	The following settled their accounts by cheque S. Williams £590; W. Churchill £810.
December 31	Refund of rates overpaid received by cheque £15.

Chapter 6

Balancing off Accounts and the Trial Balance

Learning Objectives:

At the end of your study of this chapter you should:

1. be able to make the entries in an account at the end of a period known as 'Balancing off',
2. understand that mechanised accounting 'Balances off' after every set of entries,
3. be able to extract a Trial Balance and understand any errors relating to it.

In the previous chapters you have read about how to make debit and credit entries in accounts. You will want to know periodically what the cumulative effect of the debit and credit entries has been. This is done by finding the 'balance' on each account. The word 'balance' is an accounting term meaning the difference between amounts entered on each side of the account.

If the total of the debit entries exceeds the total of the credit entries, the account is said to have a 'Debit Balance'.

If the total of the credit entries exceeds the total of the debit entries, the account is said to have a 'Credit Balance'.

It is usual for the accounts for customers and suppliers to be 'balanced off' at the end of each month. We can now look at the balancing off process:

Accounts before being balanced off on 31 May 19-5

C. Willis

19-5		£	19-5		£
May 1	Sales	192	May 27	Cash	192
" 14	Sales	300			
" 30	Sales	156			

A. Mayall

19-5		£	19-5		£
May 24	Bank	200	May 2	Purchases	310
			" 20	Purchases	144

They are now balanced off, i.e. the difference found in each case, by first of all adding up the side of the account with the greatest total and then inserting the balance (the difference) so as to make the totals of both sides equal. When this is being done you should so arrange it so that the two totals are written on the same level as each other.

After the balance is found and entered it must also be entered on the other side of the books to preserve double entry. This is effected by making the opposite entry, on the line immediately under the totals. In the details column, in the account above the total the words 'balance carried down' are inserted, whilst on the line under the totals the words entered are 'balance brought down'.

C. Willis

19-5		£	19-5		£
May 1	Sales	192	May 27	Cash	192
" 14	Sales	300	" 31	Balance carried down	456
" 30	Sales	156			
		648			648
June 1	Balance brought down	456			

Notes

1. In theory the balance is calculated as at the end of the last day of the period, in this case May 31st. It is then carried down as the opening balance of the next day, in this case June 1st. To put it another way, the closing balance of one period is the opening balance for the next period.

2. The words 'balance carried down' are usually abbreviated to 'balance c/d', whilst 'balance brought down' becomes 'balance b/d'.

3. In the case of C. Willis the total of the debit side originally exceeded the total of the credit side. In such a case the balance is said to be a debit balance. The account being that of a customer then he can be said to be a debtor. The use of the term debtor for a customer who has a debit balance can thus be seen, the balance indicating we are owed money.

A. Mayall

19-5		£	19-5		£
May 24	Bank	200	May 2	Purchases	310
" 31	Balance c/d	254	" 20	Purchases	144
		454			454
			June 1	Balance b/d	254

In A. Mayall's account the total of the credit side exceeded the total of the debit side, and the balance is said to be a credit balance. Here the use of the word 'creditor' for a supplier with a credit balance can be seen, for such a credit balance indicates that we owe money to this particular supplier.

Where accounts only have one entry it is completely unnecessary to enter the total. A double line ruled under the entry will mean that the entry is its own total. This is the case with the account shown of R. McNeill.

R. McNeill

19-5		£	19-5		£
May 16	Sales	220	May 31	Balance c/a	220
June 1	Balance b/d	220			

Where an account contains one entry only of equal figures on each side then all that is needed again are double lines ruled under each entry.

M. Beet

19-5		£	19-5		£
May 30	Bank	346	May 2	Purchases	346

Three column ledger accounts

The way that accounts are normally shown in this book is that the left-hand side of the account is the debit side, whilst the right-hand side of the account is the credit side. When accounting machinery is used the style of displaying accounts is usually different. It is shown as three columns of figures, one column being for debit entries, one for credit entries, and the remaining column for the balance.

The accounts already shown in this chapter, using the conventional method, are now shown redrafted using the typical machine accounting display.

C. Willis

19-5		Debit	Credit	Balance (and whether debit or credit)
		£	£	£
May 1	Sales	192		192 Dr
" 14	Sales	300		492 Dr
" 27	Cash		192	300 Dr
" 30	Sales	156		456 Dr

A. Mayall

19-5		Debit	Credit	Balance
		£	£	£
May 2	Purchases		310	310 Cr
" 20	Purchases		144	454 Cr
" 24	Bank	200		254 Cr

R. McNeill

19-5		Debit	Credit	Balance
		£	£	£
May 16	Sales	220		220 Dr

M. Beet

19-5		Debit	Credit	Balance
		£	£	£
May 2	Purchases		346	346 Cr
" 30	Bank	346		0

You can see that the balance is calculated afresh after every entry. When manual methods are in use it is often time-wasting to do this, and it is also frequently difficult in a classroom situation. The more calculations have to be made manually then the more errors are likely to be made. Students therefore are usually asked to use two-sided accounts instead.

There is absolutely no difference in principle, it is simply a matter of display. The final balances are exactly the same no matter which type of account is used.

The Trial Balance

We have already seen that every transaction has been recorded by using the double entry method of bookkeeping. Every credit entry has had a corresponding debit entry made, and every debit entry has a corresponding credit entry. If therefore all of the debit entries are totalled, then compared with the total of the credit entries, it is obvious that the two totals should equal each other.

To check that the two totals are equal, or as accountants would say to see if the books 'balance' a Trial Balance would be drawn up periodically.

In fact a form of trial balance could be drawn up listing down all of the accounts, and showing how much was entered on each side of each account. If the worked example shown on pages 27 and 28 has such a trial balance drawn up in respect of the entries, it would appear as in Exhibit 6.1.

Exhibit 6.1

Trial balance as on 31 August 19-5

	Dr £	Cr £
Purchases	1,125	
Sales		891
Returns Outwards		25
Returns Inwards	44	
J. Oliver Ltd.	480	850
K. Walsh & Son	25	145
B. Perkins	175	44
F. Mathis	496	496
Cash	716	610
	3,061	3,061

This is not however the usual way of drawing up a trial balance. Instead a trial balance is a *list of balances only,* shown as to whether they are debit or credit balances. Instead of the trial balance as shown in Exhibit 6.1 the normal type of trial balance would be as per Exhibit 6.2.

Exhibit 6.2

Trial balance as on 31 August 19-5

	Dr £	Cr £
Purchases	1,125	
Sales		891
Returns Outwards		25
Returns Inwards	44	
J. Oliver Ltd.		370
K. Walsh & Son.		120
B. Perkins	131	
Cash	106	
	1,406	1,406

In Exhibit 6.2 the trial balance also 'balances'. Various items have however been cancelled out from each side because the balances only have been taken.

In all the amount cancelled out, as you can see if you inspect both exhibits, amount to £1,655. This consists òf J. Oliver Ltd. £480, K. Walsh & Son £25, B. Perkins £44, F. Mathis £496, Cash £610 = £1,655. As equal amounts have been cancelled out from each side it obviously means that the new totals should also 'balance'.

The trial balance in Exhibit 6.2 is the easiest one to draw up in a real-life situation. In addition the balances are used later, either when the profits are being calculated, or also when the balance sheet is being drawn up. Thus the trial balance is not just drawn up simply to check the arithmetical accuracy of the bookkeeping records.

Errors and trial balances

You would be forgiven for thinking that, at first sight anyway, the balancing of a trial balance proves that the bookkeeping records are correct. You would however be wrong. It means that certain types of errors have not been made, but there are several types of errors which could still exist even though the trial balance totals agree. These are:

1. *Errors of omission—* where an item is completely omitted from the books.

2. *Errors of commission—* where the correct amount is entered but in the wrong person's account, e.g. a sale of £100 to J. Carter is entered in the account of J. Hardacre. The correct class of account has been used, they are both accounts for customers, what is incorrect is the identity of the customer.

3. *Errors of principle—* where a transactions is entered in the wrong class of account. Instances would be where an asset is charged to an expenses account, e.g. if a motor van was charged to a motor expenses account.

4. *Errors of original entry*— where the double entry has been properly observed, but the figures originally entered were incorrect. An instance of this would be sales for £404 being incorrectly entered in the sales account and the customer's account as £440.

5. *Compensating errors*— these are where errors cancel out each other. For example, if the motor expenses account was added up to be £100 too much and the sales account was also overadded by £100, then these two errors would cancel out in the trial balance.

6. *Reversal of entries*— the correct amounts are entered in two accounts, but on the wrong side of each account. Suppose purchases account had been credited and the supplier's personal account debited instead of vice-versa.

Assignment Exercises

6.1 Enter up the requisite accounts for the following transactions, then balance off the accounts and extract a trial balance as at 30 June 19-5:

19-5

June 1	Started firm with £5,000 in the bank.
June 2	Bought goods on credit from the following organisations: J. Halifax & Co. £675; P. York Ltd. £800; T. Sheffield & Son £360; R. Selby £150; N. Thirsk & Co. £75.
June 3	Sold goods on credit to I. Bury & Son £270; P. Salford Ltd. £495; J. Blackpool & Co. £246.
June 8	Paid insurance by cheque £177.
June 10	Cash Sales £290.
June 15	Paid rent by cash £100.
June 18	Paid the following by cheque J. Halifax & Co. £675; T. Sheffield & Son £360.
June 24	Paid wages in cash £170.
June 28	Sold goods on credit to J. Blackpool & Co. £178.
June 30	I. Bury & Son paid us by cheque £270.

6.2x The following transactions are to be entered in the records of J. Berkshire, the accounts balanced off and a trial balance extracted as at 31 March 19-3:

19-3

March 1	Began business with £10,000 in the bank and £700 cash.
March 2	Bought goods on credit from the following: P. Slough Ltd. £244; J. Taplow £376; D. Langley £506.
March 3	Paid rent in cash £300.
March 4	Sold goods on credit to: C. Iver Ltd. £400; J. Burnham & Co. £341; R. Beaconsfield £219.
March 5	Bought goods for cash £114.
March 10	Paid wages in cash £120.
March 15	Bought motor van, paying by cheque £3,141.

March 20	J. Buckingham gave us a loan by cheque £5,000.
March 22	We returned goods to J. Taplow £50; D. Langley £26.
March 26	The following paid us by cheque C. Iver Ltd. £400; R. Beaconsfield £100 (part payment).
March 29	Bought goods on credit from D. Langley £305; K. Winslow Ltd. £210.
March 31	We paid J. Taplow £326 by cheque.

6.3   Enter the following transactions in the books of I. K. Brunel & Co., balance off the accounts at the end of the month and extract a trial balance as at 31 December 19-4.

19-4

December 1	Started in business with £8,000 in the bank.
December 1	Bought fixtures on credit from A. Bell & Son £1,750.
December 2	Credit purchases from S. Morse £305; G. Stephenson & Co. £600; R. Arkwright £840.
December 3	Bought motor van by cheque £2,950.
December 5	Cash sales £410.
December 6	Paid rates by cheque £310.
December 8	Paid motor expenses in cash £12.
December 10	Cash taken for own use (drawings) £100.
December 11	Credit Sales to: S. Crompton £349; J. Dunlop & Co. £420; B. Franklin & Son. £220.
December 14	Goods returned by us to: R. Arkwright £30; S. Morse £21.
December 15	Credit sales to: F. Whittel Ltd. £380; A. Fleming £70.
December 18	Paid insurance by cheque £116.
December 19	Paid motor expenses by cheque £24.
December 21	Credit purchases from B. Wallis & Son £115; S. Morse £280.
December 23	Paid for postages by cash £28.
December 26	Goods returned to us by J. Dunlop & Co. £30.
December 29	Received cheques from: S. Crompton £349; J. Dunlop & Co. £390.
December 30	Paid cheque to G. Stephenson & Co. £600.
December 31	Received commission by cheque £110.

6.4x   The following details are to be entered in the books of J. Price for the month of June 19-7, balance off the accounts, and then extract a trial balance as on 30 June 19-7:

19-7

June 1	Firm started with £7,500 in the bank and £250 in cash.
June 2	Bought office machinery on credit £880 from L. Waterhouse & Co.
June 2	Bought goods on credit: R. Touche £405; D. Ross Ltd. £340; K. Peat £200; C. Marwick & Co. £90.
June 3	Paid rent by cheque £80.
June 4	Cash Sales £122.

June 6	Sales on credit to: D. Anderson £340; K. Grenside £500; L. Thornton £102; J. Baker £71; T. Cooper & Son £195.
June 8	Bought goods paying by cash £58.
June 11	Paid for postages £35 by cash.
June 14	Paid insurance by cheque £130.
June 16	Goods bought on credit: D. Ross £70; G. D. May £304.
June 18	Goods returned to: R. Touche £35; K. Peat £10.
June 20	Paid rent by cash £80.
June 22	Goods returned to us by J. Baker £12; K. Grenside £30.
June 24	Paid for lighting and heating £34 by cheque.
June 26	Paid the following by cheque: R. Touche £370; C. Marwick & Co. £90.
June 29	Bought stationery paying by cash £68.
June 30	Cash taken for own use £100.

Chapter 7

Trading and Profit and Loss Accounts and Balance Sheets

Learning Objectives:

At the end of your study of this chapter you should:

1. understand some of the uses of a Trading Account and how Gross Profit is calculated,

2. be able to prepare both a Trading and Profit and Loss Account with a Balance Sheet,

3. be able to properly classify the balance sheet items. Assets into Fixed Assets and Current Assets. Liabilities into Current and Other Liabilities,

4. be able to distinguish Capital and Revenue Expenditure,

5. be able to make end of year adjustments to revenues and expenses.

6. be aware of the meaning of Capital Invested, Capital Employed and Working Capital.

The calculation of the profits earned by a business or the losses incurred by it, can probably be said to be the main objective of the accounting function. After all, the business was set up in the first place in the hope that profits could be earned, and the proprietor will want to know for various purposes how much profit has been made. Some of these reasons may be:

1. To compare how much profit has been made with what he had expected.

2. So as to enable him to plan ahead.

3. To show to his bank manager as and when he wants to borrow money from the bank.

4. For income tax purposes.

5. To show to a prospective partner or purchaser of the business.

In chapter five you saw how the expenses and revenues were collected together in appropriately named accounts prior to them being brought together to calculate profits or losses. For traders, meaning by this someone who mainly buys and sells goods, the profits or losses are calculated by using a special account called a Trading and Profit and Loss Account. This is dealt with in this chapter. For those who will carry on further studies in accounting next year, accounts for manufacturing businesses will be dealt with then.

One of the most important uses of the Trading and Profit and Loss Account is that of comparing the results of one period with those of other periods, also comparing results actually achieved against those expected. This is one of the areas which helped influence the Business Education Council to devise a core module called *'Numeracy and Accounting'*. The field of numeracy, Statistics, has a considerable part to play in helping the reader of accounts to interpret them.

A large number of businesses attach a great deal of importance to their gross profit percentage. This is the amount of profit made for every £100 of Sales, before deducting the running expenses of the business. This means that if sales are £10,000 and the cost of the goods sold (*not* including other expenses such as lighting, heating, motor expenses etc.) is £8,000, then the profit before the other expenses is £2,000. Expressed as a percentage of sales it is 20 per cent, i.e. for every £100 of sales the business made £20 profit before other expenses. The firm would compare this period's gross profit percentage with that of the previous periods.

So that the firm can more easily make comparisons, the practice exists of splitting up the account in which profit is calculated into two sections. The first section is called the Trading Account and is the one in which the Gross Profit is found, and the other section is used for the calculation of the Net Profit. Gross Profit, as already indicated, is the excess of the sales over the cost of goods sold. The net profit is found when the Profit and Loss Account part is completed. This part consists of the gross profit plus any revenue other than sales, such as commissions received or rent received, less the total costs used up in the period.

Where the cost of goods sold during a period exceeds the sales then this result is known as a Gross Loss, although such an occurrence would not normally happen very often. Where the other expenses exceed the Gross Profit plus other revenues then the result is Net Loss. You can see that, as the cost of goods sold figure is the one that is used in the calculation of gross profit, the accounting custom is to calculate profits only when the goods have been disposed of and not before.

We can now look at Exhibit 7.1 which is the trial balance of J. Morgan drawn up as on 31 December 19-3 after the completion of his first year in business.

Exhibit 7.1

J. Morgan
Trial Balance as on 31 December 19-3

	Dr. £	Cr. £
Sales		54,000 ✓
Purchases	42,400	
Rent and Rates	3,000	
Office Expenses	3,850	
General Expenses	150	
Fixtures and Fittings	5,000	
Creditors		5,600
Debtors	7,200	
Bank	900	
Cash	250	
Drawings	6,850	
Capital		10,000
	69,600	69,600

The first step in the calculation of profit is to draw up the Trading Account with the help of the information given in the Trial Balance. The definition of gross profit is 'sales less cost of goods sold', but on reflection you should be able to see that purchases will only equal cost of goods sold if all of the goods bought had been sold by 31 December 19-3. However, it would usually be the case that a trader would keep a stock of goods for resale, as the goods sold are normally being replenished all the time.

You may well ask where in the trial balance is the figure for the stock of goods? As this is a new business J. Morgan had started up, on 1st January 19-3, without a stock of goods. There is no record of stock of goods at 31 December 19-3, as what has been recorded as far as goods are concerned are (i) goods sold, i.e. sales, and (ii) goods bought, i.e. purchases. The only way left for Morgan to find the value of the stock of goods is by a stocktaking on 31 December 19-3 after the business for that day has been completed. The act of stocktaking is that of making a list of all the unsold goods in his possession, and then placing a value on them. The value normally used is that of the cost price of those goods. Let us assume that for Morgan's business this was calculated as £6,400. This will then mean that the cost of purchases less the cost of unsold goods will equal the cost of goods sold, if we ignore losses by wastage or theft. If this figure is deducted from the figure of sales we would arrive at the gross profit.

This could be calculated using ordinary arithmetic:

Sales	−	Cost of Goods Sold (Purchases − unsold stock)	=	Gross Profit
£54,000	−	£36,000 (£42,400 − £6,400)	=	£18,000

However, this is not performing the task by using double entry accounts. In double entry the balance of the sales account would be transferred to the trading account by debiting the sales account (thus closing it) and crediting the trading account. The balance on the purchases account would then be transferred to the trading account by crediting the purchases account (thus closing it) and debiting the trading account.

The accounts concerned with the movement of stock during the period have now been closed, and a trading account is being drawn up to a particular date, in this case 31 December 19-3. On this date Morgan has an asset for which now no account exists, namely stock (of unsold goods). To rectify this a stock account must be opened, and as this is an asset the amount of stock must be debited to it. You have already seen that the stock needs to be brought into the calculation of gross profit. Such a calculation is performed in the trading account, and therefore the corresponding credit for the closing stock should be in the trading account and this completes the double entry for the item.

It is usual for the trading account and the profit and loss account to be combined under one heading. The trading account is the top section whilst the profit and loss account is the lower section of the combined account. The balance on the trading account is described as 'gross profit' rather than simply as 'balance'. When calculated the gross profit is carried down to the profit and loss section of the account.

Exhibit 7.2

J. Morgan

Trading and Profit and Loss Account for the year ended 31 December 19-3

	£		£
Purchases	42,400	Sales	54,000
Gross Profit c/d	18,000	Closing Stock	6,400
	60,400		60,400
		Gross Profit b/d	18,000

So far the accounts used will appear as follows:

Sales

19-3	£	19-3	£
Dec. 31 Trading A/c	54,000	Dec. 31 Balance b/d	54,000

Purchases

19-3	£	19-3	£
Dec. 31 Balance b/d	42,400	Dec. 31 Trading A/c	42,400

Stock

19-3	£
Dec. 31 Trading A/c	6,400

Entering the closing stock on the credit side of the trading account is really a deduction from the purchases on the debit side. In accounting nowadays it is normal practice to show the closing stock as a deduction from the purchases in the trading account. This method then throws up a figure which can be described as 'cost of goods sold'. This can be seen in Exhibit 7.3.

We can now turn to the preparation of the profit and loss account. Apart from sales which has already been dealt with, all other revenue accounts should be transferred to the credit of the profit and loss account. Examples would be rent received and commission received.

The costs of the year which have been used up, in other words the expenses of the year, are transferred to the debit of the profit and loss account. You may also think, and you would be correct, that as the fixtures and fittings have been used throughout the year that they will have deteriorated, and consequently something should be charged for this fact. There are methods of charging for this but the methods are left until Chapter 11 where a full discussion of this factor takes place.

Now we can look at Exhibit 7.3 where the revised trading account is shown.

Exhibit 7.3   *J. Morgan*
Trading and Profit and Loss Account for the year ended 31 December 19-3

	£		£
Purchases	42,400	Sales	54,000
Less Closing Stock	6,400		
Cost of Goods Sold	36,000		
Gross Profit c/d	18,000		
	54,000		54,000
Rent and Rates	3,000	Gross Profit b/d	18,000
Office Expenses	3,850		
General Expenses	150		
Net Profit	11,000		
	18,000		18,000

The figure of £11,000 is a debit in the profit and loss account, and accordingly a credit is needed elsewhere. As capital of the proprietor is increased by the net profit, this means, using the accounting formula, that the credit entry of £11,000 for the profit should be in the capital account.

The trading and profit and loss account, plus all the revenue and expense accounts, can be seen to be devices to save unnecessary detail being entered in the capital account. Every sale at a profit and every other revenue increases the capital of the proprietor. Every sale of goods at a loss and every expense reduces the capital. Instead of the impractical task of altering the capital after every transaction the various items of profit and loss, of revenue and expense, are collected in suitably named accounts. Then they are all brought together in the trading and profit and loss account where the net increase/reduction in the capital is calculated.

Keeping a separate account for drawings can also be seen to be so as to avoid unnecessary detail in the capital account. Accordingly there will be just one total figure for drawings transferred to the debit of the capital account.

We can now look at the expense accounts after they have been closed also the capital account with the entries for drawings and profit.

Rent and Rates

19-3		£	19-3		£
Dec. 31 Balance b/d		3,000	Dec. 31 Profit and Loss A/c		3,000

Office Expenses

19-3		£	19-3		£
Dec. 31 Balance b/d		3,850	Dec. 31 Profit and Loss A/c		3,850

General Expenses

19-3		£	19-3		£
Dec. 31 Balance b/d		150	Dec. 31 Profit and Loss A/c		150

Capital

19-3		£	19-3		£
Dec. 31 Drawings		6,850	Jan. 1 Cash		10,000
Dec. 31 Balance c/d		14,150	Dec. 31 Net Profit from Profit and Loss A/c		11,000
		21,000			21,000

The Balance Sheet

After the trading and profit and loss account has been completed, a statement is drawn up in which the balances still remaining in the books are listed according to whether they are asset, liability or capital balances. The name given to this statement is 'balance sheet'. Chapter 2 gave examples of balance sheets. On the right-hand side of the balance sheet the assets are shown, whilst the left-hand side is for liabilities and capital.

You should note that the balance sheet is not part of the double entry system of bookkeeping, it is not an account, it is simply a statement showing the remaining balances arranged in a particular order. This is in direct contrast to the trading and profit and loss account. The very use of the word 'account' means that something is part of the double entry system. As the balance sheet is not part of the double entry system no entries are made in the actual asset, liability or capital accounts when the balance sheet is drawn up.

You might notice that in the accounting records an asset is shown as a debit balance, on the left hand side of an account, whereas in a balance sheet an asset is shown on the right-hand side. Why this inconsistency? There is no logical reason for this, in fact it would make the work of lecturers, teachers and textbook authors that much easier. As the balance sheet is not part of the double entry system there is no need to keep to the rules affecting accounts. Most countries in the world in fact do show assets on the left-hand side of the balance sheet. In the United Kingdom custom simply allocated the items the other way around.

There is no legal need to show assets on the right-hand side of a balance sheet and liabilities and capital on the left-hand side. It will be seen later that most large companies do not show them in either of these two ways. Usually, when these companies publish their balance sheets, they list them one under the other. Possibly, therefore, assets may be shown first with capital and liabilities shown underneath, or vice-versa. It is however possibly easier for you to visualise a balance sheet with two sides to it, as you will have become used to accounts with two sides to them. This method will therefore be the one adhered to in the rest of this volume.

We certainly do not have to redraft the trial balance after the trading and profit and loss account have been completed. It will be quite useful to do so, as it will reveal exactly which balances still remain in the accounting records. These are shown in Exhibit 7.4.

Exhibit 7.4

J. Morgan

Trial Balance as on 31 December 19-3
(after Trading and Profit and Loss Account completed)

	Dr. £	Cr. £
Fixtures and Fittings	5,000	
Creditors		5,600
Debtors	7,200	
Bank	900	
Cash	250	
Stock	6,400	
Capital		14,150
	19,750	19,750

One point needing special note is that the stock account was not in the original trial balance, but as it has been created since then we have now shown it in the redrafted trial balance.

Marshalling the assets, liabilities and capital in the balance sheet

The two main classifications of assets are those of Fixed Assets and Current Assets. Fixed Assets are those assets which are of long-life, are material items, are held to be used in the business and are not primarily for resale or for conversion into cash. Some examples are buildings, machinery, motor vehicles and fixtures.

Assets are called current assets when they represent cash or are primarily for conversion into cash or have a short life. An example of a short-lived asset is the stock of heating oil which will be used up in the near future. Other examples of current assets are stock of goods, debtors, cash and bank balances.

It is best if the assets in the balance sheet are shown under the separate headings of Fixed Assets and Current Assets. In doing this there are two ways of listing the assets under the two headings. The method preferred, because it helps to standardise the accounts of sole traders with those of limited companies, is that under each heading you start with the most permanent asset, or to define it in a different way the asset which is most difficult to turn into cash, and finishing with the asset which is the least permanent or easiest to turn into cash. The first assets to be shown are fixed assets, under the heading 'Fixed Assets' clearly stated. Current assets under their own heading are then shown.

The other main way of showing the assets in the balance sheet is the complete opposite to that described. This starts off with current assets, with the least permanent asset shown first, progressing to fixed assets, and the last item shown is the most permanent fixed asset. This method has been used by banks but has, in the main, fallen into disuse in the United Kingdom.

The reason why it is important that items should be given a particular place to be displayed is for convenience. If standardisation is maintained a comparison of a balance sheet of one firm with another is made that much easier, as you immediately know exactly where to look for particular items.

The first method is the one that will be kept to in this book. Using this method Exhibit 7.5 shows the order in which assets may be displayed.

Exhibit 7.5

> *Fixed Assets*
> Land and Buildings
> Fixtures and Fittings
> Machinery
> Motor Vehicles
>
> *Current Assets*
> Stock
> Debtors
> Bank
> Cash

Looking at the order in which the assets have been listed, the one that you would probably think that the authors have got wrong is that of stock. At first sight stock would seem to be more easily realisable than debtors. However, in fact debtors could probably be turned into cash by many businesses more easily than could stock. The debtors could be turned into cash by selling the rights to receive the debts to special finance firms called credit factors. On the other hand, to dispose of all the stock of a business is a difficult and long-winded task. The order in fact also follows the order in which full realisation of the stock takes place. Before any sale takes place there must be stock, when sold on credit this becomes debtors, when they pay by cheque, it becomes money in the bank, and when withdrawn from the bank it becomes cash.

If we now look at the other side of the balance sheet the first item is preferably that of capital. The next item would be long term liabilities such as loans not requiring payment for at least a year, and finishing with current liabilities, these being such things as debts for goods which will have to be paid in the near future. The other method is the complete reversal of this, but as this method conflicts with most company accounts it is best avoided.

If the balance sheet of J. Morgan is now drawn up to conform with these methods it will appear as in Exhibit 7.6.

Exhibit 7.6

J. Morgan
Balance Sheet as at 31 December 19-3

	£				£
Capital			*Fixed Assets*		
Cash Introduced	10,000		Fixtures and Fittings		5,000
Add Net Profit	11,000				
	21,000		*Current Assets*		
Less Drawings	6,850		Stock	6,400	
		14,150	Debtors	7,200	
Current Liabilities			Bank	900	
Creditors		5,600	Cash	250	
					14,750
		19,750			19,750

The following notes are applicable.

1. For capital, each class of liabilities and each class of assets, a separate total is needed. An instance of this is the £14,750 total for current assets. To do this the individual items are inset and the resultant totals extended into the end columns.

2. For each item normally just the final balance for the period is shown, e.g. bank £900. In the case of capital in a sole trader's balance sheet a summary of the account is shown. The capital will obviously be something in which the proprietor is very interested. If we had simply put only the final balance of £14,150 in the balance sheet then the balance sheet would 'balance'. The proprietor would however almost certainly ask "Where do you get the figure of £14,150 from?" Accountants over the years naturally got fed up with answering that question for a considerable number of people. They therefore evolved the custom of stating how the capital has changed over the year by means of profits/losses and drawings.

3. The word account is not shown after each item.
4. If you will compare the date on the balance sheet with that on the trading and profit and loss account, the basic difference between these two financial statements can be illuminated. The trading and profit and loss account is a *period statement,* in that it shows what has happened during a specified lapse of time, in this case the complete year of 19-3. The balance sheet is the opposite to this, it is a position statement drawn up *at one particular moment in time,* in this case the precise end of 19-3.

Capital and Revenue Expenditure

Capital expenditure can be said to be either that which is incurred in the purchase of fixed assets or that which adds to the value of fixed assets. Examples of capital expenditure are the purchase of machinery, the purchase price of a building, the legal costs incurred in the purchase of the building, costs of improvements to buildings.

Revenue expenditure does not add to the value of fixed assets. It consists of the costs actually incurred in running the business during a particular period.

The distinction between the two forms of expenditure is of extreme importance. It is the revenue expenditure which is chargeable to the trading and profit and loss account when the net profit is being calculated. Capital expenditure on the other hand reflects itself in the balance sheet. Should capital expenditure be incorrectly treated as revenue expenditure then too much will be charged as expenses, and consequently the net profit will be understated. On the other hand, if the opposite happens and too little gets charged as expenses then profit will be overstated. The calculation of the net profit is therefore dependent on the correct allocation of expenditure between capital and revenue expenditure.

There will be some items which are part capital expenditure and part revenue expenditure. An instance of this may be a building which has work done on it which is partly repairs (revenue expenditure) and partly improvements (capital expenditure). In these cases the expenditure is divided between the two forms of expenditure. The repairs part would be charged to a building repairs account, this would be charged as an expense in the Profit and Loss Account at the end of the financial period. The improvement part would be debited to the Buildings Account and would be shown as an increased amount in the balance sheet.

J. Morgan's Second Year

When J. Morgan has completed his second year in trading, on 31 December 19-4, a trial balance is drawn up. This is shown as Exhibit 7.7. You will notice that new sorts of accounts are shown for transactions which did not occur in the first year.

Exhibit 7.7

J. Morgan
Trial Balance as on 31 December 19-4

	Dr. £	Cr. £
Sales		87,500
Returns Inwards	1,500	
Purchases	55,600	
Returns Outwards		900
Rates	1,200	
Office Expenses	5,120	
Wages	6,840	
General Expenses	310	
Carriage Inwards	1,300	
Carriage Outwards	2,450	
Buildings	25,000	
Fixtures and Fittings	8,000	
Creditors		8,800
Debtors	12,350	
Bank	3,700	
Cash	300	
Drawings	8,280	
Capital		34,150
Stock	6,400	
Loan from B. Kilvert		7,000
	138,350	138,350

Notes:

1. The carriage (cost of transport) of goods into a firm is called Carriage Inwards, whilst the carriage of goods out of the firm to customers is called Carriage Outwards.

   When a firm buys goods some of them are bought 'carriage paid'. This means that the cost of the goods is that of the goods actually delivered to the buyer's place of business. Other goods are bought 'carriage forward'. This means that the buyer has to pay separately for carriage.

   All of this means that the purchases account will contain some goods which are carriage paid and some which are carriage forward, and consequently the goods bought are shown at two different price levels. To ensure that the purchases in one period are properly comparable with another period, the cost of carriage inwards is added to the purchases figure in the trading account. The resultant figure is then the cost of the goods as delivered to the business.

   Carriage outwards, on the other hands, is charged to the profit and loss account as an expense.

2. The stock figure in the trial balance is that from the previous year, it is therefore the opening stock for 19-4. From what you have read already you will know that the stock at the end of 19-4 can only be found by conducting a stocktaking. Assume that it amounts to £8,400.

3. When the gross profit is being calculated the figure of sales needed is that of the net sales, as some of the goods sold by Morgan were returned to him later. Similarly, the figure of purchases needed is that of the net purchases, because here also returns have been made, this time to the suppliers. To find these figures the returns inwards should be deducted from the sales figure, whilst the returns outwards should be deducted from the purchases figure.

4. You should also show as a charge in the trading account any wages of a productive nature, or any other expenses which are concerned with putting the product into a condition which makes it saleable. In Morgan's business we can assume that the wages are those of sales assistants, they are therefore non-productive and will be charged as such in the profit and loss account.

5. The increase in capital to £34,150 has occurred because J. Morgan has put another £20,000 into the business bank from his private resources outside the business.

We can first of all calculate the gross profit using ordinary arithmetic, and then draw up the trading and profit and loss accounts using double entry.

	£	£
Sales: are Total Sales	87,500	
less Returns Inwards	1,500	86,000
Opening Stock	6,400	
Add Total Purchases	55,600	
Less Returns Outwards	900	54,700
Add Carriage Inwards	1,300	
Cost of Goods Available for Sale	62,400	
Less Closing Stock	8,400	
Cost of Goods Sold		54,000
Gross Profit		32,000

J. Morgan
Trading & Profit & Loss Account for the year ended 31 December 19-4

		£		£
Opening Stock		6,400	Sales	86,000
Add Purchases	55,600			
Less Returns Outwards	900	54,700		
Carriage Inwards		1,300		
		62,400		
Less Closing Stock		8,400		
Cost of Goods Sold		54,000		
Gross Profit c/d		32,000		
		86,000		86,000
Wages		6,840	Gross Profit b/d	32,000
Office Expenses		5,120		
Rates		1,200		
Carriage Outwards		2,450		
General Expenses		310		
Net Profit		16,080		
		32,000		32,000

Now we can use the balances remaining, including the new balance on the stock account, to draw up a balance sheet as on 31 December 19-4.

J. Morgan
Balance Sheet as at 31 December 19-4

Capital		£	Fixed Assets		£
Balance 1.1.19-4	14,150		Buildings		25,000
Add Net Profit	16,080		Fixtures and Fittings		8,000
Add Cash Introduced	20,000				33,000
	50,230		Current Assets		
Less Drawings	8,280	41,950	Stock	8,400	
			Debtors	12,350	
Long Term Liability			Bank	3,700	
Loan from B. Kilvert		7,000	Cash	300	24,750
Current Liabilities					
Creditors		8,800			
		57,750			57,750

Final Accounts

Very often the collective name given to the Trading and Profit and Loss Account, together with the Balance Sheet, is that of 'Final Accounts'. This terms is rather misleading, as the balance sheet is not an account.

Stock Account

We can now look at the stock account for both years.

Stock

19-3	£	1 9 - 4	£
Dec. 31 Trading A/c	6,400	Jan. 1 Trading A/c	6,400
19-4			
Dec. 31 Trading A/c	8,400		

Adjustments at the end of a period

You have seen that the trading and profit and loss account have contained the revenue for a particular period, and that deducted from this has been the expenses for the period, the final result being a net profit or a net loss.

To this point in the book it has been assumed, for the sake of simplicity, that the revenue expenditure was entirely used up during the period of the trading and profit and loss accounts. Quite obviously however, this will not always be the case, as the amount in an expense account may cover more than the period covered by the trading and profit and loss account being drawn up.

An expense account will contain all the cash and cheque payments made in respect of that expense. If the whole of these costs are used up during the period, then the balance on that account can be transferred as an expense to the debit of the profit and loss account. On the other hand, when the costs used up and the amount paid are not equal to each other, then an adjustment will have to be made in respect of the overpayment or underpayment of costs used up in the period.

Underpayment of Expenses

Let us look at a firm where the rent is £4,000 per annum. It is payable every three months, on the last day of March, June, September and December. Tenancy commenced on 1st January, 19-6. The rent was paid in 19-6 on 29 March, 28 June, 2 October and 7 January 19-7.

The rent account will appear as follows for the year ended 31 December 19-6.

Rent

19-6	£
Mar. 29 Bank	1,000
Jun. 28 Bank	1,000
Oct. 2 Bank	1,000

The rent paid in 19-7 will appear as the part of the double entry in 19-7.

The rent costs used up in 19-6 amount to £4,000, as the premises have been occupied for a full year, and this therefore is the amount required to be transferred to the profit and loss account. To make the account balance the £1,000 rent owing at the end of 19-6 must be carried down to 19-7 as a credit balance, as the rent owing is a liability on 31 December 19-6.

The balance carried down could be described as "Rent Owing c/d", "Rent Accrued c/d", or "Accrued c/d". The latter description will be used now in showing the completed account.

Rent

19-6	£	19-6	£
Mar. 29 Bank	1,000	Dec. 31 Profit and Loss A/c	4,000
Jun. 28 Bank	1,000		
Oct. 2 Bank	1,000		
Dec. 31 Accrued c/d	1,000		
	4,000		4,000
		19-7	£
		Jan. 1 Accrued b/d	1,000

Expenses Prepaid

Now let us look at another firm where rent is also payable every 3 months, on the first day of January, April, July and October. The rent is £2,000 per annum. The property is occupied from 1 January 19-8. The account for the first year is now shown:

Rent

19-8	£
Jan. 1 Bank	500
Apl. 4 Bank	500
Jul. 11 Bank	500
Oct. 2 Bank	500
Dec. 28 Bank	500

The last item, paid on 28 December, is in fact completely for 19-9. The figure of expense needed for rent in the profit and loss account is £2,000. To achieve the balancing off of the account the prepayment of £500 is carried forward as such to 19-9. It can be seen to be an asset at 31 December 19-8 and as such it therefore needs to be carried forward as a debit balance.

The account can be shown.

Rent

19-8	£	19-8	£
Jan. 1 Bank	500	Dec. 31 Profit and Loss A/c	2,000
Apl. 4 Bank	500	Dec. 31 Prepaid c/d	500
Jul. 11 Bank	500		
Oct. 2 Bank	500		
Dec. 28 Bank	500		
	2,500		2,500
19-9			
Jan. 1 Prepaid b/d	500		

Prepayment will also occur when items, other than purchases, are bought for a business, and these items have not been fully used up in the business.

For instance suppose that oil is used for heating. During the year a total of £740 is spent on the purchase of oil. At the end of the year £160 stock of oil still remains. The stock is therefore a form of prepayment and will have to be carried to the next period where it will be used up.

Heating

19-8	£	19-8	£
Dec. 31 Total of Payments	740	Dec. 31 Profit and Loss A/c	580
		Dec. 31 Stock c/d	160
	740		740
19-9			
Jan. 1 Stock b/d	160		

The stock of oil is not added to the stock of goods (purchases) in the balance sheet, but is added to the other prepayments of expenses.

Revenue items outstanding

Sales revenue itself which is outstanding is already shown as balances on the customers' personal accounts, i.e. these are debtors. We must now consider other kinds of revenue such as commission receivable or rent receivable.

The revenue to be brought into the profit and loss account is that which has been earned during the period. If all the revenue earned is actually received during the period, then that will be the amount to be transferred to the credit of the profit and loss account. However, when all the revenue earned has not been received in the period an adjustment must be made. The amount receivable is the amount needed for the profit and loss account.

Let us look at a case where commission is earned and payment is made on a quarterly basis. The details are:

3 months to:
31 March 19-4   £290, received   6 April 19-4
30 June 19-4   £420, received 17 July 19-4
30 September 19-4 £505, received 10 October 19-4
31 December 19-4   £480, received 16 January 19-5

The account in the books for the year to 31 December 19-4, will appear as now shown.

Commissions Receivable

19-4	£
Apl. 6 Bank	290
Jul. 17 Bank	420
Oct. 10 Bank	505

The amount needed for the profit and loss account for 19-4 is £290 + £420 + £505 + £480 = £1,695. The amount needed to bring up the account total to this figure is £480, this being the amount owing for commission on 31 December 19-4. This balance is carried forward as a debit balance, as it represents an asset.

Commissions Receivable

19-4		£	19-4		£
Dec. 31 Profit and Loss A/c		1,695	Apl. 6	Bank	290
			Jul. 17	Bank	420
			Oct. 10	Bank	505
			Dec. 31	Accrued c/d	480
		1,695			1,695
19-5					
Jan. 1 Accrued b/d		480			

The balance sheet and expense and revenue account balances

Where there are balances on revenue and expense accounts, after the profit and loss account has been drawn up, then such balances have to be shown in the balance sheet.

The amounts owing by the firm are usually added together and shown as one figure. These could be listed as 'Expense Creditors', 'Accrued Expenses', or 'Expenses Owing'. The item would appear under current liabilities as they are expenses which would have to be paid in the near future.

The prepaid items are added together and are called 'Prepaid Expenses', 'Prepayments', or 'Payments in Advance'. Sometimes they are added to the debtors in the balance sheet, sometimes they are shown next under debtors.

Any amounts owing for rent receivable or commissions receiveable are usually added to debtors.

The following items of Rent Receivable £500 owing, Insurance owing £270, Rates prepaid £130, Stock of Stationery £180, Wages owing £600 would appear in a balance sheet as follows:

Balance Sheet as at 31 December 19-7

Current Liabilities	£	Current Assets	£
Trade Creditors		Stock	180
Accrued Expenses	870	Debtors	500
		Prepayments	130
		Bank	
		Cash	

Various kinds of capital

The claim of the proprietor is represented by the capital account. The word 'Capital' is, however, often given different meanings. The main meanings are:

1. Capital invested. By this is meant the actual amount of money, or money's worth, which has been brought into the business by the proprietor from his outside interests.

2. Capital employed. This term has quite a few meanings, and it is often used quite loosely. At an elementary level it is usually taken to mean the difference between the assets and liabilities of the business at a particular point in time. You will undoubtedly realise that at a balance sheet date this is represented by the closing balance on the capital account. It is sometimes called 'Net Assets'.

3. Working capital. This is a term which simply means the excess of the current assets over the current liabilities of a business.

Working capital in the balance sheet

It is increasingly common to find that the amount of Working Capital is shown as a figure in the balance sheets of firms. The balance sheet of J. Morgan at 31 December 19-4 is now redrafted to illustrate this point, the figure of £15,950 being displayed separately.

J. Morgan
Balance Sheet as at 31 December 19-4

Capital		£	Fixed Assets		£
Balance 1.1.19-4	14,150		Buildings		25,000
Add Net Profit	16,080		Fixtures and Fittings		8,000
Add Cash Introduced					33,000
	20,000				
	50,230		Current Assets		
Less Drawings	8,280	41,950	Stock	8,400	
			Debtors	12,350	
Long Term Liability			Bank	3,700	
Loan from B. Kilvert		7,000	Cash	300	
				24,750	
			Less Current Liabilities		
			Creditors	8,800	15,950
		48,950			48,950

Sufficiency of working capital

The Working Capital should be adequate to be able to finance the business without too much strain. Exactly what this should be will vary with different types of business. This will be examined in more detail later in the book.

Goods for own use

Very often the proprietors of businesses will take goods for their own use without actually paying for them. There is certainly nothing illegal about this if entries are made to record such an action. The normal action taken is to credit the purchases account and to debit the drawings account.

Those of you who work in accounting practices may well know that in the U.K. any goods taken by the proprietors should, for tax purposes, be charged out at selling prices. The choice is between showing the transfers at selling price in the accounts, or instead showing the transfers at cost, leaving the profit difference to be shown in tax calculations completely outside the double-entry bookkeeping system. In examination questions the transfers should be shown at the figures as given.

The valuation of stock

In the interests of simplification it has been assumed that giving a value to the stock is something that could be done very easily. Thus it has been stated that the stock is valued at 'cost'. However the word 'cost' has quite a few different meanings. This will be looked at later in your studies.

Assignment Exercises

7.1   From the following trial balance of F. Chaplin draw up a trading and profit and loss account for the year ended 31 December 19-8 and a balance sheet as at that date.

Trial Balance as at 31 December 19-8

	Dr. £	Cr. £
General Expenses	210	
Rent and Rates	400	
Motor Expenses	735	
Salaries	3,560	
Insurance	392	
Purchases	14,305	
Sales		26,815
Stock 1 January 19-8	4,080	
Motor Vehicle	2,800	
Creditors		5,160
Debtors	4,090	
Premises	20,000	
Cash at Bank	1,375	
Cash in Hand	25	
Capital		24,347
Drawings	4,350	
	56,322	56,322

Stock at 31 December 19-8 was £4,960

7.2x Extract a trading and profit and loss account for the year ended 30 June 19-4 for F. Kidd. The trial balance as at 30 June 19-4 was as follows:

	Dr.	Cr.
	£	£
Rent and Rates	1,560	
Insurance	305	
Lighting and Heating	516	
Motor Expenses	1,960	
Salaries and Wages	4,850	
Sales		35,600
Purchases	21,650	
Trade Expenses	806	
Motor Vans	3,500	
Creditors		3,250
Debtors	6,810	
Shop fixtures	3,960	
Shop buildings	28,000	
Stock 1 July 19-3	9,320	
Cash at bank	1,134	
Drawings	6,278	
Capital		51,799
	90,649	90,649

Stock at 30 June 19-4 was £9,960

7.3 The financial year of J. Thomas ended on 31 December 19-6. Show the ledger accounts for the following items including the balance transferred to the necessary part of the final accounts, also the balances carried down to 19-7.

(a) Motor Expenses: Paid in 19-6 £744; Owing at 31 December 19-6 £28.

(b) Insurance: Paid in 19-6 £420; Prepaid as at 31 December 19-6 £35.

(c) Rent: Paid during 19-6 £1,800; Owing as at 31 December 19-5 £250; Owing as at 31 December 19-6 £490.

(d) Rates: Paid during 19-6 £950; Prepaid as at 31 December 19-5 £220; Prepaid as at 31 December 19-6 £290.

(e) Thomas sub-lets part of the premises. Receives £550 during the year ended 31 December 19-6. Tenant owed Thomas £180 on 31 December 19-5 and £210 on 31 December 19-6.

7.4x J. Percival's year ended on 30 June 19-4. Write up the ledger accounts, showing the transfers to the final accounts and the balances carried down to the next year for the following:

(a) Stationery: Paid for the year to 30 June 19-4 £855; Stocks of stationery at 30 June 19-3 £290; at 30 June 19-4 £345.

(b) General expenses: Paid for the year to 30 June 19-4 £590; Owing at 30 June 19-3 £64; Owing at 30 June 19-4 £90.

(c) Rent and Rates (combined account): Paid in the year to 30 June 19-4 £3,890; Rent owing at 30 June 19-3 £160; Rent paid in advance at 30 June 19-4 £250; Rates owing 30 June 19-3 £205; Rates owing 30 June 19-4 £360.

(d) Motor Expenses: Paid in the year to 30 June 19-4 £4,750; Owing as at 30 June 19-3 £180; Owing as at 30 June 19-4 £375.

(e) Percival earns commission from the sales of one item. Received for the year to 30 June 19-4 £850; Owing at 30 June 19-3 £80; Owing at 30 June 19-4 £145.

7.5   The following is the trial balance of P. Peterson, drawn up as on 31 December 19-7. Draw up a trading and profit and loss account for the year ended 31 December 19-7 and a balance sheet as at that date.

	Dr. £	Cr. £
Capital		65,697
Drawings	6,300	
Fixtures and fittings	3,250	
Motor Vehicles	4,180	
Creditors		12,253
Premises	30,000	
General Expenses	745	
Lighting and Heating	1,217	
Insurance	408	
Debtors	13,100	
Rent and Rates	2,316	
Office expenses	605	
Bank	1,153	
Motor expenses	2,175	
Salaries and wages	6,297	
Carriage Inwards	404	
Sales		122,050
Purchases	101,300	
Stock 1 January 19-7	26,550	
	200,000	200,000

Notes at 31 December 19-7:
1. Stock £28,480.
2. Rates owing £204.
3. Motor expenses owing £110.
4. Insurance prepaid £58.
5. Ignore depreciation of fixed assets.

7.6x   L. Cox draws up his trial balance as at 31 December 19-4 as shown below. Draw up a set of final accounts for the year.

	Dr. £	Cr. £
Packing Expenses	525	
Sundry Expenses	190	
Lighting & Heating Expenses	416	
Insurance	205	
Rent	1,800	
Rates	906	
Salaries and Wages	5,689	
Motor Expenses	1,416	
Sales		68,300
Purchases	51,150	
Returns Inwards	200	
Returns Outwards		350
Stock 1 January 19-4	15,690	
Debtors	16,314	
Creditors		10,170
Fixtures and Fittings	4,300	
Drawings	6,950	
Capital		29,256
Cash in hand	150	
Cash at bank	2,175	
	108,076	108,076

Notes at 31 December 19-4:

1. Expenses which have been prepaid: Insurance £19; Rates £150.
2. Expenses which are owing: Rent £600; Sundry Expenses £15; Motor Expenses £210.
3. Stock £17,170.
4. Ignore depreciation of fixed assets.

7.7 The following is the trial balance of F. Larkin as at 31 March 19-6. Draw up a set of final accounts for the year ended 31 March 19-6.

	Dr.	Cr.
	£	£
Stock 1 April 19-5	18,160	
Sales		92,340
Purchases	69,185	
Carriage Inwards	420	
Carriage Outwards	1,570	
Returns Outwards		640
Wages and Salaries	10,240	
Rent and Rates	3,015	
Communication Expenses	624	
Commissions Payable	216	
Insurance	405	
Sundry Expenses	318	
Buildings	20,000	
Debtors	14,320	
Creditors		8,160
Fixtures	2,850	
Cash at bank	2,970	
Cash in hand	115	
Loan from K. Blake		10,000
Drawings	7,620	
Capital		40,888
	152,028	152,028

Notes at 31 March 19-6:
1. Prepaid expenses: Insurance £29; Sundry Expenses £22.
2. Expenses owing: Rent £250; Communication Expenses £85; Commissions Payable £24.
3. Stock £22,390.
4. Ignore depreciation of fixed assets.

7.8x J. Goodier drew up the following trial balance as at 30 September 19-8. You are to draft trading and profit and loss accounts for the year to 30 September 19-8 and a balance sheet as at that date.

	Dr. £	Cr. £
Loan from P. Parkin		5,000
Capital		25,955
Drawings	8,420	
Cash at Bank	3,115	
Cash in Hand	295	
Debtors	12,300	
Creditors		9,370
Stock 30 September 19-7	23,910	
Motor Van	4,100	
Office Equipment	6,250	
Sales		130,900
Purchases	92,100	
Returns Inwards	550	
Carriage Inwards	215	
Returns Outwards		307
Carriage Outwards	309	
Motor Expenses	1,630	
Rent and Rates	2,970	
Telephone Charges	405	
Wages and Salaries	12,810	
Insurance	492	
Office Expenses	1,377	
Sundry Expenses	284	
	171,532	171,532

Notes at 30 September 19-8:

(a) Prepaid expenses: Insurance £105; Rates £405.

(b) Expenses owing: Rent £300; Telephone £85.

(c) Stock £27,475.

(d) Ignore depreciation of fixed assets.

Chapter 8

Concepts and Conventions

Learning Objectives:

At the end of your study of this chapter you should:

1. **understand the significance of the basic Concepts and Conventions of Accounting for the preparation of Trading and Profit and Loss Accounts and Balance Sheets.**

So far the main part of accounting in this book has been concerned with the entering of transactions in the accounting records. We will later get to the parts of accounting which deal with the classifying, summarising and interpreting of the accounting records. Before proceeding on to such aspects we will now look at the basic concepts and conventions of accounting.

You must not be surprised if you do not agree with all of the concepts and conventions. You may well think that something could be better done in some other way. Accounting is not a static subject, it is constantly undergoing change. Some of the changes are as a result of outside pressure from non-accountants, whilst others stem from within the accountancy profession itself.

The final accounts shown in chapter seven were drawn up for the benefit of the owner of the business, Mr. Morgan. You will see later on that a business can be owned by more than one person, and in such a case the final accounts will be for the benefit of them all. Let us consider a few other uses to which Mr. Morgan's final accounts can be put. One fairly obvious one is that they would be used by the Inspector of Taxes when Mr. Morgan's profits for Income Tax were being calculated. The bank manager would also want to see a copy of the final accounts if Mr. Morgan wanted to borrow money from the bank. In addition Morgan may want to show them to a prospective purchaser of the business, a prospective partner or to one of his suppliers if he wanted to be given quite a lot of goods on credit terms. In the cases of partnerships and limited companies, each partner or each shareholder would also want a copy.

A little reflection on your part might well bring home to you that in fact it would be better if different sets of accounts were prepared for different purposes. For instance the bank manager's view of the accounts would largely be concerned about whether Morgan would be able to repay the money borrowed from the bank if his firm suddenly ceased trading. The asset values which would be of more interest to the bank manager would therefore be how much they would fetch on sale rather than what they had cost. Similarly the prospective buyer would rather know how much profits he could make from the business instead of simply seeing how Morgan had fared. However, accounting has basically been concerned with accounts simply for the proprietors' use only. As matters stand therefore this one set of accounts has to be used for all the other purposes, and this accordingly is not an ideal situation. There is nothing to prevent alternative accounts being drafted, it is simply that the normal procedure, especially in a small firm, is for only one set of final accounts to be drawn up to serve all purposes.

What all of this means is that Trading and Profit and Loss Accounts are multi-purpose documents. If these have to be of any use to the various parties then these parties have to agree to the way that they are drawn up. Let us look at what this means. Assume that you are in a class of students, and that you are faced with the problem of valuing your assets, which consist simply of 5 textbooks. The first sort of value you decide to put on them is the saleable value. Your own assessment is £8, but other members of the class may give figures ranging from £3 to £14. Suppose instead that the value you will give them is the value of their use to you. In your own estimation you think that the use of these books will help you pass your examinations and so pave the way to an extremely good job. Another person in the class may have completely the opposite view of the value of the books to him. The use values of the books to the different members of the class will therefore differ very widely between members of the class. Then finally you decide to value them by reference to their cost. You have in fact got the receipts for the money paid by you for the books, and these show that you paid out a total of £24. The other members of the class agree that this was the price paid for the books.

The cost price of the books is therefore the only value to which all members of the class could agree. If a multi-purpose document has to be accepted in general use there is no point in having as values figures which cannot be agreed to by all. The cost price is therefore the value given to assets in the accounting records of a firm.

If a measure is used to gain a consensus of opinion, rather than to use one's own measure which might conflict with other people's, it is said to be objective. In contrast with this, the using of your own measure, whether other people agree with it or not, is said to be subjective. The desire to provide one set of accounts for a number of different users, and consequently gains their consensus of opinion, means that objectivity is sought after in financial accounting. If you can understand this desire for objectivity then you will understand many of the contradictions that there appear to exist in accounting.

Financial accounting seeks objectivity, and consequently rules have to be laid down as to the ways in which financial activities are entered in the accounting records. Such rules are generally known as concepts.

Basic Concepts

1. *The Cost Concept*

   You have just already read the need for this earlier in this chapter. It means that assets are normally recorded at cost, and this value is that which is used for assessing the future usage of an asset.

2. *The Money Measurement Concept*

   Accounting is only concerned with those items which can measured in monetary terms, and in addition the monetary value placed on the item has to be measured objectively. This means that the full picture of the state of a business can never be seen in Accounting, nor can it show fully how well or otherwise the business is being conducted. Accounting does not itself show you whether or not the firm has a good workforce or whether the management is of a high calibre. It would not show that discontent amongst the workers is just about to lead to a strike, or that the firm's best customer is going to become bankrupt next week. It does not reveal that the firm's biggest competitor is just about to launch a first-class product on to the market which will take a lot of business away from the firm whose accounts we are considering.

   Looking therefore at a set of accounting figures does not give you the full story of what is happening to a business. Those people who think that it does are simply deluding themselves. Others maintain that accounting should endeavour to place a monetary value on these other factors, but the argument against that is that it would lead to a severe loss of objectivity. Try placing a value on the services which will be given to the firm by one of its workers, or of putting a monetary value on the fact that the firm has just placed a new product on to the market and the initial reactions to the product are very unclear as yet. Certainly,different people would give different figures for these items, and therefore as the accounts are of a multi-purpose nature which need to be acceptable to the many parties involved, such a placing of values cannot be undertaken. In accounting as it stands, if an acceptable figure for all parties cannot be agreed to, then the task will not be undertaken at all.

3. *The Going Concern Concept*

   If the opposite is not known Accounting will always assume that the business will continue to exist for an indefinitely long period of time. Only if the business was going to be disposed of would it be necessary to show how much the assets would fetch. In the accounting records normally this is to be assumed to be of no interest to the firm. All of this is obviously connected with the cost concept. If firms were not assumed to be going concerns the cost concept could not really be used, as if the firms were always to be treated as though they were going to be sold immediately after the balance sheet date, then the saleable values of the assets would be much more relevant than cost.

4. *The Business Entity Concept*

The only transactions that are entered in the accounting records of a firm are those that affect the firm itself. The only way that an attempt is made to show anything about the financial position of the proprietor is limited to showing how his capital in the firm is affected. If he puts another £10,000 cash into the business the accounting records will show that the firm has £10,000 more cash and that his capital has increased by £10,000. The accounting records do not show he has £10,000 less in his private resources. The accounting records are limited to the firm itself as a separate entity.

5. *The Realisation Concept*

In accounting, profit is normally regarded as being earned at the time when the goods or services are passed to the customer and he incurs liability for them. The profit is treated as being realised on that date. You must notice very carefully that it is not when the order is received from the customer, not when the contract is signed, nor is it dependent on waiting until the customer pays for the goods or services.

This can mean that profit can be taken as being realised in one account period, and then it is discovered to have been incorrectly taken as such when the goods are returned as being faulty in a later period. Alternatively the services could have been subject to an allowance in the later period because the services had been poorly performed. If the returns or allowances could have been estimated with reasonable accuracy, then an adjustment could have been made to the calculated profit in the period when the goods or services passed to the customer.

6. *The Dual Aspect Concept*

This concept states that there are two aspects to Accounting. One aspect is represented by the assets of the business and the other by the claims against them. The aspects are always equal to each other, and in chapter two it has been called the accounting equation. It can be written:

$$\text{Assets} = \text{Liabilities} + \text{Capital}$$

7. *The Accrual Concept*

Net profit is said to be the difference between revenues and expenses rather than that between cash receipts and expenditures. This concept is known as the Accrual Concept. When the actual mechanics of carrying out the accrual concept are being performed, then this is known as 'matching' expenses against revenues.

For people not well versed in accounting this concept is often quite puzzling. Many of these people imagine that expenses in a period consists of the actual payments made. Instead the fact is that expenses consists of the assets used up in a particular period in the obtaining of the revenues for that period, and normally cash paid in a period and expenses of a period are not equal to each other.

The Assumption of the Stability of Currency

Most readers will be very aware of the fact that a few years ago many goods could be bought for much less money than today. Accounting, however, uses the cost concept. This means that over a period accounting statements will show distorted figures, because assets bought at different times, at the prices then ruling, will be added up to show the total of the assets in cost terms.

Suppose for instance you bought a building 10 years ago for £50,000, and then now, 10 years later, you buy another building which is identical in every way except for the price, £100,000. The two figures are added up to show buildings at a figure of £150,000. The figure £150,000 is correct historically, but apart from that the total figure cannot be said to be particularly valid for any other purpose.

To get a proper assessment of accounting records one must therefore bear in mind the distorting effects of changing price levels. The techniques of making amendments to correct such distortions are outside the scope of this volume.

The Conventions of Accounting

The concepts of accounting have been accepted for many years. They are, however, capable of being interpreted in many ways. There has accordingly grown up generally accepted approaches to the application of the concepts. The main conventions are 1. Materiality, 2. Conservatism (alternatively called Prudence), 3. Consistency.

1. *Materiality*

   The effort of recording a transaction in a particular way should always be worthwhile doing, barring some cases where legal needs have to be observed. If it is not worthwhile then accounting would not be serving a useful purpose.

   Let us look at a few obvious items which are not worthwhile recording in a certain way. For instance a box of paperclips may last a very small firm for more than one accounting period. Every time you clip one piece of paper to another you will use up part of this cost of paperclips. To record this as an expense every time a paperclip is used would simply not be worthwhile, as the price of the paperclips would be so little. Instead, as the box of paperclips is not a material item, the cost of the box of paperclips would be charged as an expense in the period it was bought, irrespective of the fact that it could last for more than one accounting period. We could put it another way, do not waste your time in the elaborate recording of trivial items.

   In a similar way a cheap waste-bin would be charged as an expense in the period it was bought, irrespective of the fact that the waste-bin could last for fifty years. Compared with this a machine costing many thousands of pounds would be deemed to be a material item, and consequently, as you will read in the chapter on depreciation, we attempt to charge each accounting period with the cost consumed in each period of use.

You may well ask, and you would be very sensible to do so, exactly what amount would be considered to be a material item. Is it £5, £50 or £500? The answer is that there are no exact rules at all. The decision as to what is material and what is not is totally dependent on judgement. One firm may well decide that all items under £50 should be treated as expenses in the period in which they were bought, even though in fact the items may stay in use in the firm for many years. A different firm, and this would be especially true of a large firm, may well fix the limit at £500, or even £1,000. Different limits may well be fixed by a firm for different types of items.

The size and type of firm will obviously affect their judgement as to what is, or is not, a material item. For you, as a student, £50 would probably be a material item. For a millionaire £50 would be a relatively insignificant amount. Just as people vary in their opinions as to what is and what is not material, then so do firms.

In fact, with two firms having the same amount of sales and net profit, in one firm having a lot of machinery an item of £300 may well be treated as not being material, whereas the other firm has very little machinery and might treat even as small a figure as £100 for a machine as being material.

2. *Conservatism (or Prudence)*

An accountant very frequently has to choose which figure to take for a particular item. The concept of conservatism, or prudence as it often known, establishes that under normal conditions he will take the figure which will understate rather than overstate profits. Another way of stating this is to say that he would choose the figure which would cause the capital to be shown at a lower rather than a higher figure.

Following this same approach it could also be said that accountants ensure that all losses are recorded in the books, but profits should not be anticipated by recording them prematurely.

It is undoubtedly this convention that has often led people in the past to think of accountants as being rather miserable by nature, as they favour showing lower rather than higher profits by generally looking at financial affairs rather sceptically. This convention has however seen considerable changes in the past 30 years, as it is becoming more evident that accountants will turn away from such gloomy points of view and move towards showing a brighter picture when it is warranted.

Before you make up your mind that accountants are unnecessarily pessimistic, it should be pointed out that the history of business is littered with bankruptcies and company liquidations brought about by businessmen with over-optimistic ideas about the progress of their organisations. The accountant does not run the organisation, he will simply advise the owner(s). It is his duty therefore to try to bring the owner(s) of the business to a proper and sober appraisal of the affairs of the business. Naturally, the owner(s) can ignore the accountant's advice if they so wish. The accountant can also help when the opposite applies in that the owner(s) under-appraise the progress of the business.

3. *Consistency*

You can see that the conventions and concepts already listed are so broad in nature that each of them could affect the accounting records in many detailed different ways. There is no doubt that each firm should use the concepts and conventions so that the picture of the activities of the business are shown in an equitable fashion.

This cannot be done if one method is used one year and a different method in the next year, and so on. If the methods are changed constantly then the profits shown would be completely distorted. It would not be possible to compare one year's profits with another.

There is consequently a convention of consistency. This states that when a firm has started to use a method for the accounting treatment for particular items then it will enter all similar items that follow in exactly the same way.

This does not mean that the firm always has to use the particular methods until eventually the firm closes down. A firm can change the methods used, but this should not be effected until it has received a great deal of consideration. Where such a change is made, and the profits or losses are altered by a material amount, then, either in the profit and loss account or in notes attached to it, the effect of the change(s) should be clearly stated.

Accounting Terminology

Many of the terms used in accounting theory unfortunately mean different things to different people. What one person may call principles someone else may describe as concepts and conventions, whilst another person will list them all as concepts. If you understand that this is so, then you should not get too confused by terminology being used in different ways.

Chapter 9

The Division of the Ledger: Cash Books

Learning Objectives:

At the end of your study of this chapter you should:

1. understand the division of ledgers into specialised functions,
2. be able to prepare two and three column cash books,
3. understand the importance of folio referencing,
4. be aware of and able to handle a Petty Cash Book using the Imprest System.

Whilst the firm is still a small one, entering into a relatively few transactions, all of the double entry accounts could be kept within one book called the ledger. You will easily appreciate that when the firm grows and the number of transactions increase, that one book would soon become too bulky for convenient use. Naturally, accountants have arrived at a solution to this problem.

One way would be to have two ledgers, then three ledgers and so on as the firm grew, with the accounts contained in them being chosen at random. It would however be difficult to remember exactly which accounts were in which ledger, and a lot of time would be wasted in tracing exactly where the accounts were.

The solution that accountants arrived at was to divide the ledger up into its different functions. For the personal accounts, we could have two ledgers, one for the customers' personal accounts which we could call the Sales Ledger, and one for the suppliers' personal accounts called the Purchases Ledger. Another function which takes up quite a lot of space is that in respect of the receipt and payment of money. Therefore for the receipt and payment of cash and cheques the cash account and the bank account are taken out of the ledger and combined together in one book called the Cash Book. The rest of the accounts, these are the expense, revenue and asset and liability accounts, could be retained in the one ledger which could be called either a General Ledger or a Nominal Ledger. It is important to realise that the ledgers and the cash book contain accounts, in other words they are all part of the double entry.

The division of the ledger makes the division of work simpler if more than one person is needed to enter transactions in the accounting records. Each of the book-keepers could be allocated their work by functions, each bookkeeper taking over the book or books for the function(s) covered by him.

The general ledger, in its new state, would still need to be used quite extensively. After all it would contain the sales account, purchases account, returns inwards account, returns outwards account, all of the expense and revenue accounts, assets other than cash, bank and debtors, and liabilities other than creditors.

So that the general ledger does not have to be continually used by more than one person, another technique is used to save the sales, purchases, returns inwards and returns outwards accounts from containing unnecessary detail. For this purpose four new books are opened. These are for credit transactions only. One book is used for credit sales, one for credit purchases, one for returns inwards and another for returns outwards. All of these books are dealt with in detail in chapter ten. The idea behind this is that when a credit sale is made, an entry for this is made in the customer's personal account but an entry is not made in the sales account. Instead the credit sale is listed in the sales book. Periodically the total of the sales book is transferred to the credit side of the sales account in the general ledger. Only at the time when that total was being transferred would the general ledger need the collaboration of two people, one being the person whose job it is to look after the general ledger and the other being the person who looks after the sales book. Similar actions would be used for purchases, returns inwards and returns outwards.

As the firm grows therefore, each book-keeper would move towards specialising in the different functions recorded in the books. Just how far this proceeds depends on how large the firm grows, and the exact requirements of the business. For instance it might become impossible for one book-keeper to look after the sales ledger as the number of customers continued to increase, as the number of entries simply could not be handled by one person. The solutions to this could vary. It might be resolved simply by having one sales ledger which contained customers' accounts with names commencing A to M, and another sales ledger with letters N to Z. However, it might be better for the firm if it was split on a geographical basis, say one sales ledger for the United Kingdom customers, and another for overseas customers. Any other suitable method would suffice. In the same way the cash book could be split into a Cash Payments Book and a separate Cash Receipts Book.

At this juncture however we are concerned with the basic division of the ledger, rather than how these can be sub-divided later. These can be summarised:

The Ledger is divided into:

Sales Ledger Purchases Ledger General Ledger Cash Book	All of these contain accounts and are therefore part of the double-entry system.
Sales Book Purchases Book Returns Inwards Book Returns Outwards Book	These are simply listing devices to save the relevant double entry accounts from containing unnecessary details

The Cash Book

The Two Column Cash Book

The Cash Book consists simply of the cash account and the bank account put together to form one book. Up to now these have been on separate pages of the ledger. You can see that it is in fact more convenient to place the account columns together so that all the money received and all the money paid, whether in cash or by cheque, can be found on one page. To do this the cash book is ruled so that the debit column of the cash account and the debit column of the bank account are placed alongside each other, and the credit columns of the cash and bank accounts are also placed alongside each other.

Exhibit 9.1 shows a cash account and a bank account as if they have been kept as separate accounts in a ledger, and then shown as they would be displayed in a cash book.

Exhibit 9.1

Cash

19-4		£	19-4		£
May 1	Balance b/d	80	May 7	Stationery	20
May 7	K. Fleming	130	May 14	J. Sharp	22
May 18	B. Smith˙	34	May 30	Wages	180
May 31	K. Sellars	46	May 31	Balance c/d	68
		290			290
Jun 1	Balance b/d	68			

Bank

19-4		£	19-4		£
May 1	Balance b/d	2,360	May 6	Rent	150
May 5	E. Schofield	495	May 15	P. Quinn	424
May 22	R. Mason	305	May 28	A. Daley Ltd.	576
May 30	R. Eastman	160	May 31	Balance c/d	2,170
		3,320			3,320
Jun 1	Balance b/d	2,170			

Cash Book

19-4		Cash £	Bank £	19-4		Cash £	Bank £
May 1	Balance b/d	80	2,360	May 6	Rent		150
May 5	E. Schofield		495	May 7	Stationery	20	
May 7	K. Fleming	130		May 14	J. Sharp	22	
May 18	B. Smith	34		May 15	P. Quinn		424
May 22	R. Mason		305	May 28	A. Daley Ltd.		576
May 30	R. Eastman		160	May 30	Wages	180	
May 31	K. Sellars	46		May 31	Balance c/d	68	2,170
		290	3,320			290	3,320
Jun 1	Balances b/d	68	2,170				

Cash Paid into the Bank

In Exhibit 9.1 the payments into the bank have consisted entirely of cheques received by the firm which have been banked immediately. We must now look at cash being paid into the bank. Consider now the case of a customer paying his account in cash, and then later part of the cash is paid into the bank. The cash banked affects the records as follows:

Effect	Action
1. Asset of cash is reduced.	Credit the asset account, this being represented by the cash column in the cash book.
2. Asset of bank is increased.	Debit the asset account, this being represented by the bank column in the cash book.

If £500 cash is received from J. Wright Ltd. on 1 May 19-4, and then £440 of that is banked on 2 May 19-4 the cash book will appear as follows:

		Cash	Bank			Cash	Bank
19-4		£	£	19-4		£	£
May 1	J. Wright Ltd.	500		May 2	Bank	440	
May 2	Cash		440				

As you know, the details column should give the name of the account where the corresponding part of the double entry has been recorded. Against the cash payment of £440 appears the word 'Bank' meaning that the debit of £440 is to be found in the bank column, and the converse applies.

If the whole of the cash received is banked immediately then the receipt can be shown as a direct entry into the bank column on the debit side of the cash book, i.e. it is treated for entry purposes in the same manner as a cheque.

When the firms needs cash for payment, but has insufficient cash in hand for the purpose, then the firm may withdraw cash from the bank. The way that this is done is by making out a cheque to pay itself a certain amount of cash. The proprietor, or an authorised employee, will visit the bank and exchange the cheque for the amount of cash stated on it. This is usually known as 'cashing a cheque'.

This may be summarised:

Effect	Action
1. Asset of cash is increased	Debit the asset account, which is represented by the cash column in the cash book.
2. Asset of bank is reduced	Credit the asset account, which is represented by the bank column in the cash book.

If £250 cash is withdrawn on 1 July 19-6 from the bank it would appear as follows:

		Cash	Bank			Cash	Bank
19-6		£		19-6			£
Jul 1	Bank	250		Jul 1	Cash		250

When an item does not need entering in another book as part of the double entry because it had been completed within the cash book itself, then this is known as a 'contra' item, the Latin word for 'against'. The cash paid into the bank, and the cash withdrawn, are both contra items.

The Use of Folio Columns

You have already seen that the details column in an account contains the title of the account in which the other half of the double entry has been completed. It is therefore possible when looking at the account to see where the completion is of the other part of the double entry.

However, with an increase in the number of books in use, the simple mention of the other title may not be sufficient to give a quick reference to the location of the account. An extra aid is required and this is brought about by the use of a 'folio' column. In each account, in each book, an extra column is printed, this is always shown on the immediate left-hand side of the money columns. This column is used to enter the name of the other book in an abbreviated form, plus the number of the page in the other book where double entry is completed.

An entry of a receipt of cash from D. Towers whose account was on page 189 of the sales ledger, and the cash is recorded on page 77 of the cash book, would use the folio colums as follows:

In the sales ledger. In the folio column alongside the entry of the amount would appear CB 77

In the cash book. In the folio column alongside the entry of the amount would appear SL 189.

A full cross-reference is thus given. For contra items the letter 'C' is shown in the folio column.

The folio columns are only filled in when double entry has been completed. The act of using one book as a medium for entering the items to the relevant accounts to complete double entry is known as 'posting' the items. This also means it will be simpler to notice when the book-keeper has forgotten to complete double entry, by the fact that such entries will not contain anything in the folio column.

Exhibit 9.2 shows the following items written up in the form of a cash book. The folio columns are entered up as though double entry has been completed to the other ledgers.

19-4		£
August 1	Balance brought forward from last month:	
	Cash	48
	Bank	1,930
August 2	Received cheque from M. Evans	306
August 5	Cash Sales	276
August 8	Paid rent in cash	180
August 9	Banked £100 of the cash held by the firm	100
August 16	Cash Sales paid direct into the bank	192
August 20	Paid cheque to J. Taylor	89
August 30	Withdrew cash from the bank for business use	200
August 31	Paid wages in cash	192

Exhibit 9.2

Cash Book

	Folio	Cash £	Bank £			Folio	Cash £	Bank £
19-4				19-4				
Aug 1 Balances	b/d	48	1,930	Aug 8	Rent	GL 45	180	
Aug 2 M. Evans	SL114		306	Aug 9	Bank	C	100	
Aug 5 Sales	GL 22	276		Aug 20	J. Taylor	PL188		89
Aug 9 Cash	C		100	Aug 30	Cash	C		200
Aug 16 Sales	GL 22		192	Aug 31	Wages	GL212	192	
Aug 30 Bank	C	200		Aug 31	Balances	c/d	52	2,239
		524	2,528				524	2,528
Sept 1 Balances	b/d	52	2,239					

The Three Column Cash Book

Cash Discounts

It is very important for most firms for their customers to pay their accounts promptly. To encourage customers to pay promptly a firm may offer to accept a lesser amount if the account is paid within a specified time. The amount of the deduction allowed is known as a 'cash discount'. It is still called a 'cash discount' when the customer pays by cheque.

The rate of cash discount is normally quoted as a percentage. Full details of the percentage to be allowed, and the period within which payment has to be made, are given on all sales documents.

A firm will possibly encounter discounts from two points of view. First, the firm may allow cash discounts to its own customers. Second, the firm may receive cash discounts from its suppliers from whom it buys goods. To distinguish easily between the two, the first kind of discounts are known as 'Discounts Allowed', whilst the second kind are known as 'Discounts Received'.

We can now examine what the effect of discounts are by looking at two examples.

Exhibit 9.3

We are owed £200 by D. Whalley. He pays this on 4 May 19-5 by cash within the time limit specified by us, and we therefore allow him a 5 per cent cash discount. He will therefore pay £200 − £10 = £190 as full settlement of his account.

Effect	*Action*
1. Of cash:	
Cash is increased by £190.	Debit cash account with £190.
Asset of debtors is reduced by £190.	Credit D. Whalley £190.
2. Of discounts:	
Asset of debtors is reduced by £10. (After the cash was paid of £190 a balance still showed of £10.	Credit D. Whalley £10

As the account is deemed
to be settled, this asset
must be cancelled)

Expense of discounts   Debit discounts allowed account £10.
allowed increased by £10.

Exhibit 9.4

We owed £200 to A. Marple Ltd. We paid this on 6 May 19-5 by cheque within the time limit laid down. Marple Ltd therefore allow us a 2½ per cent cash discount. We therefore pay a cheque of £200 − £5 = £195 as full settlement of the account.

	Effect	*Action*
1.	Of cheque:	
	Asset of bank is reduced by £195.	Credit bank account £195.
	Liability of creditors is reduced by £195.	Debit A. Marple Ltd. account £195.
2.	Of discounts:	
	Liability of creditors reduced by £5.	Debit A. Marple Ltd. account £5.
	(After cheque was paid the balance of £5 still remained. As the account is now deemed to be settled the liability must be cancelled).	
	Revenue of discounts received increased by £5.	Credit discounts received account £5.

In the firm's books the account would appear as follows:

Cash Book (page 87)

		Folio	Cash	Bank				Folio	Cash	Bank
19-5			£	£	19-5				£	£
May 4	D. Whalley	SL47	190		May 6	A. Marple Ltd.				
							PL114			195

Discounts Received (General Ledger, page 39)

				19-5			£
				May 5	A. Marple Ltd.		
						PL114	5

Discounts Allowed (General Ledger, page 40)

19-5			£
May 4	D. Whalley	SL47	10

D. Whalley (Sales Ledger, page 47)

19-5			£	19-5				£
May 1	Balance b/d		200	May 4	Cash	CB 87		190
				May 4	Discount	GL 40		10
			200					200

A. Marple Ltd. (Purchases Ledger, page 114)

19-5			£	19-5		£
May 5	Bank	CB 87	195	May 1	Balance b/d	200
May 5	Discount	GL 40	5			
			200			200

It is not necessary to write 'Discount Allowed' or 'Discount Received' in full in the personal accounts, the word 'Discount' on its own is sufficient. After all, the sales ledger will only contain discounts allowed and the purchases ledger will only contain discounts received.

The Discounts Received Account and the Discounts Allowed Account are both to be found in the General ledger, along with the other expense and revenue accounts. Now you have already been told that every effort should be made to prevent constant reference to the general ledger. As far as discounts are concerned this is managed very easily by adding an extra column on each side of the cash book for discounts. Discounts allowed are entered in the discounts column on the debit side of the cash book, whilst discounts received are entered in the discounts column on the credit side of the cash book.

If such a cash book is completed from the facts in Exhibit 9.4 it will appear as follows:

Cash Book

		Discount	Cash	Bank			Discount	Cash	Bank
19-5		£	£	£	19-5		£	£	£
May 4	D. Whalley				May 5	A. Marple Ltd.			
	SL87	10		190		PL 114	5		195

In the personal accounts of customers and suppliers the method of showing discounts would not alter.

To enter the discounts in the cash book in this way can be seen as a technique for saving time. When money is being paid, or received, it is precisely at this point in time that the discount will have to be calculated. The cash book therefore has to be used in any case. The amount of cash or cheque received or paid is entered and the discount slotted into the discount column. Thus for both cash (or cheque) and discount only one date has to be written, and only one completion of a details column.

The discounts columns are not part of the double entry system, as they are not accounts, unlike the cash and bank columns. The columns for discounts are simply listing devices, or they could be called collection points. Half of the double entry has been made in the personal accounts. It therefore now needs an entry in the discounts account. This is done by entering the total of the discounts received columns to the credit of a discounts received account, and the total of the discounts allowed columns to the debit of a discounts allowed account.

At first sight this appears to be incorrect. Why should a credit total be transferred to the credit of an account? To check whether this is correct or not, we must look at the entries in the personal accounts. Discounts received will all have been shown on the left-hand side in the supplier's accounts, therefore what is required is the total of all these discounts received entered on the credit side to preserve double entry balancing. The converse applies to discounts allowed.

We can now look at Exhibit 9.5 details to be entered in such a cash book, with the ultimate transfer of the discounts total to the requisite accounts.

Exhibit 9.5

19-5		£
May 1	Balances brought down from April:	
	Cash Balance	38
	Bank Balance	1,560
	Creditors' accounts:	
	G. Hallworth	80
	R. Skermer	360
	A. Chatwood	480
	Debtors' accounts:	
	K. Platt	120
	G. Slack	640
	R. Wright	200
May 3	R. Wright pays us by cheque having deducted 2½ per cent cash discount £5	195
May 5	We pay A. Chatwood by cheque less 5 per cent cash discount £24	456
May 12	We withdrew £100 cash from the bank for business use	100
May 15	We pay G. Hallworth by cash less 2½ per cent cash discount £2	78
May 20	K. Platt pays us by cash after having deducted 5 per cent cash discount	114
May 24	We paid wages in cash	132
May 29	G. Slack pays us by cheque, having deducted 2½ per cent cash discount £16	624
May 31	We pay R. Skermer by cheque after having deducted 5 per cent cash discount £18	342

Cash Book
Page 85

19-5		Folio	Discount £	Cash £	Bank £	19-5		Folio	Discount £	Cash £	Bank £
May 1	Balances	b/d		38	1,560	May 5	A. Chatwood	PL49	24		456
May 3	R. Wright	SL88	5		195	May 12	Cash	C			100
May 12	Bank	C		100		May 15	G. Hallworth	PL72	2	78	
May 20	K. Platt	SL141	6	114		May 24	Wages	GL61		132	
May 29	G. Slack	SL116	16		624	May 31	R. Skermer	PL95	18		342
						May 31	Balances	c/d		42	1,481
			27	252	2,379				44	252	2,379
Jun 1	Balances	b/d		42	1,481						

Sales Ledger

R. Wright   Page 88

19-5			£	19-5				£
May 1	Balance	b/d	200	May 3	Bank		CB 85	195
				May 3	Discount		CB 85	5
			200					200

G. Slack   Page 116

19-5			£	19-5				£
May 1	Balance	b/d	640	May 29	Bank		CB85	624
				May 29	Discount		CB85	16
			640					640

K. Platt   Page 141

19-5			£	19-5				£
May 1	Balance	b/d	120	May 20	Cash		CB85	114
				May 20	Discount		CB85	6
			120					120

Purchases Ledger

A. Chatwood   Page 49

19-5			£	19-5				£
May 5	Bank	CB85	456	May 1	Balance		b/d	480
May 5	Discount	CB85	24					
			480					480

G. Hallworth   Page 72

19-5			£	19-5				£
May 15	Cash	CB85	78	May 1	Balance		b/d	80
May 15	Discount	CB85	2					
			80					80

R. Skermer   Page 95

19-5			£	19-5				£
May 31	Bank	CB85	342	May 1	Balance		b/d	360
May 31	Discount	CB85	18					
			360					360

General Ledger

Wages   Page 61

19-5			£	19-5	£
May 24	Cash	CB85	132		

Discounts Received   Page 69

				19-5		£
				May 31	Total for the month	
					CB85	44

Discounts Allowed

19-5		£		
May 31	Total for the month			
	CB85	27		

You can now see that the total of the discounts received on the debit side of the accounts in the Purchases Ledger amounted to £24 + £2 + £18 = £44. The total entered in the discounts received account is also £44 so that double entry principles have been observed. A check on discounts allowed will disclose a similar picture.

Bank Overdrafts

A firm may be allowed to have a bank overdraft. This means that the firm can draw cheques for a sum greater than the amount of money that it has put in the account, so that the balance on the account will represent money owing to the bank. It is a liability and it will be a credit balance.

Taking the last cash book illustrated, if the amount paid by cheque to R. Skermer was £2,342, instead of £342, then the amount placed in the account totalling £2,379 would be exceeded by the amounts withdrawn. The cash book would appear as in Exhibit 9.6.

Exhibit 9.6

Cash Book

	Folio	Discount £	Cash £	Bank £		Folio	Discount £	Cash £	Bank £
19-5					19-5				
May 1 Balances b/d			38	1,560	May 5 A. Chatwood				
May 3 R. Wright SL88		5		195		PL49	24		456
May 12 Bank C			100		May 12 Cash C				100
May 20 K. Platt SL141		6	114		May 15 G. Hallworth				
May 29 G. Slack SL116		16		624		PL72	2	78	
May 31 Balance c/d				519	May 24 Wages GL61			132	
					May 31 R. Skermer				
						PL95	18		2,342
					May 31 Balance c/d			42	
		27	252	2,898			44	252	2,898
Jun. 1 Balance b/d			42		Jun. 1 Balance b/d				519

The Petty Cash Book and the Imprest System

A further progression of preventing various books from containing a great deal of unnecessary detail is the keeping of a Petty Cash Book. When the firm starts to get larger the receipt and payment of items may be given to a person whom we will call the cashier. He will be a fairly senior member of the accounts staff.

To save the cashier wasting his time handling small cash payments, the task could be handed over to a junior member of his staff who would then be known as the petty cashier. A separate book for these small items, called the Petty Cash Book, could be kept by him.

The normal form of a petty cash book is that it is analytical in form. This is to save a lot of unnecessary record-keeping. For instance suppose that small amounts of travelling expenses are paid, and that in any one year the petty cashier makes 1,000 small payments of travelling expenses. For the account in the general ledger for travelling expenses to contain 1,000 entries would be ridiculous. Instead, by the use of analytical columns in the petty cash book, the petty cashier needs only to post the total of the petty cash book say once per month. The general ledger would contain only 12 entries therefore, instead of 1,000 entries for these small items of expense.

Each person claiming payment from the petty cashier will have to complete a petty cash voucher. This should show the reason for payment, any necessary proof of incurring the expense, and should be signed by the recipient.

The Imprest System

The basic idea underlying this system is for the cashier to give the petty cashier an adequate amount of cash to cover the expenses for the ensuing period. When the end of the period arrives the cashier ascertains the amount of cash paid out by the petty cashier. He then gives the petty cashier an amount equal to that spent, and the amount of petty cash then in hand should be equal to the original amount given by the cashier. Let us look at Exhibit 9.7 to see an example.

Exhibit 9.7

		£
1st Period.	The cashier gives the petty cashier	500
	The petty cashier pays out in the period	463
	Petty cash left in hand	37
	Add reimbursement from the cashier	463
	Petty cash in hand end of period 1	500
2nd Period.	Petty cashier pays out in this period	414
	Petty cash left in hand	86
	Add reimbursement from the cashier	414
	Petty cash in hand at end of period 2	500

Sometimes it is necessary to increase the fixed amount at the start of the period, i.e. the £500 shown in the exhibit. This fixed amount is often known as a cash 'float'. If the firm had wanted to increase the float to £600 at the end of the second period then the cash paid by the main cashier would have been £414 + £100 = £514.

A considerable advantage of the imprest system is the control that can be exercised. At any time it is capable of being checked, for the petty cash in hand at any time should be equal to the cash float less the amount paid out per the cash vouchers during the period up to the date of the checking.

We can now look at a typical month of petty cash transactions in a firm, and then compare this with the Analytical Petty Cash Book shown as Exhibit 9.8

19-4

May 1	The main cashier gives £250 as float to the petty cashier.	
	Payments out of petty cash during May:	£
May 2	Postages	16
May 3	B. Smith — travelling expenses	14

May 4	Cleaning Expenses	13
May 6	Petrol	9
May 8	H. Harkness — travelling expenses	21
May 9	Settlement of N. Potter's account in the Purchases Ledger	18
May 11	Cleaning Expenses	17
May 14	Postages	3
May 15	W. Howard — travelling expenses	6
May 18	Settlement of J. Kent's account in the Purchases Ledger	8
May 18	Cleaning Expenses	22
May 20	Postages	7
May 22	P. Poulson — travelling expenses	11
May 24	Petrol	5
May 25	Cleaning Expenses	19
May 28	Postages	2
May 30	Petrol	12
May 31	The cashier reimburses to the petty cashier the amount spent in the month.	

The receipts side of the petty cash book shown represents the debit side.

The payments side is the credit side of the petty cash book. The items are first entered in the total column and then extended into the relevant expense column. When the period comes to an end the total column is added and compared with the sum of the totals of all the other columns on the payments side, obviously the two total figures should agree. In this case £26 + £52 + £71 + £28 + £26 = £203.

In order that double entry should be completed, the total of each expense column should be transferred to the debit of the relevant expense account in the general ledger. The folio column for the respective expense account is shown directly underneath the expense column, for instance the Motor Expenses account is found in the general ledger on page 36. This is abbreviated to GL36.

The end column has been chosen as a ledger column. Items paid out of petty cash which needed posting to a ledger other than the general ledger are shown there. Such items would be those such as if a purchases ledger account was settled from petty cash.

Exhibit 9.8

Receipts £	Folio	Date 19-4	Details	Voucher No.	Total £	Motor Expenses £	Travelling Expenses £	Cleaning £	Postages £	Ledger Folio	Ledger Accounts £
250	CB88	May 1	Cash								
		May 2	Postages	1	16				16		
		May 3	B. Smith	2	14		14				
		May 4	Cleaning	3	13			13			
		May 6	Petrol	4	9	9					
		May 8	H. Harkness	5	21		21				
		May 9	N. Potter	6	18					PL142	18
		May 11	Cleaning	7	17			17			
		May 14	Postages	8	3				3		
		May 15	W. Howard	9	6		6				
		May 18	J. Kent	10	8					PL72	8
		May 18	Cleaning	11	22			22			
		May 20	Postages	12	7				7		
		May 22	P. Poulson	13	11		11				
		May 24	Petrol	14	5	5					
		May 25	Cleaning	15	19			19			
		May 28	Postages	16	2				2		
		May 30	Petrol	17	12	12					
203	CB95	May 31	Cash		203	26	52	71	28		26
		May 31	Balance	c/d	250	GL36	GL42	GL76	GL95		
453					453						
250		Jun. 1	Balance	b/d							

Assignment Exercises

9.1 A two column cash book is to be written up from the following, carrying the balances down to the following month:

19-4

January 1	Started business with £4,000 in the bank.
January 2	Paid for fixtures by cheque £660.
January 4	Cash sales £225.
January 5	Paid rent by cash £140.
January 6	T. Thomas paid us by cheque £188.
January 8	Cash sales paid direct into the bank £308.
January 10	J. Kramer paid us in cash £300.
January 12	Paid wages in cash £275.
January 14	J. Walters lent us £500 paying by cheque.
January 15	Withdrew £200 from the bank for business use.
January 20	Bought stationery paying by cash £60.
January 22	We paid J. Flowers by cheque £166.
January 28	Cash Drawings £100.
January 30	J. Scott paid us by cheque £277.
January 31	Cash Sales £66.

9.2x Write up a two-column cash book from the following:

19-6

November 1	Balances brought forward from last month: Cash £105; Bank £2,164.
November 2	Cash Sales £605.
November 3	Took £500 out of the cash till and paid it into the bank.
November 4	J. Matthews paid us by cheque £217.
November 5	We paid for postage stamps in cash £60.
November 6	Bought office equipment by cheque £189.
November 7	We paid J. Little by cheque £50.
November 9	Received rates refund by cheque £72.
November 11	Withdrew £250 from the bank for business use.
November 12	Paid wages in cash £239.
November 14	Paid motor expenses by cheque £57.
November 16	L. Lawrence lent us £200 in cash.
November 20	R. Norman paid us by cheque £112.
November 28	We paid general expenses in cash £22.
November 30	Paid insurance by cheque £74.

9.3 Enter up a three column cash book from the details following. Balance off at the end of the month, and show the relevant discount accounts as they would appear in the general ledger.

19-7

May 1	Started business with £6,000 in the bank.
May 1	Bought fixtures paying by cheque £950.
May 2	Bought goods paying by cheque £1,240.

May 3	Cash Sales £407.
May 4	Paid rent in cash £200.
May 5	N. Morgan paid us his account of £220 by a cheque for £210, we allowed him £10 discount.
May 7	Paid S. Thompson & Co. £80 owing to him by means of a cheque £76, they allowed us £4 discount.
May 9	We received a cheque for £380 from S. Cooper, discount allowed £20.
May 11	The following accounts were paid by our customers by cheque, in each case we deducted a cash discount of 5 per cent: C. Ball £80; R. Lucas £300; T. Ford £180.
May 12	Paid rates by cheque £410.
May 14	L. Curtis pays us a cheque for £115.
May 16	Paid M. Monroe his account of £120 by cash £114, having deducted £6 cash discount.
May 20	P. Exeter pays us a cheque for £78, having deducted £2 cash discount.
May 27	We paid the following accounts by cheque, in each case we first deducted a cash discount of 2½ per cent: T. Starr £280; C. Green £440; R. Johnson £520.
May 31	Cash Sales paid direct into the bank £88.

9.4x A three column cash book is to be written up from the following details, balanced off and the relevant discount accounts in the general ledger shown.

19-5

March 1	Balances brought forward: Cash £230; Bank £4,756.
March 2	The following paid their accounts by cheque, in each case deducting 5 per cent cash discounts; Accounts: R. Burton £140; E. Taylor £220; R. Harris £300.
March 4	Paid rent by cheque £120.
March 6	J. Cotton lent us £1,000 paying by cheque.
March 8	We paid the following accounts by cheque in each case deducting a 2½ per cent cash discount; N. Black £360; P. Towers £480; C. Rowse £800.
March 10	Paid motor expenses in cash £44.
March 12	H. Hankins pays his account of £77 by cheque £74, deducting £3 cash discount.
March 15	Paid wages in cash £160.
March 18	The following paid their accounts by cheque, in each case deducting 5 per cent cash discount: Accounts: C. Winston £260; R. Wilson & Son £340; H. Winter £460.
March 21	Cash withdrawn from the bank £350 for business use.
March 24	Cash Drawings £120.
March 25	Paid T. Briers his account of £140, by cash £133, having deducted £7 cash discount.
March 29	Bought fixtures paying by cheque £650.
March 31	Received commission by cheque £88.

9.5 The following details are to be entered up into a three column cash book, balanced off, and the discount accounts to be shown in the general ledger.

19-7

June 1   Balances brought forward: Cash £205; Bank £1,460.

June 2   The following accounts were paid by our customers by cheque, in each case a discount of 5 per cent was deducted: D. Hawkins £540; P. Grogan £600; L. Dennis £1,000.

June 3   Paid stationery by cash £62.

June 4   R. Jones lent us £2,000 by cheque.

June 5   We paid the following accounts by cheque, in each case deducting a 2½ per cent discount: F. Toner & Co. £40: J. Mottershead £360; P. Hobbit £480; R. Tootal £800.

June 6   We paid F. Glass & Co. a cheque £319.

June 8   We paid J. Bickerstaffe's account of £320, by cheque £310 having deducted £10 cash discount.

June 12   Withdrew cash from the bank for business use £400.

June 15   The following accounts were paid by our customers in cash, in each case deducting 5 per cent cash discount: C. Potter £20; N. Reader £40; T. Cook £100.

June 16   Bought motor van paying in cash £500.

June 18   Paid rent by cheque £800.

June 24   Bought premises paying by cheque £10,000.

June 29   R. Smithers paid us in cash £63.

June 30   Paid W. Whitelaw by cheque £167.

9.6x Enter the following in a three column cash book. Balance off the cash book at the end of the month and show the discount accounts in the general ledger.

19-8

June 1   Balances brought forward: Cash £97; Bank £2,186.

June 2   The following paid us by cheque in each case deducting a 5 per cent cash discount: R. Harty £1,000; C. White £280; P. Peers £180; O. Hardy £600.

June 3   Cash Sales paid direct into the bank £134.

June 5   Paid rent by cash £88.

June 6   We paid the following accounts by cheque, in each case deducting 2½ per cent cash discount J. Charlton £400; H. Sobers £640; D. Shallcross £200.

June 8   Withdrew cash from the bank for business use £250.

June 10   Cash Sales £206.

June 12   D. Deeds paid us their account of £89 by cheque less £2 cash discount.

June 14   Paid wages by cash £250.

June 16   We paid the following accounts by cheque: L. Lucas £117 less cash discount £6; D. Fisher £206 less cash discount £8.

June 20   Bought fixtures by cheque £8,000.

June 24   Bought motor lorry paying by cheque £7,166.

June 29   Received £169 cheque from D. Steel.

June 30   Cash Sales £116.

June 30   Bought stationery paying by cash £60.

9.7 The following transactions are to be entered in a petty cash book, with analysis columns for Postages, Travelling Expenses, Cleaning, Sundry Expenses and a ledger column. It is to be kept on the imprest system, the amount spent being reimbursed by the chief cashier on the last day of the month. The opening petty cash float is £300.

19-3		£
January 1	Postage	26
January 2	J. Short — travelling expenses	11
January 4	Gratuity to refuse collectors	1
January 5	R. Gratrix — ledger account	14
January 7	C. Smart — travelling expenses	29
January 8	Postages	15
January 10	A. Jowett — travelling expenses	6
January 12	T. Johnson — ledger account	12
January 13	Poison licence	2
January 15	Postages	20
January 17	Cleaning Materials	4
January 18	D. Jardine — travelling expenses	17
January 20	Clock repair	3
January 21	C. Travis — ledger account	14
January 23	Postages	29
January 24	Desk Diary	5
January 26	D. Bracknell — ledger account	15
January 27	Postages	22
January 28	Cleaning materials	6
January 30	H. Jordan — travelling expenses	14

9.8x Rule up a petty cash book with analysis columns for office expenses, motor expenses, cleaning expenses, and casual labour. The cash float is £350 and the amount spent is reimbursed on 30 June.

19-7		£
June 1	H. Scraggs — casual labour	13
June 2	Letterheadings	22
June 2	Unique Motors — motor repairs	30
June 3	Cleaning Materials	6
June 6	Envelopes	14
June 8	Petrol	8
June 11	J. Higgins — casual labour	15
June 12	Mrs. Body — cleaner	7
June 12	Paper clips	2
June 14	Petrol	11
June 16	Typewriter repairs	1
June 19	Petrol	9
June 21	Motor Taxation	50
June 22	T. Sweet — casual labour	21
June 23	Mrs. Body — cleaner	10
June 24	P. Dennis — casual labour	19
June 25	Copy paper	7
June 26	Flat Cars — motor repairs	21
June 29	Petrol	12
June 30	J. Young — casual labour	16

Chapter 10

The Division of the Ledger: Sales, Purchases, Returns Inwards and Returns Outwards Books

Learning Objectives:

At the end of your study of this chapter you should

1. **understand and be able to prepare the Sales and Purchases Books and the respective Returns books,**
2. **know how Value Added Tax is recorded by firms on Sales and Purchases.**

In the last chapter it was stated that the recording of transactions gets divided up into the various functions of the business. In order that the general ledger could be kept free from unnecessary detail it was stated that separate books could be kept for credit transactions concerned with sales, purchases, returns inwards and returns outwards. We can now look at these books in detail.

The Sales Book

For many businesses a high proportion of the sales will be on credit terms instead of being sold for immediate cash. Quite a lot of firms in fact sell only on credit terms. For each such credit sale the seller will send to the buyer a document known as an invoice. The invoice gives full details of the goods and the prices. The seller will also keep one or more copies of the invoice for his own use. Exhibit 10.1 is an example of such an invoice.

To the seller of the goods the invoice is called a sales invoice, whilst the buyer, when he receives his copy, would regard it as a purchases invoice. We are here concerned with the seller's accounting records and we will therefore call it a sales invoice.

The sales invoices will be used by the seller to enter up his sales book. All that the book comprises is a list of each invoice, showing the date, the name of the firm to whom the goods had been sold, the number of the invoice for reference purposes, and the net amount of the invoice. It is pointless to show a detailed description of the goods sold in the sales book, as this could be found by examining the sales invoice itself.

Exhibit 10.1

Invoice No. 18612
Your Purchase Order 164/720

P.A.C. LTD.
HIGHSIDE WORKS,
DEEPSIDE,
STOCKPORT,
CHESHIRE SK8 1DB
1 May 19-3

INVOICE

Messrs A. Taylor & Sons,
86 Keswick Road,
MANCHESTER M13 1JP

				£
20 Overhead Rods	×	£8		160
16 Pairs Tru-clips	×	£2		32
8 Linkpins	×	£1		8
				200
Less 25% trade discount				50
				150

Terms: 2½% cash discount if paid within 1 month

We will leave the consideration of Value Added Tax, V.A.T., until later in the chapter, as not all firms have to add V.A.T. to the value of their sales invoices. Looking at the specimen invoice shown as Exhibit 10.1, a deduction of £50 is shown. This illustrates one of the two methods of pricing the goods sold. On the one hand an invoice could be sent just showing the actual amount at which the goods have been charged to the customer. The other way is that shown in Exhibit 10.1 where the goods are shown at one figure and an amount then deducted for trade discount, the net figure being the amount actually charged for the goods.

The reasons for allowing trade discounts are as follows:

(a) Traders are often charged out at the full retail price by wholesalers and manufacturers, but a trade discount is then deducted equalling the difference between the manufacturer's/wholesaler's price and the full retail price. The net figure is consequently the price payable by the trader, whilst the trade discount will equal the amount of gross profit that the trader will make if he sells the goods at the full retail price. Thus the invoice gives information as to the retail price, and this will also make it easier to handle for a firm which sells both to traders and to the general public. All goods are charged out at full retail price to both kinds of customers, but in the case of traders a deduction is made for trade discount in the form of a percentage. Sales staff will consequently only have to consult one set of sales price lists, the adjustments of the prices between the two sorts of customers being made by the use of trade discounts.

(b) Different traders may be given different rates of trade discounts. In addition a higher rate of trade discount may be given to traders buying goods in large quantities.

As trade discount is simply a means of calculating the net selling price of the goods no entry is made anywhere in the books for it. Compare this with cash discounts which are a vital part of the double entry system.

Exhibit 10.2 is an example of a sales book. The first item shown is that of the sales invoice from Exhibit 10.1.

Exhibit 10.2

	Sales Book			Page 92
19-3		*Invoice No.*	*Folio*	*£*
May 1	A. Taylor & Sons	18612	SL 59	150
May 9	P. Saunders Ltd.	18613	SL 125	315
May 24	R. Robertshaw	18614	SL 198	84
May 31	J. Willans & Co.	18615	SL 217	630
	Transferred to Sales Account		GL 86	£1,179

When entering these credit sales in the sales ledger, we adhere to the principles of personal accounts outlined in earlier chapters. Apart from the fact that the reference numbers will be different the other items in the personal accounts will remain the same. To use the sales book when entering up the individual items in the customers' accounts in the sales ledger is known as 'posting' the sales book.

Sales Ledger

A. Taylor & Sons Page 59

19-3			£
May 1	Sales	SB92	150

P. Saunders Ltd. Page 125

19-3			£
May 9	Sales	SB 92	315

R. Robertshaw Page 198

19-3			£
May 24	Sales	SB 92	84

J. Willans & Co. Page 217

19-3			£
May 31	Sales	SB 92	630

You can see that the personal accounts have been debited with a total of £1,179. No credit entry has as yet been made for these items. The sales book itself is simply a list, it is not an account and is therefore not a part of the double entry system. We must obviously complete double entry, and this is done by taking the total of the sales book and entering this amount on the credit side of the sales account in the general ledger. This is done periodically, usually monthly, but it could be done weekly or for some other period of time.

General Ledger

Sales Page 86

19-3 £

May 31 Credit Sales for
the month   SB 92   1,179

If you will compare this with the entries made when all the accounts were kept in one ledger, you should be able to see the differences. The final answer is the same, personal accounts would have been debited with £1,179 and the sales account credited in total with £1,179. The differences are that the personal accounts are now kept in a separate ledger, and also that the sales account now shows total figures instead of details of the individual sales.

The Sales Book is also often called the Sales Day Book or the Sales Journal.

The Purchases Book

In most firms a large proportion of the purchase of goods will be credit purchases. The sales invoice sent by one firm will be the purchases invoice in the hands of the recipient. This causes some confusion to students on occasion. You should bear in mind that the invoice must be identified from the point of view of the firm whose books are being written up. If the firm is selling then the invoice is a sales invoice, if it is buying it is a purchases invoice.

Credit purchases follow a similar plan to that of credit sales. The net amount of each invoice, after trade discount is entered in a purchases book, and the items are then posted to the purchases ledger. The invoice is then filed away for future reference. At the end of the period the total of the purchases book is entered on the debit side of the purchases account in the general ledger. An example is now given:

Purchases Book Page 115

19-3		Invoice No.	Folio	£
May 1	N. Marsland & Son	3079	PL 29	88
May 14	W. Pritchard Ltd.	3080	PL 77	304
May 22	J. Coy & Co.	3081	PL 95	486
May 31	F. Livesey	3082	PL 129	600
	Transferred to Purchases Account		GL 87	1,478

Purchases Ledger

N. Marsland & Son

Page 29

19-3 £

May 1 Purchases PB 115   88

W. Pritchard Ltd. Page 77

19-3 £

May 14 Purchases PB 115   304

J. Coy & Co.   Page 95
                    19-3   £
          May 22 Purchases   PB 115   486

F. Livesey   Page 129
                    19-3   £
          May 31 Purchases   PB 115   600

General Ledger

Purchases   Page 87
19-3   £
May 31 Credit Purchases
    for the month PB 115   1,478

The Purchases Book is often also called the Purchases Day Book or the Purchases Journal.

Returns Inwards Books

If goods are returned by customers, or else there is a dispute concerning the goods, or an allowance is made by the firm, a document known as a credit note is sent by the firm to the customer. The 'credit note' takes its name from the fact that the customer's account will be credited by the amount of the allowance, thus reducing his indebtedness to the firm. Credit notes are often printed in red to distinguish them easily from invoices.

Exhibit 10.3 shows a credit note sent to A. Taylor and Sons in respect of goods returned by them. You can consult Exhibit 10.1 to see the sales invoice in respect of which some goods were returned later.

Exhibit 10.3

Credit Note No. CN/937 Your ref. no. A/489	P.A.C. LTD. HIGHSIDE WORKS, DEEPSIDE, STOCKPORT, CHESHIRE SK8 1DB 12 May 19-3

CREDIT NOTE

Messrs A. Taylor & Sons,
86 Keswick Road,
MANCHESTER M13 1JP

				£
1 Overhead Rod	×	£8		8
2 Pairs Tru-clips	×	£2		4
				12
Less 25% trade discount				3
				9

The credit notes are listed in a returns inwards book, and this is then used to post the items to the credit of the personal accounts in the sales ledger. The total of the returns inwards book for the period is transferred to the debit of the returns inwards account in the general ledger to complete double entry.

An example of a returns inwards book, showing the items posted to the sales and general ledgers is now shown:

Returns Inwards Book			Page 15
19-3	Note No.	Folio	£
May 12 A. Taylor & Sons	937	SL 59	9
May 20 K. Inman Ltd.	938	SL 90	35
May 23 J. Swinburne & Co.	939	SL 109	66
May 29 P. Saunders Ltd.	940	SL 125	40
Transferred to Returns Inwards Account		GL 93	150

Sales Ledger

A. Taylor & Sons		Page 59
19-3		£
May 12 Returns Inwards		
	RI 15	9

K. Inman Ltd.		Page 90
19-3		£
May 20 Returns Inwards		
	RI 15	35

J. Swinburne & Co.		Page 109
19-3		£
May 23 Returns Inwards		
	RI 15	66

P. Saunders Ltd.		Page 125
19-3		£
May 29 Returns Inwards		
	RI 15	40

General Ledger

Returns Inwards			Page 93
19-3		£	
May 31 Returns for the			
month	RI 15	150	

Returns Outwards Book

When goods are returned to a supplier a document called a debit note is sent to him giving details of the amount of allowance to which the firm is entitled. Such a debit note can also cover allowances where goods were not returned but an allowance was due, e.g. because of short supply or of some other deficiency. The very use of the term 'debit note' can be seen to have originated from the fact that the supplier's account will be debited, as our indebtedness to them has accordingly been reduced.

The returns outwards books is the place where the debit notes are listed. The items are then posted to the debit of the personal accounts in the purchases ledger. To complete double entry the total of the returns outwards book for the period is transferred to the credit of the Returns Outwards Account in the general ledger. An example now follows:

Returns Outwards Book

			Page 14
19-3	Note No.	Folio	£
May 10 N. Marsland & Son	1864	PL 29	16
May 16 G. Lester & Co.	1865	PL 35	104
May 23 W. Pritchard Ltd.	1866	PL 77	14
May 30 A. Clark	1867	PL 106	29
Transferred to Returns Outwards Account		GL 94	163

Purchases Ledger

N. Marsland & Son   Page 29

19-3   £
May 10 Returns Outwards
     RO 14   16

G. Lester & Co.   Page 35

19-3   £
May 16 Returns Outwards
     RO 14   104

W. Pritchard Ltd.   Page 77

19-3   £
May 23 Returns Outwards
     RO 14   14

A. Clark   Page 106

19-3   £
May 30 Returns Outwards
     RO 14   29

General Ledger

Returns Outwards   Page 94

19-3   £

May 31 Returns for the
       month RO 14   163

Other names commonly in use for the returns outwards book are the Purchases Returns Book or the Returns Outwards Journal.

Books as Collection Points

You can see the Sales, Purchases, Returns Inwards and Returns Outwards books are in fact collection points for data connected with these particular activities. Their main purpose is that they save the various accounts in the general ledger from containing unnecessary detail. This means in turn that they facilitate the division of work between members of the accounting staff.

In this book you are given the basic mechanics of keeping a set of accounting records. What you have to bear in mind is that the accounting records do not have to be kept exactly as described in this book. The answers that should be obtained, whatever system is in use, are those that would be obtained from using the system written about in this book.

This means that in fact you do not have to keep a Sales Book as described in this chapter. Instead the entries in the customer's accounts can be posted direct from the sales invoices. The sales invoices could be collected together, and then, at the end of the period, they could be added up using an adding machine. The resultant total would then be credited to the sales account. The end result is therefore exactly the same as if a sales book had been written up.

The types of short-cuts taken will vary tremendously between firms. As it is impossible to look at all of these, in this book we examine instead the basic methods. If you can understand the basic principles, you will be able to understand any other method without too much difficulty.

Value Added Tax

Value Added Tax, which we will abbreviate as V.A.T., is chargeable in the United Kingdom on a wide variety of goods and services. Some goods and services are not liable to V.A.T., these include food and bank charges. The government department which deals with V.A.T. in the United Kingdom is the Customs and Excise department. The rates at which V.A.T. is charged varies from time to time. Some goods will carry a different rate than others. In the past motor-cars and electrical goods have been charged at different rates.

Throughout this book the rate of V.A.T. used in all examples will be that of 10 per cent. Most examining bodies have used questions assuming that the rate was 10 per cent, as it is easy to perform the calculations.

Taxable Firms

Suppose that firm A takes raw materials it has grown, it then processes them and wishes to sell them. If there was no V.A.T. the firm would sell them for £1,000, but V.A.T. has to be added and so firm A sells them to firm B for £1,000 + V.A.T. £100 (10%) = £1,100. Firm A will now have to pay £100 V.A.T. collected to the Customs and Excise. Firm B, having bought the goods for £1,100 alters them slightly and then sells them to firm C for £1,300 + V.A.T. £130 = £1,430. Firm B now has to pay the Customs and Excise a cheque for the amount added less the amount paid to A for V.A.T. The cheque payable is therefore £130 − £100 = £30. Firm C then sells the goods to the general public for £1,700 + V.A.T. £170. Firm C then has to pay to the Customs and Excise the amount of V.A.T. added by it less the V.A.T. paid to B, £170 − £130 = £40.

You can see from all this that the V.A.T. tax has all been suffered by the final customer, who suffered V.A.T. of £170. The way that the Customs and Excise collected this tax was by way of A handing over £100, B £30 and C £40 = £170 total.

Exempted Firms

What is meant by an exempted firm is one which does not have to add V.A.T. on to the price at which it sells its goods or services. On the other hand such a firm cannot obtain a refund of the V.A.T. it has paid itself on goods and services it has acquired. Such a firm may therefore buy goods for £2,000 plus V.A.T. £200 = £2,200, and may sell them for £3,000 without adding V.A.T. It will not however get a refund of the £200 V.A.T. paid.

Instances of exempted firms are banks and insurance companies. Very small firms with a low turnover (the limit is changed from time to time), do not have to register for V.A.T. if they do not wish to, and therefore do not charge V.A.T. on their goods or services.

Zero Rated Firms

These firms do not have to add V.A.T. to the selling prices of their goods or services. They do however obtain a refund of all V.A.T. paid by them. If one of such firms buys goods for £3,000 + V.A.T. £300, and later sells them for £4,000 it will not add V.A.T. to the £4,000 selling price. It will however be able to obtain a refund of the V.A.T. £300 paid when the goods were bought. This distinguishes a zero rated firm from an exempted firm.

The fact that a firm is zero rated relates to the goods or services which a firm deals in. Instances are food firms and publishers.

Partly Exempt Traders

Some traders will sell goods on which they charge V.A.T. and some which are exempted or zero rated. These firms will have to apportion their turnover, and follow the rules already described for each part of the turnover.

Recording V.A.T. in the Accounts

Other than firms which are exempted, firms do not suffer V.A.T. as an expense. They either obtain a refund of the V.A.T. they have paid, as is the case in zero rated businesses, or else they charge V.A.T., deducting what they have paid themselves in V.A.T. The latter firms therefore simply act as unpaid tax collectors.

From an accounting point of view therefore, the discussion which follows is split between those firms which (A) Do not suffer V.A.T. as an expense, and (B) Exempted firms which actually suffer V.A.T.

(A) Firms which can recover V.A.T. paid

1. Taxable Firms

(a) Value Added Tax and Sales Invoices

Such a firm has to add V.A.T. to its Sales Invoices. The V.A.T. is based on the net amount of the sales invoice after any discounts have been deducted.

Exhibit 10.4 is an example of a sales invoice incorporating V.A.T. Details are as follows:

May 5 19-6. C. Mayall & Co., 15 High Lane, Keswick, sold the following goods to R. Willis Ltd, 34 Hazel Grove, Leicester. All goods are subject to a 20 per cent trade discount.

100 rolls T14 Paper at £2 per roll

3,000 sheets A3 Art paper at £10 per 100 sheets

500 boxes PP Envelopes at £1 per box.

All of these goods are subject to V.A.T. at the rate of 10 per cent.

Exhibit 10.4

C. Mayall & Co. 15 High Lane, Keswick	
	Date: 5 May 19-6
Invoice No. 6476	Your order No. A/1422

To: R. Willis,
     34 Hazel Grove,
     Leicester

	£
100 Rolls T14 Paper at £2 per roll	200
3,000 Sheets A3 Art paper at £10 per 100 sheets	300
500 boxes PP Envelopes at £1 per box	500
	1,000
Less Trade Discount 20%	200
	800
Add V.A.T. 10%	80
	880

There will normally be an extra column in the Sales Book for V.A.T. This will make it easier to account for V.A.T. We can now look at a Sales Book written up for the month of May 19-6.

Sales Book

Page 79

19-6	Invoice No.	Folio	Net £	V.A.T. £
May 5 R. Willis (see Exhibit 10.4)	6476	SL 84	800	80
May 11 M. McNeill Ltd.	6477	SL 118	240	24
May 20 M. Brown & Son	6478	SL 156	330	33
May 31 M. Sinclair Ltd.	6479	SL 199	160	16
Transferred to General Ledger		GL 69	1,530 GL 82	153

The items can now be posted to the Sales Ledger. Each of the customers' accounts are charged simply with the full amounts of each invoice including V.A.T.

Sales Ledger

		R. Willis	Page 80
19-6		£	
May 5 Sales	SB 79	880	

		M. McNeill Ltd.	Page 118
19-6		£	
May 11 Sales	SB 79	264	

		M. Brown & Son	Page 156
19-6		£	
May 20 Sales	SB 79	363	

		M. Sinclair Ltd.	Page 199
19-6		£	
May 31 Sales	SB 79	176	

You can see that, in total, the various personal accounts have been debited with £1,683, this being the total of the accounts payable by the customers. Of the figure of £1,683, the amount of £1,530 represents the actual figure of sales, the other £153 being for V.A.T.

The transfer to the credit of the Sales account is restricted to the actual figure of sales £1,530. The other £153 being V.A.T., is then posted to the credit of a V.A.T. account.

General Ledger

	Sales		Page 69
	19-6		£
	May 31 Credit Sales for the month	SB 79	1,530

	Value Added Tax		Page 82
	19-6		£
	May 31 Sales Book: V.A.T.	SB 79	153

Value Added Tax and Cash Discounts

If a cash discount is offered, even though payment is not made within the time limit and the chance of a cash discount is lost, V.A.T. is based on the net amount of the invoice *less* cash discount.

In the case of Exhibit 10.4, if a cash discount of 5 per cent had been offered, i.e. 5% × £800 = £40, then the V.A.T. would be based on the figure of £800 — cash discount £40 = £760, so that V.A.T. would be £760 × 10% = £76. Contrast this with the V.A.T. of £80 which was charged when a cash discount was not offered.

Value Added Tax and Purchases

A taxable firm will have to add V.A.T. to its sales invoices, but it will also be able to claim a refund on the V.A.T. it had paid on its purchases. Normally the V.A.T. added to Sales will be greater than that of V.A.T. on Purchases, and this means that there will be periodic payments to the Customs and Excise. If V.A.T. on Purchases did in fact exceed V.A.T. on Sales then the firm would obtain a refund from the Customs and Excise.

The actual recording of Purchases in the Purchases Book and Purchases Ledger follow the same pattern as that for Sales, except obviously the double-entry items are shown in a reverse fashion. A Purchases Book for the firm of Mayall & Co., and the Purchases Ledger, for the month of May 19-6 might appear as follows:

	Purchases Book		Page 62
19-6	*Folio*	*Net*	*V.A.T.*
		£	£
May 2 J. Stanley & Co.	PL 61	150	15
May 8 R. Oliver Ltd.	PL 77	200	20
May 21 K. Hardy	PL 95	660	66
May 31 T. Laurel & Son	PL 121	80	8
Transferred to General Ledger	GL 77	1,090 GL 82	109

Purchases Ledger

J. Stanley & Co.			Page 61
19-6			£
May 2	Purchases	PB 62	165

R. Oliver Ltd.			Page 77
19-6			£
May 8	Purchases	PB 62	220

K. Hardy			Page 95
19-6			£
May 21	Purchases	PB 62	726

T. Laurel & Son			Page 121
19-6			£
May 31	Purchases	PB 62	88

The personal accounts have thus been credited with a total of £1,199. The actual purchases are £1,090 and this is the amount to be transferred to the debit side of the Purchases Account. The other £109 being V.A.T., is transferred to the debit of the V.A.T. account. You will remember that the V.A.T. account already contains a credit of £153 being the V.A.T. on Sales.

General Ledger

Purchases			Page 77
19-6	£		
May 31 Credit Purchases for the month PB 62	1,090		

Value Added Tax			Page 82
19-6	£	19-6	£
May 31 Purchases Book:		May 31 Sales Book:	
V.A.T. PB 62	109	V.A.T. SB 79	153
May 31 Balance c/d	44		
	153		153
		Jun. 1 Balance b/d	44

If a Trading and Profit and Loss Account was being drawn up for the month, then the Trading Account would contain a credit of £1,530 transferred from the Sales Account, also a debit of £1,090 transferred from the Purchases Account. The £44 V.A.T. owing would appear in the Balance Sheet as at May 31 19-6 as a creditor.

2. Zero Rated Firms

These firms do not have to add V.A.T. on their sales, as the rate of V.A.T. is zero. They can however claim back any V.A.T. suffered on purchases and services bought. This puts such firms in an enviable position. There will accordingly be no V.A.T. column in the Sales Book. The Purchases Book and the Purchases Ledger will appear exactly as you have just seen in the firm of Mayall & Co. The V.A.T. owing by the Customs and Excise at the end of each period will be shown as a debtor in the Balance Sheet.

(B) *Firms which cannot recover V.A.T.*

These firms do not add V.A.T. on to their sales invoices. In addition they are unable to reclaim V.A.T. paid on Purchases. In this sort of firm there is no V.A.T. account, the V.A.T. paid is counted as part of the cost of purchases. Therefore if purchases of £200 + V.A.T. £20 = £220 are made, the purchases book will contain one figure of £220 and the supplier will be credited with £220.

V.A.T. on items other than Sales or Purchases

Value Added Tax is not just paid on purchases, it is also paid on the purchase of fixed assets and many other items of expense. The treatment of V.A.T. for these items will depend on whether or not V.A.T. can be reclaimed or not. The rule is that if V.A.T. can be reclaimed then the item should be shown net, i.e. V.A.T. should be excluded from expense accounts or asset accounts. When V.A.T. cannot be reclaimed then the expense or fixed asset account should be shown gross, i.e. V.A.T. should be included. The following example of two firms buying similar items should illustrate this point.

	Firm which can reclaim V.A.T.		Firm which cannot reclaim V.A.T.	
Buys Machinery £800 + V.A.T. £80	Debit Machinery £800 Debit V.A.T. account £80		Debit Machinery	£880
Buys Stationery £400 + V.A.T. £40	Debit Stationery £400 Debit V.A.T. account £40		Debit Stationery	£440

Assignment Exercises

10.1 Enter up sales, purchases, returns inwards and returns outwards books, post the items to the relevant personal accounts in the sales and purchases ledger, and show the transfers to the general ledger.

19-7

April 1	Credit sales to L. Nelson £105.
April 2	Credit purchases from F. Drake £800.
April 4	Credit sales to H. Frobisher £306; W. Raleigh £208.
April 15	Credit purchases from C. Wellington £125; J. Napoleon £305; J. Hastings £201; K. Gladstone £550.
April 16	Returns inwards from L. Nelson £12; W. Raleigh £44.
April 18	Credit sales to W. Raleigh £905; D. Columbus £289; A. Bruce £400.
April 21	Credit purchases from J. Napoleon £609; T. Palmerston £106; J. Disraeli £300.
April 24	Returns outwards to C. Wellington £15; J. Hastings £19; K. Gladstone £60.
April 30	Returns inwards from D. Columbus £66.

10.2x You are to enter the following items in the books, post to personal accounts, and show transfers to the general ledger.

19-5

July 1	Credit purchases from K. Hill £380; M. Norman £500; N. Senior £106.
July 3	Credit sales to E. Rigby £510; E. Petch £246; F. Thompson £356.
July 5	Credit purchases from R. Morton £200; J. Coutts £180; D. Ellerby £410; C. Davies £66.
July 8	Credit sales to A. Green £307; H. Gough £250; J. Freestone £185.
July 12	Returns outwards to M. Norman £30; N. Senior £16.
July 14	Returns inwards from E. Petch £18; F. Thompson £22.
July 20	Credit sales to E. Petch £188; F. Powers £310; E. Large £420.
July 24	Credit purchases from C. Ferguson £550; K. Entwistle £900.
July 31	Returns inwards from E. Petch £27; E. Rigby £30.
July 31	Returns outwards from J. Coutts £13; C. Davies £11.

10.3 Enter up the following transactions, using separate sales, purchases, returns inwards and returns outwards books, and show the necessary accounts in the general ledger.

19-1

May 1	Credit sales: R. Jones £120; V. Smythe £95; P. Donaldson £160.
May 3	Credit purchases: J. Kelly £88; W. Greaves £200; L. MacMahon £104.
May 5	Credit sales: I. Shaw £116; N. Rossiter £216; P. Ramsbottom £300.
May 6	Credit purchases: T. Cartwright £100; W. Greaves £144; R. Joiner £72; H. Carter £550.
May 10	Goods returned by us to V. Smythe £13; I. Shaw £10.
May 19	Goods returned by us to J. Kelly £15; L. MacMahon £6.
May 23	Credit sales: J. Pitt £390; T. McDowell £64; A. Lean £109.
May 24	Credit purchases: W. Johnson £1,000; E. Holt £44.
May 30	Goods returned to us by J. Pitt £120.
May 31	Goods returned by us to H. Carter £50.

10.4x Now enter the following in the requisite books:

19-3

December 1	Credit sales to F. Hargreaves £170; P. Shaw £440; W. Dinsdale £115.
December 4	Credit purchases from D. Garner £63; A. Kirk £80; J. Young & Co. £500.
December 6	Credit sales to: F. Hargreaves £195; J. & M. Cutler £300; P. Gibbs £666.
December 11	Credit purchases from: G. Hollings £420; T. Hulse & Son £175.
December 13	Returns made to us by: F. Hargreaves £25; P. Shaw £100.
December 15	Credit sales to: H. Cowan £40; W. Dyke £330.
December 16	Returns sent by us to: D. Garner £11; T. Hulse & Son £25.
December 20	Credit sales to D. Singer £164.
December 21	Returns sent to us by: F. Hargreaves £28; P. Shaw £31; P. Gibbs £14.

Chapter 11

Depreciation of Fixed Assets

Learning Objectives:

At the end of your study of this chapter you should:

1. **understand some of the causes of depreciation and why it is required in the preparation of accounts,**
2. **be able to calculate commonly used accounting methods of providing for depreciation,**
3. **be able to record depreciation provisions and entries for sales and additions to fixed assets in the accounts.**

Fixed assets should fulfil the requirements that they are of long-life, of material value, are held to be used in the business, and are not primarily for resale.

With the exception of land, most fixed assets have a limited number of years of useful life to the business. Machinery, motor vehicles, fixtures and buildings do not last for ever. Land itself may become used up after a number of years, as may be true of quarries, mines and land used for similar purposes.

When a fixed asset is bought, and then later disposed of by the firm, that part of the original cost that is not recovered on disposal is known as depreciation. You will be able to see that the only time that depreciation can be calculated accurately is when the asset is disposed of and the difference between the cost and the disposal price calculated. If a machine is bought for £10,000 and then disposed of 10 years later for £200, the amount of depreciation will be £10,000 − £200 = £9,800.

This means that depreciation is as much a cost for services, in this case the service given by the machine, as costs are consumed for services such as wages, lighting, rent etc. Depreciation is therefore an expense, and it will have to be charged in the profit and loss account, along with other expenses before ascertaining the net profit. This charge will have to be made so that the net profit will be the profits remaining after charging all expenses for the period.

The causes of Depreciation

These may be broken down into the main classifications of physical deterioration, economic factors, depletion, and the time factor.

Physical deterioration. Caused by wear and tear when the asset is in use, and also by erosion, rusting, rotting and decay from being exposed to the elements of nature such as rain, wind and sun.

Economic factors. These may see an asset put out of use by a firm even though the asset itself may still be in quite a good physical condition. These can mainly be put under the headings of obsolescence and inadequacy.

Obsolescence means the act of becoming obsolete or out of date. When newer and later models of machines are introduced then it will often be uneconomic to carry on using the old models. Obvious examples are such items as computers, aircraft, manually operated machines which can be replaced by automatic machinery which can do the job more cheaply, and so on.

Inadequacy on the other hand refers to the asset being put out of use because of the growth of a firm or by changes in its requirements. For instance a small aircraft may be used by a firm to fly people to a particular holiday destination. When the holiday resort becomes much more popular a larger aircraft is needed, and the small aircraft sold.

Simply because assets are put out of use by a firm does not mean that they are scrapped. For instance a computer may be sold to another firm which may get quite a few years good use out of it. The small aircraft just mentioned may be bought by another firm and used for many years until it is no longer fit to fly.

Depletion. Some assets are of a wasting character, very often because of the extraction of raw materials from them. These raw materials are either then sold to other firms or used as a basis for making something else. Natural resources such as quarries, mines and oilwells fit under this heading. To provide for the depreciation of such wasting assets is called provision for depletion.

The Time Factor. Quite obviously the time factor is associated with all the factors mentioned already. There are in addition certain fixed assets in which the time factor is associated in a different way. These consist of assets with a fixed period of life by law, such as leases, copyrights and patents. An agreement for a lease can be entered into for any agreed period. A patent's life is normally sixteen years, there are certain grounds on which this may be extended. Copyright exists for such things as publishing or playing music or for publishing books. Copyright in the case of books extends to 50 years after the author's death. Provision for the consumption of these assets is usually called amortisation rather than the term depreciation.

Appreciation

You may well have asked yourself the question as to what accounting treatment is given to assets that appreciate (increase) in value. In fact basic accounting practice would ignore such an appreciation, as to bring appreciation into the accounts would be to go against both the cost concept and the convention of conservatism, both described in chapter eight.

However, in certain circumstances appreciation is taken into the accounts. This is especially true of limited company and partnership accounts. We will leave a consideration of the procedures to be followed in those circumstances until a later stage of your studies.

Provisions for Depreciation

Over the whole of the life of an asset the depreciation is calculated as cost less amount received when the asset is put out of use by the firm. If the item was bought and sold within one accounting period, then the depreciation can be charged as an expense in that period when calculating the period's net profit. The real difficulties start when the asset is kept for several accounting periods and an attempt has to be made to charge depreciation as an expense against each period. We can now examine some of these difficulties:

1. Only with a few assets, such as a lease or a patent, is it possible to assess an asset's useful life. Even a lease may be put out of use if the premises become inadequate. A patent may become useless if a new invention appears.

2. No one knows how much a firm will receive in x years time when the asset is put out of use.

3. How do you measure use? Suppose that a firm buys a motor-van which it owns for three years. In the first year it is driven by a most careful driver, the second year by a clumsy and reckless driver, and the third year by an average driver. The way that the van has been driven will affect the motor-van and consequently the cash receivable on disposal. How should the firm apportion the costs of using the motor-van and consequently the cash receivable on disposal? How should the firm apportion the motor-van's depreciation costs for each of the three years? The same problem would occur with machines operated by different workers.

4. Besides depreciation, there are also the repairs and the maintenance of the asset to consider. These both affect the length of economic use of the asset, and also the eventual disposal price. Should these not therefore affect the depreciation provision calculations?

Having examined some of the difficulties you will probably not be surprised to find out that the methods of calculating provisions for depreciation are mainly accounting customs rather than there be any 'true' methods.

Methods of Calculating Provisions for Depreciation

There are two methods which are used far more than any others. The first method, used more than any other, is the Straight-Line Method, whilst the other main method is the Reducing Balance Method.

1. *Straight Line Method.*

   This is generally regarded as the most suitable method. It allows an equal amount to be charged as depreciation for each year of the expected use of the asset.

   It is found by the use of the formula:

   $$\frac{\text{Cost} - \text{Estimated Residual Value}}{\text{Number of years of expected use}} = \text{Depreciation provision per annum}$$

   As an example, if a machine with an expected life of 4 years cost £50,000 and it has an estimated residual value of £1,280, the depreciation provision per annum would be:

   $$\frac{£50,000 - £1,280}{4} = £12,180$$

   The residual value is often ignored in practice if it is likely to be a relatively small amount.

2. *Reducing Balance Method*

   In calculating the annual depreciation provision, a fixed percentage is applied to the balance of the costs remaining at the end of the previous accounting period. The balance of unallocated costs should therefore show a reduction each year, and because a fixed percentage is used the depreciation provision will be smaller as each year passes. In theory the balance of the unallocated costs at the end of the expected life of the asset should equal the estimated residual value.

   The formula used to find the necessary percentage is:

   $$r = 1 - \sqrt[n]{\frac{s}{c}}$$

   where n = the number of years
   s = the net residual value (this must be a significant amount or the answers will be absurd, since the depreciation rate would amount to nearly one)
   c = the cost of the asset
   r = the rate of depreciation to be applied.

If we use the figures for the machine in which the straight-line method was used, the calculations become:

$$r = 1 - \sqrt[4]{\frac{£256}{£10,000}} = 1 - \frac{4}{10} = 0·6 \text{ or } 60 \text{ per cent.}$$

When applied to each of the four years of use the depreciation provisions would be:

	£
Cost	50,000
Year 1. Depreciation Provision 60% of £50,000	30,000
Cost not yet allocated, end of year 1	20,000
Year 2. Depreciation Provision 60% of £20,000	12,000
Cost not yet allocated, end of year 2	8,000
Year 3. Depreciation Provision 60% of £8,000	4,800
Cost not yet allocated, end of year 3	3,200
Year 4. Depreciation Provision 60% of £3,200	1,920
Cost not yet allocated, end of year 4	1,280

In this particular case the percentage used conveniently worked out to be a round figure. Naturally the answer will usually come out to several places of decimals. It would be usual for the percentage figure to be taken to be the nearest whole figure.·

Advocates of this method usually point out that it helps to even out the total amount of costs charged as expenses for the use of the asset each year. They argue that in addition to depreciation such assets have running costs in addition, with the repairs and maintenance expenses usually increasing each year. To have equal total costs each year therefore, the depreciation provisions should fall. However, as you can see from the depreciation figures given each year in the example shown, the repairs and maintenance expenses would have to be of considerable amounts to bring about an equal total charge for each year of use.

The use of this method has fallen in recent years, with an increase in the use of the Straight Line Method. In fact many small firms use the reducing balance method because it is the basic method used by the Inland Revenue when calculating tax allowances for the depreciation of fixed assets.

Incorrect Estimates of Depreciation

Naturally it often happens that the asset is kept in use longer than expected. In such a case the total provisions for depreciation should not exceed the expected total depreciation. In the example given, once the total depreciation provisions amount to £48,720 then further provisions for depreciation are not needed, no matter how many more years the asset is kept in use. Quite simply the objective of allocating the total depreciation has already been achieved. It is not that the total depreciation provisions are wrong, but that the provisions for each period have been overstated by the expected life of the asset being exceeded by the actual life.

Where the actual period of use is less than the expected period then the provisions charged will be less than the depreciation actually suffered. This is corrected by the use of the Assets Disposals Account, mentioned later.

The year in which the asset is disposed of is charged not only with the provision for that year, but also with the amount by which the total provisions for depreciation have fallen short of the depreciation suffered.

Correction is also made by using the Assets Disposal Account when the actual amount received on disposal varies from the estimated amount, but the expected life and the actual life are the same as one another. Where the amount received on disposal is less than that estimated then a further charge needs to be made to the profit and loss account. If the opposite applies and more cash is received than the estimated residual amount, too much will have been charged for depreciation over the years and this needs correction by a credit in the profit and loss account.

The Adjustment of Depreciation Provision Rates

Quite frequently it will become apparent, well before the asset is put out of use, that the depreciation provision rates are either excessive or inadequate. Consequently they should be revised. The ways of performing all of the necessary adjustments are outside the scope of this book.

Monthly and Annual Calculations

For assets bought or sold within an accounting period there are two main ways in which the calculations are performed.

1. Provision for depreciation made on the basis of one month's provision for every one month of ownership. Fractions of months are usually ignored.

2. On the basis that provision is made only on the assets in use at the end of the period, and for these a full year's depreciation is charged. Assets sold during the period will therefore not have a provision charged, no matter how many months they were in use. Conversely, assets bought in the year will have a full period's depreciation charged even though they were in use for only part of the period.

In an examination, when the dates on which assets are bought or sold are given, then the examiner will expect method No. 1. If dates are not given you should use method No. 2.

Recording Depreciation Provisions

After the arithmetic has been done to work out the depreciation provision there remains the recording of the provision in the books. It is now common practice to have Depreciation Provisions in separate accounts away from the asset accounts. However, you may well come across firms in which the depreciation provisions are entered direct in the asset accounts. We will therefore look at one instance using this outdated method, which we will show as the old method, and the same details using completely separate accounts, which we will call the modern method. After this example we will show all of the records using the modern method.

In a business, with a financial year end of December 31, a machine is bought for £5,000 on 1 January 19-2. It is to be depreciated at the rate of 20 per cent using the reducing balance method. The records for the first two years, using both methods, now follow.

Old Method

Machinery

19-2			£	19-2			£
Jan. 1	Bank		5,000	Dec. 31	Depreciation		1,000
				Dec. 31	Balance	c/d	4,000
			5,000				5,000
19-3				19-3			
Jan. 1	Balance	b/d	4,000	Dec. 31	Depreciation		800
				Dec. 31	Balance	c/d	3,200
			4,000				4,000
19-4							
Jan. 1	Balance	b/d	3,200				

Depreciation

19-2		£	19-2		£
Dec. 31	Machinery	1,000	Dec. 31	Profit and Loss	1,000
19-3			19-3		
Dec. 31	Machinery	800	Dec. 31	Profit and Loss	800

Profit and Loss Account for the year ended 31 December

		£
19-2	Depreciation	1,000
19-3	Depreciation	800

This is usually shown on the balance sheet as follows:

Balance Sheets

As at 31 December 19-2	£	£
Machinery at cost	5,000	
Less Depreciation for the year	1,000	4,000

As at 31 December 19-3	£	£
Machinery as at 1 January 19-3	4,000	
Less Depreciation for the year	800	3,200

Modern Method

Machinery

19-2		£
Jan. 1	Bank	5,000

Provision for Depreciation: Machinery

19-2		£	19-2		£
Dec. 31 Balance	c/d	1,000	Dec. 31 Profit and Loss		1,000
19-3			19-3		
Dec. 31 Balance	c/d	1,800	Jan. 1 Balance	b/d	1,000
			Dec. 31 Profit and Loss		800
		1,800			1,800
			19-4		
			Jan. 1 Balance	b/d	1,800

Profit and Loss Account for the year ended 31 December

19-2 Depreciation	1,000
19-3 Depreciation	800

In the balance sheet the balance on the Machinery Account is shown, less the balance on the Provision for Depreciation Account.

Balance Sheets

	£	£
As at 31 December 19-2		
Machinery at cost	5,000	
Less Depreciation to date	1,000	4,000
As at 31 December 19-3		
Machinery at cost	5,000	
Less Depreciation to date	1,800	3,200

Without carrying on entering up all the double entry accounts, let us look at how the balance sheet entries would appear using both methods, as follows on 31 December 19-5. Before showing the balance sheets we can work out the depreciation provisions for 19-4 as 20% × £3,200 = £640, and for 19-5 as 20% × (£3,200 − £640) £2,560 = £512.

Balance Sheets as at 31 December 19-5		£	£
(Old Method)	Machinery as at 31 December 19-4	2,560	
	Less Depreciation for the year	512	2,048
(Modern Method)	Machinery at cost	5,000	
	Less Depreciation to date	2,952	2,048

You can see that the modern method gives you a better view of the machinery as an asset. The modern method is far more revealing as to the relative age of the asset, as you can get a good idea by comparing the total depreciation to the original cost. This comparison is not available from the balance sheet if the old method is used.

Disposal of an asset

Once an asset is put out of use, its cost is transferred to the debit of an Assets Disposal Account. The depreciation provided on the asset from the date bought to the date of disposal is transferred from the provision for depreciation account to the Assets Disposal Account. By the use of this method the balance on the asset account will represent the cost of the assets retained, whilst the balance on the provision for depreciation account is solely that of the provisions on the retained assets.

Any cash received is credited to the Assets Disposal Account. If the Assets Disposal Account has a difference on the credit side, then that amount should be transferred to the debit side of the profit and loss account. The difference will represent the amount by which actual depreciation has exceeded depreciation provisions on the asset. If the difference instead had been on the debit side of the Assets Disposal Account, that amount would be transferred to the credit side of the profit and loss account. This amount represents how much depreciation provisions have exceeded actual depreciation.

Exhibits 11.1 and 11.2 give illustrations of the disposals of assets.

Exhibit 11.1

A machine was bought on 1 January 19-2 for £1,000 and another on 1 July 19-3 for £1,500. The first machine was sold on 1 October, 19-4 for £480. The machinery is to be depreciated at 20 per cent, using the straight line method and based on assets in use at the end of each financial year ignoring items sold in the year. The financial year end is December 31st.

Machinery

19-2			£	19-3			£
Jan. 1	Bank		1,000	Dec. 31 Balance		c/d	2,500
19-3							
Jul. 1	Bank		1,500				
			2,500				2,500
19-4				19-4			
Jan. 1	Balance	b/d	2,500	Oct. 1	Asset Disposals		1,000
				Dec. 31 Balance		c/d	1,500
			2,500				2,500
19-5							
Jan. 1	Balance	b/d	1,500				

Provision for Depreciation: Machinery

			£	19-2		£
				Dec. 31 Profit and Loss		200
19-3				19-3		
Dec. 31 Balance		c/d	700	Dec. 31 Profit and Loss		500
			700			700

19-4				19-4			
Oct. 1	Asset Disposals (2 years × 20% × £1,000)		400	Jan. 1	Balance	b/d	700
				Dec. 31	Profit and Loss		300
Dec. 31	Balance	c/d	600				
			1,000				1,000
				19-5			
				Jan. 1	Balance	b/d	600

Asset Disposals: Machinery

19-4		£	19-4		£
Oct. 1	Machinery	1,000	Oct. 1	Bank	480
			Oct. 1	Provision for Depreciation	400
			Dec. 31	Profit and Loss	120
		1,000			1,000

Profit and Loss Accounts for the year ended 31 December

	£
19-2 Provision for Depreciation	200
19-3 Provision for Depreciation	500
19-4 Provision for Depreciation	300
Previous under-provision for Depreciation on Machinery sold	120

Balance Sheet (extracts) as at 31 December

	19-2	19-3	19-4
Machinery at cost	1,000	2,500	1,500
Less Depreciation to date	200	700	600
	800	1,800	900

Exhibit 11.2

This is a more complicated example. First, more items are dealt with and second, the depreciation provisions are to be based on one month's depreciation for one month's ownership. A business having a financial year end of December 31 buys two machines on 1 January 19-4. No. 1 costs £1,000 and No. 2 costs £3,000. It buys machine No. 3 on 1 April 19-6 for £3,500 and No. 4 on 1 October 19-6 for £2,500. Machine No. 2 is sold on 1 July 19-7 for £1,250 and No. 1, after constantly breaking down, is sold for £10 on 30 September 19-8. Depreciation is at the rate of 20 per cent per annum, ignoring scrap value, using the straight line method.

Machinery

			£				£
19-4							
Jan. 1	Bank		4,000				
19-6							
Apl. 1	Bank		3,500	19-6			
Oct. 1	Bank		2,500	Dec. 31	Balance	c/d	10,000
			10,000				10,000
19-7				19-7			
Jan. 1	Balance	b/d	10,000	Jul. 1	Asset Disposals		3,000
				Dec. 31	Balance	c/d	7,000
			10,000				10,000
19-8				19-8			
Jan. 1	Balance	b/d	7,000	Sep. 30	Asset Disposals		1,000
				Dec. 31	Balance	c/d	6,000
			7,000				7,000
19-9							
Jan. 1	Balance	b/d	6,000				

Provision for Depreciation: Machinery

			£				£
				19-4			
				Dec. 31	Profit and Loss		800
19-5				19-5			
Dec. 31	Balance	c/d	1,600	Dec. 31	Profit and Loss		800
			1,600				1,600
19-6				19-6			
				Jan. 1	Balance	b/d	1,600
Dec. 31	Balance	c/d	3,050	Dec. 31	Profit and Loss		1,450
			3,050				3,050
19-7				19-7			
Jul. 1	Asset Disposals		2,100	Jan. 1	Balance	b/d	3,050
Dec. 31	Balance	c/d	2,650	Dec. 31	Profit and Loss		1,700
			4,750				4,750
19-8				19-8			
Sep. 30	Asset Disposal		950	Jan. 1	Balance	b/d	2,650
Dec. 31	Balance	c/d	3,050	Dec. 31	Profit and Loss		1,350
			4,000				4,000
				19-9			
				Jan. 1	Balance	b/d	3,050

Workings:	*Depreciation Provisions*	£	£
19-4	20% of £4,000		800
19-5	20% of £4,000		800
19-6	20% of £4,000	800	
	20% of £3,500 × 9 months	525	
	20% of £2,500 × 3 months	125	1,450
19-7	20% of £7,000 × 12 months	1,400	
	20% of £3,000 × 6 months	300	1,700
19-8	20% of £6,000 × 12 months	1,200	
	20% of £1,000 × 9 months	150	1,350

Workings: *Transfers of Depreciation Provisions to Asset Disposals*

Machine 2:   Bought 1 January 19-4 at cost £3,000
Sold 1 July 19-7. Ownership 3½ years.
Depreciation 3½ × 20% × £3,000 = £2,100

Machine 1:   Bought 1 January 19-4 at cost £1,000
Sold 30 September 19-8. Ownership 4¾ years.
Depreciation 4¾ × 20% × £1,000 = £950.

Assets Disposals: Machinery

19-7		£	19-7		£
Jul. 1	Machinery	3,000	Jul. 1	Provision for	
Dec. 31	Profit and Loss	350		Depreciation	2,100
			Jul. 1	Bank	1,250
		3,350			3,350
19-8			19-8		
Sep. 30	Machinery	1,000	Sep. 30	Provision for	
				Depreciation	950
			Sep. 30	Bank	10
			Dec. 31	Profit and Loss	40
		1,000			1,000

Profit and Loss Accounts (extracts) for the year to 31 December

	£			£
19-4 Provision for Depreciation	800			
19-5 Provision for Depreciation	800			
19-6 Provision for Depreciation	1,450			
19-7 Provision for Depreciation	1,700	19-7 Previous over-provision for Depreciation on machine sold		350
19-8 Provision for Depreciation	1,350			
Previous under-provision for Depreciation on machine sold	40			

Balance Sheet (extracts) as at 31 December

	19-4	19-5	19-6	19-7	19-8
Machinery at cost	4,000	4,000	10,000	7,000	6,000
Less Depreciation to date	800	1,600	3,050	2,650	3,050
	3,200	2,400	6,950	4,350	2,950

In practice the figures of £350 overprovision and of £40 underprovision may not necessarily be shown as separate items in the profit and loss account. In such cases 19-7 might show a charge of 'Depreciation 1,350' which is 1700 − 350, and 19-8 might show 'Depreciation 1,390' i.e. 1,350 + £40.

Relationship between asset replacement and depreciation provisions

Provision for depreciation is made to ensure that the cost of an asset is charged as an expense over its useful life to the firm in an equitable fashion. Depreciation provisions of themselves do not provide funds with which to replace the assets when they are put out of use. This is something that is much misunderstood by members of the general public, and also by a not inconsiderable number of accountancy students.

Providing for depreciation may possibly affect the proprietor's actions so that funds are available to replace the asset, but this is certainly not true in a great many cases. Suppose a machine is bought for £5,000 and is expected to be used for 5 years at the end of which it is expected to be put out of use and no money will be received for the scrapped machine. Assuming provision for depreciation has been provided on the straight-line basis then £1,000 per annum has been charged for each of 5 years. The net profit will have been reduced £1,000 for each year as a result of the depreciation having been charged. The proprietor may therefore, because his recorded profits are £1,000 less each year, also reduce his drawings by £1,000 a year. If that was true, then the consequence of £1,000 less drawings could mean his bank balance would be increased (or his bank overdraft reduced) by that amount. Therefore at the end of the 5 years he could accordingly be in a position to have the £5,000 cash available to replace the machine.

This however does not have to be true at all. The proprietor may still take the same drawings whether or not a provision for depreciation is charged. There is nothing in law which says that if recorded profits are £x then you should not have drawings of more than £y. In one business earning £20,000 profit a year the proprietor may well take £5,000 in drawings. In another business earning £20,000 profit the proprietor may take £30,000 drawings. In the long-term a proprietor may well go bankrupt if his drawings continually exceed net profits. In the short term there may be no relationship whatsoever between drawings and net profits. Accordingly this means that the amounts charged as depreciation provisions, which affects the amounts of net profits recorded, may not affect the drawings in the short term at all.

Assignment Exercises

11.1 K. Smart started in business on 1 January 19-2. Write up the machinery account and the provision for depreciation account for the years ended 31 December 19-2 and 19-3 from the following information. Depreciation is at the rate of 10 per cent, using the straightline basis and where 1 month's ownership equals 1 month's depreciation provision, and eventual scrap value is to be ignored.

    19-2   January 1   Bought machine for £2,000

    19-3   January 1   Bought two machines for £1,500 each

           July 1   Bought machine for £1,800

11.2x Delight & Co. started in business on 1 January 19-5. For the years ended 31 December 19-5, 19-6 and 19-7 you are to show (i) The motor vehicles account, (ii) Provision for depreciation account, (iii) The balance sheet extracts.

Motor vehicles bought:

    19-5   1 January   1 motor costing £4,000

    19-6   1 April   1 motor costing £4,200

           1 October   2 motors costing £5,000 each

    19-7   1 July   1 motor costing £4,800

Depreciation is at the rate of 20 per cent per annum using the straight line method, motors being depreciated for each proportion of a year.

11.3 Young & Co. has bought the following fixed assets:

    19-1   1 January   Bought fixtures £500; Machinery £2,000

           1 June   Bought machinery £2,500

    19-2   1 March   Bought fixtures £600

           1 November Bought machinery £3,000; fixtures £700

Machinery is to be depreciated at the rate of 20 per cent, fixtures 10 per cent, both using the reducing balance method. It is to be based on assets in existence at the end of a year, irrespective of the date when the asset was bought during the year.

The financial year end of the business is 31 December. Show for the above two years:

(i) The machinery account. (ii) The fixtures account, (iii) The provision for depreciation accounts. (iv) Balance sheet extracts.

11.4x A company depreciates its machinery at the rate of 12½ per cent per annum, straight line method, for each month of ownership. Draw up the Machinery Account, the Provision for Depreciation Account, the Machinery Disposals Account, and the balance sheet extracts, for each of the four years ended 31 December 19-1, 19-2, 19-3 and 19-4 from the following:

    19-1   Bought machinery costing £4,000 on 1 January, and £6,400 on 1 October

    19-2   Bought machinery costing £2,400 on 1 July

    19-3   Sold machinery bought on 1 January 19-1 for £4,000 for the sum of £2,300 on 30 September 19-3

11.5 Diddle & Co. keeps its fixed assets at cost. At 31 December 19-4 the accounts for fixed assets and for depreciation provisions are:

	Total Cost to date £	Total Depreciation to date £
Motor Vehicles	89,450	30,850
Fixtures	17,400	6,300

The following additions were made during the year ended 31 December 19-5: Motor Vehicles £5,500, fixtures £2,100.

Some motors bought in 19-1 for £6,500 were sold for £2,050 during the year.

The rates of depreciation are: Motor Vehicles 20 per cent, Fixtures 10 per cent, using the straight line basis, calculated on the assets in existence at the end of the year irrespective of the date of purchase or sale.

You should show the necessary accounts (and balance sheet extracts) for the year ended 31 December 19-5.

11.6x Carriers and Co. makes up its accounts to 30 June annually. It depreciates its machinery using the reducing balance method, at a rate of 25 per cent, with a full year's charge made in the year of purchase, depreciation being ignored in the year of sale. Fixtures are depreciated using the straight-line basis at the rate of 10 per cent per annum, using one month's ownership equals 1 month's depreciation. The following transactions occurred:

19-4 July 1 Bought machinery £4,000; fixtures £2,000.
      December 1 Bought machinery £2,400.
19-5 October 1 Bought fixtures £3,600.
      December 1 Bought machinery £4,800.
19-6 January 1 Bought machinery £1,200.
19-7 January 1 Sold machinery costing £4,000 on
      1 July 19-4 for the sum of £1,980.
      April 1 Sold fixtures costing £2,000 on
      1 July 19-4 for the sum of £1,810

Show the necessary accounts for the years ended 30 June 19-5, 19-6 and 19-7.

11.7 M. Foot & Co. owned 4 lorries at 1 April 19-6

Lorry A	Bought 18 May 19-3	£6,300
Lorry B	Bought 16 June 19-4	£5,500
Lorry C	Bought 28 March 19-5	£5,750
Lorry D	Bought 31 December 19-5	£7,500

Depreciation is taken straightline 20 per cent per annum, giving a full year's depreciation on assets in use at the end of each year, ignoring depreciation in year of sale.

During the year to 31 March 19-7 the following occurred:

(i)   16 April 19-6   E was bought for £7,000.
(ii) 30 November 19-6   B was involved in an accident and was a total write-off. Insurance company paid us £1,350 in full settlement.
(iii) 6 December 19-6   F was bought for £7,200
(iv) 14 January 19-7   A was sold for £2,925.

Record these in the requisite accounts for the year ended 31 March 19-7, together with balance sheet extracts as at 31 March 19-7.

11.8x L. Silkin & Co. owned 3 aircraft at 31 December 19-7.

Aircraft A   which had cost £36,000 on 1 April 19-5

Aircraft B   which had cost £54,000 on 1 January 19-6

Aircraft C   which had cost £108,000 on 1 October 19-6

Depreciation is on a monthly basis, using the reducing balance basis at a rate of 33⅓ per cent.

During the year to 31 December 19-8

(i)   On 1 January 19-8 aircraft D bought for £84,000.

(ii) On 31 March 19-8 aircraft B was lost whilst flying over the Pacific. Insurance compensation for the aircraft received £19,600.

(iii) On 1 July 19-8 aircraft E bought for £81,000.

(iv) On 30 September 19-8 aircraft A sold for £9,750.

Write up the requisite accounts for the year to 31 December 19-8, and show the balance sheet extracts as at that date.

Chapter 12

Bad Debts and Doubtful Debts

Learning Objectives:

At the end of your study of this chapter you should:

1. **understand the need to make provisions for bad and doubtful debts.**
2. **be able to make the entries in the accounts to make the necessary provisions for bad debts.**

In many businesses the majority, sometimes all, of the sales are on a credit basis. Such a business is taking a normal risk that some of the customers may never pay for the goods sold to them. As this is a normal risk, when customers do not pay their accounts then this is a normal business expense. We call these non-payments 'bad debts', and they must be charged as expenses when calculating the profit or loss for the period.

If we find a debt to be bad, then the asset is not worth anything, and the account must accordingly be cancelled. To do this we credit the debtor's account to cancel the asset, and then increase the expenses account called bad debts by debiting it there. If the debtor has paid part of the debt then it is the remainder which will be written off as a bad debt. When the profit and loss account is being drawn up the total of the bad debts account is transferred there. Exhibit 12.1 shows the treatment of bad debts.

Exhibit 12.1

C. Mariner
19-2		£	19-2		£
Feb. 16 Sales		90	Dec. 31 Bad Debts		90

R. Shaw
19-2		£	19-2		£
Mar. 17 Sales		360	Apl. 12 Bank		100
			Dec. 31 Bad Debts		260
		360			360

Bad Debts
19-2	£	19-2	£
Dec. 31 C. Mariner	90	Dec. 31 Profit and Loss	350
Dec. 31 R. Shaw	260		
	350		350

Profit and Loss Account for the year ended 31 December 19-2

	£
Bad Debts	350

Provision for Bad Debts

Accountants, in using the matching concept, endeavour to match up against the revenue of a period the expenses which have helped to create it. Ideally a bad debt would be shown as such in the same period as that in which the relevant sale was made. The snag here, is that it is quite frequently the case that it is not until a period later than that when the sale is made is it realised that the debt is a bad debt.

The accountant therefore tries to match bad debts against sales, by making a provision for bad debts at the end of each accounting period. The amount of the provision is based on experience, a knowledge of the customers, and of the economic climate. Sometimes the list of debtors is scrutinised and a list made of the likely bad debts. For some firms an overall percentage is used for the bad debts provision. Another, and rather more scientific basis than that of an overall percentage, is that of different percentages for debts owing for different lengths of time. This assumes, normally quite rightly so, that the longer a debt is owed the more chance there is of the debt turning out to be a bad debt. The schedule might appear as in Exhibit 12.2.

Exhibit 12.2

Ageing Schedule for Estimated Bad Debts

Period debt has been owing	Amount	Estimated percentage bad	Provision for bad debts
	£	%	£
Less than one month	10,000	1	100
1 month to 2 months	4,000	2	80
2 months to 3 months	2,000	3	60
3 months to 6 months	1,000	5	50
Over 6 months	500	8	40
	17,500		330

Provisions for Bad Debts can be recorded either just in the Bad Debts Account, or alternatively a separate Provision for Bad Debts Account will be used for the provision. Exhibit 12.3 will show the use in Method A where a Bad Debts Account alone is used, and Method B is used where separate accounts are used for Bad Debts and for the provision for Bad Debts.

Exhibit 12.3

A business started on 1 January 19-5 and its financial year end is 31 December. A list of the debtors, bad debts and the estimated bad debts for the first four years is now given.

Year to 31 December	Debtors at end of year (after Bad Debts written off)	Bad Debts written off during year	Debts at end of year thought to be impossible to collect
	£	£	£
19-5	8,000	279	200
19-6	9,000	410	250
19-7	11,000	590	320
19-8	9,600	605	280

Method A (One Account only for bad debt records)

Bad Debts

19-5		£	19-5	£
Dec. 31 Various		279	Dec. 31 Profit and Loss	479
Dec. 31 Provision	c/d	200		
		479		479
19-6			19-6	
Dec. 31 Various		410	Jan. 1 Provision b/d	200
Dec. 31 Provision	c/d	250	Dec. 31 Profit and Loss	460
		660		660
19-7			19-7	
Dec. 31 Various		590	Jan. 1 Provision b/d	250
Dec. 31 Provision	c/d	320	Dec. 31 Profit and Loss	660
		910		910
19-8			19-8	
Dec. 31 Various		605	Jan. 1 Provision b/d	320
Dec. 31 Provision	c/d	280	Dec. 31 Profit and Loss	565
		885		885
			19-9	
			Jan. 1 Provision b/d	280

Profit and Loss Account for the year ended 31 December (extracts)

	£
19-5 Bad Debts	479
19-6 Bad Debts	460
19-7 Bad Debts	660
19-8 Bad Debts	565

Balance Sheets as at 31 December (extracts)

	19-5	19-6	19-7	19-8
	£	£	£	£
Debtors	8,000	9,000	11,000	9,600
Less Provision for Bad Debts	200	250	320	280
	7,800	8,750	10,680	9,320

Method B (using a Bad Debts Account and a separate Provision for Bad Debts Account)

Bad Debts

19-5	£	19-5	£
Dec. 31 Various	279	Dec. 31 Profit and Loss	279
19-6		19-6	
Dec. 31 Various	410	Dec. 31 Profit and Loss	410
19-7		19-7	
Dec. 31 Various	590	Dec. 31 Profit and Loss	590
19-8		19-8	
Dec. 31 Various	605	Dec. 31 Profit and Loss	605

Provision for Bad Debts

				19-5		
				Dec. 31 Profit and Loss		200
19-6				19-6		
Dec. 31 Balance c/d			250	Dec. 31 Profit and Loss		50
			250			250
				19-7		
19-7				Jan. 1 Balance b/d		250
Dec. 31 Balance c/d			320	Dec. 31 Profit and Loss		70
			320			320
19-8				19-8		
Dec. 31 Profit and Loss			40	Jan. 1 Balance b/d		320
Dec. 31 Balance c/d			280			
			320			320
				19-9		
				Jan. 1 Balance b/d		280

Profit and Loss Account for the year ended 31 December (extracts)

	£		
19-5 Bad Debts	279		
Provision for Bad Debts	200		
19-6 Bad Debts	410		
Provision for Bad Debts	50		
19-7 Bad Debts	590		
Provision for Bad Debts	70		
19-8 Bad Debts	605	19-8 Reduction in Provision	
		for Bad Debts	40

The balance sheet for Method B will appear exactly as in Method A.

If you compare the amounts charged as an expense to the Profit and Loss Account, you will see that the amounts charged are the same whichever method is used.

	Method A	*Method B*
19-5	479	279 + 200 = 479
19-6	460	410 + 50 = 460
19-7	660	590 + 70 = 660
19-8	565	605 − 40 = 565

Assignment Exercises

12.1 A firm makes a provision for doubtful debts of 3% of debtors.

At 31 December 19-4 debtors amounted to £15,600. During the year ended 31 December 19-5 debtors written off as being irrecoverable amounted to £915. At 31 December 19-5 debtors amounted to £21,400.

Show the appropriate entries in the bad debts account, assuming that provisions are shown therein.

12.2x Starting on 31 December 19-2 a firm decided to create a provision for bad debts based on 5 per cent of debtors and to maintain that percentage provision at the end of each year. The provisions are to be adjustments to the bad debts account.

After bad debts had been written off debtors balances at 31 December each year were: 19-2 £56,000; 19-3 £63,600; 19-4 £48,400; 19-5 £71,000. Bad debts written off each year to 31 December were 19-2 £3,465; 19-3 £4,906; 19-4 £3,624; 19-5 £5,602.

Draw up the bad debts accounts for each of the four years.

12.3 J. Sparkes started a firm on 1 January 19-3.

As economic conditions changed he altered his bad debt provisions. The debtors, after bad debts had been written off, and the requisite percentage provision required were as follows:

	Debtors	% provision
31 December 19-3	£79,500	4%
31 December 19-4	£84,100	3%
31 December 19-5	£106,800	2½%
31 December 19-6	£96,000	3⅓%

Bad Debts written off were:
31 December 19-3	£3,720
31 December 19-4	£3,690
31 December 19-5	£4,862
31 December 19-6	£3,909

Write up the bad debts account for each of the four years.

12.4x At 31 December 19-4 the balance of the provision carried forward on the bad debts account amounted to £1,565. During the following 3 years the following debts were written off as being bad debts, subject to the notes below: 19-5 £2,244; 19-6 £2,784; 19-7 £3,806.

A provision should be made based on 2 per cent of the debtors outstanding at the end of each year. Debtors at 31 December 19-5 £105,000; 19-6 £96,400; 19-7 £120,800.

The following additional information is also available, and as yet the only entries have been made in the cash book:

(i) A debt of £58 written off in 19-2 as being a bad debt, was paid by the debtor in 19-5.

(ii) For one debt of £360, the debtor was made bankrupt in 19-6. A dividend of 40% = £144 was received from the official receiver in bankruptcy in 19-6. Nothing else will be received in future. Write up the bad debts account for each of the three years ended 31 December 19-5, 19-6 and 19-7.

12.5 The trial balance now shown was extracted from the books of J. Wenham as at 31 December 19-3:

	Dr.	Cr.
	£	£
Purchases	60,800	
Sales		91,400
Returns Inwards	1,200	
Returns Outwards		1,350
Carriage Inwards	450	
Carriage Outwards	310	
Motor Expenses	1,864	
Salaries	5,310	
Discounts Allowed	309	
Discounts Received		210
Rent and Rates	810	
Insurance	204	
Bad Debts written off	1,516	
Provision for bad debts, 1 January 19-3		805
Stock-in-trade, 1 January 19-3	31,630	
Debtors	22,460	
Creditors		11,960
Drawings	7,155	
Cash in Hand	150	
Cash at Bank	5,850	
Fixtures at cost	11,000	
Motor vans at cost	9,400	
Provision for depreciation as at 31 December 19-2:		
Fixtures		4,400
Motor Vans		2,360
Capital		47,933
	160,418	160,418

The following are to be taken into account as at 31 December 19-3.
(i) Stock-in-trade £36,530.
(ii) Insurance prepaid £44.
(iii) Salaries outstanding £506.
(iv) Provision for bad debts to be increased to £880.
(v) Provide for depreciation for the year: Fixtures £2,200; Motor Vans £1,620.

You are required to prepare a Trading and Profit and Loss Account for the year ended 31 December 19-3 and a Balance Sheet as at that date.

12.6x The following trial balance was extracted from the records of J. Jordan, a trader, as at 31 December 19-1:

	Dr.	Cr.
	£	£
Discounts Allowed	410	
Discounts Received		506
Carriage Inwards	309	
Carriage Outwards	218	
Returns Inwards	1,384	
Returns Outwards		810
Sales		120,320
Purchases	84,290	
Stock 31 December 19-0	30,816	
Motor Expenses	4,917	
Repairs to Premises	1,383	
Salaries and Wages	16,184	
Sundry Expenses	807	
Rates and Insurance	2,896	
Premises at Cost	40,000	
Motor Vehicles at Cost	11,160	
Provision for depreciation motors as at 31.12.19-0		3,860
Debtors and Creditors	31,640	24,320
Cash at Bank	4,956	
Cash in Hand	48	
Drawings	8,736	
Capital		50,994
Loan from P. Holland		40,000
Bad Debts	1,314	
Provision for bad debts at 31 December 19-0		658
	241,468	241,468

The following matters are to be taken into account at 31 December 19-1:

(i)   Stock £36,420.

(ii) Expenses owing: Sundry Expenses £62; Motor Expenses £33.

(iii) Prepayment: Rates £166.

(iv) Provision for bad debts to be reduced to £580.

(v)   Depreciation for motors to be £2,100 for the year.

(vi) Part of the premises were let to a tenant who owed £250 at 31 December 19-1.

(vii) Loan Interest owing to P. Holland £4,000.

You are required to prepare a Trading and Profit and Loss Account for the year ended 31 December 19-1 and a Balance Sheet as at that date.

Chapter 13

The Evolution of Modern Methods of Processing Data

Learning Objectives:

At the end of your study of this chapter you should:

1. **be aware of how technological and other factors are currently playing a part in changing accounting systems and numerate analysis.**

The accounting content of this book so far has dealt mainly with the principles of double entry, and the accounting records have been shown in the form of the basic conventional system. It would be a mistake to think that all firms and organisations maintain their accounting records exactly as shown in this book. However, although the actual methods by which the accounts are maintained may be different, the main ends which the accounting system exists to serve remain the same. No matter whether the accounting system is maintained manually by bound books or loose-leaf ledgers, by keyboard machines or by a computer of any sort, the answers obtained should not alter. For instance questions such as "What is the total of debtors?", "What is the total of creditors?", "What is the bank balance?" should receive the same answers whichever method is maintained. The final accounts will also remain the same.

The changes take place in the means by which the information is collected and processed, also the speed by which all of this can be done. With the more advanced systems however, extra information can be extracted from the data collected, and this can all be obtained as an automatic by-product of the basic book-keeping system. You should always bear in mind that such information must satisfy cost-benefit criteria. This quite simply is that (barring information that has to be produced by law) the benefit to be obtained from possessing certain information must exceed the cost of obtaining it. The accounting systems should therefore be designed with that in mind.

Why then have you been studying just the basic conventional double-entry book-keeping system? Is this not a waste of time when firms use computers for their book-keeping? You have already read earlier in this chapter that the answers from the modern systems are the same as the answers you would have got from the basic system, albeit not so quickly. Any system of accounting or book-keeping is still concerned with recording changes in assets, liabilities and capital. The double-entry system is consequently capable of being used by any form of organisation. When you learn book-keeping for the first time you simply do not know what systems will be in use at firms that you will meet in your working life. In four years time a firm using manually written records may be using a computer. If you had a job with a firm with computerised records you may well leave and start up your own small firm, and you might do the book-keeping manually in a few hours per week. If you learn the basic system properly you will make it much easier to move from simple systems to sophisticated systems and vice-versa.

Possibly it is best to introduce modern methods to you by tracing their development from the conventional double entry system. The firm where you are employed, or will be employed, will be at some stage along this span of development. You will thus be able to relate what you are doing with what used to be done, and possibly with what you will be doing in the future.

1. Bound Books

Until the typewriter appeared in 1866, bound volumes were universally in use for book-keeping records. The accounts were in the same basic double-entry as described in this book. However as carbon paper had not been invented there was much more manual copying of items than is now the case. Sales invoices, credit notes and debit notes had to be copied by hand into the sales book and the returns books before they were sent out. Of course carbon paper or specially treated paper is used now so that the making of the original copy also makes further copies automatically.

2. Loose-Leaf Ledgers and Carbon Paper.

The development of the typewriter and of carbon paper led to the transition from bound books to loose-leaf ledgers, as obviously loose-leaves and carbon paper can be inserted into a typewriter.

Initially the loose-leaf ledgers were kept in covers which could be opened and closed only by using a special key. Loose leaves therefore had to be extracted from the ledger and then placed in the typewriter. After use it was removed from the typewriter and replaced in the ledger. It was soon seen that this wasted a lot of time. The loose-leaves were therefore replaced by cards which could be kept in trays.

The next step was in experimentation as to how one operation could produce several different records. Special stationery was designed with interleaved carbon, or with carbon backing on one or more of the sheets. This stationery was in the form of sets. A sales set might produce the following from one typing operation:

Two sales invoices (one for our own copy, one to be sent to the customer).

An advice note for the customer.

Instructions to the warehouse staff to send the goods.

3. The Typewriter and the Adding Machine to the Accounting Machine

In the latter part of the nineteenth century adding machines were in use. In the U.S.A. in 1901 an accounting machine was manufactured which was a combination of the adding machine and the typewriter. Other machines, were based primarily on the typewriter and others based primarily from the adding machine also came into use.

Multicopy carbon stationery allied to these machines came into use. This was much more sophisticated than the sales set already described. Different coloured paper to distinguish one type of form from another started to be used. One operation could produce several records, and could also at the same time calculate the new balance on an account after an entry was made, and could accumulate totals of entries for control purposes.

4. Punched Card Accounting Machines

In 1884 in the U.S.A. Dr. Hollerith developed a machine which worked in a completely different way. This was based on information which was recorded by punching holes into cards in a set way.

The system could be summarised as:

(i) Punching holes into cards to represent the information being dealt with.

(ii) Sorting the cards into a required order.

(iii) Getting the cards put through a machine which would print the information out in a tabulated form.

The firm needed three basic types of machines to do this: (a) A punch, (b) A sorter and (c) A tabulator.

The most important part of the system were the actual punched cards themselves. They were all of the same size with one corner cut off so that you could see if any of them was facing the wrong way or was upside down.

The considerable advances in the field of computers and the reductions in cost, have now made most punched card machinery obsolete.

5. Electronic Computers

For accounting work computers follow on logically from punched cards. Computers were first used for business purposes around the year 1952.

The first computers were quite large machines. As a rough illustration of the comparison with today, a machine that would fill up the whole of the space in a room could today have its work performed quicker and more efficiently by a machine that would easily fit on to the top of your desk.

A computer has five basic component parts:

(i) An input unit.

(ii) A store or memory unit.

(iii) An arithmetic unit.

(iv) An output unit.

(v) A control unit.

When computers were first used the input was made by using punched cards or punched paper tape. The 1960's and 1970's saw considerable changes, both as regards the input to computers and the capabilities of them, so that such an input is now more or less obsolete.

What we are now seeing is a whole new world of mini-computers. These were a 'spin-off' from the technology employed in outer space and in defence. Whereas at one time it would only be the larger firms which had computers, we are now witnessing the introduction of computers into all but the very small organisations. The use of micro-circuits has meant a considerable reduction both in the size of computers and of their costs.

The world of computers is changing so rapidly that whatever was written now would be outdated to some extent by the time that the textbook was printed. As already stated input into a computer used to be by way of punched card or punched paper tape. Some computers now can have data and control instructions fed into them by using a keyboard with a sort of typewriter layout. On top of the central processing unit of the computer will be a visual display unit, rather like a television. Instructions fed in, and a certain amount of computer output information can be viewed on the visual display unit.

With certain types of computers input can be put onto a disc, weighing under 2 ozs, and known as a 'floppy disk' or diskette. This small disc can hold a considerable amount of information. The floppy disks are then used as input instead of punched cards etc.

Computers should be seen as more than just machines which can handle book-keeping. They are tools of management, and a large number of problems can be solved by using them correctly. Some of these can be as automatic by-products of the book-keeping system. Stock control is an obvious choice, as this is done in so many firms.

Modern developments in statistical methods, allied with the computer's ability to handle vast quantities of data quickly and efficiently, has given a new dimension to accounting data. For many years, statistical theory has known *how* to analyse and present information as a basis for decision taking and control. But it is only with the advent of the computer that it has been possible to handle efficiently the mass of data that such theory demands. The drudgery and inaccuracy of data collection, once employing an army of clerks, has been all but eliminated. Never before has management had at its fingertips so much relevant information. Without doubt, the speed and accuracy of the modern digital computer has made statistical information cost effective.

We can leave this chapter by saying that the developments now in hand are revolutionising the world of book-keeping and accounting. At the same time you should not think that the basis of accounting has changed, but simply that the recording function and the automatic reproduction of certain desirable information as a by-product of the accounting system is now capable of being performed by a computer, cheaply and easily, in all but the smallest firms.

140

Chapter 14

An Introduction to Partnership Accounts

Learning Objectives:

At the end of your study of this chapter you should:

1. understand the main accounting provisions of the Partnership Act 1890,
2. be able to calculate the distribution of profit between partners having taken into account interest on capital and drawings,
3. be able to produce final accounts for a partnership.

The sort of final accounts which you have read about so far have been those concerned with businesses each owned by one person only. Obviously in most businesses there comes a time when it would be beneficial for more than one person to participate in the ownership of the business. Perhaps the amount of capital required cannot all be supplied by one person alone, or maybe the experience and abilities needed to run the business properly are such as to necessitate more than one person being involved in ownership. Sometimes people simply prefer to share the joys and problems of running a business. In many cases there will be a family relationship between the owners. If there is to be more than one owner of a business the form of business organisation needed is either that of a partnership of or a limited company. This chapter deals with partnerships, chapter fifteen will be concerned with limited companies.

The act which governs partnerships is the Partnership Act 1890. A partnership may be defined as an association of two to twenty persons (but see next sentence) carrying on business in common with a view of profit. The maximum limit of twenty does not apply to firms of accountants, solicitors, stock exchange members or members of other professional bodies which receive the approval of the Board of Trade for this purpose. For the non-exempt organisations a limited company would have to be formed if it was desired to have more than twenty owners.

Excepting one special type of partner, known as a limited partner, each partner is liable for the debts of the partnership to the full extent of his private possessions should the firm be unable to meet its debts. Apart from limited partners, each partner would have to pay his share of any deficiency. A limited partner is one who is registered under the provisions of the Limited Partnership Act 1907. His liability is limited to the amount of capital invested by him in the partnership; he can lose that amount but his personal possessions cannot be taken to pay any debts of the firm. Limited partners however may not take part in the management of the partnership business. There must be at least one general partner in a limited partnership.

People can enter into partnership with each other without any form of written agreement. However, it is much wiser to have an agreement drawn up by a solicitor, as this will lead to a tendency to have fewer misunderstandings and disagreements between the partners. A partnership deed or articles of partnership can contain as much, or as little, as the partners desire. It does not have to cover every eventuality. The usual accounting requirements contained can be listed as follows:

1. How much capital is to be contributed by each partner.
2. The ratio in which profits or losses are to be shared.
3. The rate of interest, if any, to be given on capital, before profits are shared.
4. The rate of interest, if any, to be charged on partners' drawings.
5. Salaries, if any, to be paid to partners.

We can now examine some of the thinking underlying these requirements.

(a) *Ratio in which profits are to be shared*

Students often think that profits should be shared in the same ratio as that in which capital is contributed by the partners. As an example suppose that in a two-man partnership Webb had contributed £20,000 and Burns £10,000, would you advise them to share the profits Webb ⅔rds and Burns ⅓rd even though the work to be performed by each partner is the same? Let us look at the first few years of the business and see how it works out.

Year	1	2	3	4	Total
	£	£	£	£	£
Net Profit	12,000	15,000	18,000	19,500	
Shared:					
Webb ⅔	8,000	10,000	12,000	13,000	43,000
Burns ⅓	4,000	5,000	6,000	6,500	21,500

You can see that Webb would receive £43,000, which is £21,500 more than Burns. In fact, if the profits are shared equitably, as the work of the partners is exactly the same, the extra profits given to Webb should be just enough to compensate him for putting in the extra capital. Surely giving Webb £21,500 extra over four years because he had put £10,000 extra into the firm cannot be fair to Burns.

Suppose instead that if Webb had put in £29,000 and Burns £1,000, would you give Webb $\frac{29}{30}$ths of the profits?

To overcome this problem we use the concept of interest on capital.

(b) *Interest on Capital*

We start off with the premise that if the work to be performed by the partners is of equal value to the firm, but that the capital contributed is unequal, it would then be equitable if interest was given on the partners' capital. The interest so calculated would then be deducted from the net profit and the remainder divided in their profit-sharing ratios.

The rate of interest given will have to be agreed to by the partners. In theory, it should equal the return they would have got if they had invested the capital in something else.

Looking at Webb and Burns again, but this time sharing the profits equally *after* charging 10 per cent interest on capital, the division of profits would become:

Years	1	2	3	4	Total
	£	£	£	£	£
Net Profit	12,000	15,000	18,000	19,500	
Interest on Capitals:					
Webb 10% on £20,000	2,000	2,000	2,000	2,000 =	8,000
Burns 10% on £10,000	1,000	1,000	1,000	1,000 =	4,000
Remainder shared:					
Webb ½	4,500	6,000	7,500	8,250 =	26,250
Burns ½	4,500	6,000	7,500	8,250 =	26,250

Summary	Webb	Burns
	£	£
Interest on Capital	8,000	4,000
Remainder of Profits	26,250	26,250
	34,250	30,250

Consequently, Webb has received £4,000 more than Burns, this being an adequate reward in the opinion of the partners.

(c) *Interest on Drawings*

Under normal circumstances, it will be better for a partnership if the partners leave as much of their cash in the business for as long as possible, instead of taking it out as drawings. If more cash is left in the firm the greater will be the opportunities of taking advantage of various bargains, more goods can be bought in bulk at cheaper prices, the firm will not have to miss out on cash discounts, and so on.

To deter the partners from taking cash out unnecessarily the procedure is used of charging the partners interest on their drawings, calculated from the date of withdrawal to the end of the financial year. The interest charged to them will then be added to the profits available for division between the partners. The rate of interest should be that as agreed by the partners would be sufficient to encourage partners to leave cash in the firm.

Assume that Webb and Burns decide to charge interest at 10 per cent per annum, and that their drawings during the financial year ended 31 December are as follows:

Webb

Drawings		Interest					£
1 January	£1,500	£1,500 × 10% ×	12 months	=	150
1 April	£400	£400 × 10% ×	9 months	=	30
1 June	£600	£600 × 10% ×	7 months	=	35
1 September	£3,000	£3,000 × 10% ×	4 months	=	100
1 October	£2,000	£2,000 × 10% ×	3 months	=	50
		Interest charged to Webb		=	365

Burns

Drawings		Interest					£
1 January	£500	£500 × 10% ×	12 months	=	50
1 March	£600	£600 × 10% ×	10 months	=	50
1 May	£300	£300 × 10% ×	8 months	=	20
1 August	£2,400	£2,400 × 10% ×	5 months	=	100
1 October	£1,600	£1,600 × 10% ×	3 months	=	40
		Interest charged to Burns		=	260

(d) *Salaries*

One partner may have some extra task or responsibility. It could of course be temporary in nature. In giving him some compensation for this it is best not to disturb the profit and loss sharing ratio. A better way is to give him a salary sufficient to compensate him for the duties performed. The salary is deducted before arriving at the balance of profits to be divided in the profit and loss sharing ratios.

A change in the profit and loss ratios for this purpose could have meant that the partner may be inadequately compensated if the profits are low. It could also mean a larger share of a loss. A salary is therefore a much more suitable method.

The Distribution of Profits

We can now look at a full illustration. Palmer and Hogan are in partnership sharing profits and losses in the ratio of Palmer 2/3rds, Hogan 1/3rd. They are entitled to 10 per cent interest on capital. Palmer having £40,000 capital and Hogan £32,000. Hogan is to have a salary of £2,000 per annum. Interest is being charged on drawings, Palmer being charged £500 and Hogan £300. The net profit, before any allocations to the partners amounted to £24,000 for the year ended 31 December 19-2.

	£	£	£
Net Profit			24,000
Add Charged as Interest on Drawings:			
Palmer		500	
Hogan		300	800
			24,800
Less Salary: Hogan		2,000	
Interest on Capital:			
Palmer	4,000		
Hogan	3,200	7,200	9,200
			15,600
Balance of Profits Shared:			
Palmer 2/3rds		10,400	
Hogan 1/3rd		5,200	15,600

Consequently the £24,000 profits have been shared as follows:

	Palmer	*Hogan*
	£	£
Balance of Profits	10,400	5,200
Interest on Capital	4,000	3,200
Salary	—	2,000
	14,400	10,400
Less Interest on Drawings	500	300
	13,900	10,100

£24,000

Final Accounts of Partnerships

If the sales, purchases, stock and expenses of a partnership were exactly the same as that of a sole trader, then the trading and profit and loss accounts would be the same for both the sole trader and for the partnership. However, a partnership will have an extra section shown immediately under the normal profit and loss account, this section will be called the profit and loss appropriation account. In this account the distribution of the profits will be shown. The heading to the trading and profit and loss account in a partnership will not include the words 'appropriation account'. The fact that it is not included is simply an accounting custom.

Now the trading and profit and loss account of Palmer and Hogan from the details already shown can be given:

Palmer and Hogan
Trading and Profit and Loss Account for the year ended 31 December 19-2

	£			£
(Trading Account − same as for sole trader)				
	£			£
(Profit and Loss Account − same as for sole trader)				
Net Profit c/d	24,000			
		£		£
Interest on Capitals:		Net Profit b/d		24,000
Palmer	4,000	Interest on Drawings:		
Hogan	3,200 7,200	Palmer	500	
Salary: Hogan	2,000	Hogan	300	800
Balance of Profits:				
Palmer 2/3rds	10,400			
Hogan 1/3rd	5,200 15,600			
	24,800			24,800

Fixed and Fluctuating Capital Accounts

In a sole trader's business the capital account changes each year as net profit is added and drawings deducted. In a partnership there is a choice between (a) Fluctuating Capital Accounts or (b) Fixed Capital Accounts plus Fluctuating Current Accounts. Let us look at both of these methods, using the partnership of Palmer and Hogan as an example, and with the assumption that the drawings for the year ended 31 December 19-2 were Palmer £8,000 and Hogan £6,000.

(a) Fluctuating Capital Accounts

The distribution of profits would be credited to the capital accounts, one for each partner, and the drawings and the interest on drawings debited. This means that the balance at the end of each year will alter i.e. it will fluctuate.

Capital: Palmer

19-2	£	19-2	£
Dec. 31 Drawings	8,000	Jan. 1 Balance b/d	40,000
Dec. 31 Profit and Loss		Dec. 31 Profit and Loss	
Appropriation:		Appropriation:	
Interest on Drawings	500	Share of Profits	10,400
Dec. 31 Balance c/d	45,900	Interest on Capital	4,000
	54,400		54,400
		19-3	
		Jan. 1 Balance b/d	45,900

Capital: Hogan

19-2		£	19-2		£
Dec. 31 Drawings		6,000	Jan. 1 Balance b/d		32,000
Dec. 31 Profit and Loss			Dec. 31 Profit and Loss		
Appropriation:			Appropriation:		
Interest on Drawings		300	Share of Profits		5,200
			Salary		2,000
Dec. 31 Balance c/d		36,100	Interest on Capital		3,200
		42,400			42,400
			19-3		
			Jan. 1 Balance b/d		36,100

(b) *Fixed Capital Accounts Plus Current Accounts*

Capital: Palmer

			19-2		£
			Jan. 1 Balance b/d		40,000

Capital: Hogan

			19-2		£
			Jan. 1 Balance b/d		32,000

Current Account: Palmer

19-2		£	19-2		£
Dec. 31 Drawings		8,000	Dec. 31 Profit and Loss		
Dec. 31 Profit and Loss			Appropriation:		
Appropriation:			Share of Profits		10,400
Interest on Drawings		500	Interest on Capital		4,000
Dec. 31 Balance c/d		5,900			
		14,400			14,400
			19-3		
			Jan. 1 Balance b/d		5,900

Current Account: Hogan

19-2		£	19-2		£
Dec. 31 Drawings		6,000	Dec. 31 Profit and Loss		
Dec. 31 Profit and Loss			Appropriation:		
Appropriation:			Share of Profit		5,200
Interest on Drawings		300	Salary		2,000
Dec. 31 Balance c/d		4,100	Interest on Capital		3,200
		10,400			10,400
			19-3		
			Jan. 1 Balance b/d		4,100

In both of the methods described, if the salary had been paid to Hogan then there would have been a further debit in the Current Account/Fluctuating Capital Account of Hogan. It has been assumed that the salary has not in fact been paid, it being merely credited to his account.

The use of fixed capital accounts plus current accounts is preferred for two main reasons. The balance of the current account will show how much of the profits, to which a partner is entitled, have been left in the firm. If a current account turns out to have a debit balance then this can act as a warning that the partner is taking more cash out of the business than he is entitled to as his share of the profits.

The second reason is rather more complicated, and some of you will come across a rule in 'Garner v. Murray' later in your studies. This is concerned with the distribution of losses when a partner has become bankrupt. Suffice to say here that the use of separate capital and current accounts will help to bring some equity into the situation in a firm with three partners or more.

The Balance Sheet

The capital and liabilities side of the balance sheet, using fixed capital accounts, would be as follows:

Palmer and Hogan

Balance Sheet as at 31 December 19-2

		£	£
Capitals:	Palmer	40,000	
	Hogan	32,000	72,000

Current Accounts	*Palmer*	*Hogan*	
	£	£	
Share of Profits	10,400	5,200	
Salary	—	2,000	
Interest on Capital	4,000	3,200	
	14,400	10,400	
Less Drawings	8,000	6,000	
Interest on Drawings	500	300	
	5,900	4,100	10,000

Current Liabilities		
Creditors (say)		5,000
		87,000

If one of the current accounts had finished in debit then the total figure shown in the final column would be a net figure. If Hogan had finished £600 in debit then Dr would be shown after the £600 and the final column would show £5,300 for the total of both current accounts.

Absence of Partnership Agreement

You will wonder what happens if an agreement does not exist, express or implied. This is governed by Section 24 of the Partnership Act 1890. If an agreement does not exist for any one of the points now listed, then for that particular item the following will apply:

1. Profits and losses are to be shared equally.
2. No interest is to be allowed on capital.
3. No interest to be charged on drawings.
4. Salaries are not allowed.
5. Where a partner puts money into a firm in excess of the capital he has agreed to subscribe, then he is entitled to interest at the rate of 5 per cent on such an advance.

The above apply where there is no agreement. The agreement does not have necessarily to be a formal agreement drawn up by a lawyer. It may instead be contained by evidence in a letter, or it may be implied by conduct, such as when partners sign final accounts when they show profits shared in some ratio other than equally. In many cases only the courts would be able to decide on exactly whether or not agreement existed.

Assignment Exercises

14.1 Draw up a profit and loss appropriation account for the year ended 31 December 19-7 and balance sheet extracts at that date, from the following:

    (i)   Net Profits.

    (ii) Interest to be charged on capitals: Williams £2,000; Powell £1,500; Howe £900.

    (iii) Interest to be charged on drawings: Williams £240; Powell £180; Howe £130.

    (iv) Salaries to be credited: Powell £2,000; Howe £3,500.

    (v) Profits to be shared: Williams 50%; Powell 30%; Howe 20%.

    (vi) Current Accounts: Williams £1,860; Powell £946; Howe £717.

    (vii) Capital Accounts: Williams £40,000; Powell £30,000; Howe £18,000.

    (viii)Drawings: Williams £9.200; Powell £7,100, Howe £6,900.

14.2x Dent, Bishop and White are in partnership. They share profits and losses in the ratio 3:2:1 respectively. Interest is charged on drawings at the rate of 10 per cent per annum and credited at the same rate in respect of the balances on the partners' capital accounts.

Bishop is to be credited with a salary of £2,000 per annum.

In the year to 31 December 19-4 the net profit of the firm was £50,400. The partners drawings of Dent £8,000; Bishop £7,200; White £4,800 were taken in two equal instalments by the partners on 1 April 19-4 and 1 October 19-4.

The balances of the partner's accounts at 31 December 19-3 were as follows:
(all credit balances)

	Capital Accounts £	Current Accounts £
Dent	30,000	750
Bishop	28,000	1,340
White	16,000	220

You are required to:

    (i) Prepare the firm's profit and loss appropriation account for the year ended 31 December 19-4,

    (ii) Show how the partners' capital and current accounts are shown in the balance sheet as at 31 December 19-4.

14.3 Melton and Mowbray are in partnership sharing profits and losses equally. The following is their trial balance as at 30 June 19-6:

	Dr. £	Cr. £
Buildings at cost	50,000	
Fixtures at cost	11,000	
Provision for Depreciation: Fixtures		3,300
Debtors	16,243	
Creditors		11,150
Cash at Bank	677	
Stock at 30 June 19-5	41,979	
Sales		123,650
Purchases	85,416	
Carriage Outwards	1,288	
Discounts Allowed	115	
Loan Interest: Kipling	4,000	
Office Expenses	2,416	
Salaries and Wages	18,917	
Bad Debts	503	
Provision for Bad Debts		400
Loan from J. Kipling		40,000
Capitals: Melton		35,000
Mowbray		29,500
Current Accounts: Melton		1,306
Mowbray		298
Drawings: Melton	6,400	
Mowbray	5,650	
	244,604	244,604

Prepare a trading and profit and loss appropriation account for the year ended 30 June 19-6, and a balance sheet as at that date.

(i) Stock, 30 June 19-6 £56,340.

(ii) Expenses to be accrued: Office Expenses £96; Wages £200.

(iii) Depreciate fixtures 10 per cent on reducing balance basis.

(iv) Reduce provision for bad debts to £320.

(v) Partnership salary: £800 to Melton. Not yet entered.

(vi) Interest on drawings: Melton £180; Mowbray £120.

(vii) Interest on capital account balances at 10 per cent.

14.4x Oscar and Felix are in partnership. They share profits in the ratio: Oscar 60 per cent; Felix 40 per cent. The following trial balance was extracted as at 31 March 19-6:

	Dr. £	Cr. £
Office Equipment at cost	6,500	
Motor Vehicles at cost	9,200	
Provisions for depreciation at 31.3.19-5:		
Motor Vehicles		3,680
Office Equipment		1,950
Stock 31 March 19-5	24,970	
Debtors and Creditors	20,960	16,275

Cash at Bank	615	
Cash in Hand	140	
Sales		90,370
Purchases	71,630	
Salaries	8,417	
Office Expenses	1,370	
Discounts Allowed	563	
Current Accounts at 31.3.19-5:		
Oscar		1,379
Felix		1,211
Capital Accounts: Oscar		27,000
Felix		12,000
Drawings: Oscar	5,500	
Felix	4,000	
	153,865	153,865

Draw up a set of final accounts for the year ended 31 March 19-6 for the partnership. The following notes are applicable at 31 March 19-6.

(i) Stock 31 March 19-6 £27,340.

(ii) Office Expenses owing £110.

(iii) Provide for depreciation: Motors 20 per cent of cost, Office Equipment 10 per cent of cost.

(iv) Charge Interest on capitals at 10 per cent.

(v) Charge Interest on drawings: Oscar £180; Felix £210.

14.5 Menzies, Whitlam and Gough share profits and losses in the ratios 5:3:2 respectively. Their trial balance as at 30 September 19-5 was as follows:

	Dr.	Cr.
	£	£
Sales		210,500
Returns Inwards	6,800	
Purchases	137,190	
Carriage Inwards	1,500	
Stock 30 September 19-4	42,850	
Discounts Allowed	110	
Salaries	18,396	
Bad Debts	1,234	
Provision for Bad Debts 30.9.19-4		800
General Expenses	945	
Rent and Rates	2,565	
Postages	2,450	
Motor Expenses	3,940	
Motor Vans at cost	12,500	
Office Equipment at cost	8,400	
Provisions for Depreciation at 30.9.19-4:		
Motor Vans		4,200
Office Equipment		2,700
Creditors		24,356
Debtors	37,178	
Cash at Bank	666	

		Dr.	Cr.
Drawings: Menzies		12,610	
Whitlam		8,317	
Gough		6,216	
Current Accounts: Menzies			1,390
Whitlam		153	
Gough			2,074
Capital Accounts: Menzies			30,000
Whitlam			16,000
Gough			12,000
		304,020	304,020

Draw up a set of final accounts for the year ended 30 September 19-5. The following notes are relevant at 30 September 19-5:

(i)   Stock 30 September 19-5 £51,060.

(ii) Rates in advance £120; Stock of postage stamps £190.

(iii) Increase provision for bad debts to £870.

(iv) Salaries: Whitlam £1,200; Gough £700. Not yet recorded.

(v)   Interest on Drawings: Menzies £170; Whitlam £110; Gough £120.

(vi) Interest on Capitals at 10 per cent.

14.6x Robinson and Rhodes share profits and losses in the ration 3:2 respectively. The trial balance as at 31 December 19-4 was drawn up as follows:

	Dr.	Cr.
	£	£
Bank		22,001
Cash	150	
Debtors and Creditors	14,796	9,444
Buildings at Cost	30,000	
Fixtures at cost	9,000	
Provision for Depreciation on Fixtures: 31.12.19-3		2,700
Stock at 31 December 19-3	28,465	
Purchases and Sales	70,300	96,420
Returns Inwards and Outwards	1,155	945
Carriage Outwards	456	
Carriage Inwards	234	
Discounts Allowed and Received	565	1,420
Repairs to Fixtures	118	
Salaries and Wages	4,920	
General Expenses	306	
Bad Debts	1,270	
Current Accounts as at 31.12.19-3:		
Robinson		1,370
Rhodes	145	
Drawings: Robinson	10,470	
Rhodes	6,950	
Capital Accounts: Robinson		25,000
Rhodes		20,000
	179,300	179,300

Draft a set of final accounts for the year to 31 December 19-4, also using the following information as at that date:

(i) Stock at close £34,016.

(ii) Depreciation of fixtures: 10 per cent of cost.

(iii) Expenses owing: Repairs to Fixtures £38; Carriage Outwards £38.

(iv) Establish a bad debts provision of £500.

(v) Salary not yet recorded: Rhodes £2,000.

(vi) Interest on capitals at 8 per cent.

(vii) Interest on drawings: Robinson £195; Rhodes £114.

Chapter 15

An Introduction to Limited Company Accounts

Learning Objectives:

At the end of your study of this chapter you should:

1. **understand some of the more important accounting provisions of the law relating to limited companies,**
2. **understand the main features of Share Capital and Dividends,**
3. **be able to prepare final accounts for a limited company.**

Partnerships have two main disadvantages. The first is that in most cases the number of owners cannot exceed twenty, the exceptions have been explained in chapter fourteen. This means that if a large amount of capital is needed, more than could be supplied by twenty people, then this would render the business unviable.

The other disadvantage is that the liability of partners (barring limited partners) for debts of the partnership is not limited to the amount invested in the partnership. The failure of a partnership business could result in the partner losing not only his share of the partnership assets, but also part or even all of his private assets in addition.

The organisation which is not subject to both of these disadvantages is the Limited Liability Company. There are also a relatively few companies which have unlimited liability but these are not dealt with in this book. From here on any reference to a company will mean that we are dealing with a limited liability company.

A limited company's capital is divided into shares. These can be of any denomination such as 10p, 50p, £1, £5 or £10 shares. All that you have to do to become a member of a limited company, alternatively called a shareholder, is to buy one or more shares in the company. You may then pay for the share(s) in full, or else you may sometimes pay part of the money, the balance to be paid as and when the company may arrange. The most that you, as a shareholder, can lose is the share(s) that you hold, except that when the share(s) are only partly-paid you can be asked to pay the amount owing by you on the shares. Thus if a company loses all of its assets and still has debts outstanding by it, a member's private possessions cannot be touched to pay the company's debts, except for money owing on partly-paid shares. The member's liability is therefore a limited one in a limited liability company.

Companies therefore meet the needs of starting and running an organisation needing a lot of capital, or where it is desired that the members have limited liability.

Private and Public Companies

There are two types of company, the Private Company and the Public Company. Private companies outnumber public companies by a ratio of more than 20 to 1, and there are in fact over 500,000 private companies.

A private company is one which:

(a) Has a minimum membership of two.
(b) Limits the number of members to fifty, excluding present and past employees of the company.
(c) Restricts the right to transfer its shares.
(d) Prohibits any invitation to the public to subscribe for any shares or debentures in the company.

A company which does not fulfil the above conditions is a public company. These must also have a minimum number of two members, there being no maximum limit. It must also have a minimum issued share capital of £50,000.

From 1980 public companies have been required to end their names with the words 'public limited company'. This can be abbreviated as 'plc' or in capitals PLC. If the registered office is in Wales the Welsh equivalent is permitted, this is 'cwmni cyfyngedig cyhoeddus'.

The company's day-to-day business is not run by the shareholders. The fact that you own a share will normally give you voting rights, and you will then be able to attend general meetings of the company. At general meetings the directors of the company are appointed, and it is the directors to whom the shareholders entrust the day-to-day running of the business. Once a year, at an Annual General Meeting, the directors have to report on their stewardship to the shareholders. This report is accompanied by a set of final accounts for the year.

Share Capital and Dividends

The shareholder obtains his share of the profits in the form of a dividend. After the profits have been calculated the directors meet to decide how much of the profits shall be used to provide dividends for shareholders and how much will be retained in the business. The amount of the proposed dividend(s) is then put to the members at the Annual General Meeting for their approval. The shareholders can approve the dividend, they can propose a lower dividend although this latter action obviously doesn't happen very often. What they can't do is to propose a higher dividend for themselves than that proposed by the directors. Should the directors propose no dividend at all then the shareholders have no power to alter the decision. They could of course vote to change the directors, so that future decisions by directors about dividends might be different.

The decision by the directors about the amount of dividends is normally quite a complex one. Factors which have to be taken into account are such as (i) the availability of cash and bank balances to pay a dividend, (ii) the tax position of the company, (iii) effect of any government directives on dividends, (iv) the forecasts of future cash flows and profits, (v) the possibility of take-over bids, and so on.

Dividends are normally expressed as a percentage. If income tax is ignored, a dividend of 20 per cent in Firm A with 100,000 ordinary shares of £1 each will amount to £20,000. A dividend of 5 per cent in Firm B with 20,000 shares of £2 each will amount to £2,000. Someone with 10 shares in each firm would receive £2 from Firm A and £1 from Firm B.

There are various types of shares. The two main kinds are preference shares and ordinary shares. A preference share is one where the holder is entitled to a dividend at a specified percentage rate before the ordinary shareholders receive anything. The ordinary shares will be entitled to the remainder of the profits which have been appropriated as dividends.

Exhibit 15.1 shows what dividends would be payable if a company had 10,000 10 per cent preference shares of £1 each, and 10,000 ordinary shares of £1 each.

Exhibit 15.1

Years	1	2	3	4
	£	£	£	£
Profits appropriated for Dividends	1,300	2,400	1,600	2,200
Preference Dividends (10%)	1,000	1,000	1,000	1,000
Ordinary Dividends	(3%) 300	(14%) 1,400	(6%) 600	(12%) 1,200

Preference shares come in two main types, these are non-cumulative preference shares and cumulative preference shares. A non-cumulative preference share is one which ranks before ordinary shares for a yearly dividend of a specified percentage amount. However, should the profits in any year be so low that they are not sufficient to cover the full percentage of the preference dividend, the deficiency *cannot* be carried forward and paid from future year's profits. With cumulative preference shares on the other hand any deficiencies are carried forward, and these are then paid before the ordinary shares get anything.

Let us look at a company with 10,000 £1 ordinary shares and 5,000 10% preference shares of £1 each. Profits available for dividends are: year 1 £1,700: year 2 £300: year 3 £2,800: year 4 £100: year 5 £4,000. Exhibit 15.2 shows the results (a) if the preference shares were non-cumulative whilst (b) shows the situation if the preference shares were cumulative.

Exhibit 15.2

(a) Year	1	2	3	4	5
	£	£	£	£	£
Profits	1,700	300	2,800	100	4,000
Non-cumulative Preference Dividend (limited in years 2 and 4)	500	300	500	100	500
Dividends on Ordinary Shares	1,200	—	2,300	—	3,500

(b) Year	1	2	3	4	5
	£	£	£	£	£
Profits	1,700	300	2,800	100	4,000
Preference Dividends	500	300	700*	100	900*
Dividends on Ordinary Shares	1,200	—	2,100	—	3,100

*including arrears

Classes of Capital

The total of the share capital which the company is authorised to issue is known as the Authorised Share Capital. An alternative name for this is the Nominal Capital. The amount of shares actually issued is known as the Issued Share Capital. If the whole of the Authorised Capital has been issued then Issued Share Capital and Authorised Share Capital will be one and the same amount.

Where the company has requested that only a part of the amount of each share be paid, then the total asked for on all shares is the Called-Up Capital. You can obviously deduce that the amount not yet requested is the Uncalled Capital. Calls in Advance refers to amounts paid in advance before being requested, whilst calls in arrear refer to amounts requested but not yet paid.

Trading and Profit and Loss Accounts

When limited companies send copies of their final accounts to their shareholders, as they have to do by law, they do not have to give full details of every item in their trading and profit and loss accounts. To do so might give rival organisations information which the company may wish to keep secret. The Companies Acts therefore insist on only a limited amount of information being shown.

In calculating the profits of a company which can be appropriated, there are two types of expenses which can only be found in the accounts of limited companies.

1. Debenture Interest. The term debenture is one used for companies only, and it refers to money received on loan by a company, written acknowledgement being given under the company's seal. A loan to a partnership or a sole trader is known simply as a loan, whilst a loan to a company is usually known as a debenture. The interest payable for the use of such a loan is an expense of the company and is accordingly charged as

an expense in the Profit and Loss Account. Debenture interest is payable whether or not profits are made, as compared with dividends which are dependent on available profits.

2. Directors' remuneration. As directors are found only in companies then obviously this form of expense is in company accounts only.

The Appropriation of Profits

After charging all expenses, including directors' remuneration and debenture interest, the net profit can be calculated. It is then the task of the directors to decide how these profits should be appropriated.

The first charge on these profits will be the amount of Corporation Tax payable to the Inland Revenue. The amount of Corporation Tax is based on the profits made by the company.

Secondly, if any profits are to be put to reserve then the transfer is shown. Such a transfer is not one of putting cash itself on one side. All it involves is that part of the profits made, in the opinion of the directors, should not be regarded as being available for dividend purposes in that year. Such a transfer may be for a specific purpose, and the reserve named accordingly, e.g. a Fixed Assets Replacement Reserve. It may not be so specified and could be a transfer to a General Reserve.

From the balance of profits that still remains the dividends are proposed. The remainder which is the unused balance of profits is carried forward to the following year's appropriation account. There it goes to swell the total profits available for appropriation in that year. There is usually a balance of such unappropriated profits to be carried forward, assuming that the company has not been making losses. Even if it was the policy of the company to pay as high a dividend as possible, because dividends are payable to a rounded figure or percentage per share, there will still be a balance. This is because it would be very uncommon to find that the profit figures remaining after transfers to reserves exactly equalled, to round figures, an amount payable to shareholders.

Exhibit 15.3 shows the appropriation of profits for the first three years of a company's life.

Exhibit 15.3

Unique Ltd has an Ordinary Share Capital of 100,000 ordinary shares of £1 each and 50,000 10 per cent preference shares of £1 each.

For the first three years of trading ended 31 December the net profits are 19-2 £37,874: 19-3 £59,661: 19-4 £33,286.

The Corporation Tax which will become payable will be: 19-2 £15,500: 19-3 £21,180: 19-4 £13,470. Transfers to reserves are 19-2 Nil: 19-3 General Reserve £12,500: 19-4 Foreign Exchange Reserve £3,000. Dividends were proposed each year both on preference shares and on ordinary shares. For these latter shares the rate of dividends proposed were 19-2 15 per cent: 19-3 20 per cent: 19-4 12 per cent.

Appropriation of Profits
(1)   *For the year ended 31 December 19-2*

	£	£
Net Profit for the year		37,874
Less Appropriations:		
Corporation Tax	15,500	
Preference Dividend 10%	5,000	
Ordinary Dividend 15%	15,000	35,500
Unappropriated Profits carried to next year		2,374

(2)   *For the year ended 31 December 19-3*

	£	£
Net Profit for the year		59,661
Add Unappropriated Profits from last year		2,374
		62,035
Less Appropriations:		
Corporation Tax	21,180	
General Reserve	12,500	
Preference Dividend 10%	5,000	
Ordinary Dividend 20%	20,000	58,680
Unappropriated Profits carried to next year		3,355

(3)   *For the year ended 31 December 19-4*

	£	£
Net Profit for the year		33,286
Add Unappropriated Profits from last year		3,355
		36,641
Less Appropriations:		
Corporation Tax	13,470	
Foreign Exchange Reserve	3,000	
Preference Dividend 10%	5,000	
Ordinary Dividend 12%	12,000	33,470
Unappropriated Profits carried to next year		3,171

The Final Accounts of Limited Companies: Profit and Loss Accounts

When a company draws up its own Final Accounts, purely for internal use by the directors and the management, then it can draft them in any way which is considered most suitable. Drawing up a Trading and Profit and Loss Account and Balance Sheet for the firm's own use is not necessarily the same as drawing up such accounts for examination purposes. If a firm wishes to charge something in the Trading Account which perhaps in theory ought to be shown in the Profit and Loss Account, then there is nothing to prevent the firm from so doing. The examinee, on the other hand, must base his answers on accounting theory and not on the practice of his own firm.

When it comes to publication, i.e. sent to the shareholder or to the Registrar of Companies, then the Companies Act, 1981, Schedule 1, lays down the information which *must* be shown and also *how* it should be shown. Prior to the 1981 Act, provided the necessary information was shown it was completely up to the company exactly *how* it was shown. The provisions of the 1981 Act bring the United Kingdom into line with the Fourth Directive of the EEC, and therefore the freedom previously available to companies on *how* to show the information has been taken away from them. There are however some advantages to be gained from such standardisation.

The 1981 Act however does give companies the choice of two alternative formats (layouts) for balance sheets, and four alternative formats for profit and loss accounts. As the reader of this chapter will most probably be studying this for the first time, it would be inappropriate to give all the details of all the formats. Only the far more advanced student would need such details. In this book therefore the reader will be show an internal profit & loss account which can easily be adapted to cover publication requirements under the 1981 Act, also a balance sheet.

All companies, even the very smallest, have to produce accounts for shareholders giving the *full* details required by the 1981 Act. 'Small' and 'medium' companies, can however file 'modified' accounts with the Registrar of Companies. These will be examined later in your course.

The format that will be used for the published profit and loss account in this book, out of the four formats which could be used, is Format 1. The reasons for this choice are that it is in a vertical style, which is much more modern, and in addition is much more like common UK practice before the 1981 Act.

The Companies Act 1981, Schedule 1, shows Format 1 as in Exhibit 15.4.

Exhibit 15.4

Profit and loss account formats
Format 1

1. Turnover
2. Cost of sales
3. Gross profit or loss
4. Distribution costs
5. Administrative expenses
6. Other operating income
7. Income from shares in group companies
8. Income from shares in related companies
9. Income from other fixed asset investments
10. Other interest receivable and similar income
11. Amounts written off investments
12. Interest payable and similar charges
13. Tax on profit or loss on ordinary activities
14. Profit or loss on ordinary activities after taxation
15. Extraordinary income
16. Extraordinary charges
17. Extraordinary profit or loss
18. Tax on extraordinary profit or loss
19. Other taxes not shown under the above items
20. Profit or loss for the financial year

Obviously this is simply a list, and it does not show where sub-totals should be placed. The important point is that the items 1 to 20 have to be displayed in that order. Obviously if some items do not exist for the company in a given year then those headings will be omitted from the published profit and loss account. Thus if the company has no sorts of investments then items 7, 8, 9, 10 and 11 will not exist, so, that item 6 will be followed by item 12 in that company's published profit and loss account. The actual numbers on the left hand side of items do not have to be shown in the published accounts.

Exhibit 15.5 shows a Trading and Profit and Loss Account drawn up for internal use by the company. This could be drawn up in any way as far as the law is concerned because the law does *not* cover accounts prepared solely for the company's internal use. If the internal accounts were drawn up in a completely different fashion to those needed for publication, then there would be quite a lot of work to do to re-assemble the figures, into a profit and loss account for publication. In Exhibit 15.5 the internal accounts have been drawn up in a style which makes it much easier to get the figures for the published profit and loss account. As examination questions may ask for both (i) internal and (ii) published accounts, it makes it simpler for the students if the internal *and* published accounts follow a similar order of display.

Exhibit 15.5 (Accounts for internal use)

Block plc

Trading & Profit & Loss Account for the year ended 31 March 19-8

	£	£
Turnover		765,000
Less Cost of Sales:		
Stock 1 April 19-7	105,000	
Add Purchases	460,000	
	565,000	
Less Stock 31 March 19-8	126,000	439,000
Gross Profit		326,000
Distribution Costs:		
Salaries & Wages	50,000	
Motor Vehicles Costs: Distribution	21,000	
General Distribution Expenses	15,000	
Depreciation: Motors	4,000	
Machinery	3,000	93,000
Administrative Expenses:		
Salaries & Wages	44,000	
Directors' Remuneration	20,000	
Motor Vehicle Costs: Administrative	8,000	
General Administrative Expenses	31,000	
Auditors' Remuneration	2,000	
Depreciation: Motors	3,000	
Machinery	2,000	110,000	203,000
		123,000
Other Operating Income: Rents Receivable		7,000
		130,000
Income from shares in related companies	2,500	
Income from shares from non-related companies	1,500	
Other Interest Receivable	1,000	5,000
		135,000
Interest Payable:		
Loans Repayable within five years	500	
Loans Repayable in ten years time	1,500	2,000
Profit on ordinary activities before taxation		133,000
Tax on Profit on ordinary activities		48,000
Profit on ordinary activities after taxation		85,000
Undistributed profits brought forward from last year		55,000
		140,000
Transfer to General Reserve	15,000	
Proposed ordinary dividend	60,000	75,000
Undistributed profits carried forward to next year		65,000

Exhibit 15.5 is redrafted into a form suitable for publication and shown as Exhibit 15.6.

Exhibit 15.6 (Accounts for publication)

Block plc

Profit and Loss Account for the year ended 31 March 19-8

		£	£
1.	Turnover		765,000
2.	Cost of Sales		439,000
3.	Gross Profit		326,000
4.	Distribution Costs	93,000	
5.	Administrative Expenses	110,000	203,000
			123,000
6.	Other Operating Income		7,000
			130,000
8.	Income from Shares in Related Companies	2,500	
9.	Income from Other Fixed Asset Investments	1,500	
10.	Other Interest Receivable	1,000	5,000
			135,000
12.	Interest Payable:		2,000
	Profit on Ordinary Activities before Taxation		133,000
13.	Tax on Profit on Ordinary Activities		48,000
14.	Profit for the year on Ordinary Activities after Taxation		85,000
	Undistributed Profits from last year		55,000
			140,000
	Transfer to General Reserve	15,000	
	Proposed Ordinary Dividend	60,000	75,000
	Undistributed Profits Carried to Next Year		65,000

The Final Accounts of Limited Companies: Balance Sheets

The Companies Act 1981 sets out two formats for the balance sheet, one vertical and one horizontal. The method chosen for this book is that of Format 1 because this most resembles U.K. practice. As it is the vertical style format it will also be looked upon with favour by examiners.

Format 1 is shown as Exhibit 15.7. Monetary figures have been included to illustrate it more clearly.

Exhibit 15.7   Balance Sheet – *Format 1*   £000's

		£	£	£
A. CALLED UP SHARE CAPITAL NOT PAID*				10
B. FIXED ASSETS				
I	Intangible assets			
	1. Development costs	20		
	2. Concessions, patents, licences, trade marks and similar rights and assets	30		
	3. Goodwill	80		
	4. Payments on account	5	135	
II	Tangible assets			
	1. Land and buildings	300		
	2. Plant and machinery	500		
	3. Fixtures, fittings, tools and equipment	60		
	4. Payments on account and assets in course of construction	20	880	
III	Investments			
	1. Shares in group companies	15		
	2. Loans to group companies	10		
	3. Shares in related companies	20		
	4. Loans to related companies	5		
	5. Other investments other than loans	30		
	6. Other loans	16		
	7. Own shares	4	100	1,115
C. CURRENT ASSETS				
I	Stock			
	1. Raw materials and consumables	60		
	2. Work in progress	15		
	3. Finished goods and goods for resale	120		
	4. Payments on account	5	200	
II	Debtors			
	1. Trade debtors	200		
	2. Amounts owed by group companies	20		
	3. Amounts owed by related companies	10		
	4. Other debtors	4		
	5. Called up share capital not paid*	–		
	6. Prepayments and accrued income**	–	234	
III	Investments			
	1. Shares in group companies	40		
	2. Own shares	5		
	3. Other investments	30	75	
IV	Cash at Bank and in Hand		26	
			535	
D. PREPAYMENTS AND ACCRUED INCOME**			15	
			550	
E. CREDITORS: AMOUNTS FALLING DUE WITHIN ONE YEAR				
	1. Debenture loans	5		
	2. Bank loans and overdrafts	10		
	3. Payments received on account	20		
	4. Trade creditors	50		
	5. Bills of exchange payable	2		
	6. Amounts owed to group companies	15		
	7. Amounts owed to related companies	6		
	8. Other creditors including taxation and social security	54		
	9. Accruals and deferred income***	–	162	
F. NET CURRENT ASSETS (LIABILITIES)				388
G. TOTAL ASSETS LESS CURRENT LIABILITIES				1,513

H. CREDITORS: AMOUNTS FALLING DUE AFTER MORE
THAN ONE YEAR

1.	Debenture loans	20	
2.	Bank loans and overdrafts	15	
3.	Payments received on account	5	
4.	Trade creditors	25	
5.	Bills of exchange payable	4	
6.	Amounts owed to group companies	10	
7.	Amounts owed to related companies	5	
8.	Other creditors including taxation and social security	32	
9.	Accruals and deferred income***	–	116

I. PROVISIONS FOR LIABILITIES AND CHARGES

1.	Pensions and similar obligations	20	
2.	Taxation, including deferred taxation	40	
3.	Other provisions	4	64

J. ACCRUALS AND DEFERRED INCOME***

	20	200
		1,313

K. CAPITAL AND RESERVES

I	Called up share capital		1,000
II	Share premium account		100
III	Revaluation reserve		20
IV	Other reserves:		
	1. Capital redemption reserve	40	
	2. Reserve for own shares	10	
	3. Reserves provided for by the articles of association	20	
	4. Other reserves	13	83
V	PROFIT AND LOSS ACCOUNT		110
			1,313

(*); (**); (***) These items may be shown in either of the two positions indicated.

Chapter 16

Interpretation of Accounting Information

Learning Objectives:
At the end of your study of this chapter you should:
1. **be able to analyse variations in the gross and net profits,**
2. **understand and be able to calculate some key accounting ratios.**

Accounting information is intended to be used in a number of ways. In this chapter some of the methods which are used to interpret accounts will be explained. Firstly analysis of the Trading and Profit and Loss Account then the Balance Sheet.

	19-1	19-2
	£	£
Sales	10000	20000
Cost of Goods Sold	5000	12000
Gross Profit	5000	8000
Expenses	2000	5000
Net Profit	3000	3000

The profit has remained the same but the other figures comprised in the profit calculation have changed significantly. One convenient way of looking at this difference is by expressing the figures in the Profit and Loss Account as a percentage of the sales. The result would be in this example:-

	19-1	19-2
	%	%
Sales	100	100
Cost of Goods Sold	50	60
Gross Profit	50	40
Expenses	20	25
Net Profit	30	15

In the period under review the total sales have doubled but the gross margin percentage has reduced from 50% to 40% and expenses have increased from 20% to 25%. The Net margin which reflects these changes has thus fallen from 30% to 15%.

How can these differences have arisen? If we examine the change in Gross Profit the differences can be the result of many different influences. For example it could be due to deliberate changes in management's policy in fixing prices. In 19-1 they may have added 100% to the cost price of a good to reach the selling price, whereas in 19-2 they may have decided to become more competitive and only add ⅔ or 66·7%. Thus an item which costs £12 in both 19-1 and 19-2 would be sold for £24 in 19-1 and £20 in 19-2. Provided that the volume of sales goes up the management might think this is worthwhile. In our example it might have been responsible for sales doubling and gross profit going up by £3000.

	19-1			19-2	
	£	%		£	%
Cost	12.00	50	Cost	12.00	60
Margin 100%			Margin		
on cost	12.00	50	⅔ (66.7%)	8.00	40
			on cost		
Selling Price	24.00	100		20.00	100

The same result as management changing its pricing policy might arise if the cost of the goods being sold rises, whilst the selling price remains the same. For example if the item costing £12 and sold for £24 in 19-1 increased in cost to £14.40 with the selling price kept at £24, the profit on sales in 19-2 would have fallen from 50% to $\dfrac{9.60}{24.00} \times \dfrac{100}{1} = 40\%$.

	19-1			19-2	
	£	%		£	%
Cost	12.00	50	Cost	14.40	60
+ Margin 100%	12.00	50	Margin on		
			Cost		
			⅔		
			(66.7%)	9.60	40
Selling Price	24.00	100		24.00	100

There may be various other reasons for the change in gross margin in relation to sales. In particular in many businesses the calculation of the Cost of Goods Sold figure depends heavily on the calculation:- Opening Stock in Trade plus Purchases less Closing Stock in Trade equals Cost of Goods Sold. Frequently the exact counting of stock in trade is difficult and may not be accurate. Let us examine and example where the effect of stock undervaluation is shown.

Example
In 19-1 1200 units are bought @ £10
500 units are sold @ £20.

The stock at cost price should therefore be 700 units valued at £10 each = £7000.

The correct gross profit is thus

		19-1	
		£	%
Sales		10000	100
Purchases	12000		
less Stock in Trade	7000		
Cost of Goods Sold		5000	50
Gross Profit		5000	50

Suppose that 100 units of stock in trade were misplaced at the time of physically counting stock. The recorded closing stock is thus valued as only 600 units at £10 each = £6000.

The gross profit now will be shown as:-

		19-1	
		£	%
Sales		10000	100
Purchases	12000		
less Stock in Trade	6000		
Cost of Goods Sold		6000	60
Gross Profit		4000	40

The consequences for profits would have been exactly the same if 100 units of stock in trade had been destroyed or stolen. In all these cases the closing stock is at a lower value than it ought to be and gross profit is understated as a consequence. Exactly the reverse would be true if the stock value were overstated. i.e. profit would be too high. Overstatement is not going to arise from theft however!

If the example is now continued for another year it can be seen that the consequences of the error will affect the next year.

Example

In 19-2 the business buys a further 600 units @ £10 and sells 800 units @ £20. The stock in trade at the end of 19-2 should be 500 units at £10 = £5000. The position if all had been correct in 19-1 would be:-

		19-2	
		£	%
Sales		16000	100
Opening Stock	7000		
Purchases	6000		
	13000		
less Closing Stock	5000	8000	50
Gross Profit		8000	50

However if the profit is calculated with the incorrect figure of 19-1 stock but assuming that a correct physical count for 19-2 of 500 units was completed then the results would be (Opening Stock 700 units + Purchases 600 units — Sales 800 units = 500 units).

		19-2	
		£	%
Sales		16000	100.00
Opening Stock	6000		
Purchases	6000		
	12000		
less Closing Stock	5000	7000	43.75
Gross Profit		9000	56.25

The profits for 19-1 and 19-2 together add to the same total:-

	Correct Annual Profits	*Incorrect Annual Profits*
	£	£
19-1	5000	4000
19-2	8000	9000
	13000	13000

This would not be the case if the shortage of stock in 19-1 had been due to loss or theft since the subsequent calculation of 19-2 stock in trade would also have been short of the missing goods. Thus if the difference in stock in trade is due either to calculation errors or short counting the effect on one year will be corrected in the next, but the proper comparison of margins in both years will be impossible.

Another reason why the gross profit position can change over two periods is a change in the items which make up the sales. Most businesses sell more than one item and usually different items are sold at different profit margins. Thus if there is an increase in the proportion of units sold at a higher margin the total margin should increase.

Example

A business sells products X and Y

X costs £30 and the markup on cost is 50% thus selling for £45.

Y costs £15 and the markup on cost is 100% thus selling for £30.

In period 1.	sales are	1000 units of X
	and	500 units of Y
In period 2.	sales are	800 units of X
	and	800 units of Y

				£	%
Period 1.	Sales	X	£45000		
		Y	£15000	60000	100.0
	Cost of				
	Sales	X	£30000		
		Y	£7500	37500	62.5
	Gross Profit			22500	37.5
Period 2.	Sales	X	£36000		%
		Y	£24000	60000	100.0
	Cost of				
	Sales	X	£24000		
		Y	£12000	36000	60.0
	Gross Profit			24000	40.0

Notice that the margin in Period 2 has improved because of more sales of Y. This is true despite the fact that there is an equal profit of £15 per unit on both X and Y.

The Management of a business in addition to wanting explanations for variations in the gross profit will also want to know in detail how the other expenses have changed between the gross profit and net profit levels. Again by breaking down the expenses as a percentage of sales it is possible to see from year to year which items are giving rise to variations. For example the Profit and Loss Account of B. Broughton is as follows for three years:-

	19-1		19-2		19-3	
	£	%	£	%	£	%
Sales	20,000	100.0	30,000	100.0	40,000	100.0
Cost of Goods Sold	10,000	50.0	15,000	50.0	20,000	50.0
Gross Profit	10,000	50.0	15,000	50.0	20,000	50.0
Salaries	3,000	15.0	4,000	13.3	8,000	20.0
Motor Expenses	2,000	10.0	3,000	10.0	4,000	10.0
Heating	1,000	5.0	1,500	5.0	2,000	5.0
Rent	3,000	15.0	3,000	10.0	3,000	7.5
Total Expenses	9,000	45.0	11,500	38.3	17,000	42.5
Net Profit	1,000	5.0	3,500	11.7	3,000	7.5
	10,000	50.0	15,000	50.0	20,000	50.0

The percentage figures show that Gross Profit Margins have been constant but that the expenses have varied. Two of the expenses Motor Expenses and Heating have remained a constant proportion of sales, but Salaries and Rent have varied. Salaries first reduced then increased in proportion to sales. Rent which has remained at a fixed money amount presumably under a lease has reduced as a percentage as sales increased.

Only someone with a detailed knowledge of the business can say whether the changes in these expenses are acceptable. The accountant's job is to prepare the analysis which allows someone with the appropriate knowledge to judge whether the changes are satisfactory or not.

The importance of the stock in trade figure has already been pointed out in relation to the calculation of Gross Profit. Its importance can be further emphasised if you realise that it represents in many businesses one of its largest and most important investments. In a retail business for example very large amounts of money may have to be laid out to purchase stock in trade. In this type of business therefore it is useful to calculate the relationship between stock in trade and sales. The business man will be interested in keeping his stock in trade low and his sales high, but he will probably have to offer his customer choice and quick delivery if he is to keep his sales high. The relationship between stock in trade and sales is called the stock turnover or stockturn. It is measured by dividing the sales by the average stock in trade. For example if sales are £1000 and average stock in trade £200 the stockturn is 5 times. This means that on average the stock in trade is replaced five times each year.

The calculation of Stockturn if it is to be accurate needs to take account of the fact that the selling price of goods is marked up from the cost value of stock in trade. If we want to measure stockturn accurately then either stock in trade must be valued at selling prices before dividing into sales or sales need to be valued at cost (i.e. Cost of Goods Sold) before dividing by stock in trade at cost. Since detailed accounts give the figure of Cost of Goods Sold the best method therefore is to use:-

$$\frac{\text{Cost of Goods Sold}}{\text{Average Stock in Trade.}}$$

The Average Stock figure should be based on the average of regular stock in trade counts. If a business counts its stock quarterly then it would be as follows:-

		£
Stock in trade @	1 January	20,000
	31 March	30,000
	30 June	50,000
	30 September	15,000
	31 December	25,000

The average of the five figures is $\frac{140,000}{5}$ = £28,000. In this business the stock in trade fluctuates and the more stock counts that are obtained the more accurate the average.

Some businesses only count stock in trade at the end of the year and thus the average stock in trade can only be taken from the average of the opening and closing figures for the year. In the example just given the average would have been £22,500   i.e. $\frac{45000}{2}$ rather than £28,000. This would clearly be misleading as it ignores the big changes in stock levels during the year.

Whilst accuracy is always very desirable in accounting interpretation sometimes for purposes of comparison between different firms easily obtained ratios are useful. Stockturn is one illustration of this because detailed figures for the average stock in trade and cost of goods sold figures may not be obtainable. In this situation the analyst may gain a useful impression or approximation to stockturn by dividing sales by the average of opening and closing stock in trade figures at cost.

The relationship between average stock in trade and sales which has just been described is called an accounting ratio. A ratio is a convenient way of expressing the way in which two significant accounting numbers are related.

The idea of calculating the ratio between stock in trade and sales is useful because it helps us to understand an important factor in business activity. Stock in Trade is an asset and for similar reasons that stockturn was calculated so too can the relationships between other business assets and sales.

The assets in a simple Balance Sheet will be classified as Fixed Assets or Current Assets for example as follows:-

	£	£
Fixed Assets		
Land and Buildings	100,000	
Plant and Machinery	50,000	
Fixtures and Fittings	10,000	160,000
Current Assets		
Stock in Trade	28,000	
Debtors	20,000	
Cash at Bank	2,000	50,000

If the sales for the year ending at the Balance Sheet date were £500,000 then the following ratios can be calculated:-

Land and Buildings	: Sales	100,000: 500,000	= 1:5
Plant and Machinery	: Sales	50,000: 500,000	= 1:10
Fixtures and Fittings	: Sales	10,000: 500,000	= 1:50
Total Fixed Assets	: Sales	160,000: 500,000	= 1:3.125
Stock in Trade	: Sales	28,000: 500,000	= 1:18.57
Debtors	: Sales	20,000: 500,000	= 1:25
Cash at Bank	: Sales	2,000: 500,000	= 1:250
Total Current Assets	: Sales	50,000: 500,000	= 1:10

These ratios you will recognise are approximations since we are taking the asset value at the year end rather than the average assets held during the year. Ideally we should do as was done for the Stockturn ratio and calculate the average. Often the year end figure of assets is taken if there has not been a material change in the assets during the year.

The ratios which have been calculated are of interest because they bring together in the ratio the investment a firm has made in particular resources (i.e. assets) against an accounting measure of the firms output (i.e. sales). From this can be assessed the effectiveness of investment in assets in producing sales. If the firm has assets such as investments in shares of other firms which do not give rise to sales then the ratio would not be appropriate for such assets. It is also important to remember that assets bought in different time periods may if they are valued at cost no longer represent the current value of the asset. Thus if a ratio is to be compared with others it is important to make sure that asset values are comparable.

The Balance Sheet of a business contains not only Assets but Capital and Liabilities. The relationship between these component parts of the balance sheet is another area where ratios are useful. Consider the following Balance Sheet for Juniper Company at 31st December 19-1:

Juniper Company
Balance Sheet at 31 December 19-1

	£		£
Fixed Assets	12,000	Capital	9,000
		Loan	7,000
Current Assets	8,000	Current liabilities	4,000
	20,000		20,000

Like the Profit and Loss Account the Balance Sheet can be expressed in percentage terms:-

Juniper Company
Balance Sheet at 31 December 19-1

	%		%
Fixed Assets	60	Capital	45
Current Assets	40	Loan	35
		Current Liabilities	20
	100		100

There are a number of ways in which this can be used. Firstly we might try to assess the company's ability to pay creditors. The creditors requiring payment in the immediate future are included in Current Liabilities. The company will pay its creditors from current assets which include bank and cash balances as well as from assets that will have changed into cash (e.g. by selling stock in trade for cash) by the time the creditors are due to be paid. Thus the relationship of Current Assets to Current Liabilities is a useful measure of the firms ability to meet its liabilities in time. For Juniper Company the ratio is:-

Current Assets £8000 : Current Liabilities £4000

= 2 : 1

or expressed from the percentages 40%:20% = 2:1. This ratio is known as the Current Ratio.

From the creditors point of view he is interested in ensuring that Current Assets exceed Current Liabilities by a clear margin. A ratio of 2:1 is frequently thought of as appropriate but it is not really satisfactory to use rule of thumb figures like this without thought. In particular it is often necessary to look at the composition of Current Assets more closely. In one company the Current Assets may be 80% Stock in Trade in another 80% Cash. From a creditor's point of view the Stock in Trade may represent a risk because it could be very hard to sell if trade for this business becomes bad. He may therefore prefer to see a high cash figure. However holding cash is not likely to be profitable in itself and company will not wish to hold more cash than necessary. The level of stock in trade needs to be assessed in terms of its turnover and profitability as well as in terms of the Current Ratio.

If you refer back to the Balance Sheet for Juniper Limited note that the assets other than Current Assets are Fixed Assets which comprise 60% of the total Assets. This means that these Fixed Assets are part of the structure of the firm and unless the firm reduces in size by selling part of its structure this part will remain fixed over a number of years.

On the other side of the Balance Sheet it can be seen that Capital represents only 45% of the total. Notice that this is less than the percentage for Fixed Assets. The Loan represents 35% of the total and this with Capital amounts to 80%. The point which is important here is the terms of the loan with regard to repayment. If the lender is entitled to repayment in the near future the business may be in trouble. It will either have to raise a new loan or Capital or the business will need to be sold off. The loan is being used to fund fixed assets which probably have a long life and may not be readily sold if the lender wants repayment.

The most important lesson is that the capital and loans of a business are matched to its investments in assets. In our example if the loan is for a longer period than the assets it is financing, the firm will have an opportunity to recover its cash in time to refund the loan, and all should be well. But if the firm borrows on a short term loan and invests these funds in long lived assets it may well get into difficulty, because the loans will need to be renewed before the assets life has ended, yet because of a Credit squeeze or some such reason new loans on capital may not be available when required.

The final measure of business performance in this section brings together the other analysis. At the start of the chapter we looked at $\dfrac{\text{Profit}}{\text{Sales}}$ and the various ways in which this could be analysed. Then measures of $\dfrac{\text{Sales}}{\text{Assets}}$ were described. If these two approaches to analysis are brought together we have:-

$$\frac{\text{Profit}}{\text{Sales}} \times \frac{\text{Sales}}{\text{Assets}} = \frac{\text{Profit}}{\text{Assets}}$$

i.e. if sales is cancelled on the left hand side the measure of profit over asset remains. This is often called 'Return on Capital Employed.'

When using the general description 'Return on Capital Employed' it is important to define exactly what is meant since the definitions of both 'Profit' and 'Assets' can vary considerably. In the broadest definition 'Net Profit after Taxation' in relation to 'Total Assets' may be used. Total Assets is most commonly defined as Fixed and other non-current assets plus working capital (i.e. Current Assets less Current Liabilities). For example the abridged accounts for Ace Ltd. were as follows at 31 December 19-1:

Balance Sheet at 31 December 19-1

	£		£
Fixed Assets (net)	1,500,000	Share Capital	850,000
		Reserves	800,000
			1,650,000
Current Assets	800,000	Loans	350,000
		Current Liabilities	300,000
	2,300,000		2,300,000

The Net Profit after tax for the year to 31 December 19-1 before appropriation of dividends was £300,000. The Return on Capital employed would be:

$$\frac{\text{Net Profit after tax}}{\text{Fixed Assets} + \text{Current Assets} - \text{Current Liabilities}} = \frac{300,000}{1,500,000 + 800,000 - 300,000} = \frac{300,000}{2,000,000}$$
$$= 15\%$$

There are several other ways of calculating the Return on Capital Employed and great care must be taken to ensure that the same definition has been used when comparing different firms. You will learn more about these different approaches at a later stage in your studies.

In any ratio analysis that you undertake you must clearly understand the definition and limitation of the information you are analysing. Within the same firm you must ensure that the information is consistent over time. For example if a firm changes its method of stock valuation or depreciation between one period and the next the accounting results may not be comparable.

Care must also be taken to see that the accounting data is representative. In the example just dealt with on Return on Capital Employed the balance sheet data at 31 December was compared with a year's profit. This is only appropriate if the year end figure for assets is representative of the year as a whole. If it is not then average figures for Capital Employed for the whole year should be used; as was the case for Stockturn earlier in the chapter.

When comparing different firms it is even more difficult to ensure that these points of consistency and validity hold. In particular the valuation of assets of firms which have been bought in widely different time periods may cause problems. If firm A bought a building 5 years ago for £500,000 and firm B bought an exactly similar building this year for £750,000 any comparison of the return on these investments between A and B can be very misleading unless an adjustment for changing market values is made.

Despite these pitfalls for the unwary, ratio analysis is a very useful way of interpreting accounting information. Whether you are an investor, creditor or manager the current results of a firm need to be assessed in conjunction with evidence from previous years and from other firms. Ratios are a method of doing this efficiently by concentrating a quantity of detailed information into relatively few key statistics.

Assignment Exercises

16.1 You are examining the accounts of the Super Sweet Company for three years and have been asked to report briefly to the management on the differences in the net profits.

Super Sweet Company

	19-1	19-2	19-3
	£	£	£
Sales	200,000	250,000	300,000
Opening Stock in Trade	50,000	80,000	30,000
Purchases	130,000	100,000	140,000
	180,000	180,000	170,000
Less Closing Stock in Trade	80,000	30,000	50,000
Cost of Goods Sold	100,000	150,000	120,000
Gross Profit	100,000	100,000	180,000
Administration Expenses	20,000	25,000	30,000
Selling Expense	30,000	29,000	52,000
Net Profit	50,000	46,000	98,000
	100,000	100,000	180,000

In your report calculate the profit margins as a percentage of sales, and present the results in graphical form.

16.2x The Sales Manager of Juniper Limited has come to you for advice about the results which would arise from a change in the selling prices of the firm's products. At the present time all goods sold by Juniper Limited are priced at cost plus 50%. Currently, sales are as follows:

Product	Unit Selling Price	Total Sales
	£	£
A	15	45,000
B	12	60,000
C	9	54,000
		159,000

What is the unit cost of products A, B and C?

What should the gross profit be on total sales of £159,000 in £ and percentage terms?

The Sales Manager wants to alter the pricing policy, giving you expected new sales figures as follows:

Product A	Cost + 30%	Expected sales 4,000 units
B	Cost + 60%	Expected sales 3,500 units
C	Cost + 40%	Expected sales 8,000 units

Assume Cost remains constant.

What would expected total sales be?

What should the gross profit be on the expected sales figures in £ and percentage terms?

16.3 The accounts of Aglow Torch Company Limited are in preparation and the first draft for 19-2 has been prepared and compared with the accounts for 19-1. These are as follows, at Gross Profit level:-

	19-1	%	19-2	%
	£		£	
Sales	500,000	100	600,000	100
Opening Stock in Trade	80,000		70,000	
Purchases	290,000		360,000	
	370,000		430,000	
Less Closing Stock in Trade	70,000		130,000	
Cost of Goods Sold	300,000	60	300,000	50
GROSS PROFIT	200,000	40	300,000	50

As the accountant responsible for preparing the accounts you are unhappy about the difference in gross margins, as your pricing policy and sales mix has remained the same. On checking the stock sheets for 19-1 you discover that there was an error in the calculations and the closing stock in trade should have been £120,000, not £70,000. In addition, you find that during 19-2, £5,000 of goods had been destroyed in a warehouse due to flooding. No entries to record this loss had been made.

Restate the accounts for 19-1 and 19-2 with the adjustments for these two items included.

16.4x Uranus Products Limited sells three types of gas heater for industrial use. In 19-1, the following information on sales and costs has been collected.

Type No.	Selling Price per unit £	Cost Price per unit £	Number of units sold	Total Costs £	Total Sales £
1	50	25	10,000	250,000	500,000
2	40	30	20,000	600,000	800,000
3	80	48	4,000	192,000	320,000
				1,042,000	1,620,000

What is the gross profit margin on each type of product and in total?

In 19-2 it is expected that all costs will increase by 10%.

The mark-up on cost will be the same percentage as in 19-1.

The number of units expected to be sold will be:-

	Type 1	9,000 units
	2	21,000 units
	3	5,000 units

What is the gross profit margin on each type of product and in total which you would expect in 19-2?

16.5 The Cranborn Corporation has been examining the results of its 'Sports and Recreation' facilities over the past three years. You have been asked to prepare a report for the committee responsible which is interested to know where, if possible, savings might be made in the contribution made by the Corporation.

	19-1 £	19-2 £	19-3 £
Fees from hire of facilities	5,000	5,200	5,500
Fees from hire of equipment	600	900	1,300
Receipts from vending machines	400	450	460
	6,000	6,550	7,260
Salaries and Wages	8,000	8,800	10,200
Heating and Lighting	2,000	2,300	2,600
Repairs and Maintenance of Buildings	500	400	300
Repairs and Maintenance of Equipment	100	110	50
Goods used in vending machines	300	225	290
Telephone, Postage and Sundry Administration Costs	700	820	950
Advertising of facilities	300	100	50
	11,900	12,755	14,440
Contribution required from the Corporation	5,900	6,205	7,180

16.6x Briggs Industrial (Grippers) Limited prepares figures of its stock in trade every three months. For the past three years the figures have been as follows:

Stock in Trade at Cost

	19-1	19-2	19-3
	£	£	£
1st January	80,000	100,000	100,000
31st March	60,000	50,000	70,000
30th June	40,000	60,000	50,000
30th September	90,000	110,000	125,000
31st December	100,000	100,000	90,000

For the same period, the cost of goods sold figures were:-

	19-1	19-2	19-3
	£	£	£
Quarter ending 31st March	210,000	220,000	215,000
Quarter ending 30th June	160,000	175,000	180,000
Quarter ending 30th September	190,000	200,000	195,000
Quarter ending 31st December	290,000	270,000	250,000
Year Ending 31st December	850,000	865,000	840,000

Prepare quarterly stockturn figures and the annual stockturn for the three years using the average stock in trade.

Compare the results an external analyst would obtain using the average of opening and closing stock in trade at 1st January and 31st December, and the sales for the year which were:

$$£$$

19-1	1,125,000
19-2	1,249,000
19-3	1,058,000

16.7 The Managing Director of Agrobeans Limited has been worried about the utilisation of assets within the Company. In a conversation some time ago, you had mentioned that ratios of assets to turnover might be useful, particularly if they could be compared with another firm. The Managing Director has obtained the accounts of Quickbean Limited, a close competitor, and wants you to prepare the ratios.

	Agrobeans Limited			Quickbean Limited		
	19-1	19-2	19-3	19-1	19-2	19-3
	£	£	£	£	£	£
Fixed Assets						
Land & Buildings	101,000	120,000	120,000	—	—	—
Plant & Machinery	260,000	300,000	350,000	200,000	210,000	230,000
Motor Vehicles	70,000	72,000	74,000	60,000	80,000	90,000
Fixtures & Fittings	15,000	18,000	19,000	45,000	71,000	50,000
	446,000	510,000	563,000	305,000	361,000	370,000
Current Assets						
Stock in Trade	81,000	93,000	107,000	203,000	220,000	235,000
Trade Debtors	50,000	57,000	63,000	61,000	92,000	103,000
Cash at Bank	12,000	8,000	11,000	40,000	22,000	15,000
	143,000	158,000	181,000	304,000	334,000	353,000
Total Assets	589,000	668,000	744,000	609,000	695,000	723,000
Sales	1,767,000	1,870,000	1,890,000	2,436,000	3,130,000	3,400,000

Comment on the ratios and prepare graphs to illustrate the ratio trends.

16.8x Pobjoy Limited is a manufacturer in the Electronics Industry. Balance Sheets for the past three years are shown below. The directors are discussing a proposal to raise a loan of £500,000 at 15% interest. Prepare an analysis of the Balance Sheets, based on breaking the figures into percentages, and comment on the relationship between Assets and Capital and Liabilities. Do you think that the proposed loan can be supported from the evidence you have?

Balance Sheets (abridged)

	19-1	19-2	19-3
	£	£	£
Fixed Assets	497,000	563,000	652,000
Current Assets			
Stock in Trade	444,000	602,000	682,000
Debtors	492,000	582,000	648,000
Other	118,000	126,000	208,000
Total Assets	1,551,000	1,873,000	2,190,000
Share Capital	500,000	500,000	500,000
Retained Profit	434,000	599,000	839,000
	934,000	1,099,000	1,339,000
Current Liabilities	617,000	774,000	851,000
Total Capital and Liabilities	1,551,000	1,873,000	2,190,000
Profit before Tax for the Year	270,000	244,000	250,000

16.9x You have been offered an opportunity to purchase a business dealing in ready mixed concrete and aggregates. Balance Sheets and Profits have been projected for the next three years, as follows: –

Years from now	1	2	3
All £'000	£	£	£
Fixed Assets	146	162	159
Current Assets			
Stock in Trade	14	20	22
Debtors	63	71	74
Cash at Bank	9	9	13
	86	100	109
	232	262	268
Share Capital	70	70	70
Reserves	22	30	32
	92	100	102
10% Loan Stock	50	60	69
Current Liabilities	90	102	107
	232	262	268
Net Profit after Tax per annum	26	19	27

What is the return on Capital employed based on these figures?

Examining all the information contained in these Balance Sheets, do you consider that it would be worthwhile buying all the 70,000 £1 Ordinary Shares at the asking price of £2 per share? The average return on capital employed for the industry is 15% (using Net Profit after Tax and Fixed Assets + Current Assets – Current Liabilities).

Chapter 17

The Utopian Number System

Learning Objectives:
At the end of your study of this chapter you should be able to:
1. **understand the structure of a number system,**
2. **add, subtract, multiply and divide both positive and negative integers.**

The Utopian Number System

Some societies appear to have managed very well without developing the art of numeracy. One society in the South Pacific once used a counting system that went one, two, three — many! Surely, many schoolchildren would consider this island to be some form of paradise. Initially, we will confine our attention to a very simple counting system — though not quite so simple as the one we have just described. Utopia is a highly egalitarian society: what little it has in material goods is fairly evenly distributed among its population. There seems little point in thinking in terms of large numbers, and this viewpoint has prevailed since the dawn of history. The society has been so static and so isolated from the rest of the world that inbred into it is the inability to conceive of numbers greater than nine. Now, although this society is primitive, it still finds it convenient to trade, and so the necessity for a unit of currency arose. It was decided to use shells as the basic monetary unit, though, in line with the egalitarian viewpoint, no individual could hold more than nine shells. Now unfortunately, it seems a fact of life that as soon as a society develops trade, the loan shark also appears, and Utopia is no exception to this rule. Poor Utopia — it must now leave its 'Garden of Eden' state and come to terms with arithmetic processes and the art of numeracy. Let us set ourselves the task of explaining the basic arithmetic processes to a member of this society.

It seems reasonable to assume that the Utopians would develop the process of addition and subtraction even before the appearance of trade. After all, they will have had stocks of goods, and will have experienced both increases and decreases in these stocks. It is likely that the Utopian would soon realise that he had a built in calculator — his fingers — and would use them for performing simple sums. It is even possible that one bright Utopian would develop an *addition table* like the one in Fig. 17.1. It is also possible that a subtraction table was produced, and you should produce one for yourself that would fit into the limitations of the Utopian number system. Utopians would soon appreciate the pattern that appears in the tables.

Exhibit 17.1. Addition Table

		|First Number 1	2	3	4	5	6	7	8	9
	1	2	3	4	5	6	7	8	9	—
	2	3	4	5	6	7	8	9	—	—
	3	4	5	6	7	8	9	—	—	—
Second	4	5	6	7	8	9	—	—	—	—
Number	5	6	7	8	9	—	—	—	—	—
	6	7	8	9	—	—	—	—	—	—
	7	8	9	—	—	—	—	—	—	—
	8	9	—	—	—	—	—	—	—	—
	9	—	—	—	—	—	—	—	—	—

The appearance of trade will cause the Utopians to rethink their concept of number. Previously, their stock of goods could contain any amount up to nine items — or indeed they could have nothing. So their number system ranging between zero and nine would suffice on all occasions. But consider the case of Fred the shoemaker who has no shells. He wishes to purchase some leather worth two shells from a farmer, but he cannot afford to pay the farmer until he makes the shoes and sells them. The farmer, having surplus wealth, agrees to supply leather on credit to Fred. What is Fred's wealth now? It is not true to say that he has nothing — he cannot have nothing until he repays the farmer. To cope with such cases, it will be necessary for Utopians to make a great leap forward in their thinking and visualise numbers less than zero. We can then state that Fred's wealth is 'two shells less than zero' or minus two shells. The Utopian number system must now be extended from plus nine to minus nine.

Utopians are now faced with problems of addition and subtraction involving both positive and negative numbers — problems that create difficulties for all of us when we first meet them. Typical of such problems would be: Fred has three shells, but he owes the farmer four shells — what is Fred's present wealth? Put in this way, it is easy to see that Fred's wealth is minus one shell. Some bright individual would soon realise that the problem could be written symbolically like this:

$$(+3) + (-4) = (-1)$$

$(+3)$ represents the shells that Fred has

$+$ means that Fred borrows (we increase his debt and his stock of shells increases).

(-4) represents Fred's debt to the farmer.

(-1) represents Fred's actual wealth.

Notice that this expression tells us Fred's wealth: it does not give us his stock of shells. His stock of shells is 3 (which he originally had) + 4 (which he borrows from the farmer) = 7 shells. In the first expression, we took Fred's wealth and added a negative quantity to it. In other words we performed the arithmetic operation 'plus minus', and this caused Fred's wealth to decrease. Now as you will realise, a decrease is equivalent to a subtraction, so we can conclude that

'plus minus' means subtract.

If Fred decided to repay the farmer, then his wealth (and his stock of shells) would revert to three shells. Symbolically, it would be written like this:

$$(-1) - (-4) = (+3)$$

(-1) represents Fred's wealth before repayment
(-4) represents Fred's debt to the farmer.
— means Fred repays the debt: we reduce the debt and his stock of shells decreases.
$(+3)$ represents Fred's wealth after repaying the debt.

In this case, we perform the operation 'minus minus' and we found that Fred's wealth had increased. In other words

'minus minus' means add.

Now let use examine these transactions from the point of view of the farmer. Let us suppose that he starts with the maximum wealth of nine shells. We stated that (-4) was the amount that Fred borrowed from the farmer, so $(+4)$ must be the amount that the farmer has loaned to Fred. We said that $+$ means that Fred borrows from the farmer (Fred's stock of shells increases) so from the farmer's point of view the transaction is represented by a minus (his stock of shells decreases). On lending to Fred, the farmer's stock of shells becomes

$$(+9) - (+4) = (+5)$$

but, of course, his wealth remains fixed at nine shells. As the Farmer's stock of shells decreases, we can conclude from this arithmetic operation that

'minus plus' means subtract.

Finally, let us look again at the discharge of the debt. If minus means the farmer lends, then plus must mean that the farmer is repaid. The effect on the farmer's stock of shells is

$$(+5) + (+4) = (+9),$$

and we can conclude that

'plus plus' means add.

Let us now summarise these four operations

Operation	Action
plus minus	subtract
minus minus	add
minus plus	subtract
plus plus	add

So we can see that if the signs are the same, we add, but if the signs are different we subtract.

Despite this simple rule, Fred (in common with many people) will no doubt still have difficulty in performing such calculations. It may help Fred's understanding to illustrate the calculations on a line segment.

$$-9 \quad -8 \quad -7 \quad -6 \quad -5 \quad -4 \quad -3 \quad -2 \quad -1 \quad 0 \quad +1 \quad +2 \quad +3 \quad +4 \quad +5 \quad +6 \quad +7 \quad +8 \quad +9$$

Exhibit 17.2

The first thing to notice is that a subtraction involves a decrease, ie a movement to the left, whereas an addition involves an increase ie. a movement to the right. Let us illustrate on this line segment the calculation

$$(+3) + (-4) = (-1)$$

($+3$) locates our starting point
$+$ means face to the right
(-4) means move four numbers backwards.
This is illustrated in diag. 17.3.

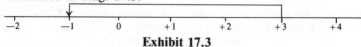

Exhibit 17.3

Likewise $(-1) - (+4) = (-5)$
(-1) locates our starting point
$-$ means face to the left
($+4$) means move four numbers forward, as illustrated in diag 17.4.

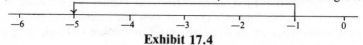

Exhibit 17.4

We shall now turn our attention to multiplication and division on the extended Utopian number system. Now Fred first met multiplication involving negative numbers when driving his ox cart to market. The ox cart travels at a speed of 2 kph. and Fred realises that by using a plus minus sign, he can indicate his direction. When travelling at $+2$kph., he is travelling to market, and at -2kph. he is travelling back from market. A highlight of Fred's journey is his drink at the public house, where he stops on both his journey to and from market. So important are the drinks to him that he measures his time travelled from the public house rather than from his home or from the market. If the time is $+2$ hours, this is two hours after he has had his drink and -2 hours is two hours before he has had his drink. Fred also measures distance from the public house: positive distances are those between the public house and the market, and negative distances are those between Fred's home and the public house. Measuring distances in this way is consistent with the construction of a line segment.

Exhibit 17.5

Suppose the time is $+3$ (ie. three hours after Fred's drink). If he is travelling to market ($+2$kph.), then he is 6km. from the public house in the direction of the market

$$\text{ie. } (+3) \times (+2) = (+6)$$

and if he is travelling back from market (-2kph.) he is 6 km. from the public house in the direction of his home

$$\text{ie. } (+3) \times (-2) = (-6)$$

Now suppose the time is —3 (ie. three hours before Fred's drink). Travelling to market, he is 6km. from the public house in the direction of his home

$$\text{ie. } (-3) \times (+2) = (-6)$$

and travelling back from market, he is 6km. from the public house in the direction of the market.

$$\text{ie. } (-3) \times (-2) = (+6)$$

Looking at these multiplications, we can deduce the rule that like signs give a plus and unlike signs give a minus.

We have just discovered that

$$(+3) \times (-2) = (-6)$$

so it follows that

$$(-6) \div (+3) = (-2)$$

and

$$(-6) \div (-2) = (+3)$$

We also discovered that

$$(-3) \times (-2) = (+6)$$

so it follows that

$$(+6) \div (-3) = (-2)$$

and we know that

$$(+6) \div (+2) = (+3)$$

So the rules for division are the same as the rule for multiplication; like signs give a plus and unlike signs give a minus. if you think back, you will realise that the rule for multiplication and division is the same as that for addition and subtraction.

Understanding these calculations is fundamental to developing the art of numeracy, and before developing the number system further, it is absolutely vital that you can cope with them. Use either the simple rules or line segments; whichever you find easier — either, rigidly applied, should ensure that you never go wrong.

Assignment Exercises

17.1   Assuming the number system is extended to include all negative and positive numbers, evaluate the following:

a.   (-8) + (-9)

bx. (-10) - (-39) + (-26) + (+19)

c.   (-12) × (+42)

dx. (+11) × (-16)

e.   (-36) × (-13) × (+2)

fx. (+144) ÷ (-16)

g.   (-625) ÷ (-25) ÷ (+5)

17.2x The temperatures at 2 a.m. in the Utopian capital during the first week in January were:

Temp. (°C) -3 -4 0 +2 -1 +1 -2

What was the average temperature during the week?

17.3 Consider the sum $5 + 4 \times 2$

It would appear that two answers are possible depending upon which operation we perform first, ie.

$5 + 4 \times 2 = 9 \times 2 = 18$

or $5 + 4 \times 2 = 5 + 8 = 13$

Which is right? Now the rule in cases such as this is that *you should multiply and divide before you add and subtract.* So the correct answer to this problem is 13. Armed with this rule can you evaluated the following?

a. $5 \times 4 + 3$

bx. $5 \times -4 + 3 \times -6$

c. $6 \div -2 - -8 \div 4$

dx. $3 \times -4 + -9 \div -3$

e. $5 + -2 \times -4 - 3 + 12 \div -6$

17.4 Consider again the sum $5 + 4 \times 2$. We know the correct answer is 13. If we wanted the answer to be 18 and the calculations to be correct we would have to use *brackets.* Brackets tell us to do that part of the sum first, ie. $(5 + 4) \times 2 = 9 \times 2 = 18$

Evaluate the following:

a. $(3 + 6) \times 4$

bx. $(3 + 6) \times (3 - 2)$

c. $(5 - 15) \div (12 - 7)$

dx. $(4 + 6) \div (8 - 13)$

e. $(5 + 3) \times (2 - 5) \div (15 - 3)$

17.5x Evaluate the following pairs of expressions.

a. i. $5 \times (4 + 2)$

b. i. $5 \times (6 - 2)$

ii. $5 \times 4 + 5 \times 2$

ii. $5 \times 6 - 5 \times 2$

What do you conclude?

Do .not attempt these revisionary assignments until you have reached Chapter 21.

Revisionary Assignments

17a Add the following:

a. 487	b. 2093	c. 3706	d. 5991	e. 2917
3964	941	5058	4006	18009
1758	5612	9116	17650	4016
4806	1306	1510	1207	9257

17bx Answer the following:

a. 3177 - 307   b. 3046 - 973   c. 5218 - 4069

d. 7916 - 3751   e. 6905 - 3006   f. 189 × 27

g. 569 × 782   h. 1489 × 236   i. 756 × 806

j. 387 × 461   k. 552 ÷ 46   l. 583 ÷ 11

m. 5022 ÷ 93   n. 1404 ÷ 27   o. 4410 ÷ 98

17c Add the following:

a. 4.87	b. 20.93	c. 5.991	d. 925.7
39.64	0.941	40.06	52.18
1.758	5.612	17.650	461.42
0.4806	13.06	0.0127	1.043

17dx a. 5.82×10 b. 76.6×10^3 c. 0.0621×10^5 d. $36.02 \div 10$

e. $0.2 \div 10$ f. $35.682 \div 10^2$ ·g. $356821 \div 10^6$

17e a. 37.5×47 b. 4.96×36 c. 38.95×76 d. 59.7×45

e. 37.5×74 f. 4.96×83 g. 38.95×67 h. 59.7×97

17fx a. 14.89×23.6 b. 9.81×0.56 c. 7.65×86.4 d. $(46.8)^2$

e. 569×7.82 f. 8.63×53.4 g. 4.93×86.2 h. $(27.6)^2$

i. 38.7×4.61 j. 0.756×806 k. 49.3×6.08 l. $(0.7)^3$

17g   a. 55.2 ÷ 46   b. 295.2 ÷ 24   c. 140.4 ÷ 27   d. 2318.8 ÷ 62
       e. 2.8 ÷ 2.5   f. 17.85 ÷ 85   g. 4.356 ÷ 3.6   h. 20.8 ÷ 6.5
       i. 53.82 ÷ 6.9   j. 73.968 ÷ 0.92   k. 2.8 ÷ 0.025   l. 4.9373 ÷ 0.97

17hx   Express the following in standard form:
       a. 890,000   b. 36210   c. 0.000086   d. 274,000,000
       e. 0.0034   f. 314700   g. 8,000,000,000   h. 0.0000002

17i   a. $\frac{1}{2} + \frac{1}{3} + \frac{1}{5}$ b. $\frac{3}{4} + \frac{2}{3} + \frac{1}{2}$ c. $2\frac{3}{4} + \frac{2}{3} - 1\frac{1}{2}$
       d. $1\frac{3}{4} - 2\frac{1}{3} + 3\frac{1}{4}$ e. $3\frac{3}{4} - 1\frac{2}{3} + 1\frac{1}{2}$ f. $3\frac{3}{4} - (1\frac{2}{3} + 1\frac{1}{2})$
       g. $3\frac{3}{4} + (1\frac{2}{3} - 1\frac{1}{2})$

17jx   a. $\frac{3}{4} \times \frac{1}{2}$ b. $1\frac{3}{4} \times 1\frac{1}{2}$ c. $2\frac{2}{3} \times 1\frac{1}{4} \times 3\frac{1}{2}$
       d. $\frac{3}{4} \div \frac{1}{2}$ e. $\frac{5}{7} \div \frac{3}{5}$ f. $3\frac{1}{2} \div 2\frac{2}{3}$
       g. $4\frac{1}{4} \div 1\frac{1}{2} \times 2\frac{1}{3} \div (1\frac{2}{3} - \frac{3}{4})$

17k   It is 215 kilometres from Calais to Rouen, 271 from Rouen to Tours and 330
       from Tours to Bordeaux. A British driver notices that as he leaves Calais his
       speedometer mileage reads 10658 miles. What will the reading be on arrival in
       Bordeaux if he makes no detours? (Assume that 1 mile = 1.6 kilometres).

       On leaving Calais he also noticed that he had 7¾ gallons of petrol in his tank.
       His car averages 40 miles per gallon and on arrival in Bordeaux he had 4
       gallons in the tank. How many litres did he buy on the way. (Assume that 1
       gallon = 4.5 litres)?

       His average speed for the journey is 34 miles per hour. How long did the
       journey take him?

       His friend drives a French car consuming 8 litres per 100 kilometres. Which car
       has the better performance?

Chapter 18

The Set of Integers

Learning Objectives:

At the end of your study of this chapter you should be able to:

1. appreciate how the number system has developed to meet the changing needs of society,

2. appreciate number systems with bases other than ten,

3. write numbers in the standard form notation,

4. manipulate simple, positive powers of numbers.

The Set of Integers

So far we would have had very little difficulty in explaining the simple arithmetic processes to primitive Utopians, and these processes would be sufficient to enable them to record the trading transactions that took place. In course of time, however, as you can imagine, a problem will emerge. In any trading society there will be gainers and losers; some people will grow richer while others grow poorer. The time will come when it will be necessary to expand the Utopian number system to include numbers greater than nine and less than minus nine. If we still confine the system to whole numbers it is called a set of integers. After all some inhabitants who are good businessmen and careful with their money will end up with many more than nine shells; others who are consistent borrowers will end up owing more than nine. Since Utopians have no ability to imagine a number greater than nine and no name for such a number exists, can you imagine the consternation when, for the first time, someone counted out nine shells and still had some left over? Not only has a new word to be invented for this new (and previously unimaginable) high number, but also a new symbol has to be devised to enable it to be recorded.

Now, you may think that this is an easy step for Utopia to take. After all, there is no great difficulty in producing new sounds to mean new numbers. In Britain we invented ten, eleven, twelve and so on; in France they decided to use dix, onze and douze. You yourself could probably produce many equally likely sounds to represent ten, eleven or twelve. No, the problem lies, not in speech, but in writing — in the development of a mathematically logical symbol. The root of the problem lies in the fact that only a society well advanced in the art of numeracy can develop the concept of a zero. It is, after all, very difficult to see the need for it. If a Utopian owed nothing there was no need to record the fact; if he possessed nothing there is equally nothing to record. Thus, in a very primitive society, the number ten had to be represented by a completely new symbol, unrelated to the previous nine.

Many signs were developed by ancient civilisation, but the only one that has come down to us in anything like general use is the Roman X to represent ten — and in its own way this is the height of logic. The symbol X, always used to represent the unknown factor, is now chosen to represent our previously unknown number.

Once this has been accepted the number system can be extended in a completely logical fashion. Eleven can become XI or ten plus one; twenty becomes XX, or two sets of ten, and so on. Of course, there also developed other symbols such as V for five. But this is not a logical necessity for the number system; it merely saves the bookkeeper the time and effort involved in writing IIII. In the same way changing the order of the symbols such as IX gives us ten *minus* one, or nine, and thus avoids the need to write VIIII. But only the symbol X was absolutely essential.

Having solved this problem, however, the Romans rapidly came up against another. Just as they needed a symbol to represent a set of ten units, so they needed additional symbols to represent ten sets of ten (C = 100), and ten sets of one hundred (M = 1000). But there is no symbol for ten sets of a thousand! Could it be that the Romans had a standard of numeracy only one step above that of the Utopians and could not imagine a number as high as this? There is little doubt, however, that with the three symbols X, C and M, and with three simplifying symbols V (5), L (50) and D (500), the Romans had developed a number system that did all that was asked of it. But what a system!

Think of a student faced with problems such as:

MDCCLIX × CDXXXIII + MCDXLVII!

Is it any wonder that while the Romans produced many famous generals, statesmen and law givers, in the whole history of their Empire they never produced any famous mathematicians? In the history of numeracy such ability is found only among societies which developed a symbol for zero. Such societies built up their number system in a completely different way, based on counting in groups of ten; or, as the mathematician puts it, they developed a number system to base ten. The odd thing is that, given the symbol 0, the number system can be extended indefinitely without the need for any further symbols. Write down any number you wish, no matter how large, and you will find that it contains only the numbers from 0 to 9.

In such a system, counting proceeds as follows:

1 2 3 4 5 6 7 8 9 10 11 12 and so on.

The number 10 can be looked at in two ways. The right hand column as you know represents units, the left hand column groups of ten. Thus 10 means, one set of ten plus no units; 23 means two sets of ten plus three units. This meaning was made clear to us in primary school when, at the head of each simple addition sum we used to put the symbols

t   u

But there is another, and more important, implication. As we move the figure in the units column one place to the left, it takes on a value ten times greater than it had, representing now groups of ten. If we move it a further place to the left it again increases in value by ten times, representing now ten groups of ten or groups of a hundred. Again this is shown clearly if we were to head the columns, indicating what they represent as follows:

	th		h		t	u
which simply means	$10 \times 10 \times 10 \times 1$		$10 \times 10 \times 1$		10×1	1

This becomes even more obvious if we break a number down into its component parts. We know that

$$26247 = 20,000 + 6000 + 200 + 40 + 7$$

but also

$$7 = 7 \times (1)$$
$$40 = 4 \times (10 \times 1)$$
$$200 = 2 \times (10 \times 10 \times 1)$$
$$6000 = 6 \times (10 \times 10 \times 10 \times 1)$$
$$20000 = 2 \times (10 \times 10 \times 10 \times 10 \times 1)$$

Thus, using this number system, we have a means of expressing numbers of any magnitude merely by adopting the convention that each time we move a number one place to the left it increases in value by ten times.

We are so accustomed to using *denary* system that it appears to us to be the simplest of all methods of counting. But there is no obligation to count in tens. We probably in the beginning began to count in fives because we had five fingers on each hand, and transferred to ten when this was insufficient merely because we had ten fingers in all. Some Eastern societies, however, still count in sixes rather than in tens, and we understand that some tribes in Central Africa use what we call the binary system, counting in twos. They are in fact, in some ways, more up to date than most of us. Because a computer can recognise only that a current is flowing or it is not flowing it is forced to use the binary system also, in which there are only two numbers, zero and one. Let us compare the method of counting in each of these three number systems.

Base 10	1	2	3	4	5	6	7	8	9	10	11	12	13	14
Base 6	1	2	3	4	5	10	11	12	13	14	15	20	21	22
Base 2	1	10	11	100	101	110	111	1000	1001	1010	1011	1100	1101	1110

Note that when you are counting in a system other than the denary we do not say ten, eleven, twelve and so on, but one zero, one one, one two and so on.

Whatever base we use, however, the principle of construction of the number system is the same. If we are using base 6, as we move figures to the left their value increases by SIX times (*not* ten times). Thus, if we want to express in our normal denary system

$$1354_6 \qquad \text{(this merely means 1354 using base 6)}$$

we get:

$$1354_6 = 1000_6 + 300_6 + 50_6 + 4_6$$

4_6	$= 4 \times (1)$	$=$	4
50_6	$= 5 \times (6 \times 1)$	$=$	30
300_6	$= 3 \times (6 \times 6 \times 1)$	$=$	108
1000_6	$= 1 \times (6 \times 6 \times 6 \times 1)$	$=$	216
			358

Thus 1354_6 is equal to 358 to base ten.

Powers of Integers

As all Utopia knows, Fred the shoemaker has very little patience and is always thinking of easier and quicker ways of doing things. He understands the number system we have developed and can use it, but each time he has to trade with those who use base six and he has to convert their figures into the denary system used by Utopia he begins to lose patience. When his customer orders 1250_6 pairs of shoes and he begins the conversion $1000_6 = 1 \times 6 \times 6 \times 6 \times 1$, he considers it a waste of time. So he has developed his own shorthand form. Instead of writing $6 \times 6 \times 6$ he writes 6^3, meaning "six multiplied by itself three times". In the same way he would write 4^2 instead of 4×4, or 3^4 instead of $3 \times 3 \times 3 \times 3$. But the first time he tried to write the number 6 in this form he was a little confused, until he realised that in this shorthand form $6 = 6^1$.

What possibly began as a type of convenient mathematical shorthand turned out in the end to be a very important and very powerful mathematical tool. Most important concepts in mathematics are simple when you get down to it. When Fred wrote 7^5, he would say to himself "seven to the power five", or more usually simply "seven to the fifth"; when he wrote 2^3, he would say "two to the power three", or "two cubed." What do you think he would call 5^2? Obviously "five to the power two", or usually "five squared." The smaller number telling us how many times we should multiply a number by itself is known as the power to which the number is raised, or more simply as the index of the number, and what began as merely a convenient expression ends up as the theory of indices, (indices is the plural of index.)

The importance of indices lies not only in the usefulness of the technique of using them but also in the fact that they give us the only way of conveniently expressing very large or very small numbers. In astronomy for example, we make use of the 'light year' as a unit of distance. This is the distance that light travels in a year and is approximately equal to $300000 \times 60 \times 60 \times 24 \times 365$ kilometres, about 9460800000000 kilometres.

Think of the problem of writing this number time after time. Worse still, try to say it. Is it not better to say that in a year light will travel approximately 9.5×10^{12} kilometres. Written in this way a number is said to be in *standard form*. Any number can be expressed in standard form by expressing it as a number between 1 and 10 multiplied by 10 raised to some power. Thus if we wish to express 3654 in standard form we would first write down 3.654. Now as we have divided by 1000 we must multiply by 1000 and $3654 = 3.654 \times 1000 = 3.654 \times 10^3$. We will not, of course, ask you to handle numbers as large as 9.5×10^{12} but you will find the idea of standard form very useful when you are considering logarithms. Let us for the moment, however, return to Utopia where problems are simpler.

Firstly we will try to develop some simple rules about the arithmetic of indices. Suppose we start with the very easy expression $10 \times 10 = 100$. Now, as we have seen this can also be written in index form as $10^1 \times 10^1 = 10^2$. Take also the equally simple $4 \times 2 = 8$. This is the same as $2^2 \times 2^1 =$

2^3. In the same way $9 \times 9 = 81$ is $3^2 \times 3^2 = 3^4$. Can you see a pattern emerging? In each case, if we add the indices of the numbers we are multiplying, we obtain the index of the answer.

Thus $2^2 \times 2^1 = 2^{2+1} = 2^3$
and $3^2 \times 3^2 = 3^{2+2} = 3^4$

We can now state a rule that applies to all indices:

> If we are multiplying a number raised to a given power by the same number raised to a different power, add the indices"

We must be careful, of course, to make sure that the numbers we are multiplying together *are* the same. $3^3 \times 3^4 = 3^7$, but $3^3 \times 2^4$ does *not* equal 6^7.

If we add the indices when we are multiplying you can probably guess what we are doing when we are dividing. Yes, we subtract the indices, but let us prove it by taking a simple division $100 \div 10 = 10$ or
$$10^2 \div 10^1 = 10^1 = 10$$
As you can see the answer 10^1 results from 10^{2-1}, the difference between the two indices. In the same way $81 \div 27 = 3$ is obtained by
$$3^4 \div 3^3 = 3^{4-3} = 3^1 = 3$$
The general rule is that

> If we are dividing a number raised to a given power by the same number raised to a different power subtract the indices.

The mathematicians of Utopia were so impressed by these new techniques that they played around with them endlessly, until one day one of them hit upon a surprising result. He found that $3^2 \div 3^2 = 3^0$ and for the first time they had to consider the possibility of a zero as an index as well as a number. Fortunately its meaning is not difficult to find. $3^2 \div 3^2$ is the same as $9 \div 9 = 1$. Once you see the point it is obvious that the power zero can occur only when the power of the number being divided is the same as the power of the divisor, that is, the numbers are the same. As you know, any number divided by itself gives the answer one. So

> Any number raised to the power zero is equal to one.

Thus, $3^0 = 1$; $27^0 = 1$; $2456^0 = 1$ and so on.

Once mathematicians have got as far as this in the development of indices, it is highly likely that they will search for the next step. In developing the number system they moved from positive numbers, 3, 2, 1 through zero to negative integers -1, -2, -3. In the same way, having discovered a meaning for positive indices (10^2, 5^3) and for a zero index (10^0), it is only natural that they should ask if a negative index can exist, and if it does exist, what can it mean?

A moment's thought will convince you that we can easily obtain a negative index. If the index of the divisor (the number we are dividing by) is greater than the index of the quotient (the number we are dividing into), the index of the answer must be negative. For example
$$10^0 \div 10^1 = 10^{0-1} = 10^{-1}$$

and using this example it is easy to see exactly what 10^{-1} means. 10^0 is, as we know equal to 1, and 10^1 is equal to 10, so $10^0 \div 10^1$ is the same thing as $1 \div 10$, or, as it is more usually put $\frac{1}{10}$. The negative sign in the index merely means "one divided by" and we divide by what is left when we take away the minus sign. 10^{-1} means then $\frac{1}{10}$ and we have discovered what mathematicians call the *inverse* of a number, that is, one divided by that number.

While we can see the meaning of 10^{-1} easily enough, does the same argument apply to 10^{-2}, 10^{-3} and so on.

Suppose we take

$$10^0 \div 10^2 \text{ we get an answer } 10^{0-2} = 10^{-2}$$

Now $10^0 \div 10^2 = 1 \div 100$ so $10^{-2} = 1 \div 100 = \frac{1}{100} = \frac{1}{10^2}$ and exactly the same rule applies. The minus sign means "one divided by" and we divide by what is left after eliminating the minus sign, i.e. 10^2. It makes no difference how we arrive at 10^{-2}. We know that $10^2 \div 10^4$ is equal to 10^{-2}, so $100 \div 10,000 = 10^{-2} = \frac{1}{10^2} = \frac{1}{100}$.

Those of you who have used logarithms to aid your calculations may have noticed a remarkable similarity between indices and logarithms. The usual logarithms you use at school are only one form of logarithms — they are in fact logarithms to base 10. The way in which they are obtained is easy to understand even if their calculation is not all that easy. The logarithm of a number may be defined as

The power to which ten must be raised to equal the number.

So if we want the logarithm of 100 we ask to what power we must raise 10 to make it equal to 100. We know that 10^2 is equal to 100, and so the logarithm of 100 is exactly 2. In the same way the logarithm of 1000 is 3 ($10^3 = 1000$) and the logarithm of 1 is 0 ($10^0 = 1$).

Can you see why, when we wish to multiply two numbers together we add the logarithms? If the logarithm of a number is merely the power to which we raise 10, we have already seen that to multiply we must add the indices.

Suppose we wish to multiply 100 by 1000 using logarithms.

$100 = 10^2$ so the logarithm of 100 is   2
$1000 = 10^3$ so the logarithm of 1000 is   3
$100 \times 1000 = 10^2 \times 10^3 = 10^5$ —
so log (100×1000) is equal to   5

Now, if the logarithm of (100×1000) is equal to 5,
100×1000 is equal to $10^5 =$ 100,000

We have gone a long way towards the understanding of indices, and in so doing have paved the way for a great leap forward, the development of logarithms. This however was only to come many centuries later with the work of Napier. Our mythical Utopian society has raised far more immediate problems for itself. For centuries they have dealt only in integers, and now they have come up against the expression 10^{-1}. While they can express this in terms of integers such as $1 \div 10$, how does this fit into their number system? What does it mean? To discover this Fred the shoemaker and his friends must go right back to the number system and rethink its implications.

Assignment Exercises

18.1x The following table gives the mean distance of planets from the sun (in miles). Express the numbers in standard form.

Mercury	36,000,000	Jupiter	483,300,000
Venus	67,200,000	Saturn	886,200,000
Earth	92,820,000	Uranus	1,783,000,000
Mars	141,600,000	Neptune	2,793,500,000

18.2 Convert the following numbers into denary numbers.

a. 12_3 bx. 12_8 c. 21_3

dx. 121_8 e. 27_8 fx. 132_4

g. 112_3 hx. 111_2 i. 413_5

18.3 Find the exact value of each of the following and, where possible express the answer in index form.

a. $2^3 \times 2^4$ bx. $3^2 \times 3^5$ c. $2^4 + 2^5$

dx. $3^2 + 2^2$ e. $4^2 \div 4^2$ fx. $3^6 \div 3^4$

gx. $2^5 - 2^3$ hx. 9×3^2 ix. $\dfrac{2^3 \times 2^4 \times 2^5}{2^2 \times 2^6}$

18.4x Assuming that numbers like 2^{-3} have a meaning and that the laws of indices hold for such numbers, simplify the following.

a. $2^4 \times 2^0$ b. $3^0 \times 3^5$ c. $3^{-1} \times 3^4$

d. $2^5 \times 2^{-3}$ e. $4^6 \div 4^{-1}$ f. $5^{-2} \div 5^{-4}$

18.5 Use your knowledge of indices to find the logarithm of the following expressions.

a. 1000   bx. 10,000   c. $10,000 \div 100$

dx. $10 \times 100 \times 1$ e. $1000 \div 100 \times 10$

Do not attempt these revisionary assignments until you have reached Chapter 21.

Revisionary Assignments

18a Convert the following fractions to decimals.

a. $^{12}/_{25}$ b. $^9/_{32}$ c. $^{55}/_{64}$ d. $^4/_{25} + ^5/_8$

e. $^{189}/_{288}$

18bx Evaluate the following correct to three decimal places.

a. $37 \div 45$ b. $263 \div 9$ c. $32 \div 114$

d. $56 \div 47$ e. $21.3 \div 4,185$.

18c Convert the following decimals to fractions.

a. 0.012   b. 26.375   c. 0.00366

d. 0.65625   e. 0.5515   f. 0.25

18dx Certain fractions were taken and converted into decimals. Each fraction had a numerator equal to one, and a denominator less than twenty. Decide which fraction each of the following decimals represents.

a. $0.11\dot{1}$ b. $0.09090\dot{9}$ c. $0.\dot{1}4285\dot{7}$

d. $0.07692\dot{3}$ e. 0.052631579 (correct to 9 decimal places)

18e Evaluate the following, expressing your answer as i) a fraction, and ii) a decimal.

a. $0.375 \times \frac{1}{4}$ b. $0.55 \div ^1/_{11}$ c. $0.36 + ^5/_8$

d. $^9/_{13} - 0.142857$

18fx   Tom, Dick and Harry each own shares in Jumbo Enterprises. Tom owns $\frac{2}{35}$ of the equity, Dick owns 0.0572, and Harry owns 57.1%. Who owns the largest share and who owns the smallest?

18g   Ruritania has five daily newspapers, and the average circulation is as follows.

The Gazette	537,000
The News	895,000
The Journal	986,000
Ruritanian Times	2,327,000
Ruritanian Express	3,423,000

Express the readership of each newspaper a) as a fraction of total readership b) as a decimal (correct to three decimal places).

18hx   The issued capital of Jumbo Enterprises is:

	£
Preference Shares	575,000
Cumulative Preference Shares	386, 000
Ordinary Shares	4,272,000

Fred owns $\frac{2}{5}$ of the preference shares, $\frac{1}{4}$ of the cumulative preference shares, and $\frac{1}{3}$ of the ordinary shares. Find the fraction of issued capital owned by Fred. Express this as a decimal.

18i   A shareholder is entitled to one vote for each cumulative preference share, two votes for each preference share and five votes for each ordinary share. If individual shares are valued at £1 each, express the votes controlled by Fred as a decimal of all votes.

18jx   Cost of North Sea Oil (per barrel)

	$
Operating Costs	1.54
Capital Cost	1.18
Interest	0.34
Profit	2.64
Tax	6.80

Source: Kitcat and Aitkin
Report on North Sea Oil.

Express the individual costs as a) a fraction and b) a decimal of the total cost per barrel.

Chapter 19

Decimals

Learning Objectives:

At the end of your study of this chapter you should be able to:

1. understand the extension of the number system into decimal fractions,
2. perform arithmetic operations with decimal fractions.

Decimals

When they first considered the extension of their number system, the Utopians had discovered the key that gave unity to the whole system — at least so far as integers were concerned. They knew that as a number was moved row by row to the left it increased in value by ten times on each occasion it was moved. Once the theory of indices was understood they would be quick to realise two things: every digit in a number obtains its value by being multiplied by 10 raised to some power. And secondly, the power to which ten is raised depends on the column in which the digit is placed. Thus a 5, placed in the fourth column from the right would take on a value of 5×10^3 or 5000. It would be noticed too that as we moved to the left the power to which ten is raised is increased by one as we move from one column to the next.

Now, none of this directly helps us to move to non integers, until someone looks at the number system and realises that it can be looked at in a different way. Suppose an integer is moved to the *right* rather than to the left. Now as it enters each successive column the power to which ten is raised is *decreased* by one, that is, the value of the number is *divided* by ten. If we move far enough to the right, we will eventually reach the units column, that headed 10^0. But what lies beyond this? If we maintain the logical pattern of our number system, any further columns we reach must surely be headed 10^{-1}, 10^{-2}, 10^{-3} and so on. Any figure in the column headed 10^{-1} will be multiplied by 10^{-1}, that is by $1/10$. Thus in the number below, in the column headed 10^{-1}, we have the integer 5, and this will take the value 5×10^{-1}, that is, $5 \times 1/10 = 5/10$. In the same way the final integer, 2, has a value of 2×10^{-2} which is equal to $2 \times 1/100 = 2/100$. Utopians can not yet fully understand these numbers less than one, but they can fit them quite comfortably into the existing number system.

Value	10^5	10^4	10^3	10^2	10^1	10^0		10^{-1}	10^{-2}
Number	1	1	2	4	6	3		5	2

There is still a minor problem of how to distinguish figures in these new columns from the original ones, but this is easy to solve. If we put a dot (or a decimal point as we call it) after the figure in the units column, we can work outward from this. Moving to the left we have increasing powers of ten, to the right we have decreasing powers of ten. To distinguish it from all others, the integer which is in the first column after the decimal point we describe as being in the first decimal place; the integer in the second column after the decimal point is said to be in the second decimal place and so on.

Thus a number such as 62.43 would mean

$$(6 \times 10^1) + (2 \times 10^0) + (4 \times 10^{-1}) + (3 \times 10^{-2})$$
$$= 60 + 2 + {}^4\!/_{10} + {}^3\!/_{100} \text{ and since } {}^4\!/_{10} = {}^{40}\!/_{100}$$
$$62.43 = 60 + 2 + {}^{43}\!/_{100}$$

It must have seemed to the Utopians that they now had a number system that would enable them to express any number, however large or however small. Actually they were wrong. There are many numbers which we cannot express exactly even in the twentieth century. With hindsight, however we can see that Utopia was well on the way to developing fractions, but at this point in time, it was more important for them to master the art of using decimals. For centuries man had lived using only integers. Fred could buy 8 pieces of leather at 10 shells a piece for a total of eighty shells. If he wanted less than eight pieces but more than seven he could not buy this amount, nor could he calculate its cost. Let us look first at the difference this new concept in decimals made to the ordinary processes of arithmetic. So far as addition and subtraction is concerned it makes very little difference. Provided we put the decimal points directly under each other in every number, including the answer, we add and subtract in tens just as we have always done. Thus:

$$
\begin{array}{rcr}
63.84 & \text{or} & 56.84 \\
+\ \ 28.25 & & -\ \ 27.95 \\
\hline
92.09 & & 28.89 \\
\end{array}
$$

What about multiplication? Again there will be no change in the integers in our answer merely because we are working in decimals. The problem is where to place the decimal point. Suppose we are faced by the problem of calculating 8.25×6.5. The trick is to forget the decimal points and multiply 825 by 65, giving us the answer 53625.

$$
\begin{array}{r}
8.25 \\
\times\ \ 6.5 \\
\hline
49500 \text{multiply by 60} \\
4125 \text{multiply by 5} \\
\hline
53625 \quad \text{add} \\
\end{array}
$$

We can now position the decimal point in this way. Count up how many figures occur *after* the decimal point in the question. In 8.25 there are two, and in 6.5 there is one, a total of three. There will be the same number of figures after the decimal point in the answer, giving us 53.625. There are no real problems in handling the multiplication of decimals. The rule given is valid no matter how large or how small the numbers we are multiplying, no matter how many places of decimals we are handling.

Division of decimals does, however, seem to cause some problems, especially in the placing of the decimal point. It is always as well whenever you can, to try to get some idea of the answer before you start. Let us look first at a relatively simple problem, $54.72 \div 8$. Here it is apparent that any answer we get must be greater than six. Can you see why? 8×6 equals 48 and since we are dividing eight into 54.72 this result is too low. Equally however our answer will be less than 7, since 8×7 is equal to 56, which is too high. The answer, then, is going to be six point something, and we cannot mislay the decimal point.

Initially we will lay out the problem as you would normally expect to see it, and then we will look at the reasoning behind it.

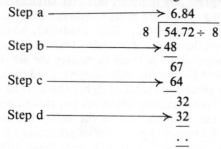

Step a. Firstly we consider dividing 8 into the first figure, 5, but quickly realise that it is not possible. Actually eight into five is equal to 0 remainder 5. Remembering our number system, you will realise that what we have said is a shorthand way of saying, "five groups of ten divided by eight makes no groups of ten, remainder 5 groups of ten."

Step b. Since we have got nowhere dividing into groups of ten we will now see if we can divide eight into the units, i.e. we will look at the first two figures. You know that these figures mean $5 \times 10^1 + 4 \times 10^0$, which is 54 units. Now 54 (units) $\div 8 = 6$ units remainder 6. The first figure of our answer is 6 units or 6×10^0.

Step c. Our answer is not yet exact so we will consider now the remainder. 6 units is equal to 60 tenths. But we also have in the question the integer 7 which has a value of 7×10^{-1} or seven tenths. So the total number of tenths we have to look at is $60 + 7$ or 67. Now 67 (tenths) divided by $8 = 8$ (tenths) remainder 3. The second figure of our answer is 8 tenths or 8×10^{-1}.

Step d. Again considering the remainder, 3 tenths = 30 hundredths plus 2 hundredths from the quotient = 32 hundredths. $32 \div 8 = 4$ hundredths, and this is the third figure of our answer, 4×10^{-2}.

There is no remainder, and we have exhausted all the digits in the quotient (54.72) so the problem is complete.

$$54.72 \div 8 = 6 \times 10^0 + 8 \times 10^{-1} + 4 \times 10^{-2} = 6.84$$

Let us now examine a problem which may look fearsome at first sight but which, as you will see, is done in exactly the same way.

$$164.8125 \div 11.25$$

Firstly, we know the answer is greater than 10 (since $10 \times 11.25 = 112.5$ which is less than 164.8125). Equally, the answer is less than 100 (since $100 \times 11.25 = 1125$ which is greater than 164.8125). So the answer lies somewhere between 10 and 99 i.e. there are two figures in front of the decimal point. It will help too if we can get rid of the decimal point in the divisor (11.25). We can do this quite easily if we multiply 11.25 by 100 to give us 1125. If we do this, however, we must also multiply the quotient by $100 - 164.8125 \times 100 = 16481.25$. Our problem becomes, then,

$$16481.25 \div 1125$$

```
                14.65
      1125 ⎡16481.25 ÷ 1125
           1125
           ‾‾‾‾
           5231
           4500
           ‾‾‾‾
            7312
            6750
            ‾‾‾‾
             5625
             5625
             ‾‾‾‾
             ....
```

Answer: $164.81 \div 11.25 = 1 \times 10^1 + 4 \times 10^0$
$$+ 6 \times 10^{-1} + 5 \times 10^{-2}$$
$$= 14.65$$

Make sure you can understand every step in the above, and if you are at all doubtful of it write down the analysis, e.g.

Step 1 1648 (tens) ÷ 1125 = 1 (ten) remainder 523 (tens)
Step 2 523 tens equal 5230 units, plus 1 unit from quotient equals 5231 units
        5231 (units) ÷ 1125 = 4 (units) remainder 731 (units)

Do this and go over it until you have completely mastered the process, and you will soon find that division of decimals creates few problems.

Both the examples we have looked at so far have exact answers. We have used every figure in the quotient and there is no remainder. But there are examples you will come across quite often in which you can carry on the process of division almost, it seems, indefinitely. We could get an answer such as, for example, 7.6418372 and still not have reached the exact result. How far do we have to go? In most questions you will be told that the result is required "correct to two (or three) places of decimals." If you are not told, you may assume that three places of decimals will be ample. Now, the expression "places of decimals" implies the number of figures after the decimal point. This is quite straightforward. It is the expression "correct to" that causes the trouble. It implies that your answer is going to be approximated, and in order to approximate accurately you will have to calculate one decimal place more than you are asked for. Suppose we obtain an answer 3.6283. Here we can approximate to one or two, or three places of decimals, but not to four places, simply because we have no means of knowing whether the final figure is in fact closer to 3 than it is to 4. So let us give the answer correct to three places of decimals. It is obvious that 3.6283 is closer to 3.628 than it is to 3.629 and we would give the answer as 3.628. If, however, we were giving the answer correct to two places of decimals, this is nearer to 3.63 than it is to 3.62 and we would give the answer as 3.63.

The general rule is:

"If the last figure calculated is less than 5 we will ignore it, but if the last figure is greater than 5, eliminate the last figure and raise the preceding figure by 1."

This rule will apply to almost all the problems you will meet, but it can leave a problem — what to do if the last figure is exactly 5? Suppose we had to give 3.6285 correct to 3 decimal places. Here we must, if we can, look at the question and our answer. If after reaching this point there is still a remainder, the correct answer will be slightly higher than 3.6285, say 3.62851. There is no doubt that this is nearer to 3.629 than it is to 3.628 and we would give 3.629 as our answer. But suppose that 3.6285 is an exact answer, or, worse still, it is given to you by an examiner. Here, our advice would be to raise the penultimate figure the first time you meet such an expression in a problem, leave it alone the next time and so on alternately. We must admit, however, that you are unlikely to meet this situation more than once in any problem. and it is, we think, better to raise the penultimate figure, to indicate to the examiner that you understand what you are doing if this is the situation you are in.

Assignment Exercises

19.1 Express the following numbers in Standard Form.
  a. 0.000123 bx. 0.456 c. 0.001
  dx. 0.00000136 e. 0.00597

19.2x a. The diameter of a molecule of water is 3.39×10^{-8}mm. Express this as a decimal.

  b. Express in decimal form,
    i. 10^{-4} ii. 10^{-6} iii. 10^{-2} iv. 10^{-1}

  c. Evaluate:
    i. $10^2 \times 10^{-4}$ ii. $10^{-3} \div 10^2$ iii. $2^3 \times 2^{-4}$

19.3 a. The profit earned by a firm last year was £10,276.96. If this profit was to be shared equally between three partners, what did each receive?

  bx. Fred the shoemaker has bought 2150 square centimetres of leather. Each pair of shoes he makes consumes 125.6 square centimetres. How many pairs of shoes can he make, and how much leather has he left over?

19.4x Find each sum.
  a. 36.49 + 18.72   b. 3.595 + 0.608 + 7.172
  c. 248.6 + 35.7   d. 7.26105 + 5.72964
  e. 0.501247 + 0.000986 + 0.720058
  Find each difference.
  f. 63.35 — 19.75   g. 926.3 — 756.4
  h. 80.05 — 26.16   i. 0.308 — 0.269
  j. 4.7902 — 0.8315

19.5 a. 0.23×0.3 bx. 3.201×0.7 c. 83.4×4.2
   dx. 5.21×0.73 e. 72.96×0.215 fx. 361.5×0.43
   g. $89.56 \div 4.6$ hx. $1.008 \div 6.3$ i. $3.708 \div 0.12$

19.6x Find each quotient
  a. $17 \div 20$ b. $4 \div 25$ c. $7 \div 8$ d. $11 \div 40$
  e. $4 \div 11$ f. $7 \div 3$ g. $5 \div 7$ h. $5 \div 6$

Do not attempt these revisionary assignments until you have reached Chapter 23.

Revisionary Assignments

19a Smith has a choice of dividing the profits of his firm with his junior partner in the ratio: 9:5, 7:4, or 16:7. State, in each case, what percentage of the profits the junior partner would receive.

  If Smith promised to give his junior partner 20% of the profits, in what ratio would the profits be divided?

19bx Eycke and Payne are in partnership, sharing profits in the ratio 5:3. Net profit last year was £24,480. Eycke has already drawn £7,500 of his share in advance and Payne has drawn £5,250.
  a. How much is each entitled to receive?
  b. By how much would Payne's income increase if he were given   45% of the profits?

19c The turnover and debtors at 31st March last for each of three departmental stores in Melchester were as follows:

	Smith Ltd.	Jones Ltd.	Brown Ltd.
	£	£	£
Turnover	12,248,300	2,461,700	7,416,200
Debtors	1,837,245	196,936	185,405

  In each case express debtors as a percentage of turnover, and comment on your figures.

19dx   Here is an extract from the profit and loss accounts and the Balance Sheets of XYZ Ltd for the last two years

Profit and Loss Accounts

	Year a (£)	Year b (£)
Sales	10200	11400
less Cost of Sales	8200	9200
	2000	2200
less Administration	730	790
Selling Expenses	510	540
Finance	310	400
	1550	1730
Net Profit	450	470
Add Undistributed Profit	900	1155
	1350	1625
less Dividend for year	195	165
Undistributed Profit	1155	1460

Balance Sheets

	Year a £		Year b £	
Fixed Assets				
Premises at cost		2380		2510
Fittings and Fixtures				
at cost	1780		1830	
less Depreciation	310	1470	400	1430
		3850		3940
Current Assets				
Stock in Trade	1001		1580	
Trade Debtors	1460		1513	
Cash	78	2539	67	3160
		6389		7100
less Current Liabilities				
Trade Creditors		2234		2640
		4155		4460
Ownership Interest				
Share Capital		3000		3000
Profit		1155		1460
		4155		4460

Below are given a number of common ratios in which the accountant is interested. Thoroughly learn the meaning of each ratio and consider for what purposes it might be useful. Calculate each ratio for the years a and b from the data above, and make comments where you feel them to be necessary.

a.   Stock Turnover ratio — cost of sales : stock in trade
       (You may use the stock in trade figure shown in the Balance Sheet for years a and b)

b.   Debtor Turnover ratio — sales : debtors

c. Creditor Turnover ratio — purchases : creditors
(You may assume that purchases in year a were £8350. You should be able to calculate year b for yourself).
d. Current ratio — current assets : current liabilities
Comment on the situation where this ratio is less than 1.
e. Liquidity ratio — debtors + cash : current liabilities

19e A man holds £16000 of British Government Stock and each quarter receives a cheque for £360 interest. What annual rate of interest is he receiving? If he had paid only £12000 for the stock what rate of return is he receiving on his investment?

19fx The figures below show the gross profit of a company and the ordinary dividend it has paid over the last 10 years. By calculating the percentage increase in profit and in dividend for each year, determine whether the dividends have been increased in line with the increase in profits.

Year	Gross Profit £000	Dividend £000
1	576	220
2	719	228
3	757	238
4	810	248
5	939	287
6	1087	382
7	1386	420
8	1501	474
9	1470	512
10	1612	552

Chapter 20

The Use of Logarithms

Learning Objectives:

At the end of your study of this chapter you should be able to:

1. appreciate the meaning of a logarithm,

2. utilise standard form notation to be able to obtain the mantissa of a logarithm,

3. manipulate logarithms to facilitate calculations throughout the course.

The Use of Logarithms

We have already mentioned, in an earlier section, the relationship between powers of ten and logarithms. In this section we will not concern ourselves with the theory of logarithms, but will concentrate on showing you how to use them. The logarithms you will be using are called common logarithms or logarithms to base 10. They are not the only logarithms, but at this stage they are all you need bother with.

Let us begin by looking at the logarithm of a number, say 124.6.

$$\text{Log } 124.6 = 2.0955$$

You can see that the logarithm consists of two parts — the integer 2, and the decimal .0955. Often it will help to think of a logarithm as consisting of these two parts rather than being a single number. Think first of the figure in front of the decimal point. What does the 2 mean? Well, as we have already seen, it is the power to which 10 must be raised to equal the number we are considering, e.g. $10 = 10^1$, so the logarithm of 10 is 1.0. Now, in the case we are looking at $10^2 = 100$. But we are looking for the logarithm of 124.6 and to obtain it we must raise 10 to a power greater than 2, yet $10^3 = 1000$ so the power we are looking for is less than 3. So, to obtain 124.6 we must raise 10 to a power greater than 2 but less than 3. It is in fact 2.0955.

$$\text{i.e. } 124.6 = 10^{2.0955} \text{ so log } 124.6 = 2.0955$$

Fortunately you do not have to bother about the precise meaning of a number raised to this peculiar power nor do you have to calculate it — our tables of common logarithms will give us all the information we need. Look now at the tables. The first column consists of two numbers ranging from 10 to 99. Then follow a number of columns headed from 0 to 9 and finally a group of columns headed 'Mean differences' again headed from 1 to 9. This enables us to find the logarithm of any four figure number. The numbers in the first column are in fact 1.0 to 9.9. Many modern books of tables do write the column in this form, but the older books range the numbers from

10 to 99 omitting the decimal point. The columns along the table headed 0 to 9 give us the second place of decimals and the Mean differences columns give us the third place of decimals. Suppose we are looking for the logarithm of 6.154. We first move down the left hand column until we reach the first two figures 6.1 (remember, 61 in the older books). Now we move

0	1	2	3	4	5	6	7	8	9

6.1   7889

along that row until we reach the column headed by the figure in the second decimal place, 5. Here we will find the number 7889. For the third decimal place we now move to the right to the mean difference columns and in the column headed 4 we find the number 3. This we ADD to 7889 to give us 7892. This figure is the decimal part of the logarithm we are seeking, but you will not find the decimal point printed in the table. This you have to insert for yourself. Nor will the table give you the integer preceding the decimal point. To obtain this we think back to the idea of Standard Form which we mentioned earlier. We know that 6.154 in Standard Form is equal to 6.154×10^0. The power to which 10 is raised is the integer preceding the decimal point in the logarithm. So Log 6.154 = 0.7892.

Suppose however that you have to find the logarithm of 61.54. The numbers in our left hand column go only to 9.9, so what do we do. The trick is to put 61.54 in standard form before we look up the logarithm tables. $61.54 = 6.154 \times 10^1$. Once again we look up the logarithm of 6.154 and find it to be .7892. This time, however the power to which 10 is raised is 1, so

Log 61.54 = 1.7892

In the same way $615.4 = 6.154 \times 10^2$ and Log 615.4 = 2.7892.

Suppose, however that the number we are considering is less than 1, possibly 0.006154. To convert this to standard form we have to multiply by 1000 or 10^3. Thus $6.154 = 0.006154 \times 10^3$
and, more important, $0.006154 = 6.154 \div 10^3$
Thus in standard form $0.006154 = 6.154 \times 10^{-3}$
and Log $0.006154 = \bar{3}.7892$

Note that we use bar three ($\bar{3}$) and not minus three (-3). The reason for this is that the decimal part of a logarithm can never be negative. When we say $\bar{3}.7892$ we mean -3 + .7892 whereas if we said the logarithm was -3.7892 we would mean -3 - .7892 which is wrong. Remember that 0.006154 is greater than $\frac{1}{1000}$ so it is greater than 10^{-3}; but it is less than $\frac{1}{100}$ so it is less than 10^{-2}. The logarithm then, lies somewhere between -3.0 and -2.0, and this is precisely what we mean by $\bar{3}.7892$. It is equal to -3 + .7892 or -2.2108. Thus we are in fact saying that $0.006154 = 10^{-2.2108}$, but for ease we say that Log $0.006154 = \bar{3}.7892$.

You should now be able to look up the logarithm of any number so try the following before you go any further:

Find the Logarithm of a) 72.61 b) 0.0154 c) 32590 d) 4.613 e) 0.5361*

It is, of course, no use learning how to look up the value of a logarithm unless we can use our results to help us in our calculations. Since we know that logarithms are based on powers of ten it will be no surprise to you to know that:

a.   To multiply two numbers together we *add* the logarithms and obtain the logarithm of the answer.

b.   To divide two numbers we subtract the logarithm of the divisor from the logarithm of the quotient and obtain the logarithm of the answer.

*Answers a) 1.8610 b) $\bar{2}$.1875 c) 4.5131 d) 0.6640 e) $\bar{1}$.7293

Exhibit 1

Suppose we wish to multiply 72.16 by 1.264 we proceed as follows:

72.16 × 1.264		Number	Log
= 91.22		72.16	1.8583
	×	1.264 +	0.1018
			1.9601

We have obtained the logarithm of the answer as 1.9601. Now we know that the integer 1 before the decimal point merely means that in its standard form the number comprising the answer is multiplied by 10^1, so we need concern ourselves only with the decimal .9601. Turn now to your antilogarithm tables. You will see they are constructed in exactly the same way as the logarithm tables and they are designed to interpret the decimal part of the logarithm. Move down the left hand column until you reach .96; now move across to the column headed 0 and we find the figure 9120. Finally move to the Mean Differences column headed 1 and we find the figure 2. This we add to 9120 to give 9122 and these are the figures we are concerned with in our answer. *Always* write these figures down in standard form i.e. as 9.122. We have already said that in the standard form we will multiply by 10^1 because the integer in the logarithm of the answer was 1. So our full answer becomes $9.122 \times 10^1 = 91.22$.

Exhibit 2

Let us look at another example. With this one work the answer out for yourself first and then check with our working.

		Number	Logarithm
		2.16	0.3345
2.16 × 4.821 × 16.45 × 0.6123	×	4.821 +	0.6831
	×	16.45 +	1.2161
	×	0.6123 +	$\bar{1}$.7870
			2.0207

Notice that when we are adding the logarithms we treat $\bar{1}$ exactly as if it were minus 1. From the antilogarithm tables 0.0207 = 1.049. The integer 2 means that we multiply by 10^2 so our answer is

$$1.049 \times 10^2 = 104.9$$

Exhibit 3

Let us now look at an example of division using logarithms.

	Number	Logarithm
$196.4 \div 38.27$		
$= 5.133$	196.4	2.2932
$\div$	38.27 —	1.5829
		0.7103

Using antilogarithm tables 0.7103 is the logarithm of
$$5.133 \times 10^0 = 5.133 \; Ans.$$

Exhibit 4

Now, consider the following example of division:

	Number	Logarithm
$6.278 \div 0.14$		
$= 44.85$	6.278	0.7979
$\div$	0.14 —	$\overline{1}$. 1461
		1. 6518

1.6518 is the logarithm of $4.485 \times 10^1 = 44.85 \; Ans.$

Note especially the way in which we handle the $\overline{1}$ in this example. We can take $\overline{1}$ as being the same as -1 for arithmetic purposes, so our calculation is 0 - (-1), and as we already know - (-1) is equal to + 1.

Exhibit 5

Occasionally you will be asked to calculate such things as $(2.86)^2$ or 2.86^5. As you know, $2.86^2 = 2.86 \times 2.86$ so

the logarithm of $2.86^2 = \log 2.86 + \log 2.86$
or more simply $2 \times \log 2.86$.

In the same way $\log 2.86^5 = 5 \times \log 2.86$

$\text{Log } 2.86 = \qquad 0.4564$ so $\log (2.86)^2 = 0.9128$ and $(2.86)^2 = 8.181$
and $\log (2.86)^5 = 2.2820$ and $(2.86)^5 = 191.4$

Exhibit 6

As a final example we will look at a problem of the type you may well have to face.

Evaluate
$$\frac{16.17 \times 8.194 \div 12.29}{(5.91)^2 \div (2.46)^3}$$

In problems such as this it is usually better to deal with the numerator and the denominator separately.

Numerator $= 16.17 \times 8.194 \div 12.29$

	Number	Logarithm	
	16.17	1.2086	
	8.194	0.9135	ADD
		2.1221	
16.17×8.194	12.29	1.0895	SUBTRACT
		1.0326	
Logarithm of the Numerator is		1.0326	

Denominator = $(5.91)^2 \div (2.46)^3$

Number	Log	Number	Log	
5.91	0.7716	$(5.91)^2$	1.5432	
2.46	0.3909	$(2.46)^2$	1.1727	SUBTRACT

Log of the denominator is   0.3705

The logarithm of the answer is

$$1.0326 - 0.3705 = 0.6621$$
$$0.6621 \text{ is the logarithm of } 4.593 \times 10^0 = 4.593 \text{ Ans.}$$

The accuracy of Logarithms

If we took the trouble to calculate it by multiplication, we would find that 5.91^2 is equal to 34.9281. Yet if we calculate it by logarithms we get 34.93. Because the tables we use have only four figures we often find that the answer we get is in an approximation, — a close one, but still an approximation. We say that the tables we have (four figure tables) are correct only to THREE significant figures. That is, in the answer 34.93 we know that the 34.9 is accurate, but the .03 is an approximation. The accurate answer could lie anywhere between 34.925 and 34.935. As we know it is 34.9281.

Normally, we will agree, the difference it makes does not matter, but just occasionally you might meet something like $5.91^4 \times 10,000$ and it is as well to be aware of the problem. By logarithms the answer is 12,200,000 but more accurately the answer is 12,199,722 a difference of 278. If this sort of difference matters it is always possible to use more accurate seven figure tables, but this need not concern you at this stage, and from hereon you can use logarithm tables with absolute confidence, giving your answer always to three significant figures.

Assignment Exercises

20.1 Assuming that log 3.142 = 0.4972 write down the logarithms of
  a. 31.42   bx.31420.   c. 0.03142   dx. 0.0003142

20.2x Given that log 2.718 = 0.4343 write down the numbers with the following logarithms.
  a. 1.4343   b. $\bar{3}$.4343   c. 4.4343   d. $\bar{1}$.4343

20.3 Find from four figure logarithm tables the logarithms of
  a. 3.875   bx. 465.9   c. 65.83   dx. 0.0763
  e. 0.8833

20.4x Given that log 2.2 = 0.3424 and log 5.5 = 0.7404 find the values of the following.
  a. Log (2.2×5.5) b. Log (22×0.55) c. Log $(2.2 \div 5.5)$
  d. Log $(0.22 \div 55)$ e. Log (2.2^2) f. Log 0.055^2

20.5 Calculate
  a. $\dfrac{14.67 \times 0.112}{883.6}$ bx. $77^3 \div 8.09^2$ c. $645 \div 163$

  dx. $496 \times 0.0367 \times 5.12$ e. $4.096 \times 10^{-7} \times 6.88 \times 10^5$

20.6x A light year is the distance travelled by light in one year. How far is this if light travels at 299800 kilometres per second and a year is taken as 365.25 days?

20.7 The mean radius of the earth is 6400 kilometers. What is its volume in cubic kilometres and its area in square kilometres? Volume = $\frac{4}{3} \times \frac{22}{7} \times$ (radius)^3
  Area = $4 \times \frac{22}{7} \times$ (radius)^2

Do not attempt these revisionary assignments until you have reached Chapter 23.

Revisionary Assignments

20a Express the following numbers in standard form
    a. 326,000   b. 4,271,326   c. 0.0367
    d. 1.372   e. 0.000278

20bx Express the following standard form numbers in the decimal system.
    a. 1.37×10^3 b. 2.786×10^4 c. 3.26×10^{-1}
    d. 4.87×10^0 e. 5.89×10^{-5}

20c Evaluate the following (answers in standard form)
    a. $(1.37 \times 10^2) + (4.36 \times 10^2)$ b. $(2.36 \times 10^3) + (4.87 \times 10^4)$
    c. $(3.24 \times 10^3) - (1.87 \times 10^3)$ d. $(4.87 \times 10^4) - (3.63 \times 10^3)$
    e. $(2.57 \times 10^2) \times (4.85 \times 10^3)$ f. $(1.44 \times 10^3) \div (1.2 \times 10^3)$
    g. $(1.44 \times 10^2) \div (1.2 \times 10^3)$

20dx Evaluate the following (answers in standard form)
    a. $(2.52 \times 10^{-2}) + (3.27 \times 10^{-3})$ b. $(2.52 \times 10^{-2}) - (3.27 \times 10^{-3})$
    c. $(2.52 \times 10^{-2}) \times (3.27 \times 10^{-3})$ d. $(1.44 \times 10^{-4}) \div (1.22 \times 10^{-5})$

20e Use logarithms to evaluate the following
    a. 3.256×357.2 b. 25.56×4892
    c. $359.6 \div 97.34$ d. $254700 \div 386.2$

20fx Use logarithms to evaluate the following
    a. $0.0375 \times 0.00576 \times 281,000$ b. $0.526 \times 0.00152 \times 37.76$
    c. $0.352 \div 0.00761$ d. $0.00386 \div 0.262$

20g Use square root tables or logarithms to find the square roots of the following numbers.
    a. 1358   b. 148,700   c. 12,350
    d. 0.037   e. 0.00275   f. 0.0000196

20hx Evaluate
    a. 10^{-3} b. $1000^{1/3}$ c. $2^{3/2} \times 2^{1/2}$
    d. $(^{169}/_{256})^{-1/2}$ e. $6^2 \times 36^{1/2}$

20i Evaluate
    a. $8^{2/3} \times \sqrt{16}$ b. $49^{1/2} \times 14^{-1}$ c. $\sqrt{5} \times (^4\sqrt{5})^3$

20jx Evaluate
    a. $\dfrac{2^3 \times 4^{-1/2}}{16 \times 8^{-2/3}}$ b. $100^{1/2} - \dfrac{12^{-1/2} \times 2^{3/2}}{2^{-3/2} \times 64^{1/2} \times 12^{-3/2}}$

Chapter 21

Rational Numbers

Learning Objectives:

At the end of your study of this chapter you should be able to:

1. understand the extension of the number system into vulgar fractions,

2. perform arithmetic operations with vulgar fractions,

3. convert fractions into decimals and vice versa.

Rational Numbers

The Utopian number system has come quite a long way from its initial range of zero to nine. New concepts in numeracy made it necessary to extend the number system, and Utopians are now able to perform many complicated types of calculation — though not quite all! There is one concept that the existing number system just cannot cope with, and, as you may have guessed, it was discovered by Fred the Shoemaker. By now he is an important man with a healthy business, a business that is expanding rapidly. He decides to take on a partner to help him find the shells necessary to finance the expansion. They will contribute an equal sum and will be joint owners of the firm. How can Fred indicate his share of ownership in the firm mathematically? Even with the existing number system, there would be no difficulty in this. He could imagine the firm split into 10 equal shares, of which he would hold five and his partner would hold five. So Fred owns 0.5 of the firm.

It is very unlikely, however, that ownership of the firm would be split up in this way. After all, Fred has worked hard in the past to build up the firm and, naturally, he will feel that he should own a larger share than his partner. In fact, he thinks that his share should be twice as big as that of his partner. But how can he express this fact in the existing number system? He could again try ten equal shares — but it won't work! If Fred has six shares (0.6) and his partner three shares (0.3), then one share will not be allocated. Fred then tries a hundred shares taking 66 or 0.66 for himself and allocating 33 or 0.33 to his partner — but again one share is not allocated. After trying 1000 shares, 10,000 shares and so on, Fred realises that, although his accuracy is improving, he just cannot express the share of ownership accurately with the existing number system.

To give the desired degree of accuracy, Fred must find some other way of writing numbers. An easy way out would be to argue that, as Fred's share is twice as great as his partner's, then Fred's share is

$$2 : 1$$

Written in this way, Fred has discovered *proportions (or ratios)*. He can visualise the time, however, when it will be necessary to perform arithmetic operations on these numbers, and it will be difficult to do this if ratios are used. Is there an alternative to this method? Fred thinks! He has met problems like this before, when dealing with division. Problems such as 10 ÷ 5 = 2 and 5 ÷ 10 = 0.5 have left him with no difficulties. But what about 17 ÷ 9, or indeed 1 ÷ 3? He cannot write down an answer to these problems using the existing number system. Realising that this type of problem arises from division, Fred looks more closely at the division sign (÷). Suppose the dot over the line represents the number he divides INTO, while the dot under the line represents the number he divides BY. Fred could then write 1 ÷ 3 = ⅓, and he can call this answer one third, i.e. the result of splitting one into three equal parts. He soon discovers that any integer can be written in many different ways using his new system. For example, he can split 4 into 2 equal parts (each of two) and express it as ⁴⁄₂; or he can split 6 into 3 equal parts (again each of two) and express it as ⁶⁄₃; and each of these expressions result in parts of the size 2. Thus he realises that 2 = ²⁄₁ = ⁴⁄₂ = ⁶⁄₃ = ⁸⁄₄ = ¹⁰⁄₅ and so on indefinitely. Numbers written in this way have been developed by considering ratios, so Fred calls them the SET OF RATIONAL NUMBERS, or, more commonly, fractions. If we consider the different ways in which we can express the integer 2, we can derive the first two rules of fractions.

Rule 1: If the top and bottom numbers of a rational number are multiplied by a constant, the fraction is unchanged.

Rule 2: If the top and bottom numbers of a rational number are divided by a constant, the fraction is unchanged.

Also, by considering division such as 1 ÷ 2, 1 ÷ 3, 1 ÷ 4 etc. on the one hand, and 17 ÷ 9, 18 ÷ 8, 4 ÷ 3 etc. on the other, a third rule can be developed.

Rule 3: If the top number (which we call the numerator) is greater than the bottom number (which we call the denominator), then the rational number is greater than 1. If the denominator is greater than the numerator, then the rational number is less than 1.

What would happen if we keep the denominator the same but change the numerator? We may experiment as follows.

$$\text{Rational Number:} \quad \frac{2}{2} \quad \frac{2\times 2}{2} = \frac{4}{2} \quad \frac{2\times 3}{2} = \frac{6}{2} \quad \frac{2\times 4}{2} = \frac{8}{2} \quad \frac{2\times 5}{2} = \frac{10}{2} \quad \text{etc}$$

$$= \qquad 1 \qquad\qquad 2 \qquad\qquad 3 \qquad\qquad 4 \qquad\qquad 5$$

Rule 4: To multiply a rational number by an integer, multiply together the numerator and the integer.

At last Fred is able to solve his original problem. He has decided that his share must be twice that of his partner. He will split the ownership into three equal shares. His partner will have one share (or 1 ÷ 3 = ⅓ of the shares), while Fred will have ⅓ × 2 = ⅔ of the shares. The answer is logical: 2 ÷ 3 must give an answer twice as large as 1 ÷ 3.

Converting decimals to this system of rational numbers will be quite easy. Let us consider the number 0.35 = 3 tenths plus 5 hundredths = 35 hundredths. As a rational number this would be 35 ÷ 100 = $^{35}/_{100}$. According to rule 3, both the numerator and the denominator can be divided by a constant without altering the value of the rational number. In this case 5 is a convenient constant to use.

$$\frac{35 \div 5}{100 \div 5} = \frac{7}{20}$$

Any decimal can be converted into a fraction in precisely this way. What if the procedure is reversed i.e. we wish to convert fractions to decimals? What we must do here is convert the denominator of the fraction into some power of ten. For example,

$$\frac{3}{8} = \frac{3 \times 125}{8 \times 125} = \frac{375}{1000} = 0.375$$

Usually it is more convenient to obtain this result by following the instruction given by the rational number, i.e. Divide 3 by 8

3 units ÷ 8 = 0 units remainder 3 units.
Considering the remainder, 3 units = 30 tenths
30 tenths ÷ 8 = *3 tenths* remainder 6 tenths.
Considering the remainder, 6 tenths = 60 hundredths
60 hundredths ÷ 8 = *7 hundredths* remainder 4 hundredths
Considering the remainder, 4 hundredths = 40 thousandths
40 thousandths ÷ 8 = *5 thousandths* with no remainder

We know then that ⅜ = 3 tenths + 7 hundredths + 5 thousandths
= 3 × 10^{-1} + 7 × 10^{-2} + 5 × 10^{-3}
= 0.375

The usual layout for the calculation is like this:

```
     0.375
  8│3.000000
    2 4
    ───
      6(0)
      5 6
      ───
        4(0)
        4 0
        ───
        . .
```

Now, of course, if we try this procedure with all rational numbers we will experience difficulty, because, as we know, it is not possible to state the result of all divisions exactly unless we use the rational number system. If we divide 1 by 3, the following would result:

```
    .3333
  3│1.0000
    9
   ──
    10
     9
    ──
    10
```

and so on indefinitely. No matter how many places of decimals we consider, we will always have a remainder. This result is called a recurring decimal, and to show that this is so mathematicians place a dot over the last digit, i.e.

$$\tfrac{1}{3} = 0.33\dot{3}$$

the dot meaning merely that the figure 3 is now repeated indefinitely. If we divide 1 by 11 the result will again be a recurring decimal.

```
         0.090909
   11 |1.00000
        99
       ----
        100
         99
        ----
         100
```

This time, instead of a single digit recurring a group of two digits recurs. To show this we use two dots.

$$\tfrac{1}{11} = 0.09090\dot{9}$$

By developing a rational number system we have now obtained a method of obtaining solutions to all problems involving division — the previous number system was not capable of doing this. However, fractions do have a disadvantage. One purpose of developing numbers is to enable us to compare, i.e. decide which of two quantities is the larger. Now with decimals it is easier to decide which of two quantities is the larger — but this may not be the case with fractions. Consider this problem.

Joe and Charlie (both friends of Fred) own shares in Utopian Leather. Joe owns $^{11}/_{36}$ ths of the shares while Charlie owns $^{7}/_{24}$ths of the shares. Who has the larger holding? Certainly $\tfrac{1}{24}$th is larger than $\tfrac{1}{36}$th but is $^{7}/_{24}$ths larger than $^{11}/_{36}$ths? To decide this it is necessary to change both types of fraction either into decimals or into the same type of fraction, i.e. to express both with the same denominator, (or, as we say, to give them a common denominator). Now 24ths and 36ths can both be changed into 72nds.

$$\frac{11}{36} = \frac{11 \times 2}{36 \times 2} = \frac{22}{72} \qquad \frac{7}{24} = \frac{7 \times 3}{24 \times 3} = \frac{21}{72}$$

So Fred can conclude that Joe has the larger share in Utopian Leather. Moreover, this analysis shows how it is possible to add or subtract fractions. Fred can conclude that the amount by which Joe's share is larger than Charlie's is

$$^{22}/_{72} - {}^{21}/_{72} = {}^{1}/_{72},$$

and the fraction of the firm owned by both Joe and Charlie together is

$$^{22}/_{72} + {}^{21}/_{72} = {}^{43}/_{72}$$

Rule 5: To add (or subtract) fractions first convert them to fractions with a common denominator and then add (or subtract) the numerators of these new fractions.

When adding or subtracting fractions it is convenient to use the "lowest common denominator" (or L.C.D.) — a number that will not always be easy to find by inspection. Suppose we wish to perform the following calculation:

$$^{33}/_{35} + {}^{29}/_{42}$$

To find the lowest common denominator it is necessary to find the lowest number that both 35 and 42 will divide into. This is done by splitting both numbers up into factors, i.e.

$$35 = 5 \times 7$$
$$42 = 6 \times 7$$

We have three separate factors, 5, 6, and 7, and the lowest common denominator must also contain these three factors. So the lowest common denominator must be $5 \times 6 \times 7 = 210 = 35 \times 6 = 42 \times 5$.

$$\frac{33}{35} + \frac{29}{42} = \frac{33 \times 6}{35 \times 6} + \frac{29 \times 5}{42 \times 5} = \frac{198}{210} + \frac{145}{210} = \frac{343}{210}$$

Using Rule 3 Fred decides that this number is greater than 1, and he would probably find it convenient to write it as a combination of integer and fraction. The line in the fraction means divide, so following this instruction:

$$210 \overline{\smash{)}343} \quad \begin{array}{c} 1 \end{array}$$

thus $343 \div 210 = 1$ remainder 133

$$\underline{210}$$
$$133$$

If the remainder is now divided by 210, we have

$$1^{133}/_{210}$$

Having mastered the technique of addition and subtraction of fractions it seems natural that we should now return our attention to multiplication and division. Now, through our experiments we have already learned something about multiplication. We discovered Rule 4 — to multiply a fraction by an integer, multiply together the integer and the numerator. For example

$$^{7}/_{12} \times 3 = {}^{21}/_{12} = 1^{9}/_{12} = 1\frac{3}{4}$$

Notice that the $^{9}/_{12}$ is simplified to $\frac{3}{4}$ by dividing 3 into both the numerator and the denominator. In fact, we could have done this before multiplying if we had set out the problem like this:

$$^{7}/_{12} \times 3 = \frac{7 \times 3 \div 3}{12 \div 3} = {}^{7}/_{4} = 1\frac{3}{4}$$

But suppose we wish to multiply together two fractions. To do this we must think carefully about the meaning of multiplication. When we say 4×3 we mean take 4 sets of 3 and add them (i.e. $3 + 3 + 3 + 3$). In the same way $\frac{2}{3} \times \frac{1}{5}$ means take $\frac{2}{3}$ of $\frac{1}{5}$th of a set of 1. Now $\frac{1}{5}$th of a set of one can be represented like this:

one fifth of a set of one

Taking two thirds of this quantity it can be represented like this:

The cross shaded area represents ⅔ of ⅕ and we can see that this represents
²⁄₁₅ of the entire set, i.e.

$$\tfrac{2}{3} \times \tfrac{1}{5} = \tfrac{2}{15}$$

Rule 6: To multiply together two fractions, multiply the two numerators
together, and multiply their denominators together.

Exhibit 1

$$\frac{3}{5} \times \frac{20}{21} = \frac{60}{105} = \frac{12}{21} = \frac{4}{7}$$

This problem could be done more directly by *cancelling,* i.e. we can divide 3
into the numerator and denominator and 5 into the other numerator and the
other denominator

$$\frac{\overset{1}{\cancel{3}}}{\underset{1}{\cancel{5}}} \times \frac{\overset{4}{\cancel{20}}}{\underset{7}{\cancel{21}}} = \frac{1 \times 4}{1 \times 7} = \frac{4}{7}$$

Notice that we have divided 3 into the numerator of the *first* fraction and
the denominator of the *second,* and 5 into the numerator of the second
fraction and the denominator of the first. This cross division is permissable
only when we are multiplying. Finally we multiply their numerators
together and their denominators together.

Exhibit 2

$$2\tfrac{2}{3} \times 1\tfrac{1}{4}$$

When you are faced with fractions such as this consisting of an integer and a
fraction we cannot begin to multiply until we have disposed of the integer.
Now if we consider 2⅔, we know that in two units there are 2 × 3 = 6
thirds. Additionally we have two thirds as a fraction so we can say 2⅔ = ⁸⁄₃.
In the same way 1¼ = ⁵⁄₄. So

$$2\tfrac{2}{3} \times 1\tfrac{1}{4} = \frac{\overset{}{\cancel{8}}}{3} \times \frac{5}{\underset{1}{\cancel{4}}} = \frac{2 \times 5}{3 \times 1} = \frac{10}{3} = 3\tfrac{1}{3}$$

When dealing with division of fractions, we can continue with the practice of writing division as one number over another. This gives a compound fraction:

$$\frac{2}{3} \div \frac{1}{5} = \frac{\frac{2}{3}}{\frac{1}{5}}$$

We can change the numerator of this compound fraction into an integer if we multiply it by 3. Of course, we must also do the same to the denominator.

$$\frac{\frac{2}{\cancel{3}} \times \cancel{3}}{\frac{1}{5} \times 3} = \frac{2}{\frac{3}{5}}$$

In the same way we can convert the denominator into an integer by multiplying both numerator and denominator by 5.

$$\frac{\frac{2}{3} \times 5}{\frac{3}{\cancel{5}} \times \cancel{5}} = \frac{10}{3}$$

so,

$$\frac{2}{3} \div \frac{1}{5} = \frac{10}{3} = 3\tfrac{1}{3}$$

Now, suppose we wish to divide ¾ by ⅖

$$\frac{3}{4} \div \frac{2}{5} = \frac{\frac{3}{4}}{\frac{2}{5}} = \frac{\frac{3}{\cancel{4}} \times \frac{\cancel{4}^{1}}{1} \times \frac{5}{1}}{\frac{2}{\cancel{5}_{1}} \times \frac{4}{1} \times \frac{\cancel{5}}{1}} = \frac{3 \times 5}{2 \times 4}$$

$$= \frac{15}{8} = 1\tfrac{7}{8}$$

Without affecting the result we can rewrite $\dfrac{3 \times 5}{2 \times 4}$ as $\dfrac{3 \times 5}{4 \times 2}$

$$= \frac{3}{4} \times \frac{5}{2} = \frac{15}{8} = 1\tfrac{7}{8}$$

So

$$\frac{3}{4} \div \frac{2}{5} = \frac{3}{4} \times \frac{5}{2}$$

Examining this enables us to derive the final rule of fractions

Rule 7: To divide a fraction by a fraction, invert the second fraction and multiply.

Exhibit 3

$$3\tfrac{1}{3} \div 2\tfrac{1}{2} = \frac{10}{3} \div \frac{5}{2} = \frac{\overset{2}{\cancel{10}}}{3} \times \frac{2}{\underset{1}{\cancel{5}}} = \frac{4}{3} = 1\tfrac{1}{3}$$

Now provided there is only one operation involved you will seldom have any difficulty in handling fractions. The trouble is that you often meet complex problems which involve several operations. For example you might be asked to evaluate something like this:

$$(2\tfrac{3}{4} + 3\tfrac{1}{2}) \div (1\tfrac{1}{4} + 2\tfrac{1}{2}) + 2\tfrac{2}{3} - 3\tfrac{3}{4}$$

You will remember in an exercise that you did earlier we indicated that you must always work out anything enclosed in brackets first. The full rule is that you must work out these complex problems in the following order:

1. First work out all expressions within the brackets.
2. Next multiply together terms separated by a multiplication sign and divide terms separated by a division sign.
3. Finally add together or subtract terms separated by a plus or minus.

Exhibit 4

$$(2\tfrac{3}{4} + 3\tfrac{1}{2}) \div (1\tfrac{1}{4} + 2\tfrac{1}{2}) + 2\tfrac{2}{3} - 3\tfrac{3}{4}$$

Firstly we must work out the terms in the two brackets

$2\tfrac{3}{4} + 3\tfrac{1}{2} = {}^{11}/_4 + {}^7/_2 = {}^{11}/_4 + {}^{14}/_4 = {}^{25}/_4$

$1\tfrac{1}{4} + 2\tfrac{1}{2} = {}^5/_4 + {}^5/_2 = {}^5/_4 + {}^{10}/_4 = {}^{15}/_4$

Our problem may now be restated as

${}^{25}/_4 \div {}^{15}/_4 + 2\tfrac{2}{3} - 3\tfrac{3}{4}$

Our rules state that we must now divide the terms separated by a division sign:

$$\frac{25}{4} \div \frac{15}{4} = \frac{\overset{5}{\cancel{25}}}{\underset{1}{\cancel{4}}} \times \frac{\overset{1}{\cancel{4}}}{\underset{3}{\cancel{15}}} = \frac{5 \times 1}{1 \times 3} = \frac{5}{3}$$

and our problem now becomes

${}^5/_3 + 2\tfrac{2}{3} - 3\tfrac{3}{4}$

We may now finally add and subtract the remaining terms, having found a suitable common denominator, in this case 12.

${}^5/_3 + 2\tfrac{2}{3} - 3\tfrac{3}{4} = {}^5/_3 + {}^8/_3 - {}^{15}/_4$

$$= \frac{5 \times 4}{12} + \frac{8 \times 4}{12} - \frac{15 \times 3}{12} = \frac{20}{12} + \frac{32}{12} - \frac{45}{12}$$

$= {}^7/_{12}$ **Answer.**

Assignment Exercises

21.1x Consider the following series
    2, 4, 5, 8, 10, 16 ....
    It represents the denominators of fractions that can be expressed exactly as decimals. Continue this series up to 100. Can you find a rule for deciding when a fraction can be expressed as an exact decimal?

21.2x It has been suggested that instead of counting to a base ten we should count to a base twelve. What advantage would this have for converting fractions to decimals? Can you find a rule for deciding which denominators can be converted into exact decimals for any given number base?

21.3 Which of the following fractions can be converted into exact decimals?
    a) $\frac{5}{8}$ b) $\frac{3}{5}$ c) $\frac{7}{9}$ d) $\frac{14}{25}$ e) $\frac{14}{35}$

21.4 Convert the fractions in question three into decimals.

21.5 Convert the following decimals into fractions
    a) 0.375   bx) 0.0105   c) 1.035   dx) 2.0018   e) 49.978

21.6 Evaluate
    a) $\frac{4}{9} + \frac{3}{5}$ bx) $\frac{13}{27} - \frac{4}{9}$
    c) $\frac{8}{27} \times \frac{9}{16}$ dx) $\frac{9}{33} \div \frac{27}{49}$.

21.7 Evaluate
    a) $\frac{7}{8} \div \frac{3}{4} + 3\frac{2}{3}$ bx) $1\frac{2}{7} \times 1\frac{5}{9} + 2\frac{1}{7} \div 5$
    c) $(2\frac{1}{4} + 3\frac{1}{3}) \div (2\frac{11}{12} + 2\frac{2}{3})$ dx) $(4\frac{1}{5} - \frac{3}{10}) \div (2\frac{1}{2} \times 4\frac{1}{3})$.

Do not attempt these revisionary assignments until you have reached Chapter 26.

Revisionary Assignments

21.a Solve the equations
    a) $2(x-3) = 3(x-1)$ b) $\frac{x}{4} - \frac{x}{5} = 2$ c) $\frac{3y}{7} - \frac{2y}{5} = \frac{4}{35}$

21.b Solve the equations
    a) $\dfrac{P+1}{7} - \dfrac{3(P-2)}{14} = 7$ b) $\frac{3}{4}(z-1) - \frac{2}{3}(3z+1) = \frac{1}{5}(z+1)$
    c) $\dfrac{2x+3}{x-2} = \dfrac{6x}{3x+2}$

21.cx Plot the following relationships
    a) $3y = 2x + 9$ b) $3y + 2x = 8$ c) $8y + 8x = 16$

21.d Find the gradient of the straight line connecting the co-ordinates
    a) (-2, 3) and (9, 4)   b) (6, -3) and (19, -3)
    c) (-3, 4) and (4, -3)   d) (0, -1) and (16, 1)

21.e With a £1200 legacy, a man buys some $3\frac{1}{2}\%$ debentures and some 4% debentures. The annual income he receives is £44. Find the amount he invested in each type of debenture.

21.fx A batsman scores 450 runs in x innings. In his next innings he scores 63 and increases his average by 2. Find x.

21.g A factory has a labour force of 400. Men are paid £1.25 per hour and women are paid £1 per hour. If the total hourly wage bill was £475, how many men does the factory employ?

21.hx 'Chocbars' sell at 5p each. To produce 'chocbars' costs £900 in overheads per week, and $\frac{1}{2}$p. per unit for raw materials.
    a) Determine the weekly level of output at which the firm would   break even.
    b) What is the profit if the firm produces 25,000 'chocbars' per   week?

21.i North West Gas used to offer its customers a choice of two tariffs. The General Tariff has a standing charge of £1 per quarter and a charge of 19.1p per therm for the first 130 therms consumed, and 16.6p per therm for subsequent therms consumed. The Gold Star Tariff has a standing charge of £3 per quarter and a charge of 14.1p per therm for all therms consumed. Obtain a rule enabling you to advise customers which tariff to chose.

21.jx It is known that the relationship between total cost and output is linear. It costs £2340 to produce 3000 units per week, and £2370 to produce 4000 units per week. If the product sells at 17p per unit, find the weekly breakeven output.

Chapter 22

Fractional Indices

Learning Objectives:

At the end of your study of this chapter you should be able to:

1. **understand the extension of the number system to include both negative and fractional indices,**

2. **use logarithms to facilitate such calculations.**

Fractional Indices

You will remember that some time ago we discussed the theory of indices. We discovered that:

$$10^3 \quad = 10 \times 10 \times 10 \quad = 1000$$
$$10^2 \quad = 10 \times 10 \qquad\qquad = 100$$
$$10^1 \qquad\qquad\qquad\qquad\quad = 10$$
$$10^0 \qquad\qquad\qquad\qquad\quad = 1$$
$$10^{-1} \quad = \frac{1}{10} \qquad\qquad = 0.1$$
$$10^{-2} \quad = \frac{1}{100} \qquad\qquad = 0.01$$

Now every index we have so far discussed has been an integer, and it seems logical that we should consider as well fractional indices to see if we can give a meaning to them. What meaning can be attached, for example, to $10^{1/2}$, $10^{1/3}$, $10^{3/4}$, and so on? However long a time we spend thinking about this problem, no obvious meaning is clear. But they are, after all, indices, and so, whatever their meaning, they must obey our rules. Let us apply these rules to see if they can throw any light on the meaning of fractional indices.

$$10^{1/2} \times 10^{2/3} = 10^{1/2 + 2/3} = 10^{7/6}$$

So what? The meaning is no clearer. But suppose we can obtain a result that does mean something — perhaps we can then reason backwards and obtain a meaning for fractional indices.

$$10^{1/2} \times 10^{1/2} = 10^{1/2 + 1/2} = 10^1$$

Now, 10^1 does mean something. It is merely another way of writing 10. Moreover the two numbers we started with are the same. The problem we are considering is to find a number which, when multiplied by itself gives 10 i.e. a number which when squared gives 10. Can you see that no integer will do this? Let us, then, shelve this problem and consider another number

$$16^{1/2} \times 16^{1/2} = 16^{1/2 + 1/2} = 16^1 = 16$$

This one is easy. The square of 4 is 16, so $16^{1/2}$ must be equal to 4. The process we are examining is called, finding the roots of a number — in this case the *square root*.

4^2 is the square of 4 i.e. 16

$4^{1/2}$ is the square root of 4 i.e. 2

Notice that squaring and square rooting are opposite (or inverse) processes, and that ½ is the inverse of 2. If 10^2 means ten squared, then in every sense it is logical to call $10^{1/2}$ the square root of ten. As a convenient shorthand form we can use the sign $\sqrt{}$ to mean 'the square root of', and so we may say, $10^{1/2} = \sqrt{10}$.

Considering the matter further, we know that

$$8^{1/3} \times 8^{1/3} \times 8^{1/3} = 8^{1/3 + 1/3 + 1/3} = 8^1 = 8.$$

Thus, when we are looking for a meaning to $8^{1/3}$, we are seeking a number which when multiplied by itself twice will be equal to 8. This number we call the *cube root* and indicate it by the sign $\sqrt[3]{}$. Thus,

$$2 \times 2 \times 2 = 8, \text{ and so } \sqrt[3]{8} = 2$$

In the same way $10^{1/4}$ means the fourth root of ten ($\sqrt[4]{10}$), $10^{1/5}$ means the fifth root of ten ($\sqrt[5]{10}$) and so on.

We have deduced the meaning of a fractional index when the numerator is equal to one, but suppose the numerator is not equal to one. What is the meaning of $10^{5/6}$? Now, looking back at $10^{1/2}$, we know it means the square root of 10 to the power one. Equally $10^{1/3}$ means the cube root of ten to the power one. If the denominator tells us which root we are seeking, it seems logical that the numerator should tell us the power. Thus $10^{5/6} = \sqrt[6]{10^5}$ or $(\sqrt[6]{10})^5$. Let us check to see whether this is so.

$64^{1/2} \times 64^{1/3} = 64^{5/6}$

$64^{1/2} = \sqrt{64} = 8$

$64^{1/3} = \sqrt[3]{64} = 4$

Hence $64^{1/2} \times 64^{1/3} = 8 \times 4 = 32$

Now, if we are right, and $64^{5/6}$ does mean the sixth root of 64 to the power five, then $(\sqrt[6]{64})^5$ should also equal 32.

$$\sqrt[6]{64} = 2 \text{ and } 2^5 = 32$$

So, in a fractional index, the denominator of the fraction indicates the root we are seeking, and the numerator indicates the power to which the number is raised.

Example 1 Evaluate $125^{1/3}$

$$125^{1/3} = \sqrt[3]{125} = 5$$

Example 2 Evaluate $32^{4/5}$

$$32^{4/5} = (\sqrt[5]{32})^4$$

$$\sqrt[5]{32} = 2 \text{ and } 2^4 = 16$$

Example 3 Evaluate $8^{-2/3}$

$$8^{-2/3} = \frac{1}{8^{2/3}}$$

$$8^{2/3} = (\sqrt[3]{8})^2$$

$$\sqrt[3]{8} = 2 \text{ and } 2^2 = 4$$

$$8^{-2/3} = \frac{1}{4} = 0.25$$

Example 4 Evaluate $4^{1/3} \times 4^{-4/3}$

$$4^{1/3} \times 4^{-4/3} = 4^{1/3 - 4/3} = 4^{-3/3} = 4^{-1}$$

$$4^{-1} = \frac{1}{4}$$

Earlier we postponed trying to evaluate $10^{1/2}$, a problem to which we must now return. We know that $3^2 = 9$ and that $4^2 = 16$, so $10^{1/2}$ must be nearer to 3 than to 4. We can pick a number close to 3, say $3\frac{1}{6}$. Now, $(3\frac{1}{6})^2 = {}^{361}/_{36} = 10\frac{1}{6}$, so $3\frac{1}{6}$ is too large to be the square root of ten. We can continue like this.

$$3\frac{1}{6} = 3\frac{6}{36} \text{ so try } 3\frac{5}{36}$$

$$(3\frac{5}{36})^2 = {}^{12769}/_{1296} = 9\frac{1105}{1296} \text{ so } 3\frac{5}{36} \text{ is too small}$$

$$3\frac{5}{36} = 3\frac{10}{72} \text{ and this is too small}$$

$$3\frac{1}{6} = 3\frac{12}{72} \text{ and this is too large}$$

so $10^{1/2}$ must lie between $3\frac{10}{72}$ and $3\frac{12}{72}$. We could try $3\frac{11}{72}$ but we would find that this is also too small. We can carry on in this way for as long as you wish, but we will never be able to express $10^{1/2}$ exactly, either as a decimal or as a rational number. So we have discovered that our rational number system, which seemed to enable us to write exactly the solution to all arithmetic operations, cannot cope with finding the square root of ten, and this is true of the square root of many other numbers. The roots of such numbers are called *irrational numbers* i.e. they cannot be expressed as the ratio of two integers. The best we can do is to express $10^{1/2}$ as a decimal, correct to say three decimal places, and to do this the easiest way is to use logarithms.

$$\text{Log } 10 = 1.0000$$

$$\text{Log } 10^{1/2} = 1.0000 \div 2 = 0.5000$$

$$\text{So } 10^{1/2} = 3.162$$

Rule: To find the logarithm of the square root of any number, divide the logarithm of the number by two.

In the same way if we are finding the cube root we would find the logarithm of the number, divide by 3, and this is the logarithm of the answer. How would you find the fourth, or the fifth root?

Example 5 Evaluate $(124.6)^{1/4}$

$$(124.6)^{1/4} = \sqrt[4]{124.6}$$

$$124.6 = 1.246 \times 10^2$$

so $\quad \text{Log } 124.6 = 2.0956$

and $\quad \text{Log } (124.6^{1/4}) = 2.0956 \div 4 = 0.5239$

Using antilogarithm tables

0.5239 is the logarithm of 3.341

so the fourth root of 124.6 = 3.34 correct to 3 significant figures.

Provided the number you are finding the root of is greater than one, the method used in example 5 is all you need. Suppose, however, that you are required to find the square root of 0.238. Now, 0.238 = 2.38 × 10^{-1} and the log of this is $\overline{1}.3766$. If you think about it you cannot divide this by 2, because as you know the expression means $-1 + .3766$. It would be possible to say that this is equal to $-0.5 + .1883 = -0.3117$. Since the decimal part of the log cannot be negative we would have to express this as $-1 + .6883$ or $\overline{1}.6883$ and this is, in fact the logarithm of the answer. It is a terribly cumbersome way to proceed, however, and the chances of making a mistake are high, so let us see if we can find an easier way.

$$\overline{1}.3766 = -1 + .3766$$

Since we cannot divide -1 by 2 and leave the answer as an whole number we proceed by saying that if we had -2 we could do the division. We can obtain this by subtracting 1 from the first digit to make it $-1 - 1 = -2$. But to keep the logarithm accurate we would have to add 1 to the decimal part of the logarithm so that we convert the logarithm into

$-2 + 1.3776$ and this can be divided with the result

$-1 + 0.6883 = \overline{1}.6883$ which is exactly what we got before. Thus the square root of 0.238 can now be obtained using our antilogarithm tables.

$\overline{1}.6883$ is the logarithm of 4.879 × 10^{-1} or 0.4879 so we can now say that $(0.238)^{\frac{1}{2}} = 0.488$

Example 6 Evaluate $(0.6843)^{\frac{1}{3}}$

$$0.6843 = 6.843 \times 10^{-1}$$
$$\text{Log } 0.6843 = \overline{1}.8352$$
$$\text{Log } (0.6843)^{\frac{1}{3}} = \overline{1}.8352 \div 3$$
$$\overline{1}.8352 = -1 + .8352 = -3 + 2.8352$$
$$(-3 + 2.8352) \div 3 = -1 + .9451$$
$$\text{So Log } (0.6843)^{\frac{1}{3}} = \overline{1}.9451$$

Using antilogarithm tables

$\overline{1}.9451$ is the logarithm of 8.813 × 10^{-1} = 0.8813

Thus $(0.6843)^{\frac{1}{3}} = 0.8813$

Most examinations will, of course, allow you to use books of tables which give you not only logarithms and antilogarithms but also squares and square roots. If you wish to find a square root using these tables the principle of looking them up is much the same as it is for logarithms — but you must be careful. As with logarithms the numbers in the left hand column range from 10 to 99, but it is best to think of them as you do with logarithms as being 1.0 to 9.9. Suppose we wished to find the square root of 3.286. We go down the left hand column until we reach the digits 32. And here comes your first shock — you will find two rows of numbers alongside

32, as you will against every other pair of digits. The top row gives the square root of 3.2, 3.21 3.22 and so on; the second row gives the square roots of 3.2 × 10, 3.21 × 10 or 32, 32.1, 32.2 and so on. Here we will use the top row, and moving along it to the column headed 8 we find the figure 1811. Moving now to the mean difference column headed 6 we find the digit 2, which we add to 1811 to give us 1813. Every figure in this table is given in its standard form, so the number 1813 means 1.813×10^0 or 1.813 which is the square root of 3.286. Thus, using these tables we can look up directly the square root of every number between 1 and 99.99. If you require the square root of numbers between 100 and 999.9, say 634.5 we can express this as 6.345×10^2. The square root of this is $\sqrt{6.345} \times \sqrt{100}$ or 2.519×10 = 25.19. For numbers between 1000 and 9999.9 again we divide by 100. Suppose we were finding the square root of 4567, we would express this as 45.67×100. The square root is $\sqrt{45.67} \times \sqrt{100} = 6.758 \times 10 = 67.58$.

Let us look now at an example of finding the square root of a number less than 1.

Example 7 Evaluate $(0.0863)^{1/2}$

$$0.0863 = 8.63 \times 10^{-2}$$
$$\text{Thus } \sqrt{0.0863} = \sqrt{8.63} \times \sqrt{10^{-2}}$$
$$= 2.938 \times 10^{-1} = 0.2938$$

Assignment Exercises

22.1 Evaluate

(a) 3^{-2} (b) 4^{-3} (c) $(1/2)^{-2}$

22.2 Evaluate

(a) $27^{4/3}$ (b) $1000^{3/2}$ (c) $256^{3/4}$

22.3x Use square root tables to find the value of

(a) $\sqrt{68}$ (b) $\sqrt{49270}$ (c) $\sqrt{123.4}$ (d) $\sqrt{1.86 \times 10^5}$

22.4 Use square root tables to find the value of

(a) $\sqrt{0.034}$ (bx) $\sqrt{0.00123}$ (c) $\sqrt{1.39 \times 10^{-4}}$ (dx) $\sqrt{4.36 \times 10^{-9}}$

22.5 Use logarithms to find the value of

(ax) $\sqrt{128.4}$ (b) $\sqrt[3]{429.8}$ (cx) $\sqrt{0.678}$ (d) $\sqrt[4]{0.0812}$

Chapter 23

Ratios and Percentages

Learning Objectives:

At the end of your study of this chapter you should be able to:

1. **appreciate the importance of ratios and percentages in the business environment,**

2. **convert decimals and fractions into percentage form, and vice-versa,**

3. **perform business calculations to find cost, profit and selling price from given information,**

4. **calculate simple interest.**

Ratios and Percentages

Earlier we met ratios when Fred was trying to quantify his, and his partner's share in the firm. If his share of the firm was twice as large as that of his partner this could be expressed by saying that their shares were *in the ratio 2:1.*

Nowadays it is quite common to express relative shares of firms in the form of ratios, especially when we are considering partnerships. But, if Fred is to use ratios he must be able to distribute his profits on the basis of the ratios. Let us suppose that Fred, Joe and Charlie decide to set up a partnership handling supplies of leather. The capital they contribute to start the firm is:

Fred	35,000 shells
Joe	25,000 shells
Charlie	15,000 shells

So the ratio showing their ownership is:

$$35000 : 25000 : 15000$$

Simplifying this $35 : 25 : 15$

or $7 : 5 : 3$

In other words, if the ownership of the firm was split into $7 + 5 + 3 = 15$ shares, of which Fred had 7, Joe had 5 and Charlie had 3, then this would accurately reflect the share of ownership.

Suppose that in a particular year the firm earned 4,500 shells profit — how should this profit be distributed? Just as it was convenient to think of the firm as being split into 15 different shares, so it will be convenient to imagine the profit being split into 15 different parts of $^{4500}/_{15} = 300$ shells. Fred's share of the profits would be $7 \times 300 = 2100$ shells; Charlie's share $5 \times 300 = 1500$ shells; and Joe's share $3 \times 300 = 900$ shells.

Now, Fred will naturally want to keep track of the profits in this firm in order to determine whether his money was well invested. Suppose that in the first year the profit earned was 3000 shells, and in the second year profit was 4500 shells. The rise in profit was 1500 shells, or profit rose by $^{1500}/_{3000} = \frac{1}{2}$. Now when dealing with business data, or when comparing the size of change between data, it is more usual to use *percentages*. We in Britain, are well used to reading about percentages — wage increases are restricted to 10%, the rate of inflation is 12%, V.A.T. is levied usually at 8% — the list is almost endless. Percentages are extremely easy to manipulate, and to calculate a percentage all that need to be done is to take a fraction and convert this into an equivalent proportion of 100. Take ½ for example, — a half of 100 is 50, so ½ = 50 per cent. You will appreciate that all "per cent" means is "out of a hundred".

Fred owned 7 shares out of a total of 15 shares so we can say his fractional share is $^7/_{15}$ and his percentage share $^7/_{15} \times 100 = 46\frac{2}{3}\%$, i.e. if the firm were divided into 100 shares, Fred would own $46\frac{2}{3}$ of them.

Rule: To convert a fraction into a percentage, multiply the fraction by 100. To convert a percentage into a fraction divide by 100.

Thus $^2/_5 = ^2/_5 \times 100 = ^{200}/_5 = 40\%$

and $48\% = ^{48}/_{100} = ^{12}/_{25}$

In a similar fashion, multiply a decimal by 100 to convert it into a percentage and divide a percentage by 100 to change it into a decimal.

Thus $0.125 = 0.125 \times 100 = 12.5\%$

and $39.7\% = 39.7 \div 100 = 0.397$

Now let us examine a few typical examples of how percentages may be used in practice.

Example 1

Fred buys shoes for 10 shells and sells them for 16 shells. What percentage profit does he make?

Actual profit earned is $16 - 10$ shells = 6 shells. Profit is normally expressed as a percentage of cost price so profit earned is $^6/_{10} \times 100 = 60\%$

Example 2

Fred buys shoes for 12 shells, and wishes to make 25% profit when selling them. Calculate the selling price.

   Cost Price = 12 shells

   Profit = 25% of 12 = $^{25}/_{100} \times 12 = 3$ shells

   Selling Price = 12 + 3 shells = 15 shells.

Example 3

Fred sells shoes for 24 shells and makes 20% profit on each pair of shoes sold. What was the cost price? What was the profit?

We will call the cost price 100% and the profit 20%
so the selling price = 100% + 20% = 120%.

> 120% = 24 shells

so   cost price (100%) = $^{24}/_{120}$ × 100 = 20 shells.

and   profit = 4 shells.

Example 4

Fred invests 130 shells at 12% per annum, but does not withdraw the interest. How much would we have available after 1 year? After 2 years? After 3 years?

After 1 year Fred has 130 + 12% of 130 = 130 + 0.12 × 130 = 145.6
(i.e. 130 × 1.12)

After 2 years Fred has 145.6 + 0.12 × 145.6 = 163.072 shells
(i.e. 130 × 1.12²)

After 3 years Fred has 163.072 + 0.12 × 163.072 = 182.64064 shells
(i.e. 130 × 1.12³)

Percentages are, without doubt, extremely important measures — especially to accountants, and you would be well advised to master their meaning and manipulation before proceeding further.

Assignment Exercises

23.1 A shopkeeper buys goods for £2.84 each, and wishes to make a profit of 25 % on his cost price. Calculate his selling price. What is his profit as a percentage of his selling price?

23.2x The same shopkeeper has goods for sale at £6.44 each. He has lost the invoice, so he does not know what the goods cost him. However, he can remember that he used a 15% mark-up. What was the cost price?

23.3 Tom, Dick and Harry are partners in a firm, and their share of ownership is in the ratio 6 : 5 : 4. In a particular year the firm earned £204,180 profit. How should the profit be distributed between the partners?

23.4x In 1960, a firm earned a profit of £25,140, and its capital was £167,600. In 1970, the figures for profit and capital were £126,390 and £972,230. Which was the better year for the firm?

23.5 If £1,320 is left invested at 5% per annum compound for six years, how much would be available at the end of the period?

23.6x At what rate of compound interest would £1320 grow to £1,662.82 in three years?

23.7 If inflation is running at 9% per annum, how long would it take for prices to double?

Chapter 24

Basic Ideas of Algebra

Learning Objectives:

At the end of your study of this chapter you should be able to:

1. **understand the basic ideas of, and the need for algebra,**

2. **express given data in a simple algebraic form,**

3. **change the subject of an algebraic expression.**

Basic Ideas of Algebra

Almost every student who has ever sat a mathematics examination must have suffered from the type of question that is half a page long and takes up valuable time in reading and deciding what it is all about. How they must have longed for some way of abbreviating mathematical problems and making them more readily understandable! Now this is precisely what algebra is. It is to the mathematician what shorthand is to the private secretary — it is a form of mathematical shorthand, and first we must learn the language.

Let us suppose that Tom, who owns a Mini, is driving along a country road at a leisurely pace, and is suddenly overtaken by Harry, who owns a Sunbeam Alpine which disappears in a cloud of dust round the bend. By some means, known only to those who set mathematical problems, we ascertain that Harry is driving exactly twice as fast as Tom. How can we express this everyday situation in mathematical form?

Firstly, from the information given, we have no means of determining either Tom's speed or Harry's speed. The situation is concerned with relative speed (Harry's speed in relation to Tom's) rather than absolute speed (so many kilometres per hour). We could, of course, prepare a table showing all possible speeds at which Tom might be travelling and the speed of Harry corresponding to each.

If Tom's speed were	Harry's speed would be
20 kph	40 kph
25 kph	50 kph
30 kph	60 kph and so on.

But this is nonsense! We have changed six lines of type into a table possibly several pages long and made our situation even worse. A mathematician would go about it differently. He would say, "I do not know Tom's speed, so let us invent a symbol for it," and he would begin

Let Tom's speed be s kilometres per hour.

There are two important things to note about this statement. The symbol 's' does not stand for any particular speed; it merely implies 'whatever speed Tom was going', and its value will change as Tom presses on the accelerator or the brake. Secondly there is no reason why we must choose s. We could have chosen a or b or x or y or any other letter. We chose s only because it is the first letter of the word speed, and so it may help us to remember what s stands for.

Now, whatever speed Tom may be doing (s) we know that Harry is moving twice as quickly, so we know that

Harry's speed is equal to 2 × s

Whenever we have a letter multiplied by a number that number is known as the COEFFICIENT of the letter. Thus, in the statement above, 2 is the coefficient of s. Moreover, in algebra, we do not place the multiplication sign between the coefficient and the letter. Thus our statement above will read Harry's speed is equal to 2s

We can now express the situation we described in words in two very brief statements:

Let s = Tom's speed

Then   2s = Harry's speed

and if we know Tom's speed we have a mathematical statement which enables us to calculate Harry's speed.

This, of course, is not the only way of expressing the situation outlined. If Harry is travelling twice as fast as Tom, then Tom is travelling half as fast as Harry and we could have said:

Let z = Harry's speed

Then   ½z = Tom's speed.

Alternatively we could have put it in this form:

Let z = Harry's speed and let s = Tom's speed

Then z = 2s

and also   s = ½z

All these different expressions are ways of expressing the same thing, and it does not matter really which expression you come up with. Sometimes one is more useful than another — that is all. If you wish to find Harry's speed (z) and we know Tom's speed (s), then z = 2s is probably the most straightforward. If, however, we wish to find Tom's speed when we know Harry's, then s = ½z is probably the easier. Now when we consider z = 2s we say that z is the SUBJECT OF THE EQUATION; when we consider s = ½z, then s is the subject. A good general rule is that you should consider what it is you are trying to discover and put that as the subject of the equation.

Suppose the equation you have come up with is z = 2s, but the problem continues, "if Harry is travelling at 54 kilometres an hour, how fast was Tom travelling?" We know that everyone will know immediately that the answer is 27 kilometres an hour, but we are not concerned with this. Not all problems are as simple as this one so let us look at the question more closely. We wish to find Tom's speed and to do this we must develop an equation with s as the subject. But the equation we have developed is z = 2s. So how do we go about changing the subject of this equation from z to s?

To learn how to do this let us take an apparently stupid equation

$$8 = 8$$

Suppose now we divide the left hand side of the equation by 2, giving us 4. To maintain the equality we must also divide the right hand side by 2, i.e.

$$^8/_2 = {}^8/_2 \text{ or } 4 = 4$$

If, instead of dividing by two, we had added 4 to the left hand side of the equation, it would have become $8 + 4$ or 12. To maintain the equality we would have had to add four to the right hand side also. So

$$8 + 4 = 8 + 4 \text{ or } 12 = 12$$

From this we can derive a fundamental rule of equations "whatever we do to one side of the equation, we must do exactly the same thing to the other side."

Let us now go back to the equation $z = 2s$ and attempt to make s the subject. We can easily obtain an s on the right hand side of the equation if we divide by two i.e.

$$2s \div 2 = 2s \times \tfrac{1}{2} = s$$

But to keep the equality we must also divide the left hand side by two.

$$^z/_2 = {}^{2s}/_2 \text{ or } z \times \tfrac{1}{2} = 2s \times \tfrac{1}{2}$$

Therefore
$$\tfrac{1}{2}z = s \Rightarrow s = \tfrac{1}{2}z.$$

Do not be worried by this peculiar sign $\Rightarrow$. It is used a great deal in mathematics, but all it means is "which is the same thing as."

If you have understood this very simple example, you will have realised that the trick in algebra is to be able to set up the model, that is, to express the problem in mathematical terms. So let us look at one or two more difficult examples to see how this is done.

Example 1

A man can run half as fast again as his daughter. In a race he gives her 22 metres start. Find an expression for the distance between them when they have been running for 20 seconds.

Here the distance between them depends on the speeds at which they are running, so

Let x metres per second be the speed of the daughter
Then $1\tfrac{1}{2}x = {}^{3x}/_2 = $ the speed of the father.

In 20 seconds the daughter will travel 20x metres, but, having been given 22 metres start she will be $20x + 22$ metres from the starting line. In the meantime the father will have run $^{3x}/_2 \times 20$ metres and so will be 30x metres from the starting line.

The distance between the two runners then will be the difference between $(20x + 22)$ metres and $(30x)$ metres. If we let d represent this distance we may say

$$d = 20x + 22 - 30x = 22 - 10x$$

Now, we cannot solve this problem unless we know the value of x, (the speed of the daughter), and you will discover later how to solve such problems. For the moment we will merely look at the expression as it stands.

Firstly we know that if (20x + 22) is greater than 30x the daughter will be in the lead, and (22 − 10x) will be positive. On the other hand if (20x + 22) is less than 30x, the father will be leading and (22 − 10x) will be negative.

Secondly you will note that we do not need to know, or to calculate the speed of the father in order to solve the problem. It is sufficient to know the speed of the daughter. Think for a minute as to why this should be so. Can you see that it is because we have expressed everything in terms of x (the daughter's speed)?

Thirdly, the expression we have tells us the value of d if we know the value of x. We can very easily find an expression which will tell us the value of x if we know what d is.

$$d = 22 - 10x$$

Subtract 22 from both sides

$$d - 22 = 22 - 10x - 22$$

so

$$d - 22 = -10x$$

Divide both sides by 10

$$\frac{d - 22}{10} = \frac{-10x}{10}$$

so

$$\frac{d - 22}{10} = -x$$

Multiply both sides by −1

$$-1 \times \frac{(d - 22)}{10} = -1 \times -x$$

so

$$\frac{22 - d}{10} = x \Rightarrow x = \frac{22 - d}{10}$$

Example 2

We know that to convert the temperature given in degrees Centigrade to the Fahrenheit scale, we multiply the temperature by ⁹/₅ and then add 32. Find an expression which will enable us to convert degrees Fahrenheit to the Centigrade scale.

We will let F be the temperature in degrees Fahrenheit and C be the temperature in degrees Centigrade.

Now we are told that:

$$F = (\tfrac{9}{5} \times C) + 32 = \tfrac{9C}{5} + 32 = \tfrac{9C}{5} + \tfrac{160}{5}$$

$$= \frac{9C + 160}{5}$$

To obtain the expression we want we must make C the subject of the equation and we proceed as follows.

$$F = \frac{9C + 160}{5}$$

Multiply both sides by 5

$$5F = \frac{9C + 160}{5} \times 5$$
$$= 9C + 160$$

Subtract 160 from both sides

$$5F - 160 = 9C + 160 - 160$$
$$= 9C$$

Divide both sides by 9

$$\frac{5F - 160}{9} = \frac{9C}{9} = C$$

$$C = \frac{5F - 160}{9}$$

Example 3

The total cost of producing a particular commodity consists of £513 per week in fixed costs, £10 per unit produced in variable costs and 50 pence per unit produced in depreciation. The revenue earned per week is equal to £15 per unit. Assuming that all goods produced are sold during the same week, find an expression for total weekly profit.

Here both the costs and the revenue depend on output, so we will begin by saying:

Let x = the number of units produced weekly.

If our revenue is £15 per unit and we sell all we produce,

Total Weekly Revenue = £15x

When we consider costs, we have to consider three different elements of cost. Our Fixed Costs are given as £513 per week, and this remains the same however much we produce. Our variable costs at £10 per unit will total £10x per week, and our depreciation charge at 50 pence per unit will total £½x or £$\frac{x}{2}$ per week. Thus

Total Weekly Cost = £513 + £10x + £$\frac{x}{2}$

Since Profit = Revenue − Costs

Total Weekly Profit = £15x − (£513 + £10x + £$\frac{x}{2}$)
$$= £(15x - 513 - 10x - \tfrac{x}{2})$$

We must now collect together all the terms containing x. Fifteen x minus ten x minus one half of x is equal to four and one half x. That is

$$15x - 10x - \tfrac{1}{2}x = 4\tfrac{1}{2}x = \tfrac{9x}{2}$$

Thus total weekly profit = £$(\frac{9x}{2} - 513)$

Notice that although we are dealing in algebraic terms, they obey all the rules of arithmetic. Thus minus plus becomes minus, when we deduct costs from revenue, and $15x - 10x = 5x$.

We cannot, of course, say $15x - 10y = 5(x-y)$. An expression such as this is the same as saying 15 overcoats minus 10 loaves. It must be left as it is because we cannot deduct loaves from overcoats. But $15x - 10x$ is the same as saying 15 metres minus 10 metres. Even in algebra we can still add like to like and subtract like from like.

Assignment Exercises

24.1x In Example 1, begin the calculation by saying
        Let y be the speed of the father.
        and carry on to derive an expression giving us the value of d. Verify that the expression you obtain is equal to that given in the text by calculating the value of the d in both cases given that the daughter is running at a speed of 2 metres per second.

24.2 My gross income is £x per year, but taxes take £t leaving an actual income of £n per year. Write down four equations corresponding to this situation.

24.3 A cricketer's batting average (a) depends on the number of innings he has played (n) and the total runs he has scored (t). Write down an equation for (n) in terms of (t) and (a) and for (t) in terms of (n) and (a).

24.4 An article is normally sold at a price £p, but in a sale it is reduced by £r and offered at £s. Write an equation giving (s) in terms of (p) and (r), an equation giving (p) in terms of (r) and (s), and an equation giving (r) in terms of (p) and (s). Can you think of a fourth equation which relates (p), (r) and (s)?

24.5x George who is younger than Fred will be exactly half Fred's age in 4 years. Let x be George's present age and y be Fred's present age. Find y in terms of x, and then change the subject of the formula, finding x in terms of y.

Chapter 25

Simple Equations

Learning Objectives:

At the end of your study of this chapter you should be able to:

1. derive simple equations from given information,

2. change the subject of such equations to solve for the unknown quantity.

Simple Equations

So far we have concerned ourselves with considering x as an unknown quantity. We shall now try to determine the actual quantity that x represents. Initially, we shall be concerned with equations with just one unknown quantity (which we shall probably call x). Moreover, the information in the equation will refer only to x to the power one: it will NOT contain x^2, x^7, $x^{1/2}$ etc. We usually call equations restricted in this way *simple equations*. The key to solving simple equations is contained in the rule we derived in the previous section: if we perform any arithmetic operation to one side of the equation, then we must perform the same operation to the other side.

Example 1

$$8x + 13 = 109 \dots \dots (i)$$

What we should do in this case is remove all 'non x' terms from the left hand side. Now, 13 is a 'non x' term, and we can remove it by subtracting 13 from the left hand side. Of course, we must also subtract 13 from the right hand side.

$$8x + 13 - 13 = 109 - 13$$
$$\Rightarrow 8x = 96 \dots \dots (ii)$$

The next stage is to remove the coefficient of x, and we can do this by dividing eight into both sides:

$$8x \div 8 = 96 \div 8$$
$$\Rightarrow x = 12 \dots \dots (iii)$$

So we can conclude that in this case, x, the unknown quantity has a value of twelve. Compare equation iii with equation i and you will notice that we have progressively simplified the left hand side until it contains simply x. If we attempt to do this with all equations, then we have a logical method for their solution.

Sometimes, however, we meet equations which have x terms on both the left hand side and the right hand side.

Example 2

$$8x - 9 = 3x + 21$$

Firstly we can remove the 'non x' terms from the left hand side by adding 9 to both sides:

$$8x - 9 + 9 = 3x + 21 + 9$$
$$\Rightarrow 8x = 3x + 30$$

Now we must remove the x term from the right hand side by subtracting 3x from both sides:

$$8x - 3x = 3x + 30 - 3x$$
$$\Rightarrow 5x = 30$$

Finally, we remove the coefficient of x by dividing 5 into both sides:

$$5x \div 5 = 30 \div 5$$
$$\Rightarrow x = 6$$

Our basic rule for handling equations is that if we perform any arithmetic operation to one side of an equation then we must perform the same operation to the other side. We must be particularly careful when we are performing multiplication or division. Let us return again to the equation:

$$8x + 13 = 109$$

We already know that in this case x = 12. Now suppose we decide to multiply both sides by 3:

$$3(8x + 13) = 3 \times 109$$
$$\Rightarrow 24x + 39 = 327$$

You should check that this equation still holds good when x = 12 Notice that if we wish to multiply both sides of an equation by some number (call it n), then *we must multiply every separate term in the equation by n*. The same applies to division. We can now use this rule to solve equations involving fractions.

Example 3 $\qquad 3x/8 - \frac{1}{2} = x/6$

The first step is to remove the fractions, and we can do this by multiplying throughout by 24, the lowest common denominator of 8, 2 and 6.

$$3x/8 \times 24 - \frac{1}{2} \times 24 = x/6 \times 24$$
$$\Rightarrow 9x - 12 = 4x$$

Adding 12 to both sides

$$9x - 12 + 12 = 4x + 12$$
$$\Rightarrow 9x = 4x + 12$$

Subtracting 4x from both sides

$$9x - 4x = 4x + 12 - 4x$$
$$\Rightarrow 5x = 12$$

Dividing both sides by 5 $\qquad 5x/5 = 12/5$
$$\Rightarrow x = 2\tfrac{2}{5}$$

Example 4

Probably the use to which you will most frequently put equations is in the solving of problems.

We know that Diophantus of Alexandria spent $\frac{1}{6}$ of his life in childhood, $\frac{1}{12}$ in youth and $\frac{1}{7}$ as a batchelor. Five years after his marriage, a son was born who died 4 years before his father. Diophantus' son lived half as long as his father. Now as Diophantus is reputed to be the first man to use a special symbol to represent an unknown quantity, it would be a fitting tribute to him to use algebra to discover how long he lived.

Let us assume that Diophantus lived for x years

He spent $\frac{x}{6}$ years in childhood

$\quad\quad\quad\frac{x}{12}$ years in youth

and $\quad\frac{x}{7}$ years as a batchelor

So he was unmarried for $\frac{x}{6} + \frac{x}{12} + \frac{x}{7} = \frac{33x}{84}$ years.

Five years after he was married a son was born — that is, when Diophantus was $\frac{33x}{84} + 5$ years old

The son died 4 years before Diophantus — that is, when Diophantus was $x - 4$ years old.

So Diophantus son lived for $x - 4 - (\frac{33x}{84} + 5)$ years.

But we also know that Diophantus' son lived for $\frac{x}{2}$ years, so it follows that

$$x - 4 - (\tfrac{33x}{84} + 5) = \tfrac{x}{2}$$

Removing the bracket $\quad x - 4 - \frac{33x}{84} - 5 = \frac{x}{2}$

Collecting together the like terms

$$\tfrac{51x}{84} - 9 = \tfrac{x}{2}$$

Adding 9 to both sides

$$\tfrac{51x}{84} = \tfrac{x}{2} + 9$$

Subtracting $\frac{x}{2}$ from both sides

$$\tfrac{51x}{84} - \tfrac{x}{2} = 9$$
$$\Rightarrow \tfrac{9x}{84} = 9$$

Multiplying both sides by 84

$$9x = 9 \times 84$$

Dividing both sides by 9

$$x = \frac{9 \times 84}{9}$$
$$x = 84$$

Now it is always advisable to check your solution to any problem, so let us check that Diophantus did indeed live for 84 years.

Diophantus was a child for $84 \times \frac{1}{6}$ years = 14 years

$\quad\quad\quad\quad$ a youth for $84 \times \frac{1}{12}$ years = 7 years

$\quad\quad\quad$ a batchelor for $84 \times \frac{1}{7}$ years = $\underline{12}$ years

$\quad\quad\quad\quad\quad\quad\quad\quad\quad\quad\quad\quad\quad\quad\quad\quad$ 33 years

So Diophantus was married at the age of 33 years, and his son was born when he was $33 + 5 = 38$ years.

His son died when Diophantus was $84 - 4 = 80$ years old, so his son lived for $80 - 38$ years $= 42$ years, or for half the lifespan of Diophantus.

Example 5

For our final example let us return to Fred whom you may remember started all this, and who has now become a wealthy man. He has holdings in three firms, though he will not reveal just how large these holdings are. We do know, however, that his holding in Acme is twice as large as his holding in Imperial, and his holding in International is four times his holding in Imperial. Tax returns tell us that Fred's total holdings in the three firms amount to 7.9 million shells, and company reports give us the following details on shares issued by the three firms:

> Acme 6.5 million shells
>
> Imperial 8.5 million shells
>
> International 4.5 million shells

What fraction of each firm does Fred own?

> Let $\frac{1}{x}$ be the fraction of Imperial owned by Fred

> So he owns $\frac{2}{x}$ths of Acme and $\frac{4}{x}$ths of International.

The value of Fred's holding in Imperial is $\frac{1}{x} \times 8.5 = \frac{8.5}{x}$ and the value of his holding in Acme and International is $\frac{2}{x} \times 6.5$ and $\frac{4}{x} \times 4.5$, that is $\frac{13}{x}$ and $\frac{18}{x}$ respectively.

The total value of his holding then is

$\frac{8.5}{x} + \frac{13}{x} + \frac{18}{x}$ million shells

and as we know the total value of his holdings is 7.9 million

$$\frac{8.5}{x} + \frac{13}{x} + \frac{18}{x} = 7.9$$
$$\Rightarrow \frac{39.5}{x} = 7.9$$

Notice that for the first time we have x as the denominator of the fraction. To remove the fraction, multiply both sides by x

$$39.5 = 7.9x$$

Dividing both sides by 7.9

$$5 = x$$

Now, as we defined $\frac{1}{x}$ as the fraction of Imperial owned by Fred, he must own $\frac{1}{5}$ of Imperial, $\frac{2}{5}$ths of Acme, and $\frac{4}{5}$ths of International. Again, let us check this result:

Value of holding in Acme	$= \frac{2}{5} \times 6.5$	$=$	2.6 million
Imperial	$= \frac{1}{5} \times 8.5$	$=$	1.7 million
International	$= \frac{4}{5} \times 4.5$	$=$	3.6 million

So the total value of his holding is 7.9 million

which agrees with the information given.

Assignment Exercises

25.1 Solve the equations

    a. $3x - 2 = 2x - 1$

    b. $3(x - 2) = 2(x - 1)$

    c. $x + \frac{x}{2} = 3$

25.2x Solve the equations

    a. $\frac{x}{2} + \frac{x}{3} + \frac{x}{4} = 1$

    b. $\dfrac{2(x - 1)}{3} - \dfrac{3(2x + 1)}{4} = \dfrac{x - 2}{5}$

    c. $\dfrac{2x + 1}{2x - 1} = \dfrac{6x + 1}{6x - 2}$

25.3 A man must go 5 kilometres to catch his train to work. He walks part of the way at 3.5 kilometres per hour and jogs the rest of the way at 6 kilometres per hour. If he takes 1 hour 15 minutes to complete his journey, find how far he walks.

25.4x £2800 is invested, partly at 5% and partly at 4%. At the end of the first year £128 is received in interest. How much is invested at 5%?

25.5 A number of two digits is such that the sum of its digits is 10. When the digits are reversed, the number is increased by 36. Find the number.

Chapter 26

Linear Equations

Learning Objectives:

At the end of your study of this chapter you should be able to:

1. **construct and interpret graphs of linear functions,**
2. **understand the meaning of co-ordinates, intercept and gradient of such graphs,**
3. **apply graphical methods to simple, commercial problems,**
4. **construct and draw conclusions from breakeven charts.**

Linear Equations

We have defined algebra as a kind of mathematical shorthand, and we have seen how algebra can be used to state a problem in a concise and convenient form. We saw that if the cost of producing a particular commodity consists of £513 per week in fixed costs, £10 per unit in variable costs and 50 pence per unit in depreciation, then if x units are produced in a week, the total weekly cost (c) is

$$c = 513 + 10x + \frac{x}{2}$$
$$\Rightarrow c = 513 + \frac{21x}{2}$$

Look carefully at this equation and compare it with the equations we examined in the last section and you will notice a significant difference. The equations we examined in the last section had only one unknown quantity, but in the equation above there are two unknown quantities: weekly cost (c) and weekly output (x). Now the difference between these two types of equations has important implications for us. With equations such as

$$8x + 13 = 109,$$

there will be one value, and only one value of x for which this equation holds true. In other words, such an equation has a unique solution. However, there are many values of c and x that satisfies the equation

$$c = 513 + \frac{21x}{2}$$

and a selection of these values is given in the table below.

Output (x)	0	20	30	40	50
Cost (c)	513	723	828	933	1038

You should realise that whatever value we select for x, there will be a corresponding value for c that satisfies the equation

$$c = 513 + \frac{21x}{2}$$

Probably the most convenient way of representing equations like these is to use a graph, so let us graph the relationship between cost and output. Take a piece of graph paper, rule a heavy line down the left hand side (called the vertical axis) and across the bottom of the page (called the horizontal axis). The vertical axis will represent weekly cost, and the horizontal axis will represent weekly output. The next stage is to decide on suitable scaling for the axis. The output is scaled in tens up to 50, and the cost axis is scaled in hundreds up to 1100. This enables us to graph the entire data given in the table. We would plot the information as follows: we notice that when output is 50, cost is £1038. Firstly, we locate the point on the horizontal axis where output is 50, and follow the line running vertically upwards from this point. Now locate the point on the cost axis where output is 1038, and follow the line running horizontally to the right from this point. We mark the place where the lines cross thus: ⊙ We now repeat this procedure for the other information that we have. We can then join up all the points and so obtain a graph of the relationship between cost and output (see Exhibit 26.1). Look carefully at this graph and you will notice that three important points emerge.

1. The graph that we have obtained is a straight line. Now not all graphs are straight lines, but at this level we would be advised to confine ourselves to the understanding of such graphs. Because we obtained a straight line when we plotted cost against output, we call the expression linking these two variables a linear equation. Now if an expression is linear, we need only plot two points in order to graph the relationship (though you would be well advised to plot a third point, as this will act as a check on the other two). So it will be useful to recognise in advance when an equation is linear. How can we do this? The secret is to examine the variables in the relationship (in this case x and c). If both variables are to the power one, the relationship is linear; otherwise, the relationship will be a curve.

2. If we consider the connection between cost and output, then you will surely agree that it makes more sense to say that cost depends on output than to say that output depends upon cost. In other words, output is the independent variable, and cost is the dependent variable. If you glance again at the graph you will notice that the dependent variable is drawn on the vertical axis and the independent variable is drawn on the horizontal axis. Now this is a well recognised convention — a convention you should stick to rigidly if you wish to avoid confusion.

3. The graph we have drawn shows the relationship between cost and output — but it is limited! It is concerned only with levels of output not exceeding 50. Using mathematical jargon, we can state that we have graphed

$$c = 513 + 21x/2$$

for the range

$$0 \leq x \leq 50$$

Now the lower end of this range clearly makes sense: we cannot have a negative output. However, there is no logical reason why the upper limit to output should be 50. Presumably, 50 units is the limit of the firm's productive capacity. This raises the problem of what limits are appropriate when drawing graphs. Now there is no hard and fast rule about this. The best advice we can give you is to examine the independent variable and try to decide what are sensible limits to impose on it. Then calculate the corresponding values for the dependent variable — this will give you limits for the dependent variable. Suppose, for example, the firm's productive capacity is limited to 120 units, then we would scale the horizontal axis from 0 to 120. Now when output is zero, cost is

$$513 + \frac{21 \times 0}{2} = £513$$

and when output is 120, cost is

$$513 + \frac{21 \times 120}{2} = £1773$$

so we could scale the vertical axis between zero and (say) 1800.

Co-ordinates

Sometimes you will meet equations where it is possible for one or both of the variables to have negative values. If we are to graph such equations, then we must extend the horizontal axis (usually called the x axis) to the left, and we must extend the vertical axis (usually called the y axis) downwards. This is done in diag. 26.2. and in fact divides the graph paper into four quadrants: A, B, C and D.

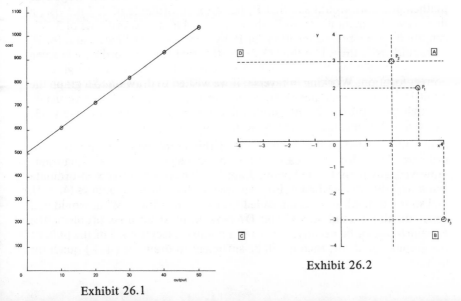

Exhibit 26.1

Exhibit 26.2

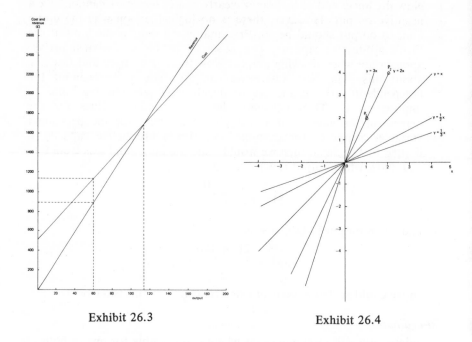

Exhibit 26.3   Exhibit 26.4

Now suppose we pick a point which we shall call P_1: using the axes of the graph it is possible to give the precise location of the point. To do this, imagine a line is drawn vertically from P_1 until it cuts the x axis. We can see that P_1 is directly in line with the value x = 3, or to use the jargon of mathematics, we would say that P_1 has an x co-ordinate of 3. Likewise, a line drawn horizontally from P_1 shows that P_1 has a y co-ordinate of 2. We can, then, give a precise location for P_1 by using its co-ordinates, and for P_1 we would write them like this: (3,2). Notice that the x co-ordinate is given first — it is obviously important to remember this if you are to give the correct location. Working in reverse, if we wished to draw on to a graph the point P_2 with co-ordinates (2,3), we would imagine a line drawn vertically through the point x = 2, and another line drawn horizontally through y = 3. The point P_2 is located at the intersection of these lines.

Any point located in the A quadrant of this graph will have positive co-ordinates, and for this reason, it is often called the (+ +) quadrant. However, any point located in quadrant B will have a positive x co-ordinate but a negative y co-ordinate. For example, P_3 had the co-ordinates (4, −3), and so the B quadrant is often called the (+ −) quadrant. What would you conclude about quadrants C and D? Now in most business problems the variables cannot be negative (profit is a notable exception). For the bulk of the graphs you draw, then it will be sufficient to draw the (+ +) quadrant only.

Breakeven Charts

Let us now return to the cost equation we considered earlier. If c is weekly cost, and x is weekly output, then

$$c = 513 + \frac{21x}{2}$$

Suppose productive capacity is limited to 200 units per week: this would involve a cost of

$$513 + \frac{21 \times 200}{2} = £2613,$$

so we can plot x = 200 against c = 2613. Now if nothing is produced, the firm would still have to incur a weekly fixed cost of £513, i.e.

$$513 + \frac{21 \times 0}{2} = £513$$

so we can plot x = 0 against c = 513, and joining these two points (as in diag. 26.3) we again have the relationship between cost and output graphed.

Now not only do we have information about the costs of the product, but also we have information about the revenue that could be earned from the sale of this product. We know that the product sells for £15 per unit, so if we call the weekly revenue R, then

$$R = 15x$$

It will be of interest to plot cost and revenue on the same graph. Now if nothing is produced, then nothing can be earned, i.e.

$$R = 15 \times 0 = 0$$

so we can plot x = 0 against R = 0. If 150 units are produced, then the revenue earned would be 15 × 150 = £2250, so we can plot x = 15 against R = 2250, and joining the two points we have graphed the relationship between revenue and cost.

Look carefully at the graphs we have drawn, and you will notice that the lines cross when x = 114, so a weekly output of 114 units must have some significance to us. As the lines intersect when x = 114, then when 114 units are produced cost must be exactly equal to revenue. We can check that this is so by substituting x = 114 in the equations for cost and revenue

$$c = 513 + \frac{21 \times 114}{2} = 1710$$

$$R = 15 \times 114 = 1710$$

Now the profit earned by the firm is the difference between the firm's cost and the firm's revenue. If cost is equal to revenue the firm must be earning a zero profit. To appreciate the significance of this output, consider any output less than 114 units — for example 60 units. Reading from the graph, the revenue earned by this output is £900, and the cost incurred is £1143. So the profit generated by this output is 900 − 1143 = −£243, i.e. a loss of £243. In fact, a little thought will tell you that any output less than 114 units will involve a loss. Look at the graph again — for any output less than 114 units, cost is greater than revenue, so the firm must incur a loss on outputs less than 114 units. Moreover, the vertical distance between the cost and revenue lines represents the amount of the loss, so we can see that the closer the output is to zero, the greater is the loss.

If we choose an output greater than 114 units, then revenue will be greater than cost, so the firm must be making a profit. Here, the vertical distance between the cost and revenue lines measures the amount of the profit. Clearly, the greater is the output above 114, the greater is the profit earned. So we can see that 114 is indeed a significant level of output — it marks the boundary between outputs that incur a loss (i.e. outputs less than 114) and outputs that generate a profit (i.e. outputs greater than 114) The output 114, then, is the output at which the firm just breaks even on its activities, and graphs drawn to determine this level of output are called breakeven charts.

The line $y = mx + c$

We have stated that it is more usual to label our axes y (for the vertical) and x (for the horizontal). Let us now examine some equations involving unknown quantities x and y.

$$y = x$$
$$y = 2x$$
$$y = 3x$$
$$y = \tfrac{1}{2}x$$
$$y = \tfrac{1}{3}x$$

As the x and y values are both to the power one, we know that if they are graphed then we would obtain 5 straight lines. The equations are graphed in diag. 26.4, and you should verify for yourself that the lines are correctly positioned. If we examine the lines, then two aspects should be apparent.

1. All of the lines pass through the point (0,0) — called the origin of the graph. Look again at the 5 equations and you will notice how similar they are. The only difference between them is the coefficient of x — in fact we can write the general form for such equations as

$$y = mx.$$

Now all equations of this form will pass through the origin — a fact that you can verify for yourself by choosing any value you wish for m and graphing the equation. A little thought will show why such lines must pass through the origin, as the implication is that in the equation when x = 0, y must equal zero, and substituting these two values in the general expression we can verify this:

$$0 = m \times 0$$

2. The greater the value of m in the equation, the steeper is the slope of the line. In fact, m measures the gradient of the line. Now what do we mean by a gradient? Suppose we saw a sign warning us that we were approaching a hill with a 'one in ten' gradient, then we would visualise a hill like this:

A mathematician, however, would not call this a 'one in ten' gradient; he would rather say that the line had a gradient of $\frac{1}{10}$. In other words, the mathematician calculates the gradient of a line by the formula:

$$\frac{\text{Vertical distance}}{\text{Horizontal distance.}}$$

How, then, would we calculate the gradient of a line drawn on graph paper? Well, the first thing to do is to select any two points on the line. The vertical distance between the points will be the difference in their y co-ordinates and the horizontal distance will be the difference in their x co-ordinates. In other words, we can calculate the gradient of the line by taking

$$\frac{\text{Change in y}}{\text{Change in x}}$$

Now we have stated that the value of m in the equation $y = mx$ measures the gradient of the line, so let us check that the line $y = 2x$ does have a gradient of 2. Selecting two points on this line (see fig. 26.4) P_1 has co-ordinates (2,4) and P_2 has co-ordinates (1,2). The change in y is $4 - 2 = 2$, and the change in x $= 2 - 1 = 1$. So

$$m = \frac{\text{Change in y}}{\text{Change in x}} = \frac{2}{1} = 2$$

We shall now consider another set of equations

$$y = 2x + 2$$
$$y = 2x + 1$$
$$y = 2x \text{ i.e. } 2x + 0$$
$$y = 2x - 1$$
$$y = 2x - 2$$

All of these equations have the same value of m, so they must all have the same gradient. In other words, if we were to graph these equations, we would obtain a set of parallel lines. All the lines have the same *slope,* it is their *position* on the graph that varies. Look again at the set of equations: in the first case, to obtain y values we add a constant amount 2 to twice the x values, in the second case we add a constant amount 1 to twice the x values. It would seem reasonable then, to state a general form for the equation as

$$y = mx + c$$

If you now carefully examine the lines and also glance at their equations, you should notice that each line cuts the y axis when y = c – for example y = 2. x + 2 cuts the y axis when y = 2, y = 2x + 1 cuts the y axis when y = 1. A little thought will show that this must be so. Any line (say, y = 2x + 2) cuts the y axis when x = 0, and when x = 0

$$y = 2 \times 0 + 2 = 2$$

Let us summarise what we have learned: plotting the equation y = mx + c will give us a straight line, m gives the line's gradient, and c tells us the intercept, i.e. where the line cuts the y axis. This information enables us to plot lines from equations quickly and efficiently. Suppose, for example, we wished to plot the equation y = 5x + 10. Well we know the line cuts the y axis at y = 10. We also know that the gradient of the line is 5 = vertical distance over horizontal distance. So from the point y = 10, move 1 unit horizontally and 5 units vertically. This enables the line to be drawn

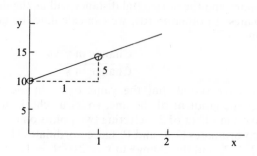

Again, using our knowledge of y = mx + c, we can find the equation of a line from seemingly limited data. Suppose we know that to produce 100 units costs £9000, and to produce 150 units costs £13,000. What is the equation linking cost and output? If we call cost y and output x, then the equation is y = mx + c, and we require values for m and c.

$$m = \frac{\text{change in y (cost)}}{\text{change in x (output)}} = \frac{4000}{50} = 80$$

So the equation is y = 80x + c, Also, we know that when x = 100, y = 9000, i.e.

$$9000 = 80 \times 100 + c$$
$$c = 1000,$$

So the equation we require is

$$y = 80x + 1000$$

Of course, we can now use this equation to find the cost of any output. To produce 180 units, for example, costs 80 × 180 + 1000 = £15,400.

Assignment Exercises

26.1x You decide to have a Spanish holiday and convert your holiday savings into pesetas. The rate of exchange obtained from your bank is 148 pesetas to the pound. Draw a graph which would enable you to convert pesetas into pounds for amounts up to £5. Read off the sterling value of 115 pesetas, 326 pesetas and 428 pesetas.

26.2x List relationships from the real world that could be described by the relationships $y = mx$ and $y = mx + c$.

26.3 Draw the graph of the line $y = -2x + 4$. What do you notice? What is the significance of the sign of m in the equation $y = mx + c$?

26.4x A transport manager is instructed to hire a car for the use of the company directors. He approaches a car hire firm who quote three different weekly tariffs.

tariff 1. A fixed charge of £20 per week.

tariff 2. A charge of 7½p per mile travelled.

tariff 3. A fixed charge of £5 per week with an additional charge of 5p per mile travelled.

Draw a graph showing how the charge varies according to mileage travelled according to which tariff is used. Prepare a set of rules for deciding which tariff should be used.

26.5 It is known that the relationship between total cost and output is linear. It costs £5350 to produce 2000 units in a week and £6100 to produce 2500 units. What are the variable costs and fixed weekly costs of production?

Chapter 27

The Organisation of Data

Learning Objectives:

At the end of your study of this chapter you should be able to:

1. **understand why and how statistical data is collected and used,**
2. **distinguish between discrete and continuous data, and between dependent and independent variables,**
3. **understand the principles of good tabular presentation,**
4. **construct tables from raw data,**
5. **interpret, analyse and present a report on tabular information.**

The modern business world has a great hunger for facts and data. Well organised data improves our understanding of problems, and helps us to take decisions wisely. Badly organised data is little better than worthless. Unfortunately, you will all-too-often come across data that is not organised – most firms have filing cabinets full of data that someone intends to organise 'one day'. In this chapter we will suggest methods of how data can be organised for meaningful analysis – we will take our first steps in the rewarding (though often confusing) world of statistics.

Most people are vaguely aware that Statistics is concerned with figures in one way or another. Equally, we think, most people are rather distrustful of the statistics that they see quoted in the press or on television. We must admit that we ourselves have some sympathy for the housewife who is told on the news one evening that the cost of living has gone up by only 2% this month, and then finds in the shops next morning that everything she buys has, in fact, risen in price by between 5% and 10%. When this sort of thing happens it is no wonder that people get the impression that statistics can be made to prove anything. And yet — if our figures are accurate and the information is presented properly — how can this be so? We would like you to believe right from the start that no genuine statistician will ever deliberately misrepresent information or use it to mislead people. It can be done of course. In life many people are unscrupulous, and later in this course we will tell you how they misrepresent information, with the strict warning that *you* must never do it.

The great weakness of Statistics, is that to the man in the street who has never studied it, the methods used by statisticians are a closed book. We hope that as you work through this course your own personal book will be opened and that you will understand the dilemma in which our housewife finds herself.

But before we begin to think of the techniques you will use and the calculations you will perform, let us stop for a minute to consider the raw material you will be dealing with.

Suppose that the student union in your school or college wishes to obtain information about its members — their age, sex, home area, whether they live in a flat, or at home, or in lodgings and so on. How would the union secretary go about collecting this information? The most obvious way is for each student to be issued with a questionnaire, posing the relevant questions, and asking for it to be returned to the secretary's office. No doubt some of the forms will be incorrectly completed: some students may genuinely misunderstand the questions: some may refuse to answer certain questions which they regard as personal: doubtless some, in the fashion of the great petitions of the nineteenth century, will be signed by Queen Victoria or Karl Marx. Yet, with all its faults, this mass of completed questionnaires is the basic raw material for the statistical report that the union secretary wishes to produce.

Raw material such as this, collected at first hand, in response to specific questions is known as *primary data*; its characteristics are that it is obtained directly for the purpose of the survey which is being undertaken, and is, as yet, unanalysed.

Now, if your union secretary is lucky, he may also be able to obtain a great deal of information from the College administration, who, using enrolment forms as their primary data, may already have produced for their own purposes a fair amount of statistical information about students. Such information will, of course, have been produced for college purposes and may not be exactly what the union wants: but it is often useful additional information. Such data, which has already been collected for another, and different purpose, we know as *secondary data*. Usually it is of less use than primary data since it has already been processed and the original questionnaire is unlikely to have asked all the questions you would like to have asked. But whether it is primary or secondary, there can be very little statistical information which was not at one time to be found only in a pile of completed forms or questionnaires. The main task of any writer on statistics is to explain what the statistician does with his raw data between collecting it and presenting his report. So let us go back to your union secretary.

It is obvious that no-one would sit down and write a report in the form of

'Mary Smith is 17, lives in Durham, and is in lodgings here; Susan Yeung comes from Singapore and is in lodgings here ...'

We might as well hand over the completed forms to anyone who is interested since all that this type of report does is detail the information which is already given in detail on the questionnaire.

We can get a clue about the next stage of the analysis if we ask ourselves what it is that the union really wants to know. Surely the sort of information that is really wanted is how many students are 16, how many are 17 and so on; what percentage of students live at home; what proportion of students come from overseas. It is not the individual we are interested in so much as total numbers in given categories. The categories in this investigation may be age, sex, type of residence, number of hours a week spent on study and so on. Within each category students will vary. Some are 16; others are 17; some live at home, others in lodgings. We call each of these categories a *variable* because within each category students will vary. So we may now say that we are interested in a number of variables such as age, and more specifically in the value we can assign to each student within the range of values over which the variable extends. We may find, for example, that when we consider the variable 'age', 267 students are aged 17, 164 are aged 18 and so on up to the eldest student. The numbers of students whom we can place at each value of the variable we will call the *frequency,* because it tells us how often we will come across a student with this particular characteristic (that is, aged 18, or doing 27 hours a week private study, or travelling more than 15 miles to college). Thus the first step we must take is to decide what aspects of student life we are interested in and count up how many students are found within each of these categories. In so doing we are simplifying our data — reducing it to a more manageable form. In the process some detail is lost. We no longer know how old Brenda Jones is; but if we are interested we still have her completed questionnaire. On the other hand we do know that 267 students are aged 17 as well as much other general information.

Once we have reached this stage we are in a position to summarise our results in the form of a table and our work begins to look more like that of a statistician. Probably as a first tentative step we would produce a simple table dealing with only one variable. It might appear like this:

Age of Students attending ABC College

Age (the Variable)	Number of Students (the Frequency)
17	267
18	164
19	96
20	74
21 and over	23
	624

There is nothing wrong with our producing 15 or 20 tables like this, each concerned with a single variable, but surely it is better for presentation purposes if we could produce a small number of compound tables each showing several variables at once. Thus we could construct a double table showing the two variables, age and sex of students at the same time.

We have constructed this table by listing one of our variables vertically (age) and the other horizontally (sex). There is no golden rule, but it generally looks better if we tabulate the variable with the greater number of values vertically and that with the smaller number of values horizontally. Notice too that we have totalled both the vertical and the horizontal columns and that this adds to our information. We not only have the age distribution of male students and of female students but also the age distribution of the entire student population, and the total number of male and female students.

Age	Number of Students		
	Male	Female	Total
17	151	116	267
18	98	66	164
19	70	26	96
20	52	22	74
21 +	18	5	23
Total	389	235	624

You may of course still argue that the table is still concerned with only one variable, age, and that all we have is two age distributions. Let us then extend our table to consider three variables, age, sex and type of accommodation. Obviously now we must further subdivide either the horizontal or the vertical columns. Again it is a good general guide to say that we believe it better to subdivide the horizontal rather than the vertical columns. But in doing this the variable in the vertical column tends to become the more important. So we must consider which is the most important variable, and this often depends on what we are trying to show. Let us suppose that in this case we are aiming to show that the type of accommodation a student occupies depends on his or her age. In this case we will list the ages vertically and subdivide the horizontal columns. Our table may now appear like this:

Age	Number of Students						
	At Home		In Lodgings		In Flat		Total
	M	F	M	F	M	F	
17	112	92	16	20	23	4	267
18	64	42	24	16	10	8	164
19	31	12	28	7	11	7	96
20	8	4	16	10	28	8	74
21 +	2	3	3	1	13	1	23
Total	217	153	87	54	85	28	—
	370		141		113		624

You will readily appreciate what a vast amount of information a table such as this can give us: the number of students who live at home, subdivided into male and female and classified according to age, as well as the same information for those who are living in lodgings or living in a flat. You can understand too how much more information could be incorporated if we subdivided further the horizontal axis as well as some subdivision of the vertical axis such as the area of origin followed in each case by the age range.

There is one problem — the more we subdivide, the more complicated our table becomes, and there comes a time when it is so difficult to read it and understand it that we find that clarity has been lost rather than gained. It is true that one treble table, such as the one above, is better than three single tables. It is equally true that if we are considering eight or nine variables, three treble tables are better than one very complex one. And if you are wondering why clarity is so important think again what we have been doing. We have collected primary data, simplified it and classified it, and are now trying to present it to our union executive in a readily digestible form. How much notice do you think the executive will take of us if they cannot understand what our tables are all about?

Just in case you are ever in the position of having to construct tables to present the raw material you have collected, there are several points you should bear in mind. Let us call them the 'Principles of Good Tabulation'.

(a) Every table should have a short explanatory title at the head. At the end you should put a note of the source of the information you have used, whether it is based on your own survey or secondary data.

(b) The unit of measurement should be clearly stated, and if necessary defined in a footnote. Not many people, for example, would know offhand what a 'Long Ton' is. In addition the heading to every column should be clearly shown.

(c) Use different rulings to break up a larger table — double lines or thicker lines add a great deal to the ease with which a table is understood.

(d) Whenever you feel it useful insert both column and row totals.

(e) If the volume of data is large, two or three simple tables are better than one cumbersome one.

(f) Before you start to draft a table be quite sure what you want it to show. Remember that although most people read from left to right, most people find it easier to absorb figures which are in columns rather than rows.

As with most things practice is the best way of learning, and these principles will soon become second nature after you have drafted a few tables for yourself.

You might well ask at this stage whether this is all there is in the subject of Statistics. If it were you would all end up with distinctions. But the most important part of the work is still to come. No statistician (or student) worth his salt is content with a mere list of figures. He now begins to ask questions, the most important of which is 'What do the figures tell me?' We now begin to analyse the figures, and statistical techniques are largely methods of extracting the utmost possible information from the data we have available. We could, for example, calculate the average age of students living at home, and compare it with the average age of students living in flats to try to determine whether we are right in assuming that the younger student will tend to live at home and the older student tend to be a flat-dweller. We can do the same thing for both male and female students to see if they behave differently. Let us simply say that there are many questions that the statistician can ask even from the simple data we have used so far.

We said earlier that the most obvious way for the union secretary to collect his data was to issue a questionnaire to each and every student. The results of his enquiry would cover every single student in the college – it will refer to what statisticians call the *population* of students. Beware of this term population. In statistics it does not mean the number of people living in a particular area. What it implies is that we have examined or obtained information about every single member of a particular group we are investigating. Thus we can talk of a population of telegraph poles, a population of shaggy-haired dogs, a population of ball-bearings and so on.

But is there any need for us to examine the population of students attending the college? If we wish to save time and money can we not do as so many public opinion polls do and take a sample of students? We could issue the questionnaire to, say 60 or 70 students only, or perhaps to every tenth student, and so reduce our raw data considerably. The *sample results* we obtain can then be applied to the population of students: if 12% of the sample live at home, we will argue that about 12% of all students in the college live at home.

Now, you may well argue that this can lead to wildly inaccurate results; and if you consider some of the results of public opinion polls in recent years it is apparent that things can, and do, go wrong. The sample chosen may be too small; it may not be representative of the population; the error arising as a result may mislead us. At this stage we will merely point out that in taking a sample we are in good company: an extremely high percentage of government statistics such as the statistics of Household Expenditure are based on samples which, on the face of it, appear to be ludicrously small.

If you think back now to the questions we suggested that you might ask about what our tables can tell us, you will realise that most of them involve a more detailed study of one variable only — the age of females living at home; the age of males living in flats. When we do begin to analyse you will appreciate that this is usual. The table presents several variables at once, but we extract just one of them at a time for further examination. In a few cases we will use two variables at once, when we are asking if there is a relationship between them such that one affects the other or that both move in sympathy. But in this foundation course we will never ask you to get involved in the analysis of three or more variables at once — which is indeed a complex matter.

The Frequency Distribution

The problems we have met so far are simple. We have had to deal with only five age groups of students, and hence our tables are compact and easily presented. Let us now turn to far more complex data collected from the community as a whole. Government departments collect a mass of detailed information on which to base future policy and one of the areas which they investigate closely is the weekly earnings of adults aged 21 and over who are in full-time employment each April. In the United Kingdom it seems that earnings in the recent past ranged from about £10 a week to £80 a week and more. You can imagine how cumbersome a table we would have if we listed every single wage level as we listed each age. Theoretically we might have to list earnings at intervals of a penny, and so have a table of over 70,000 lines — a ridiculous situation. Fortunately we can simplify this. Do you think it really matters to us whether a worker is receiving £11.90 or £12.15 a week? We would probably be content to say that they both receive about £12 a week. Extending this further, we could argue that if we are looking at the pattern of wages we would be satisfied to combine together all those who received between £10 and £12 per week, or even between £10 and £15 per week. Now this is precisely what the government does in many of its published statistics. It does not say that 157 people receive £10.21 a week, 362 receive £10.37 and so on, but merely that 100,000 people receive over £10 but less than £15 per week. Earnings are stated in convenient bands or classes, and certainly we get a much better picture of earnings from this than we could ever get from a table listing 70,000 different levels of earnings.

To show you the effect of combining different values of the variable into a single class we reproduce below a table taken from the Annual Abstract of Statistics for the United Kingdom.

Distribution of Earnings of Adults in Full-time Employment

Earnings (£)		No. of Workers (millions)
10 and under	15	0·1
15	20	1·1
20	25	2·1
25	30	2·3
30	35	1·9
35	40	1·4
40	45	0·8
45	50	0·5
50	60	0·4
60	70	0·3
70	80	0·1
		11·0

Source: U.K. Annual Abstract of Statistics

A table such as this is known as a *frequency distribution* and is very common in statistical work. The variable we are considering, earnings, can take any value within the relevant group — it need not be an integer (or whole number). You might object of course that a worker cannot be paid £12.3762 a week, and in this sense it is not true to say that wages can take *any* value. On the other hand, subject to the minimum currency unit of Britain being £0.005 or a half penny, it is a fair statement to make. This type of data is known as *continuous* data. Other examples of continuous data are ages, petrol consumption per week, miles travelled by British Rail, and you can probably think of dozens of others yourself.

We might, on the other hand, be considering a data variable which can have only set values. If we are considering the number of seats in a cinema there can only be a certain number, 875 or 358, not 364.34 or 786.93. Similarly, the number of journeys made by bus, the population of a city, the number of students sitting an examination, must be integers. Data of this kind which can have only a limited number of values is known as *discrete* data. An example of a frequency distribution using discrete data would be a frequency distribution showing the value of orders received by a departmental store during the winter months.

Orders Received

Value of Order (£000)		Number of Orders Received
0 and under	5	20
5	10	51
10	15	139
15	20	116
20	25	31
25	30	14
30 and over		5
		376

Few people would prefer to be faced with a table thousands of items long when they can have instead a manageable frequency distribution like these. Yet, something is lost. Most distributions are constructed, as was our table of wages, using groups or classes which may in some cases be very wide indeed. We have sacrificed detail for the sake of presenting a picture which can be absorbed fairly simply. It might seem, of course, that the use of class intervals will prevent our using the frequency distribution as the basis for further work. Naturally it does create a problem, and to overcome it we have to make an assumption. Going back to our wage data, we do not know the exact wages of the 1.9 million people earning between £30 and £35 a week. To enable further work to be carried out we assume that all the 1.9 million workers earn a wage precisely at the centre of the class we are considering, i.e.

$$\frac{30 + 34.99}{2} = 32.495 \text{ or } £32.50$$

Since you will be using this mid-point of a class many times, let us stress the importance of accuracy here. You must firstly consider whether the distribution is continuous or discrete. Consider a table showing cinema size determined by number of seats. One class may be cinemas ranging upwards from 200 seats but having less than 300 seats. Here the data is discrete; the minimum number of seats is 200 and the maximum is 299. The mid-point of this class is

$$\frac{200 + 299}{2} = 249.5$$

But if the same class, 200 and under 300, referred to continuous data, say the number of miles travelled by car, the minimum and maximum values of the group are 200 and 299.999. Hence the mid-point of the class becomes

$$\frac{200 + 299.999}{2} = 250$$

You will find, if you look at any published statistical tables, that in many cases no limits are given for the first and last classes. An income distribution showing annual income might begin merely with 'Under £660' and end up with the group 'Over £50,000'. Such open-ended classes create problems and we will give you a few hints on how to handle them later.

One of the most difficult problems you will have in building up a frequency distribution from raw data is to decide on what class intervals to use. Obviously, a great deal will depend on the data you have available, but a few general guidelines may help. Firstly, try not to choose class intervals which will reduce the number of groups below five or six. If you do the data will be so compressed that no pattern emerges. Naturally the rule is not infallible — E.E.C. have published statistics of farm sizes giving only three classes. These three, however, correspond to a generally accepted international definition of small, medium and large farms. Our advice is that you should try not to emulate E.E.C. Equally, at the other extreme, do not have too many classes. About fifteen or sixteen is the maximum. The problem here is not only the difficulty of absorbing lengthy tables, but also the fact that each group will have a very low, or in some cases, even a zero frequency. And this leads to another point. At the upper end of the table, if you stick slavishly to a single class interval you may well find that several consecutive groups have no members while a higher group has a frequency of two or three. In these circumstances you should sacrifice the idea of equal class widths and combine the several classes into a single wider class.

A good general guide is to take the difference between the minimum and maximum value of the variable (which we call the *range*), and divide by ten. This will give you the right class width (or thereabouts) for the majority of classes, provided that you realise that class width of five or ten, or fifty is better than one of four, or seven or sixty-two, and provided that you take care with the extreme values of the variable.

One final word of caution. Your table must be so constructed that each item of data falls clearly into a given class. Far too many tables have class intervals such as 10 − 20, 20 − 30, 30 − 40 and so on. But suppose an item is exactly 20 or exactly 30, which group do you place it in? If the distribution is continuous it is better to say, 10 and under 20, 20 and under 30; or possibly 10 – 19.9, 20 – 29.9: if the table is discrete you can give the exact limits, 10 – 19, 20 – 29 and so on.

Before we leave this brief description of the frequency distribution it would be an advantage if we show you how to tackle examination questions which ask you to construct a frequency distribution from a mass of figures. For this purpose we will look at a question recently set for the Scottish National Certificate in Business Studies examination.

Example

The following is a record of the percentage marks gained by candidates in an examination:

65	57	57	55	20	54	52	49	58	52
86	39	50	48	83	71	66	54	51	27
30	44	34	78	36	63	67	55	40	56
63	75	55	15	96	51	54	52	53	42
50	25	85	27	75	40	37	46	42	86
16	45	12	79	50	46	46	59	57	50
56	74	50	68	52	61	40	38	57	31
35	93	54	26	67	62	51	52	54	61
93	84	28	66	62	57	45	43	47	33
45	25	77	80	91	67	53	55	51	36

Tabulate the marks in the form of a frequency distribution, grouping by suitable intervals.

Looking at these figures we find that there are 100 marks given ranging from 12 to 96. We have laid down a principle of aiming at somewhere in the region of 10 classes in our frequency distributions and it certainly seems that the best class width in this example would be 10 marks. If we were to use 5 mark intervals we would end up with some 18 classes which is too many; if we use 15 mark intervals we end up with only 6 classes which is too few.

We now have to find out how many of these marks fall within each class, and we recommend that you should do this in this way. Firstly list every class vertically; now take each candidate's marks in turn, and place a dash or a 1, or some other suitable mark against the class into which it falls. Having done this for every mark we can now take each class in turn and add up how many candidates fall into each class. Your rough working will appear something like this. You will notice that for ease of counting we have divided our dashes into groups of five.

10 and under 20	111							3
20 and under 30	ЖӉ	11						7
30 and under 40	ЖӉ	ЖӉ						10
40 and under 50	ЖӉ	ЖӉ	ЖӉ	1				16
50 and under 60	ЖӉ	ЖӉ	ЖӉ	ЖӉ	ЖӉ	ЖӉ	1111	34
60 and under 70	ЖӉ	ЖӉ	111					13
70 and under 80	ЖӉ	11						7
80 and under 90	ЖӉ	1						6
90 and under 100	1111							4
								100

Before you do anything else now, check that the total frequency (that is, the number of dashes) in your rough working is the same as the number of items given in the question. Having done this you are now ready to construct your frequency distribution. Remember, though, all the things that are necessary: the heading of the table, the column headings and the source, if it is available. Getting the table correct is only one part of the answer, although it is an important part. Your final frequency distribution will appear something like this:

Percentage Marks gained by Examination Candidates

. . . . Examination . . . . 19 . .

Marks Awarded		Number of Candidates
10 and under 20		3
20	30	7
30	40	10
40	50	16
50	60	34
60	70	13
70	80	7
80	90	6
90	100	4
		100

Source: Examiners' Report 19 .

We will spend some time later on examining frequency distributions such as this to see what further information they can give us. But whatever distribution we study it has one thing in common with all other frequency distributions — it tells us the magnitude of a variable at a given point in time. There are times however when we need to look at the way the magnitude of a variable changes over fairly long periods of time — for example, we might be considering the way in which the volume of British exports to Hong Kong has changed year by year since 1960. Such a table is called a *time series*. It follows from the nature of the time series that it consists of a series of time periods: years, quarters, months, or even days, with the value of the variable given against each time period. Thus, recently, Barclays Bank conducted a survey of the output of motor vehicles quarter by quarter in each of the Common Market countries. The figures for France represent a typical time series with the value of the variable given quarterly.

Output of Motor Vehicles — France
(monthly averages — thousands)

Year 1	1st quarter	150
	2nd quarter	165
	3rd quarter	104
	4th quarter	113
Year 2	1st quarter	173
	2nd quarter	180
	3rd quarter	124
	4th quarter	184

Source: Barclays Bank Briefing No. 12

In much statistical work a time series of this nature may extend over many years, but you will find it surprising what such a series can tell us.

If you have followed carefully the argument of this chapter it should now be apparent that we are concerned with the collection, simplification, presentation and analysis of information which can be expressed quantitatively. If you do your work well you will get an accurate picture of the data you are studying. There will still be some of you who may claim that figures can be made to prove anything, and to be fair, if the data is misused this may be true. If you ignore parts of the data, and conveniently forget to include calculations and information which is inconvenient or does not support your preconceived ideas, most things are possible. But if you follow your analysis through to the bitter end, using all the information which is available, keeping an open mind and interpreting only what your figures throw up, you cannot but be somewhere near the truth. In a world in which so much reliance is placed on the work of statisticians, where government policy often depends on their findings, and where industrial decisions involving millions of pounds are taken on the basis of statistical analysis, it is important to remember that whether you like what your figures show or not, your task is to interpret what the available data tells us as honestly as you are able.

Assignment Exercises

27.1x *Average Weekly Earnings* of Administrative, Technical and*
Clerical Staff in the Public Sector and in Insurance and Banking
MALES

October	National and Local Government including Education (Teachers) and National Health Service	Nationalised Industries	Insurance and Banking
	£	£	£
1966	26.69	26.25	26.63
1967	27.88	27.13	27.73
1968	29.65	28.95	29.11
1969	32.03	31.18	30.88
1970	36.00	35.83	34.63

*Including earnings of monthly-paid employees converted to a weekly basis.

Source: Department of Employment.

Write a short report in which you bring out the main features of the data given above. Include appropriate derived statistics and illustrate your report with a suitable diagram or graph. O.N.C.

27.2x In 1951, 207 thousand persons received unemployment benefit, 906 thousand persons sickness benefit, 1437 thousand males retirement pensions, 2709 thousand females retirement pensions, 457 thousand received widows' benefit. 217 thousand persons received other National Insurance benefits. In 1971 the corresponding figures for unemployment benefit was 457 thousand, for sickness benefit was 969 thousand, for male retirement pensions 2611 thousand, for female retirement pensions 5196 thousand, for widows' benefit 448 thousand, for other National Insurance benefits 387 thousand. (Source: *Social Trends* 1972.) Tabulate this data, calculate appropriate secondary statistics and include those statistics in your tabulation. Comment briefly on your tabulation. O.N.C.

27.3x An inquiry into the population of a town at 1st April 1974 showed that the total was 297,500 persons of whom 60% were females and 40% males. 50,000 females were aged thirty and under, 60,000 were aged from 31 to 60 and the remainder were over 60 years of age. The corresponding figures for males were 60,000, 39,000 and 20,000. The average family size was 3.5. 75% of the female population lived in the northern area of the town and the remainder in the southern area. Of the males, 20% lived in the southern area. Tabulate the data given showing the analysis of each class of person into areas and age groups. Include actual figures and percentages. Show also the number of families for the town in total. O.N.C.

27.4x The Saturn Finance Company wishes to study for several years (1971, 1972, 1973, 1974) the distribution of its loans according to size of loan (under £100, £100 and under £250, £250 and under £500, £500 and over) and the purpose of the loan (home improvement, car purchase, durable household goods purchase, other).

(a) Prepare a table in which the data can be presented cross-classified by year, size of loan and purpose of loan. Include summary rows and columns for all classifications given.

(b) Insert the following figures in the appropriate cells:

    (1) In 1972, 42.7 per cent of all loans made for home improvements were for £100 and under £250.

    (2) In 1971, 31.4 per cent of all loans made for purchase of cars were for £250 and under £500.

    (3) In 1974, 29.7 per cent of all loans were under £100.

O.N.C.

27.5x While the population of the United Kingdom grew from 38.2 millions in 1901 to 55.8 m in 1972, the increase was not uniform between the regions. Seventy years ago, the south-east was the most populous region with 10.5 m. In mid-1972, its population was an estimated 17.3 m. Both the West Midlands and East Midlands have also grown quickly; the former from 3.0 m to 5.1 m and the latter from 2.1 m to 3.4 m. During the same period, East Anglia's population grew from 1.1 m to 1.7 m, whilst the south-west increased from 2.6 m to 3.8 m.

Despite its generally high birth rate, Northern Ireland's population, whilst growing from 1.2 m in 1901 to 1.5 m in mid-1972, fell as a proportion of total U.K. population. A similar trend is revealed in other economically depressed regions, and both Wales and Scotland, because of losses due to migration, have grown much more slowly than average, Wales from 2.0 m to 2.7 m and Scotland from 4.5 m to 5.2 m. (Source: *New Society and Social Trends,* Modified.) *Note:* not all regions have been included.

Arrange the above data in a suitable table, providing additional columns, in blank, appropriately headed, in which could be inserted derived statistics enabling comparisons to be made.   O.N.C.

27.6x The total number of employees of Core and Peel Ltd. at 31st December 1971 was 10,590, of which 6721 were men, 3106 women and the rest juniors. During 1971 108 men resigned and 74 men were engaged. The corresponding figures for women were 29 and 87 and for juniors 17 and 23. 1386 men, 976 women and 16 juniors were absent sometime during the year due to illness, 509 men, 876 women due to domestic circumstances and 366 men, 272 women and 3 juniors due to other causes. The average weekly wage rate paid to men was £32.00, to women £20.13 and to juniors £18.25. The company worked 50 weeks in the year. Tabulate these details showing suitable totals and sub-totals. Include also:

(a) the numbers employed at 1st January 1971,

(b) an estimate of the total annual wages paid per grade of labour and for the employees in total.   O.N.C.

27.7x (a) The records of the Family Expenditure Survey of 1971 show that in 4642 households interviewed in the survey, the head of the household was in employment. In 1236 households the occupation of the head of the household was 'professional'; 101 earned less than £30 per week; 153 earned £30 but under £40 per week; 194 earned £40 but under £50 per week; the remainder earned £50 or over per week. In 470 households the occupation of the head of the household was 'clerical'. 119 earned less than £30 per week; 129 earned £30 but under £40 per week; 90 earned £40 but under £50 per week; the remainder earned £50 or over per week. In the remaining households the occupation of the head of the household was 'manual'. 930 earned less than £30 per week; 814 earned £30 but under £40 per week; 638 earned £40 but under £50 per week; the remainder earned £50 or over per week. Tabulate this data.

(b) Using your table as an example list the basic rules which should be observed when tabulating statistical data.   O.N.C.

27.8x In 1970, 44,000 houses were purchased with a local authority mortgage (total sum advanced = £154m) and 32,000 with the help of insurance companies (£154m advanced) whilst building societies lent £1986 m to 540,000 purchasers. These figures compare with 56,000 (£168 m), 34,000 (£124m) and 504,000 (£1,477m) in 1967, and 19,000, 40,000 and 460,000 houses purchased in 1969 with the help of loans of £69m, £179m, and £1556 m from local authorities, insurance companies and building societies respectively (abridged from *New Society*).

(a) Arrange the above data in concise tabular form.

(b) Prepare a table in blank, with suitable headings in which could be inserted derived statistics from the above figures which would facilitate the making of comparisons.   O.N.C.

27.9. (a) List clearly the steps taken in forming a frequency distribution from a set of about 1000 observations giving reasons where necessary.

(b) Construct a frequency distribution using the following 100 observations:

Lives of electric light bulbs, in hours, to the last complete hour.

690	701	722	684	662	699	715	742	726	716
728	705	693	691	688	706	707	691	701	713
740	662	676	738	714	703	695	692	699	685
698	687	703	726	699	692	714	724	664	689
694	705	717	682	717	707	696	697	681	708
712	733	705	673	694	716	745	692	719	701
679	680	654	691	669	685	725	704	724	714
689	702	710	696	697	709	721	677	680	671
685	724	736	696	688	692	728	656	690	695
702	696	708	698	710	682	694	676	700	663

      O.N.C.

27.10x The following is a record of the heights in centimetres of a sample of 85 servicemen:

169 179 183 186 166 181 177 173 167 193 176 183 162 170 186 174
188 165 168 174 170 176 186 177 185 175 179 166 190 182 182 180
194 177 184 175 168 181 180 172 178 192 175 189 180 175 183 191
172 188 180 176 185 178 179 173 165 170 178 181 181 189 187 191
179 196 179 182 171 169 171 184 198 182 175 190 187 176 164 187
167 185 177 184 178

Tabulate the above data in the form of a frequency distribution, using as intervals 160 cm and under 165 cm, 165 cm and under 170 cm, 170 cm and under 175 cm, and so on.   O.N.C.

27.11x The lengths of telephone calls from a certain office were noted and the results are shown below giving the times in seconds.

141	43	203	104	82	63	24	84	41	86	47	43
100	53	139	147	137	186	214	106	150	109	170	172
194	124	175	177	162	129	128	219	40	105	48	65
105	154	154	35	149	54	104	109	119	74	140	104
168	127	191	30	109	88	104	207	38	164	182	120
166	53	145	29	112	143	49	199	130	52	109	77
142	75	146	105	125	112	40	126	67	49	90	140
132	118	134	133	159	123	161	112	157	104	92	112
151	98	156	117	156	190	122	135	116	96	163	116
186	155	106	153	69	105	136	106	131	118	94	121

Arrange these figures in a grouped frequency distribution using the intervals $0-19, 20-39$, etc.　　　　　　O.N.C.

27.12x The data below are the times for completion, rounded to the nearest hour, of a sample of fifty houses.

911 902 900 867 897 915 945 940 917 883 874 880 932 919 899 903 872
901 874 925 886 928 917 906 925 913 898 888 912 896 921 908 933 903
920 885 901 892 931 902 893 887 928 907 916 895 907 864 891 890

Classify these data into a frequency distribution.　　　　　　O.N.C.

27.13x A person's socio-economic status can be classified as either A, B, C1, C2, D or E in descending order. A random sample of 60 individuals taken in 1973 gave the following information on weekly earnings (£) in relation to socio-economic class:

45 (B)	20 (E)	16 (D)	61 (C2)	18 (E)
32 (C2)	22 (C2)	64 (C1)	62 (C1)	33 (D)
49 (D)	28 (C1)	60 (C2)	74 (B)	50 (C2)
49 (C2)	64 (B)	33 (D)	29 (C2)	21 (E)
24 (C1)	48 (C2)	23 (D)	27 (C2)	26 (E)
26 (D)	37 (C2)	85 (A)	18 (C1)	42 (C2)
43 (C1)	37 (C2)	67 (B)	19 (E)	22 (D)
17 (C2)	17 (C2)	19 (D)	23 (D)	50 (C2)
66 (C1)	74 (C1)	17 (E)	37 (C2)	55 (C1)
52 (C2)	37 (C2)	26 (D)	42 (C1)	40 (C2)
79 (B)	23 (E)	24 (D)	31 (D)	44 (C1)
15 (E)	18 (E)	40 (C2)	65 (C1)	17 (E)

Required:

(1) Compile a frequency distribution of earnings with intervals of a suitable width.

(2) By considering earnings to fall into one of three groups of less than £25, £25 – 45, and more than £45, compile a two-way table showing the frequencies in each earnings group/socio-economic class combination.

(3) Describe the main features of the data as observed from the table compiled in answer to (2) above.　　　　　　A.C.A.

Chapter 28

The Presentation of Data I

Learning Objectives:

At the end of your study of this chapter you should be able to:

1. understand the need for and the principles of diagrammatic presentation,

2. construct from given data the relevant diagram from among the following
   a) bar charts
   b) component and percentage bar charts
   c) histograms
   d) frequency polygons
   e) pie charts
   f) strata graphs

3. identify the outstanding features of the data presented in the diagram.

Numerical data, however well organised, can often fail to fulfil one of its prime functions — to communicate information. This is because many people have a positive hatred of numbers. Be honest — how often have you read a newspaper article and simply skipped over any tables it contains? It is not enough to organise data well: it must also be well presented. One of the main jobs of a statistician is to identify the main features of information given by data, and to present them in such a way that they become intelligible and interesting. In this chapter, we will examine some of the graphs and diagrams that the statistician uses to achieve this end.

Watch any television education programme and almost certainly one of the first things to strike you will be the number of devices used to present information in a vivid and interesting fashion. Graphs, diagrams, blocks of wood, animated cartoons — all play their part in putting the subject over.

Of course, television is the ideal medium for this type of visual presentation, and one of the more important developments of the second half of the twentieth century may well turn out to be the impact of television as a means of imparting information. Yet, in all this, the television producer is doing little more than statisticians have already been doing for a considerable period of time. The scale is larger; the impact is probably many times greater; but the techniques are the same.

We would like, at this point, to be able to say to you that we are going to give you a few simple rules which will enable you to master the technique of presenting diagrammatic information quickly and easily. It is not, however, as simple as that. The diagram you draw depends in part on the information you have, and what you are trying to stress. If you are trying to stress how much the government is spending annually you will produce a very different diagram from one which sets outs to examine what the government spends the money on. It might also depend on the readers you are aiming at. A diagram suitable for the readers of a mass circulation daily newspaper will be very different from one in an accounting journal; a diagram intended to extol the qualities of a particular brand of soap powder will be far removed from one designed to show the changing composition of agricultural output in the Common Market. Effective presentation is a question of flair and experience, and there is only one guideline — does the diagram present clearly and vividly the information it is designed to present?

We cannot pretend that the way in which we illustrate the presentation of particular information is the only way. You may, in fact, think it is not the best way. What we will do is to indicate the weapons you have available. The rest is up to you!

1. *The Bar Chart*

One of the most common of all techniques for presenting data is the use of the bar chart, in which the length of the bar is proportional to the size of the items we are considering. Suppose we are considering the population of some E.E.C. countries; we could be presented with a table like this:

	Population (million)		Population (million)
France	50	Denmark	4.9
Belgium	10	Britain	56
Germany	61	Holland	12.9
Italy	54		

Now, shut your eyes, and without reference to the table state which country has the highest population, which is the lowest, and where Britain comes in the league table. If you have played fair we are prepared to bet that a high proportion of you cannot answer all three questions correctly. Why? Simply because experience shows that people do not absorb lists of figures. A very different result would be obtained if we presented the same information in the form of a bar chart.

The immediate impression we get is of four giant members accompanied by a number of very small members; and it hits the eye that Britain is a giant, second only to Germany.

You will notice that the bar diagram has a heading, as should all diagrams. It is no use presenting information unless the reader knows what the information is. Note, too, that the source of the information is given as we are using secondary data. This enables the reader, if he is interested, to go back to the original figures and delve more deeply.

Here we were looking at one variable factor at a particular point in time, but we may equally use the bar diagram to show how the value of something, say the output of motor vehicles in France, has varied over time.

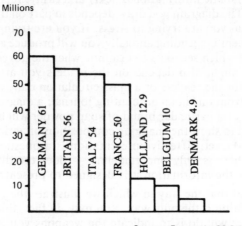

Source: Economist 26.6.71

Population of E.E.C. countries 1969 (millions)

Exhibit 28.1

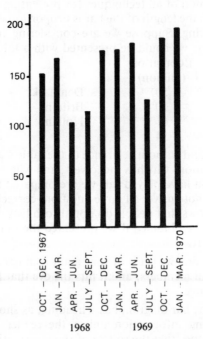

Source: Barclays Bank 3.10.70

Production of motor vehicles – France (monthly average – thousands)

Exhibit 28.2

Here you will notice that the bars are separated – this is a matter of personal preference. It is probably neater, but many statisticians say that it is more difficult to compare the height of the bars. Looking at the diagram it is immediately apparent that production in three quarters was exceptionally low; in April – June of year 2 and in the July – September quarter in years 2 and 3. Further examination may show that in the July – September quarter production is low every year, possibly due to its being the holiday season, but the April – June quarter of year 1 is clearly exceptional and one is constrained to make a more detailed examination of what happened at that time.

The bar chart is a most versatile instrument and capable of adaptation to almost any data. Three further modifications will, we think, convince you of this versatility.

Often the data we are examining includes negative figures. Profits in one year, for example, might be converted into losses the next; the balance of payments may be in surplus or deficit. Such negative figures can be represented on the bar chart quite simply by extending the bar below the zero base line as in Exhibit 28.3.

Sometimes, of course, we may be less interested in an absolute total than we are in the way that total is made up. We may wish to find out how the final cost of production is made up, where sales revenue goes to, what the government does with the money it collects. Again the bar chart proves itself equal to the task, since we can always subdivide the bar as shown in Exhibit 28.4.

Such a bar chart is often called a compound or component bar chart, since it illustrates the components that go to make a total. Sometimes we may be more interested in expressing our information in the form of percentages. It may be important to our argument that tax on North Sea Oil is 54.4% of total selling price rather than that it is 6.8 dollars. There is nothing to stop us from constructing a component bar chart the length of which represents 100% subdivided into sections to show the percentage that each component item forms of the total. In the case of tax, then, the section of the bar representing tax paid would be just over one half the length of the bar. Such a diagram, for obvious reasons, is called a percentage component bar chart.

As a final example of the use of the bar chart we will try to show how it can be used to derive information which is not immediately obvious. With Britain's entry into E.E.C. a burning question is the efficiency of European agriculture. But how can efficiency be measured? It is fair to say that if 30% of the total labour force is engaged in agriculture but the agrarian output is 10% of the Gross National Product, that country's agriculture is inefficient compared with a country for which the figures are 10% and 12% respectively, and this will be the criterion we will use.

We think you will agree that, using our criterion of efficiency, of the seven countries shown, only three — Holland, Belgium and Britain – can be said to be efficient producers in the agricultural sector, and this may well be a factor in the problems facing the common agricultural policy of the E.E.C.

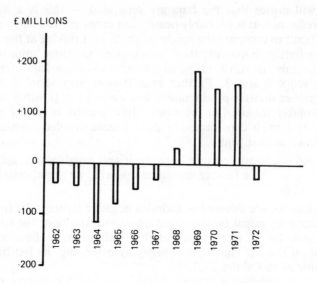

Source: Bank of England
Quarterly June 1973

U.K. net invisible earnings from non-sterling areas

Exhibit 28.3

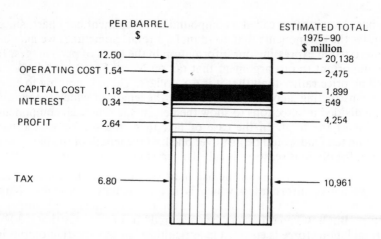

	PER BARREL $	ESTIMATED TOTAL 1975–90 $ million
	12.50	20,138
OPERATING COST	1.54	2,475
CAPITAL COST	1.18	1,899
INTEREST	0.34	549
PROFIT	2.64	4,254
TAX	6.80	10,961

Source: Kitcat and Aitkin
Report on North Sea Oil

Costs of North Sea oil

Exhibit 28.4

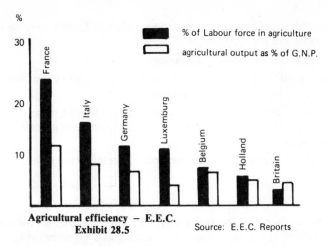

% of Labour force in agriculture

agricultural output as % of G.N.P.

Agricultural efficiency – E.E.C.
Exhibit 28.5

Source: E.E.C. Reports

2. *The Pie (or Circular) Diagram*

The circular, or pie diagram is a device beloved of those who present statistical data for the general public. It is a rare report, and a still rarer copy of the *Economist* magazine which does not contain several such diagrams. In fact, we firmly believe that the extent to which this technique is used grossly exaggerates its utility.

This diagram has only one real use – to show the relative size of the component parts of a total. A complete circle represents the total and this circle is divided into segments the size of which represents the relative importance of each constituent of the total. Thus, if we were trying to show the nature of road accidents in a particular area, we might find that of 300 accidents occurring last year, 57 involved motor-cycles. We now have to mark off a segment of the circle corresponding in size to the proportion of accidents involving motorcycles, that is, 57/300 or 19/100. Since there are 360 degrees in a circle the appropriate segment must subtend an angle of 19/100 × 360 degrees at the centre, i.e. an angle of 68.4 degrees. Our complete pie diagram will appear something like this:

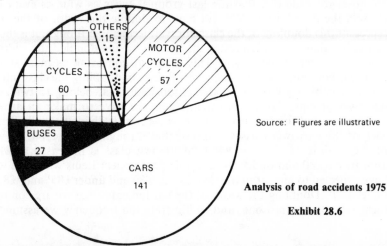

Source: Figures are illustrative

Analysis of road accidents 1975

Exhibit 28.6

Even with this single simple example you should find it easy to spot the weaknesses of the pie diagram:

(a) It involves cumbersome calculations.

(b) It is more difficult to compare segments of a circle in a pie diagram than to compare heights in a bar diagram.

(c) It gives no information as to absolute magnitude unless figures are inserted in each segment, whereas the bar diagram is scaled against a single axis.

Our own advice is not to use this method of presentation unless it is forced upon you.

3. *Plotting the Frequency Distribution – the Histogram*

You will remember that the frequency distribution examines the frequency of occurrence of different values of a variable at a given point in time, and that the values of the variable are combined together into classes of a predetermined size. It is this type of distribution that the histogram presents. The histogram is so similar to a bar chart that students often assume that they are one and the same thing. There is, however, a major difference between them. In a bar chart we are interested in only one factor, say output, the magnitude of which can be represented by the height of a bar. It does not matter how wide the bar is; we look only at the height. In a histogram, however, we are interested in two factors – the width of the classes represented by the width of the bar, and the frequency with which items within each class are found, represented by the height of the bar. In these circumstances it is the area of the bar which really interests us. Now, admittedly, in many of the cases you will deal with this distinction makes little difference. The class intervals are the same throughout the frequency distribution, so the width of the bars is the same and the relative heights of the bars will indicate directly the relative frequencies. Often, however, class intervals at the top and bottom of the distribution are left 'open', or are different from the class intervals in the main body of the table.

Suppose, for example, that the last group is twice as wide as every other class in the distribution. We will have to double the width of the bar to represent this doubling of the class interval. Remember though, it is the area of the bar that we are interested in, and so, having doubled the width, we will have to halve the height. This is not as confusing as most students believe if you think about what we are doing. In doubling the class intervals we are combining into one wider group items that belong to two of the narrower groups. To be consistent, then, we have to make an arbitrary assumption that the frequency of the wider class is divided equally between each of the narrower classes. Suppose that throughout our table the width of the class is £5, but the width of the last class is increased to £10. It appears as '£80 and under £90'. In this class appear items which we would have expected to appear in the two classes '£80 and under £85' and '£85 and under £90'. Doubling the width of the bar indicates that we are combining these two classes into one, and to illustrate the frequency we assume that each of these two 'narrow' classes contains half the number of items in the 'wider' class. That is, we halve the height of the wider bar. Be careful, however, not to draw a line down the middle of the wider bar to try to indicate this. We are only making an assumption — if you do draw such a line you are saying that if we plotted the two 'narrow' groups separately each would have exactly the same frequency, and this we cannot know.

Bearing this in mind, let us plot the histogram of the frequency distribution of weekly earnings that we obtained in the last chapter.

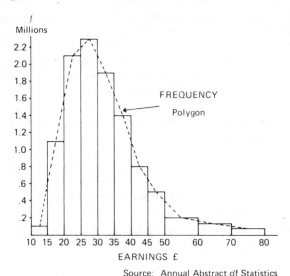

Source: Annual Abstract of Statistics

Weekly earnings of full-time adults 1971

Exhibit 28.7

Note especially the last three groups where the class interval rises from £5 to £10 and the height of the bars is halved.

A similar picture of the distribution is given by the frequency polygon which converts the histogram into a simple graph. Notice that we form the graph by joining the mid-points of the top of the bars. You will find that this convention of using the central value of the group to represent the group as a whole is a very common technique in statistical analysis. Here we are joining the mid-points by straight lines to give us the polygon, but sometimes you will be asked to construct a frequency curve and will join the mid-points of the top of the bars by a smooth curve instead of straight lines. Frequency curves of this type are very common when we wish to illustrate particular types of frequency distribution.

Finally, it is often useful to present the distribution in a different way altogether. Instead of tabulating the frequency of each class we would like to know the frequency with which the variable falls *below* a particular value. The Chancellor who wishes to help the more poorly paid in society might well propose to introduce a tax exemption bill applying to all those earning less than £35 a week. Naturally, he will wish to know firstly how many people this bill will affect, and, secondly, how many more wage earners than before will now be free of the burden of income tax.

It is, of course, simple to add up the frequencies of the first five classes of our frequency distribution, but there is more than this. For many purposes it is easier to read off directly the frequency we require, and there are measures we will introduce you to in a later chapter which are far, far easier to obtain graphically than to calculate.

To obtain information of this nature the statistician has devised the Ogive or Cumulative Frequency graph. This diagram plots, on the horizontal axis, certain values of the variable, usually the upper value of each group; on the vertical axis it shows the frequency of the items with a value less than this. Thus, in constructing the ogive, we first construct a cumulative frequency table from our frequency distribution in this way:

Wage (£)	Cumulative Frequency (millions)
Under 15	0.1
20	1.2 (i.e. 0.1 + 1.1)
25	3.3 (i.e. 0.1 + 1.1 + 2.1)
30	5.6
and so on until we reach the final group	
Under 80	11.0

It is this table that we plot as the ogive, in Exhibit 28.8.

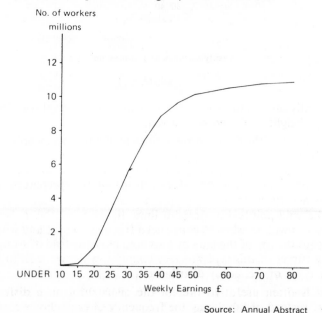

No. of workers
millions

UNDER 10 15 20 25 30 35 40 45 50   60   70   80

Weekly Earnings £

Source: Annual Abstract

Earnings of full-time adults April 1971

Exhibit 28.8

The first thing you will notice is that we have joined the points on the ogive by straight lines rather than the smooth curve that you are probably more used to. The reason for this is that we do not know how the items in any group are scattered between the upper and lower limits; so we make the only reasonable assumption that we can — that the items in any group are distributed evenly across the group. It may be a false assumption. We may find, in the group £25 and under £30, that all the 2.3 million members get a wage of £29.50; but it is not likely. So long as there is a reasonable number of members within the group, we are fairly safe in assuming an even distribution. We know that it will not materially affect our results.

4. *Plotting the Time Series*

You will remember from the last chapter that much data is given in the form of a time series, in which we take a variable and show how its magnitude has varied over a period of time. We have obtained from the United Kingdom Annual Abstract of Statistics the following table showing how consumer expenditure at constant prices varied during the period of time when prices in the United Kingdom were rising at an alarming rate, 1964 to 1974.

Consumer Expenditure at Constant Prices
(£ million)

1964	28330	1970	31472
1965	28760	1971	32397
1966	29301	1972	34318
1967	29869	1973	35962
1968	30598	1974	35741
1969	30715		

Source: Annual Abstract of Statistics

Perhaps you will agree that these figures, involving thousands of millions of pounds, mean very little; if we are honest probably very few of you even read the figures in detail.

But suppose we now draw a graph of these figures!

We are sure that even a quick glance at this graph will leave you with a permanent impression of the way in which consumer expenditure has been rising — slowly and steadily from 1964 to 1970, then much more rapidly, reaching a peak in 1973. Since we have plotted expenditure at constant prices, this represents a rising consumption of goods, i.e. a rising standard of living (it may of course be at the expense of past saving).

272

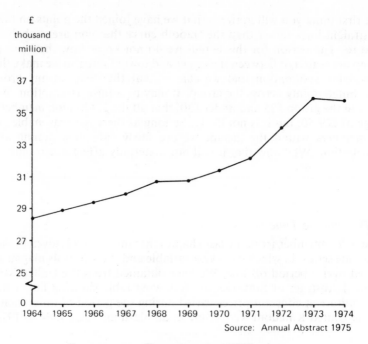

Source: Annual Abstract 1975

Consumer expenditure at constant (1970) prices
Exhibit 28.9

You will have noticed the break in the graph on the vertical axis and the sudden jump from 0 to 25. This is a device used by statisticians when every figure is high and we do not want to crush our graph into a small space at the top of the graph paper. Remember too that we could have left you with a very different impression of the behaviour of consumer expenditure by adjusting the scales on the axis. Try it for yourself by doubling the scale on the vertical axis and halving the horizontal scale; or halving the vertical scale and doubling the horizontal. We have altered the scales in exhibits 28.10 and 28.11. After looking at three graphs of consumer expenditure can you really draw any conclusions as to the rate at which consumer expenditure has been rising? We know it has gone up — and that is about all.

Now, this is all very well, but our friends, the economists, will immediately want to know what we have been spending more on. Are we buying more food and clothes, buying more houses, or wasting our resources in riotous living? For their sakes, and for yours, we add below the way in which consumption of four sub-categories of our expenditure have been behaving in the same period. Whenever we wish to compare the way in which several variables have been behaving over a period of time, it is perfectly permissable to draw as many as four or five time series on the same axes, as long as we clearly distinguish the different graphs and the diagram is not too difficult to interpret.

	Expenditure on			
	Food	Drink	Clothing	Housing
		(£ thousand million)		
1964	6080	1866	2366	3481
1965	6081	1849	2426	3597
1966	6170	1922	2425	3695
1967	6228	2001	2450	3836
1968	6260	2108	2568	3973
1969	6264	2149	2596	4106
1970	6365	2296	2693	4181
1971	6362	2463	2726	4287
1972	6320	2641	2910	4377
1973	6388	2988	3060	4483
1974	6418	3081	3039	4460

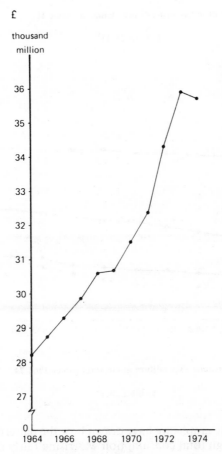

Consumer expenditure change of Scale I
Exhibit 28.10

274

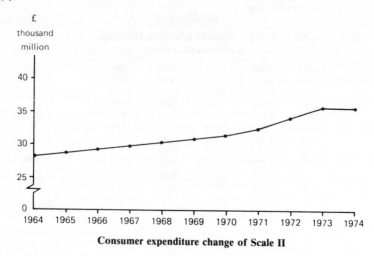

Consumer expenditure change of Scale II

Exhibit 28.11

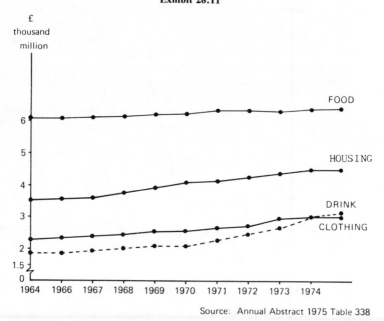

Source: Annual Abstract 1975 Table 338

Consumer expenditure at constant prices 1964-74

Exhibit 28.12

You can see from the graphs we have drawn how the pattern of expenditure is changing. Although total consumption was rising fairly rapidly over this period, expenditure on food seems to have risen very slowly indeed – the slope of the graph is almost non-existent. Far different is the case of drink. Particularly from 1969 expenditure on drink rose at an alarming rate.

Remember that this expenditure is listed at constant (1970) prices, so the rise of the graph represents increasing real consumption. Economists and sociologists would find this an interesting comment on human behaviour, and, in looking at this diagram, use your knowledge of other subjects to interpret what has been happening.

Do you remember when we discussed the bar chart we showed how it could be used to illustrate the constituents of a given total? Now, there are times when we want to illustrate how these constituents have varied over time. It may be, for example, that over the course of years road accidents involving bicycles have been forming a smaller and smaller part of total road accidents, while accidents involving motor-cars have been gradually forming an increasing proportion of total accidents. There is nothing to stop us from drawing three or four different time series, one for each type of vehicle showing the number of accidents involving that type of vehicle. We could even draw a number of graphs showing the percentage of accidents involving each type of vehicle, and we have no doubt that the diagrams would bring out the changing pattern. For this type of analysis it is far better to use a special type of diagram, the *Strata Graph,* or, if you are dealing in percentages, the *Percentage Strata Graph.* We must, however, keep the number of constituents reasonably few since otherwise the diagram may become difficult to interpret. The great advantage of this type of presentation is, as you will see, that the lines showing the magnitude of each constituent can never cross. Exhibit 28.13 is a typical strata graph, showing the constitution of road accidents over a period of time in a large city. In order to stress the points that we would like to bring out, the figures are purely imaginary, so do not think that your own town is abnormal if the pattern of accidents is different from the one we have represented.

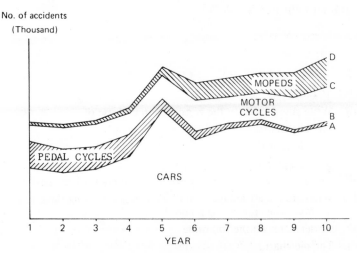

Number of road accidents 19... to 19... analysed by type of vehicle

Exhibit 28.13

The principle of the strata graph is that our totals are successively cumulated. Thus the height of line A represents the number of accidents involving motor-cars each year. When we consider those accidents involving bicycles we add together for each year those accidents involving motor-cars and those involving bicycles to produce line B, the height of which for any year tells us the number of accidents involving (motor-cars + bicycles). In the same way line C is the graph of the number of accidents involving (motor cars + bicycles + motor-cycles). Finally when we add to these figures those accidents involving mopeds, we arrive at line D, which is the total number of accidents for all vehicles. You will have realised already that the distance between each line represents those accidents involving a particular vehicle. Thus the gap between A and B shows us accidents involving bicycles and the gap between B and C those involving motor-cycles. It is, of course, desirable to distinguish each type of vehicle by distinctive shading to give the diagram clarity, but we think you will agree that such a diagram is relatively easy to interpret. Even a cursory glance tells us that the total number of road accidents has been on the increase, but within this total three distinct trends are apparent. Bicycle accidents, which were quite numerous in the early years, have dwindled away and are now very few: conversely, moped accidents, which were very few in the early years, probably because there were few moped owners, are now becoming quite an important constituent of total accidents: car accidents have increased, and although it is difficult to judge, probably remain much the same proportion of an increased total. Motor-cycle accidents, it is apparent, have remained fairly constant over the years.

If we wish to draw a percentage strata graph, it is just as easy, although the initial calculations, converting our figures into percentages, are very cumbersome. Can you see that the line D in such a graph would be a horizontal straight line at 100%?

Assignment Exercises

28.1x (i)   Write short notes on the construction and use of

    (a) bar charts,

    (b) pie charts,

    (c) line graphs,

illustrating your answer by using examples from a business environment.

    (ii) What are the advantages and disadvantages of using these diagrammatic methods when presenting reports?   O.N.C.

28.2x Write brief notes on the following:

    (a) The pie chart,

    (b) Histogram,

    (c) Band or strata chart.   O.N.C.

28.3x Indicate the more important uses of the following graphs and charts, supporting your answers with appropriate diagrammatic examples:

(i) Histogram,

(ii) Cumulative frequency curve. I.C.S.A.

28.4x (a) Statistical information is sometimes shown in the form of ideographs (pictograms). For example, pictures of sacks of different sizes or alternatively pictures of different numbers of sacks of the same size may be used to show the production of flour in different countries. Comment on the advantages and disadvantages of these pictorial forms.

(b) Describe the purpose and construction of a pie chart, illustrating your answer with a simple example of your own invention.

Scot. A.S.C.

28.5x Explain the use and method of construction of the following ways of representing data, illustrating your remarks with an example in each case:

(a) Bar charts,

(b) Pie charts,

(c) Pictogram. O.N.C.

28.6x (a) What are the advantages of using charts and graphs in statistical investigations?

(b) Describe clearly the methods to be employed in constructing:

(i) a pie chart,

(ii) a histogram.

(c) State the kind of diagram you consider most suitable to illustrate:

(i) daily hours of sunshine for a period of one month.

(ii) the number of workers, male and female, employed in a factory at each of three dates.

(iii) monthly sales, cumulative sales and a curve showing trend.

Briefly give your reasons for your choice in each case. O.N.C.

28.7x Discuss the suitability of a compound bar chart, a pie chart, and a pictogram for the presentation of data to:

(a) top management,

(b) lower management,

(c) the public.

Give examples of data which could be satisfactorily presented by each of these charts. (Do not draw the charts.) O.N.C.

28.8x A daily count of the number of rejects from the assembly line of a local manufacturer has yielded the following data:

138	164	150	132	144	125	149	157
146	158	140	147	136	148	152	144
168	126	138	176	163	119	154	165
146	173	142	147	135	153	140	135
161	145	135	142	150	156	145	128

(a) Using the data, construct a frequency distribution table and from that sketch the corresponding frequency curve.

(b) Comment on the shape of the frequency curve you have obtained and compare it with the sketched shapes of two others with which you are familiar. O.N.C.

28.9x The set of figures below shows the ages at which 50 employees were appointed to a certain grade.

```
28  27  30  27  28  28  26  27  28  28
26  28  29  31  27  28  27  29  27  29
28  27  31  27  27  29  30  27  28  28
28  29  28  29  27  30  27  28  27  29
28  27  28  29  29  28  28  28  28  27
```

Write the data in the form of a frequency table and draw the frequency curve.

Draw also the cumulative relative frequency curve. O.N.C.

28.10x   Estimates of Gross Domestic Product (GDP) in current prices from 1951 to 1972 in £m are given below.

	£m		£m
1951	12,639	1962	25,279
2	13,790	3	26,878
3	14,877	4	29,187
4	15,726	5	31,156
5	16,867	6	33,057
6	18,264	7	34,835
7	19,369	8	37,263
8	20,196	9	39,667
9	21,248	1970	43,303
1960	22,633	1	48,675
1	24,213	2	53,940

Source: National Income and Expenditure, 1973

(a) Construct a frequency distribution and a histogram of these figures and comment.

(b) Indicate how these current price estimates can be converted to real (i.e. constant price) estimates of GDP. C.I.P.F.A.

28.11x   The following is a record of marks scored by candidates in an examination:

```
77  59  84  73  51  43  50  81  61  53  69
37  58  63  67  61  90  61  50  60  84  56
77  57  42  43  41  49  37  21  24  35  34
50  11  52  30  16  33  67  87  64  47  59
37  92  88  30  38  22  22  49  46  50  64
23  73  73  48  26  36  51  85  71  57  45
```

(a) Tabulate the marks in the form of a frequency distribution, grouping by suitable intervals.

(b) Construct a histogram from your frequency distribution.

(c) Explain the essential differences between a histogram and a bar chart.

Scot. A.S.C.

28.12x   *Stocks of Coal − Great Britain, July 1972 to June 1973*
                              (thousand tons)

	Total	Opencast Sites and Central Stocking Grounds	Collieries
1972			
July	8,839	3,419	5,420
August	9,282	3,530	5,752
September	9,764	3,528	6,236
October	10,030	3,473	6,557
November	10,471	3,458	7,013
December	10,934	3,376	7,558
1973			
January	11,130	3,201	7,929
February	11,455	3,224	8,231
March	11,972	3,244	8,728
April	12,470	3,268	9,202
May	12,925	3,332	9,593
June	13,292	3,417	9,875

Source: Department of Trade and Industry.

(a) Write a short report stressing the main features of the data given above and include any derived statistics which may be appropriate.

(b) Prepare a suitable diagram or graph which will illustrate your report.

O.N.C.

28.13x

Household Expenditure in 1971

	£	Per Cent of Total
Housing	3.98	12.8
Fuel, light and power	1.85	6.0
Food	8.02	25.9
Alcoholic drink	1.46	4.7
Tobacco	1.30	4.2
Clothing and footwear	2.81	9.0
Durable household goods	2.01	6.5
Other goods	2.32	7.5
Transport and vehicles	4.26	13.7
Services	2.90	9.4
Miscellaneous	0.09	0.3
Total weekly household expenditure	30.99	100.0

Draw carefully and neatly a chart, graph or diagram to represent in visual form the household expenditure in units of actual money spent. Draw carefully and neatly a second chart, graph or diagram to represent in visual form the household expenditure in percentage terms. State the reasons for your choice.

O.N.C.

28.14x   *Unemployed in Great Britain Receiving Unemployment Benefit*
(thousands)

	Total	Unemployment Benefit Only	Unemployment Benefit and Supplementary Allowance
1970			
February	332	260	72
May	303	238	65
August	286	226	60
November	305	245	60
1971			
February	401	312	89
May	406	310	96
August	427	321	106
November	494	379	115
1972			
February	514	391	123
May	451	339	112
August	385	291	94
November	344	261	83

Source: Department of Employment.

(a) Prepare a suitable graph or chart to represent the data given above.

(b) Write a short report on the main features revealed by the table and your graph or chart using derived figures where appropriate.

O.N.C.

28.15x   *National Insurance — Great Britain: New Claims —*
Weekly Averages
(thousands)

Year	Sickness and Invalidity Benefits	Injury Benefit	Unemployment Benefit
1966	206.1	18.5	50.6
1967	193.2	18.8	63.0
1968	204.0	18.0	58.8
1969	219.4	17.9	59.6
1970	204.5	15.8	60.7
1971	169.3	14.0	68.7

Source: Department of Health and Social Security.

Prepare a suitable graph or chart to show the data given above relating to National Insurance claims in Great Britain. Write a short report on the main points revealed by your graph, using derived figures where appropriate. Explain carefully what is meant by 'Weekly Averages' and why this term is used rather than that relating to any other time period.

O.N.C.

28.16x   *Subjects studied at Britannia College of Commerce 1972*

Subject	Number of Students
Professional:	
Management	240
Banking	120
Accountancy	980
Languages:	
Spanish	20
French	220
German	100
General:	
G.C.E.	350
O.N.C.	225
H.N.C.	115

(a) Depict the data given above in the form of:

    (i)   a simple bar chart,

    (ii)   a component bar chart (actuals),

    (iii)   a percentage component bar chart,

    (iv)   a pie chart.

(b) Comment on the effectiveness of using the pie chart and the component bar chart as a means of illustrating data classification.

                                            O.N.C.

Chapter 29

The Presentation of Data II

Learning Objectives:

At the end of your study of this chapter you should be able to:

1. **understand the difference between natural and semi-log scale graphs,**
2. **plot and interpret semi-log graphs using**
   a) **natural scale paper**
   b) **semi-log scale paper,**
3. **construct and interpret the Lorenz curve,**
4. **plot scatter diagrams,**
5. **understand the importance of the Z-chart to the business world,**
6. **recognise the pitfalls to be avoided in selecting and constructing diagrams.**

The diagrams that we have examined so far are in fairly common usage. In fact we would be prepared to bet that, with the exception of strata graphs, you will have already seen all of the diagrams in the previous chapter. Basically, all of these diagrams are attempting to show the relative quantities in the data in an interesting and easily grasped manner. Yet some diagrams show much more than just the relative sizes, and we will now turn our attention to such diagrams. The chapter is concluded with a discussion on how diagrams can be made to misrepresent data.

1. *Logarithmic Graphs*

As we have seen, one of the problems with ordinary graphs is that they tend to give a false impression of the way in which figures are changing. Using a vertical scale of 1 inch = 100 units, a change from 100 to 200 units is represented by the same upward movement as a change from 1000 to 1100 units, even though it is 100% change as compared with a 10% change. The slope of the graph is the same — yet the rate of change is very different. Now, in most cases this does not matter. We may be interested only in the swings of the absolute figures; or the range of the figures may be such that the difference in the rates of change is negligible. If this is the case, we can get all we need from the graphs we have drawn. However, if we are considering inflation, for example, it is the rate at which prices are rising which is important, rather than the actual price increases.

Fortunately, if we plot the logarithms of our figures rather than the figures themselves, we can produce a graph the slope of which represents the real rate of change. Why should this be so?

Consider a case in which prices are rising by 20% a year. We can easily construct a table to show what happens to prices.

Period	Price	Log of Price	Difference of Logs
1	100	2.0000	
2	120	2.0792	0.0792
3	144	2.1584	0.0792
4	172.8	2.2375	0.0792
5	207.36	2.3167	0.0792

Don't you find it rather frightening that an inflation rate less than that of Britain in the mid 1970's will more than double prices in five years?

As you can see, the log of each price rises by 0.0792 irrespective of the magnitude of the price change, and hence we obtain a straight-line graph if we plot the logarithms. This of course tells us that the rate of change of prices is constant. It does not tell us what the rate of change is, but merely enables us to compare rates of change over time.

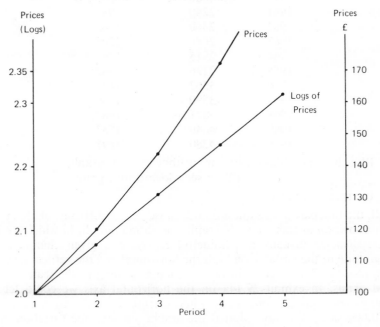

Inflation at a constant 20%

Exhibit 29.14

Strictly such a graph is known as a *semi-logarithmic* graph, as we plot logarithms only on the vertical axis. On the horizontal axis we do not plot the logarithms of the time periods.

As you can see from the diagram, if we plot the prices themselves the slope of the curve gets steeper and the fact that the rate of change is the same is completely hidden.

Often a logarithmic graph can be used also when the figures with which we are concerned range so widely that it is inconvenient to use a normal graph. Such a situation would occur if we tried to plot German price movements during the great inflation of the 1920's when prices were increasing by hundreds of times each month.

Now, although few students find difficulty in mastering the principles involved in the construction of semi-logarithmic graphs, this is such a common question in examinations at this level that we would strongly recommend you to work through the following example with us, making sure that you understand each step.

Example

Sales of Two Companies
Sales (£000)

Year	Company A	Company B
1961	2240	980
1962	2460	1082
1963	2680	1205
1964	2915	1289
1965	3136	1382
1966	3362	1476
1967	3590	1580
1968	3821	1687
1969	4049	1787
1970	4280	1891

(a) Plot the time series on (i)   an arithmetic scale graph,
                              (ii)   a semi-logarithmic graph.

(b) Interpret the results.

Well, the first part of this question will cause you no difficulty at all. As you well know, an arithmetic scale graph is a normal graph, in which we let a given distance (usually a centimetre) represent a given change in the magnitude of the variable on both the horizontal and the vertical axes. We then plot the figures given in the question according to the scale we have used. Thus, in exhibit 29.14a on the horizontal axis we could let two centimetres represent one year, while on the vertical axis it represents £500,000 sales. We have plotted the graphs showing the variation in the sales of the two companies in the normal way.

When we now come to consider the semi-logarithmic graphs, we have to be careful. In some examinations you will be issued only with the normal graph paper we have used so far; in others with graph paper already designed for semi-logarithmic use. Let us suppose firstly that you have been issued only with the normal arithmetic scale graph paper. In this case, as you know, we will plot the years along the horizontal axis as normally, but along the vertical axis you will have to plot the logarithms of the sales figure for each year. Our first step then must be to obtain these logarithms. We strongly

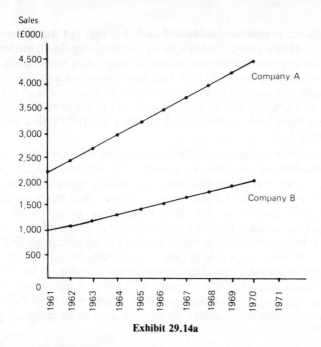

Sales
(£000)

4,500
4,000
3,500
3,000
2,500
2,000
1,500
1,000
500
0

1961 1962 1963 1964 1965 1966 1967 1968 1969 1970 1971

Company A

Company B

Exhibit 29.14a

advise you to do this as part of the answer and not on a piece of scrap paper. It is easy to make a mistake, and if you do examiners are far more inclined to be generous if they can trace easily where the mistake has arisen. So we proceed as follows:

| | Company A | | Company B | |
Year	Sales	Log	Sales	Log
1961	2240	3.3502	980	2.9912
1962	2460	3.3909	1082	3.0342
1963	2680	3.4281	1205	3.0810
1964	2915	3.4646	1289	3.1103
1965	3136	3.4964	1382	3.1405
1966	3362	3.5266	1476	3.1691
1967	3590	3.5551	1580	3.1987
1968	3821	3.5822	1687	3.2271
1969	4049	3.6073	1787	3.2521
1970	4280	3.6314	1891	3.2767

Although this seems to be a cumbersome process, almost any of the small pocket calculators you are normally allowed to use will give you the logarithms you require in a matter of seconds. All you have to do now is to scale the vertical axis to accommodate the logarithms you have obtained, and draw the graphs. We have done this in exhibit 29.14b, but you will notice that we have also inserted on the vertical axis on the right some of the absolute values of the sales. While modern management is well aware of the use of semi-logarithmic graphs they also wish to be able to see at a glance the value of the sales turnover without having to refer to a book of log tables.

Even a quick glance at exhibits 29.14a and 29.14b brings out the advantages of the semi-logarithmic graph. The graphs of the sales figures on arithmetic scale imply that the two companies increased their sales at a steady rate throughout the whole period. But as you are aware, such graphs show absolute changes, not *rates* of change, and equal absolute increases imply a declining *rate* of increase. This is well brought out in the semi-logarithmic graphs, where a close look at company A shows a marked tendency of the rate of change to fall.

More important, the two graphs give completely different impressions of the relative performance of the two companies. The arithmetic scale graph implies that company A is expanding more rapidly than company B because the slope of the graph of the former's sales is steeper. But again the use of absolute figures is deceptive. The semi-logarithmic graphs show that company B's performance is at least as good as that of company A in that it is expanding at the same rate, while on a very close examination we find that the rate of growth over the whole period is marginally better than that of company A, and from 1964 onwards growth certainly seems to be steadier and more sustained than that of company A. Thus, we may come to the conclusion that, although both companies have grown substantially in the period, company B, although smaller, appears to have done marginally the better.

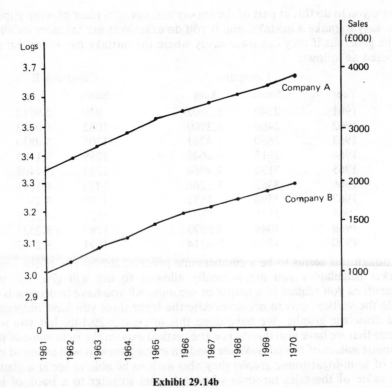

Exhibit 29.14b

Now this is all very well, but suppose you are issued with semi-logarithmic graph paper already ruled. The great advantage of this paper is that you can insert the absolute figures of sales on the graph without first having to look up the logarithms. Probably, however, few of you have had the opportunity yet of seeing semi-logarithmic graph paper, so let us explain the principles on which it is ruled. One axis is ruled normally, in centimetres and millimetres (after all, it is *semi* logarithmic). But the other axis is quite differently ruled. It is drawn on the basis that equal distances represent equal percentage changes rather than equal absolute changes. Thus, if one centimetre represents a change from 10 to 100 (an increase of 10 times), the next centimetre will represent a change from 100 to 1000 (also an increase of 10 times).

There is more to it than this, however. No-one would expect you to calculate the percentage change for each figure that you have to plot on the graph. We have merely stated the obvious − that one axis of the semi-logarithmic graph paper is scaled logarithmically. Let us take it further. If we take the first centimetre on the vertical scale to represent an increase of 1 unit (from 1 to 2), the next centimetre would represent an increase from 2 to 4. We could have obtained exactly the same effect by plotting logarithms. The log of 1 is $0 \cdot 0$, so you will realise that the logarithmic graph can range upwards only from an absolute value of 1 (not 0 as can the arithmetic scale graph). Now the logarithm of 2 is 0.30103, and the logarithm of 4 is 0.60206. Similarly the logarithm of 8 is 0.90309. Can you see that, in allowing each centimetre to represent the same proportional increase in the absolute figures, we are scaling according to the logarithms of the numbers? In this case one centimetre represents an increase in the logarithm of .30103; and when we add .30103 to a logarithm, we are in fact multiplying the previous number by two. So each successive centimetre represents an increasing change in the absolute figures − 2, 4, 8, 16 and so on.

But the logarithmic scale is not drawn in centimetres as is the arithmetic axis. Suppose once again that we take the first vertical division on the graph paper to be one centimetre long (whether it is or not depends on the graph paper with which you are issued). We can let this centimetre represent any absolute magnitude that we wish. Let us again assume that it represents an increase from 1 to 2. The next main division on our graph paper will also represent an absolute increase of one unit, from 2 to 3, but this division will not be a centimetre deep. We have already said that the second centimetre represents an increase in absolute values from 2 to 4, so you would naturally expect the second division representing an increase from 2 to 3 to be less than a centimetre deep. It will in fact be about .585 centimetres deep only. Thus each successive unit increase on the logarithmic axis will entail a smaller and smaller vertical rise, and the vertical scaling will look something like Exhibit 29.14d.

In practice, of course, the graph paper you will be given will have each main division subdivided as normal graph paper is into ten subsections to enable you to plot the intermediate figures. If you have not seen such graph paper before, we strongly recommend that you immediately study carefully exhibit 29.14c where we have drawn the two graphs we are concerned with on semi-logarithmic paper, and, most important, obtain a stock of such paper of your own and practice drawing semi-logarithmic graphs using the exercises at the end of this chapter.

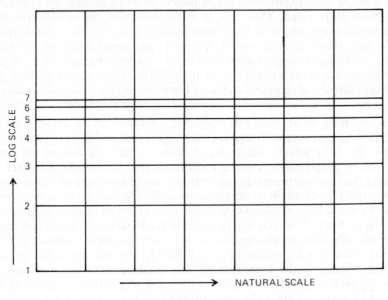

Exhibit 29.14d

2. *The Lorenz Curve*

If you look at statistics of income one of the first things that strikes you is the inequality in the distribution of incomes in most countries. Not only is the range of incomes wide, from under £1000 a year to £20,000 a year and more in the United Kingdom, but we also find that a very small percentage of the income recipients at the top of the scale receive a disproportionately large share of total income. Equally, the very large percentage of low income earners receive in total a very small percentage of the total income. You must, at some time in your life, have met such statements as 'the top 5% of income recipients receive over 70% of total income'.

Now any economist will tell you that one purpose of our taxation system, or any taxation system which is progressive, is to reduce the inequality of incomes, and naturally we would all like to know how far the system is succeeding in this objective. Statisticians have derived a diagram, the Lorenz curve, which enables us to show graphically the extent of inequality, not only of incomes, but also of many other things.

In this diagram, considering income distribution, we measure on the horizontal axis the percentage of population, and on the vertical axis the percentage of income, see exhibit 29.15a.

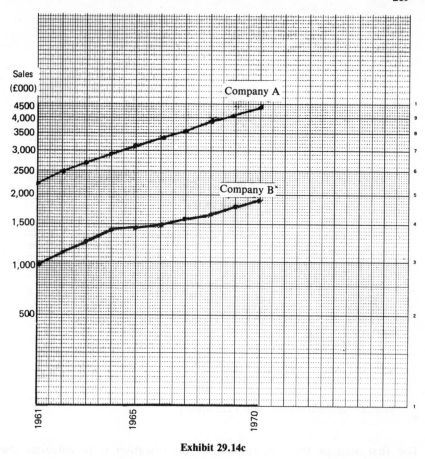

Exhibit 29.14c

Now, obviously, if incomes are distributed equally, the bottom 10% of income earners will receive 10% of total income, the bottom 20% of income earners will receive 20% of total income and so on. The graph representing such a distribution of income will be the straight line OR passing through the origin and at 45 degrees (provided, that is, that the horizontal and vertical scales are the same), and any divergence from this line will indicate some degree of inequality. The point A for example would be interpreted as 'the bottom x% of income earners receive y% of total income', and, since x is greater than y, would be derived from a situation such as 'the bottom 65% of income earners receive only 32% of total incomes'.

Let us illustrate the use of Lorenz curves by applying them to the following income statistics of the United Kingdom.

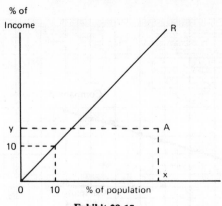

Exhibit 29.15a

Income Class	No. of Incomes		Pre-tax Income		Post-tax Income	
£	(000)	%	£m	%	£m	%
50–249	5070	18.6	991	4.9	990	5.5
250–499	6570	24.2	2590	12.8	2486	13.8
500–749	6155	22.6	4143	20.5	3844	21.4
750–999	4830	17.8	4580	22.6	4168	23.2
1000–1999	4145	15.2	5849	28.9	5113	28.5
2000–3999	353	1.3	1305	6.4	940	5.2
4000–5999	59	0.2	469	2.3	281	1.6
6000 and over	18	0.1	330	1.6	129	0.8
	27200		20257		17951	

Source: National Income and Expenditure

The first step in the construction of our diagram is to calculate the percentages appropriate to each group and each column. Thus the 5,070,000 individuals in the income class £50 – £249 comprise 18.6% of all income recipients and they received 4.9% of all pre-tax income. We have inserted the relevant percentages in the body of the table, although in an examination you would have to calculate each of them from the original figures given to you.

The next step is to cumulate the percentages you have calculated in this way:

Income Earners (%)		Pre-tax Income (%)	Post-tax Income (%)
18.6	receive	4.9	5.5
42.8		17.7	19.3
65.4		38.2	40.7
83.2		60.8	63.9
98.4		89.7	92.4
99.7		96.1	97.6
99.9		98.4	99.2
100.0		100.0	100.0

It is now easy to draw the Lorenz curves relating to pre-tax and post-tax income:

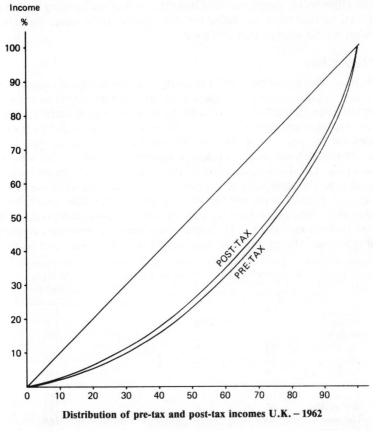

Income %

Distribution of pre-tax and post-tax incomes U.K. – 1962

Exhibit 29.15b

Now any divergence from our straight line of equal distribution of income indicates that there is inequality in the distribution of incomes, and the further the Lorenz curve is from this line of reference, the greater is the degree of inequality. It is worth noting that if the Lorenz curve is below the straight line the inequality is in favour of the upper income groups in that a high percentage of low income earners receive a small percentage of income. If, on the other hand, the Lorenz curve is above the straight line, it implies that a given percentage of the bottom income earners receive a higher percentage of total income; the inequality, that is, works in favour of the poor.

Looking at our diagram, it is apparent that at this time there was a great deal of inequality in the income structure of the United Kingdom. Although the taxation system did reduce it, the reduction seems to have been minimal.

We have not, however, asked what was done with the tax revenue. Much of it was returned to the lower income groups in the form of social benefits — family allowances, supplementary benefits, subsidised housing and so on. It may well be that when we allow for this transfer of income, the effects of taxation would appear very different.

3. *The Z Chart*

A diagram which is often used in industry and commerce, although it seems to be less popular among statisticians, is the Z Chart, so called because the completed diagram takes the form of the letter Z. This is merely a device to enable management to show concisely three different aspects of a time series plotted on the one graph. On the bottom bar of the Z we plot the time series of monthly (or weekly) sales, or output, or whatever variable we are considering. On the diagonal bar of the Z we plot the cumulative total to date, that is, the total sales or output we have achieved since the beginning of the year. Finally as the top bar of the Z we plot the total sales achieved in the last year: the first or January figure is the total sales achieved during the period 1st February last to 31st January this year; the February figure is the total from last March until the end of February this year, and so on.

	Output – ABC Limited		Cumulative Total	Moving Annual Total
	Last Year	Current Year		
January	9	11	11	146
February	8	14	25	152
March	9	12	37	155
April	13	15	52	157
May	14	16	68	159
June	18	19	87	160
July	16	18	105	162
August	15	14	119	161
September	12	14	133	163
October	10	13	146	166
November	9	11	157	168
December	11	15	172	172

We will illustrate by plotting the figures of output for a firm ABC Ltd. The figures are simplified to enable you to follow the calculations more easily. Obviously, although we are plotting figures for the current year only, if we are to obtain a running total of sales over the last twelve months we will need the figures for two years.

If you look carefully at the graph, the first thing that you will notice is that while the moving annual total and the cumulative total figures are plotted on the vertical lines representing each month, the monthly total is plotted in the middle of each month. The reason for this is easy to see. The monthly figures show performance during the whole of the month, and, as you are aware, the way to show this is by plotting points in the middle of the period. The other totals, however, represent performance over a period of time ending on a specific date, and are intended to show achievement up to and including that date. Thus these figures are more correctly plotted at the end

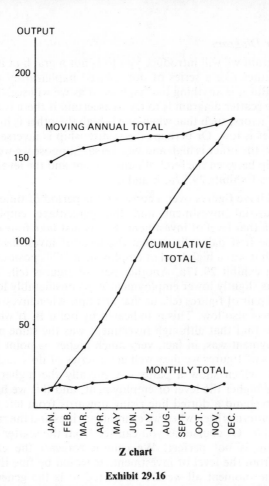

OUTPUT

200

MOVING ANNUAL TOTAL

150

CUMULATIVE
TOTAL

100

50

MONTHLY TOTAL

JAN. FEB. MAR. APR. MAY JUN. JLY. AUG. SEPT. OCT. NOV. DEC.

Z chart

Exhibit 29.16

of the months. You will see too what a vast amount of information is given by this simple diagram. The cumulative total tells us performance to date, and it is a simple matter to superimpose on the diagram a line showing planned or expected performance. Thus we can see at a glance whether our plans are being realised or whether we are falling behind. The moving annual total enables us to compare performance this year with that at a comparable time last year. If this chart is rising it means that figures in that month are higher than they were in the same month last year. Thus we have the means of making a direct comparison with last year. Finally the monthly total enables us to keep a direct check on what is happening now; and if we are falling behind our plan we can usually spot a month with low figures which has caused this and so discover why. Is it any wonder, with this wealth of information to be had, that the Z chart is so popular in industry?

4. *The Scatter Diagram*

The final diagram we will introduce you to is not a graph at all. It looks at first glance rather like a series of dots placed haphazardly on a sheet of graph paper. But it is anything but haphazard as we will see. The basic aim underlying the scatter diagram is to try to ascertain if there is a relationship between two factors, such that when one is high the other is high, when one is low the other is low. Or perhaps the relationship is inverse − when one variable is low, the other is high and vice versa. Suppose we were examining the relationship between the level of employment and the level of industrial investment, see Exhibits 29.17a, b and c.

Firstly we will have figures over a considerable period of time giving us the level of industrial investment and the percentage employment rate associated with that level of investment. Let us just take four of those pairs of figures. The first pair tells us that the level of investment is high and associated with it was a high level of employment. This position is indicated by point A in exhibit 29.17a. Another pair of figures tells us that when investment was slightly lower employment was considerably lower — point C. Still a third pair of figures tells us that at a time when investment was low employment was also low. This is indicated by point B. If we examine the last figures we find that although investment was the same as before, the level of employment was, in fact, very much higher — point D. If we plot sufficient pairs of figures we may well get a series of dots such as those on exhibit 29.17b which show a pattern. Generally the higher the level of investment the higher the level of employment, and this we have indicated by inserting freehand a dotted line rising upwards from left to right. The same sort of pattern is seen when we examine savings and the rate of interest in Exhibit 29.17c. Of course, as you can see from the scatter of the points the relationship is not perfect. We cannot forecast the exact level of employment from the level of investment. It would be fine if we could do this, but at the moment all we are interested in is the general tendency. Before you leave the scatter diagram, experiment for yourself. Draw a scatter diagram showing the relationship between investment and *un*employment. You should get an inverse relationship − the points *falling* from left to right. And finally, try to draw a scatter diagram in which there is no clear relationship shown between two variables.

Some Pitfalls to be Avoided

We must not leave the subject of graphs and diagrams without giving you some advice on what not to do. Unfortunately you will find examples every day of diagrams which illustrate what we are about to say should not happen.

A device beloved of advertisers today is to represent their information in the form of little pictures or ideograms. The sales of a particular brand of beer may be represented by the size of a foaming tankard, the amount of washing-up liquid you get for a penny by the height of liquid in a test-tube.

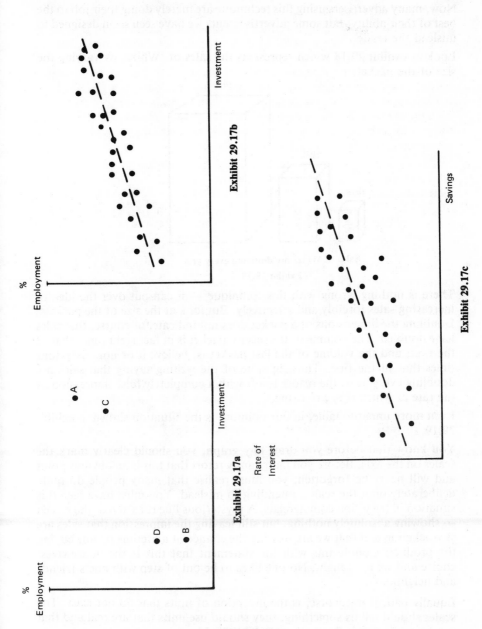

Exhibit 29.17

Now, many advertisers using this technique are merely doing their job to the best of their ability; but some advertisements we have seen seem designed to mislead the reader.

Look at exhibit 29.18 which represents the sales of 'Whizz' by varying the size of the packet.

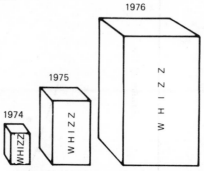

Sales of Whizz are doubling every year
Exhibit 29.18

There is nothing wrong with this technique — it can put over the idea of increasing sales forcibly and effectively. But look at the size of the packets. Doubling the dimensions of a packet does not indicate, of course, that sales have doubled. The volume of the second packet is in fact eight times that of the first, and the volume of the last packet is, believe it or not, sixty-four times that of the first. Thus, in spite of the writing saying that sales are doubling every year, the reader is left with a completely false impression of the rate at which they are rising.

Even more unpardonable, in our opinion, is the situation shown in exhibit 29.19.

You know that before you draw any graph, you should clearly mark the scales on the axis. Before you indignantly retort that this is an obvious point and will never be forgotten, you must realise that many people do quite deliberately omit the scales, intending to mislead. You must have seen this situation in television commercials. A mysterious line runs across the screen — showing absolutely nothing, but still leaving the impression that sales are skyrocketing and that we are missing the chance of a lifetime by not buying the product. Couple this with the statement that this is the housewives' choice and we are caught. No-one likes to be out of step with one's friends and neighbours.

Equally bad, if not worse, is the invention of units that do not exist. The scales should tell us something; they should use units that are real and that can be understood. But look at Exhibit 29.20.

Imagine this graph on your television screen, and the smooth voice of the announcer 'proving' by pointing to the graph that daily brushing with Gritto is bound to make our teeth whiter. But what is a unit of brightness? We are afraid that we do not know, and we very much suspect that the advertising agencies do not know either.

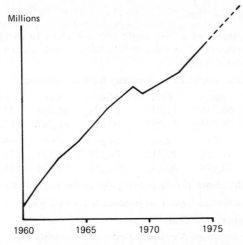

Sales of Bang show it to be the housewives' choice

Exhibit 29.19

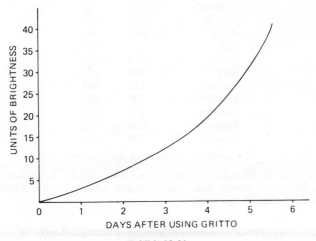

Exhibit 29.20

Students often ask us which is the best diagram to use, for a particular purpose. There is no real answer to this and we suggest that you do not waste time looking for one. Any diagram should present the salient features of the data simply and vividly. Equally, if the reader has to spend a great deal of time 'sorting out' what a diagram means, it is a bad diagram.

But do not let it stop here. Certain features of the data should be obvious from the diagram. Now ask questions. Why has the variable behaved in this manner? Why has A behaved differently from B? Is there a relationship between C and D, and, if so, what is this relationship? Only by asking questions such as these will you get full value from your diagrams.

Assignment Exercises

29.1x A sales department of a firm might plot a Z chart to check or monitor the annual performance of its sales staff. Describe such a chart with an example and explain how it is used. A.C.A.

29.2x The production figures for a company were as follows:

	Jan.	Feb.	Mar.	Apr.	May	June
1973	60,746	57,071	63,621	66,014	71,736	80,213
1974	68,123	58,983	60,693	61,247	67,778	76,567

	July	Aug.	Sept.	Oct.	Nov.	Dec.
1973	91,780	92,314	76,770	67,123	71,512	87,490
1974	92,124	99,632	104,210	99,634	88,241	107,870

(a) Round the above production figures to the nearest thousand.

(b) Use the rounded figures to produce a Z chart for 1974.

(c) Comment on your chart. Scot.A.S.C.

29.3x   *Imported Softwood Deliveries (monthly averages)*
                      (thousand cubic metres)

Month	1972	1973
January	532	882
February	667	527
March	731	828
April	629	654
May	791	940
June	746	838
July	828	870
August	553	851
September	800	833
October	919	1004
November	900	806
December	576	535

Source: Department of Industry.

From the information given, construct a Z chart for 1973. Explain when you might find such charts used and comment briefly on the advantages of representing data in this way.

O.N.C.

29.4x   *Tonnage and Service Speed of Passenger Liners of*
                          the X-Y Company

Gross Tonnage	Service Speed (knots)
26,000	25.0
21,700	24.0
26,000	25.0
21,630	24.0
20,300	19.4
15,020	21.6
15,010	21.6
20,100	20.0
26,300	24.6
21,660	20.5

10,470	19.4
20,450	22.2
11,730	20.1
12,150	19.9
16,990	19.6
19,930	19.4
14,440	19.0
9,420	19.3

(a) What is the purpose of analysing data by means of a scatter diagram?

(b) Draw a scatter diagram to illustrate the above figures.

(c) Comment on what the diagram reveals. O.N.C.

29.5x *Transport: Great Britain 1973*

	Number of New Registrations of Road Vehicles	Index of Vehicle Distances Travelled (av. 1963 = 100)
January	206,295	153
February	198,531	142
March	223,353	177
April	192,364	180
May	194,446	184
June	186,845	197
July	172,407	214
August	254,438	212
September	159,388	197

Source: Department of the Environment.

(a) The table of transport in Great Britain given above contains two sets of data expressed in different terms. By means of a ratio-scale graph show how these two sets of data may be compared. Use natural scale paper.

(b) Comment on the situation revealed by your graph. O.N.C.

29.6x (i) Describe four diagrammatic methods of presenting numerical data.

(ii) Explain how semi-logarithmic paper differs from arithmetic (or difference) graph paper and give an example of a situation in which semi-logarithmic graph paper would normally be used.

(iii) The following hypothetical data shows the state of weather in London on ten consecutive days.

Day	1	2	3	4	5	6	7	8	9	10
Noon temp. (°C)	19	18	17	20	21	19	18	20	22	19
	C	W	W	S	S	C	W	S	S	C

(C – cloudy, W – wet and S – sunny)

By using appropriate diagrammatic methods, illustrate:

(a) the proportion of days which were cloudy, wet and sunny;

(b) how the noon temperature varied from day to day. O.N.C.

29.7x (a) What advantages has semi-logarithmic graph over a natural scale graph?

(b) Plot the following two series on the same diagram using semi-logarithmic graph paper to show their relative movements and comment on the results.

How could a similar comparison be achieved without using semi-logarithmic paper?

Growth of a Company

	1970	1971	1972	1973	1974
Turnover (£)	70,000	400,000	1,200,000	1,800,000	4,100,000
Cost of materials (£)	30,000	160,000	500,000	750,000	1,400,000

O.N.C.

29.8x (a) For what reasons do we use semi-logarithmic or ratio-scale graph paper rather than the more usual arithmetic scale paper?

(b) Plot the data given below, on semi-logarithmic paper.

(c) Comment briefly on what your graph shows.

Consumers' expenditure in the United Kingdom in £m at current prices from 1960 to 1970

Item/Year	1960	1964	1968	1970
Total consumer expenditure	16,900	21,500	27,200	31,300
Food	4,200	4,900	5,700	6,400
Housing	1,660	2,340	3,290	3,900
Running costs of vehicles	450	780	1,400	1,700

Source: Annual Abstract of Statistics.   O.N.C.

29.9x The following table shows the sales of natural gas in the United States, and the natural gas sales of the Metropolitan Gas Corporation, for the period from 1956 to 1968:

Year	United States Natural Gas Sales Cubic Feet (billions)	Metropolitan Gas Corporation Natural Gas Sales Cubic Feet (billions)
1956	7,500	850
1957	8,013	1,030
1958	8,502	1,090
1959	8,750	1,150
1960	9,501	1,250
1961	10,095	1,275
1962	10,700	1,300
1963	11,030	1,350
1964	12,050	1,350
1965	12,800	1,280
1966	13,250	1,302
1967	13,900	1,390
1968	15,500	1,500

(a) Graph this data on a semi-logarithmic scale.

(b) State what the graph indicates about the comparative natural gas sales of the Metropolitan Gas Corporation and the industry as a whole, and explain the advantage of using a semi-logarithmic scale.

A.C.A.

29.10x   Using a slide rule or a table of logarithms you are required to construct semi-log graphs and plot on them the following data:

In Great Britain

Year	Total expenditure on highways (£ million)	Total number of cars licensed (thousands)	Total number of goods vehicles licensed (thousands)	Total casualties in road accidents (thousands)
1959	228.0	4,972	1,378	333
1960	238.0	5,532	1,448	348
1961	270.7	5,983	1,503	350
1962	301.2	6,560	1,522	342
1963	342.4	7,380	1,582	356
1964	405.8	8,252	1,633	385
1965	421.2	8,922	1,661	397
1966	457.4	9,522	1,639	392
1967	528.2	10,312	1,692	370
1968	580.9	10,825	1,640	349

Source: Annual Abstract of Statistics.

Interpret the graphs you have drawn and give the advantages, if any, of this type of presentation.   I.C.M.A.

29.11x   (a) Plot the following data using arithmetic scale graph paper.

Period	1	2	3	4	5	6	7	8
Data	200	320	640	1180	2080	4050	6480	9030

(b) Describe two methods of drafting a semi-logarithmic curve when no semi-logarithmic graph paper is available. Using one of those methods plot the data and state the advantages and disadvantages of using the semi-log scale over the more usual arithmetic scale.

I.C.M.A.

29.12x   *Stoppages of Work due to Industrial Disputes*

	Number of Stoppages beginning in 1973	Aggregate Number of Working Days Lost in these Stoppages (to nearest thousand)
Under 250 days	1200	125
250 and under 500	453	161
500 and under 1000	402	282
1000 and under 5000	592	1250
5000 and under 25,000	180	1844
25,000 and under 50,000	24	859
50,000 days and over	22	2625

Illustrate the above data by means of a Lorenz curve. Why is this form of graph the most suitable for displaying the above information?

O.N.C.

29.13x   (a) Construct a Lorenz curve in respect of the following data concerning the net output of manufacturing industry X:

Manufacturing Industry X

Average Number of Employees	Number of Firms	Net Output (£ million)
25 and under 100	205	16
100 and under 300	200	60
300 and under 500	35	18
500 and under 750	30	26
750 and under 1,000	20	26
1,000 and under 1,500	10	54

(b) Explain the purpose of presenting information in the form of the Lorenz curve, and comment on your answer to (a) above.

A.C.A.

Chapter 30

The Averaging of Data

Learning Objectives:
At the end of your study of this chapter you should be able to:
1. **understand the nature of statistical averages,**
2. **calculate from given data and explain the significance of**
    a) **the arithmetic mean**
    b) **the median**
    c) **the mode,**
3. **understand the circumstances in which each average is appropriate.**

So far, we have concentrated our attentions on organising and presenting data. What we shall now do is attempt to summarise the data at our disposal into a single statistic. This will certainly ease the task of making comparisons, though we must always remember that summarising data is bound to mean that something will be lost.

If you think carefully about it, you will realise that statisticians spend a great deal of their time making comparisons, and the conclusions they reach are often of fundamental importance to every one of us. Comparing income today with income ten years ago is an indicator of how our living standards have changed. Comparing incomes between regions helps the government in its regional policies. Comparing how our prices are changing over time in relation to price changes abroad indicates how competitive our industries are, and comparing our balance of payments over time indicates our ability to pay our way in the world.

Many of the comparisons made present no problems, as we are comparing a single figure value. For example, we can state that I.C.I. earned a certain profit in 1975, and compare this with the profit earned in 1976. Any problems involved in this comparison will be concerned with the calculation of the profit and the rate of inflation, and no-one will dispute that it is legitimate to compare profit in 1975 with profit in 1976 as long as inflation is taken into account. In some cases, however, the things we are trying to compare vary in themselves. Suppose, for example, we attempt to compare incomes on Merseyside with incomes in London: not only is there a variation within the regions, but also a variation within each region. In a previous chapter you saw that we could put raw data into a frequency distribution, and present it in the form of a histogram etc. No doubt we could draw histograms, showing the distribution of incomes in London and Merseyside, and this would enable us to state that incomes earned in London exceeded incomes earned on Merseyside. But is this good enough?

You can probably identify two problems in the statement above. Firstly, do we mean that *all* incomes in London exceed *all* incomes on Merseyside? Obviously not! Many people on Merseyside will earn much more than, say, a porter on the Underground. Secondly, given that incomes earned in London exceed incomes earned on Merseyside, we would wish to know by how much. In other words, we wish to *quantify* the differences in income, and we certainly will not be able to do this by just looking at a frequency distribution or a histogram. What we need is some figure that is *representative* of income in London. We can then obtain a representative figure for Merseyside incomes, compare them, and draw some conclusions as to the size of the difference in incomes.

How are we going to obtain this representative figure? Probably you have guessed already, especially in the current economic climate with our preoccupation with income levels. The TV newscaster does not state that incomes have risen by 10% over the last twelve months: he states that *average* incomes have risen. We are given information on *average* hourly rates of pay, *average* rainfall levels, batting and bowling *averages,* the *average* amount we spend on drink — and so on. The advertising men are very fond of telling us what the *average man* buys, where he goes for his holidays, and what he does with his leisure.

Three conclusions can be drawn from this last paragraph. Firstly, an average is obviously meant to tell us something about the matter under consideration, and unless it is representative of the data, it obviously cannot do this efficiently. Secondly, the word 'average' is one that we meet daily in our conversation, and is a word that is used in a very loose manner. How many times have you heard people use such remarks as 'I *think* that on average I use *about* five gallons of petrol per week'? Here the idea of an average and an *estimate* are shading into each other. We must avoid this at all costs. An average is capable of being calculated from data, and so it is precise. Thirdly, averages are used to describe a wide variety of data, and we must be really sure that we know what an average is. In fact there are many types of average, and we must be sure to select the right one for the right job. If we don't do this, then there is a great danger that the average we quote will not be representative of the data.

The Arithmetic Mean

Most people will tell you to calculate an average something like this: total all the numbers in the group and divide by how many numbers there are in the group. So the average of 5, 7, 9, and 10 is

$$\frac{5+7+9+10}{4} = 7.75$$

In fact, it is easier to demonstrate how to calculate an average than it is to explain how to calculate it. Now mathematicians have developed two useful symbols to overcome this problem. Suppose we put this group of figures we wish to average in a column, and give this column a heading x. The group we considered above would look like this:

$$x$$
$$5$$
$$7$$
$$9$$
$$10$$

If we wish to total these figures, the mathematician would state $\Sigma\ x$ — meaning take the sum of the column headed x.(Σ is a Greek capital letter pronounced *sigma*.) Also, we state that there are n figures in the column (in this case $n = 4$). So the expression

$$\frac{\Sigma x}{n}$$

tells us precisely how to calculate the average. We stated earlier that there are many forms of average, and the average we have just calculated is called the *arithmetic mean*. Statisticians use the symbol $\bar{x}$ (pronounce it 'x-bar') to stand for the arithmetic mean, so we can write

$$\bar{x} = \frac{\Sigma x}{n}$$

The arithmetic mean is certainly the most widely used average, both by statisticians and laymen. It will be useful, then, to examine in what sense it is representative. Returning to our example, we have

$$x = 5, 7, 9, 10 \quad \bar{x} = 7.75$$

Notice that the arithmetic mean represents not one single item in the group, so it cannot be representative in the sense that it is typical. It follows, then, that 'representative' means something other than typical. If we subtract the mean from each of the items in the group, we have

$$-2.75, -0.75, +1.25, +2.25$$

We call each of these differences a *deviation* from the arithmetic mean. Notice that the sum of these deviations is zero. Using the sigma notation we have

$$\Sigma(x - \bar{x}) = 0$$

So the arithmetic mean tells us the point about which the values in the group cluster ('mean' in fact means centre, and statisticians call averages measures of central tendency.) This is what we imply when we state that the mean is representative. So we now have a definition of the arithmetic mean − a measure chosen such that the sum of the deviations from it is zero.

For the moment, we shall postpone judging whether this meaning of representative is valid, and concentrate on this important definition of the mean. In fact, the definition enables us in many cases to simply our calculations of the arithmetic mean. Suppose we guess a value for the arithmetic mean (call this guess x_0). Now if our guess is correct, then the sum of the deviations from x_0 would be zero. If it isn't, then our guess was wrong, and we can adjust our guess to give the true value of the mean. Suppose, for example, we wish to find the arithmetic mean of the group

$$100.1, 100.2, 100.4, 100.8$$

If we guess the mean to be 100, then the deviations are

$$+0.1, \ +0.2, \ +0.4, \ +0.8, \text{ sum} = 1.5$$

Clearly, our guess was too low, and we must adjust our guess by

$$\frac{+1.5}{4} = +0.375$$

so the true value of the mean is

$$100 + 0.375 = 100.375$$

(You should check this value by calculating the mean directly.) We can again use the sigma sign to show precisely how to use this method to calculate the arithmetic mean.

$$\bar{x} = x_0 + \frac{\Sigma(x - x_0)}{n}$$

In other words, the arithmetic mean is the assumed mean plus a correction factor.

Now let us examine another factor of the arithmetic mean which will simplify calculations. We can multiply or divide the group of numbers we wish to average, and find the average of this adjusted group. We can then adjust the average we have calculated to the true value. Suppose, for example, we want to find the arithmetic mean of the group

$$0.0002, \ 0.0005, \ 0.0012, \ 0.0015$$

Multiplying this group by 10,000 we have

$$2, \ 5, \ 12, \ 15$$

which has a mean of 8.5. To obtain a true value for the mean, we now divide by 10,000 giving

$$\bar{x} = 0.00085$$

Of course, in many cases you would not bother to use either of the simplifications mentioned — especially if you have access to a calculating machine. Later, though, we shall meet cases where they speed up our calculations considerably, and also lessen the risk of arithmetic error.

The Arithmetic Mean of a Frequency Distribution

Earlier we recommended that you put raw data into frequency distributions wherever possible, so we must now examine how to find their arithmetic mean. If we consult the General Household Survey, we would learn that 1000 couples married in 1965 would be expected to have the following number of children in 1973.

Number of children	0	1	2	3	4
Number of families	364	362	226	44	4

We require to know the mean number of children per family. First, we will write the data into two columns, one headed x (the number of children — this is our variable) and the other headed f (frequency). If we multiply the columns together (fx) this will give the total number of children for each family size. So, for example, we see that there are a total of 132 children from 3 children families.

x	f	fx
0	364	0
1	362	362
2	226	452
3	44	132
4	4	16
	1000	962

Adding up the fx column, there are a total of 962 children in the 1000 families, which gives an average of $\frac{962}{1000} = 0.962$ children per family. Now we know that Σf means total the column headed f (this gives the total number of families) and Σfx means total the column headed fx (which gives the total number of children). So we now know how to find the arithmetic mean of a discrete frequency distribution.

$$\bar{x} = \frac{\Sigma fx}{\Sigma f}$$

Now this is all very well, but much data is in the form of grouped, continuous frequency distributions. Suppose we wished to find the average age of the male labour force. We could obtain the data we require from the Annual Abstract of Statistics. We will find the average age in 1971.

Age	Number in employment (millions)	Age	Number in employment (millions)
15, but under 20	1.1	45 –	1.5
20 –	1.7	50 –	1.3
25 –	1.5	55 –	1.4
30 –	1.3	60 –	1.1
35 –	1.3	65 but under 70	0.4
40 –	1.4		14.0

Now we have a problem here: look at the age group 20 to 25 years. Within this group there are 1.7 million men, but we have no idea what their *actual* ages are. So we are going to have to make some assumption about their ages. Probably the most sensible assumption to make is that the 1.7 million men in this group have an average age of 22.5 years — the mid-point of the group. If we do this for all groups, then we can use the formula we obtained earlier to calculate the arithmetic mean.

Mid-point	Frequency	
x	f	fx
17.5	1.1	19.25
22.5	1.7	38.25
27.5	1.5	41.25
32.5	1.3	42.25
37.5	1.3	48.75
42.5	1.4	59.50
47.5	1.5	71.25
52.5	1.3	68.25
57.5	1.4	80.50
62.5	1.1	68.75
67.5	0.4	27.00
	14.0	565.00

$$\bar{x} = \frac{\Sigma fx}{\Sigma f} = \frac{565}{14} = 40.36$$

So the average age of working males in 1971 was 40.36 years.

Now let us see if we can simplify the arithmetic involved in these calculations. Well, the first thing we can do is to multiply all the frequencies by 10: this will remove the decimal fractions and not make any difference to our answer. We can take an assumed mean (in this case we will take 42.5) and calculate the deviations of the items x from 42.5. Notice that all the deviations are divisible by 5, and if we do this we obtain a column that we head d.

x	$(x - 42.5)$	d	f	fd
17.5	-25	-5	11	-55
22.5	-20	-4	17	-68
27.5	-15	-3	15	-45
32.5	-10	-2	13	-26
37.5	-5	-1	13	-13
42.5	0	0	14	0
47.5	5	1	15	15
52.5	10	2	13	26
57.5	15	3	14	42
62.5	20	4	11	44
67.5	25	5	4	20
			140	-60

So the average deviation from the mean is $-\frac{60}{140} = -\frac{3}{7}$. But as we divided the deviation by 5, we must multiply the average deviation by 5 to give $-\frac{15}{7}$. In other words, our value for the assumed mean is $\frac{15}{7}$ greater than the true value of the mean. So the true value of the mean is

$$42.5 - \frac{15}{7} = 40.36 \text{ years}$$

which agrees with the value we obtained earlier.

Now if we say that d is the deviation from the assumed mean divided by a constant c then we can write a formula for our simplified method like this:

$$\bar{x} = x_0 + \frac{c\Sigma fd}{\Sigma f}$$

Notice that the constant c is normally equal to the class width, though you can choose any value for c which is convenient.

It will be interesting to examine the accuracy of the two means we have calculated. Considering first the mean number of children per family, the distribution gave us the exact number of children in each of the 1000 families. So our calculation of the mean number of children gave us the exact value for the mean: the same result would have been obtained if we had used the frequency distribution or the raw data. However, this is not so with the mean age of the male working population as we did not know the exact age of any of the individuals. In fact, for the members in each class we found it necessary to make an assumption about their ages, so we cannot guarantee the accuracy of the mean. You should realise that although it is much more convenient to consider grouped frequency distributions than raw data, the price we pay for this convenience is the loss of accuracy. In most cases, however, the loss in accuracy is not too serious.

So far we have considered frequency distributions with constant class widths. Now let us look at a case where the class width is uneven.

Distribution of Earnings of Weekly Paid Adults aged 21 and over, April 1971

	Frequency (millions)	Mid-point (x)
£10, but under £16	0.2	14
£16 –	0.4	17
£18 –	0.6	19
£20 –	0.7	21
£22 –	0.9	23
£24 –	1.0	25
£26 –	0.9	27
£28 –	0.9	29
£30 –	1.9	32.5
£35 –	1.4	37.5
£40 –	0.8	42.5
£45 –	0.5	47.5
£50 –	0.4	55
£60 –	0.3	65
£70, but under £100	0.1	85

Source: Annual Abstract of Statistics.

It will certainly be worthwhile multiplying the frequencies by 10, and probably taking an assumed mean (in this case we have chosen £30). However, there is no suitable constant for simplifying the deviations. So we have:

x	$(x-30)$	f	$f(x-30)$
14	-16	2	-32
17	-13	4	-52
19	-11	6	-66
21	-9	7	-63
23	-7	9	-63
25	-5	10	-50
27	-3	9	-27
29	-1	9	-9
32.5	2.5	19	47.5
37.5	7.5	14	105
42.5	12.5	8	100
47.5	17.5	5	87.5
55	25	4	100
65	35	3	105
85	55	1	55
		110	238

$$\bar{x} = 30 + \tfrac{238}{110}$$

$$= £32.16 \text{ per week}$$

So sometimes it is not practical to use the simplified method, and you should always weigh up carefully whether it is worth the labour involved. Better still, buy an electronic calculator (they are very reasonably priced these days) and it will always be worthwhile using the first method.

Limitations on the Use of the Arithmetic Mean

Earlier, we postponed judgement on just how representative was the arithmetic mean. We simply stated that 'representative' certainly doesn't mean typical. The time has now come to put the arithmetic mean through a series of tests, and see how it performs.

If you examine sources of published statistics, you will be surprised how often frequency distributions have 'open-ended' classes. We reproduce below a frequency distribution showing the estimated wealth of individuals in Great Britain in 1968.

Wealth	% of Total
Not over £5000	78.38
£5000 – £15,000	16.17
£15,000 – £25,000	2.52
£25,000 – £50,000	1.88
£50,000 – £100,000	0.70
£100,000 – £200,000	0.23
£200,000 –	0.11

Source: Annual Abstract of Statistics.

When we calculated the mean from a frequency distribution, we had to make assumptions about the values of the items in each class. We took the mid-point as the representative value of each class. But what assumptions can we make about the average wealth of individuals in the final class? It would be a brave man indeed who would estimate the upper limit for this group. Likewise, what would be a reasonable lower limit to put on the first class? Unless we have adequate information about the first and last groups, we cannot calculate the mean for this type of distribution. To obtain a mean, we must refer to the raw data (and this just is not available for government published statistics). Clearly, we need a measure that does not depend upon the adequate knowledge of extreme values of the distribution. This problem of open-ended statistics is one you will meet continually in analysis of published statistics — in fact we had quite a job finding distributions that were not open-ended! Before we leave this point, however, it should be stated that if you *must* estimate the missing limit for open-ended distributions, make sure that the frequencies in the open-ended classes are small in relation to other frequencies. Any inaccuracies due to estimates shouldn't, then, be too serious.

The second point about the arithmetic mean is that it often produces results that are not suitable from a communication viewpoint. Earlier, we found that the average number of children per family was 0.962. Most people would consider this to be a ridiculous statement. In situations like this, people expect an integer (i.e. a whole number) to be representative of the number of children per family. If we are going to ensure that all averages are integers, then we must change our idea of an average.

The third point is perhaps the most important of all: the mean is highly sensitive to extreme values. Consider the case of Fred, who at an interview for a job is told that the average income of salesmen in the company is £8000 per year. He accepts the job as he considers the firm to be very progressive with excellent prospects for himself. Although his starting salary is only £2000 a year, his salary will obviously climb very quickly. You could imagine how cheated Fred felt when he found that the sales force consisted of just five men: the sales director on £30,000 a year and four salesmen on £2500 a year! The extreme value (in this case the sales director's salary) has caused the arithmetic mean to be most unrepresentative. To examine this point further, let us return again to the distribution of weekly incomes of males over the age of 21. The cumulative frequency distribution would look like this:

	Cumulative Frequency (millions)
Under £16	0.2
Under £18	0.6
Under £20	1.2
Under £22	1.9
Under £24	2.8
Under £26	3.8
Under £28	4.7

Under £30	5.6
Under £35	7.5
Under £40	8.9
Under £45	9.7
Under £50	10.2
Under £60	10.6
Under £70	10.9
Under £100	11.0

Consulting the ogive for this distribution (Exhibit 30.1), we see that 6.45 million people earn less than the average wage of £32.16, which represents nearly 60% of all workers in this category. On this basis, many would claim that the mean is not representative of this data. Had we taken *all* incomes rather than weekly incomes only, then the average would have been much higher (and hence even more unrepresentative). This is the reason that so many people scoff at the average income figures that are quoted from time to time.

Before we search for an alternative to the arithmetic mean, we must say something in its defence. The main redeeming feature of the arithmetic mean is that its calculation involves the use of *all* the data. We will see later that this is not a characteristic of alternatives to the arithmetic mean. In other words, the weaknesses of the arithmetic mean are also its strengths. Because all the data is used, and because the arithmetic mean is capable of precise calculation, most statisticians still prefer it to other measures. In fact the arithmetic mean is capable of, and is the basis for, advanced analysis. Any alternative to the arithmetic mean cannot be used for advanced analysis, so their uses are descriptive rather than analytical.

The Median

Suppose we arranged a group of numbers in ascending order, then the median would be the value of the item in the middle. So the median of the group 3, 4, 7, 9, 11 is 7. Notice that the median is quite unaffected by extremities at either end of the group. Take the case of the sales force considered earlier: the incomes are

$$£2500, £2500, £2500, £2500, £30,000$$

and the median income is £2500. The actual size of the director's income makes no difference whatsoever to the median: if the director's salary was doubled or halved then the median would still remain £2500. So the median is quite insensitive to extreme values in the group or distribution, and certainly overcomes the major objections to the arithmetic mean. If you arrange a group of n items in ascending order, then the value of the $\frac{(n+1)}{2}$ th item is the value of the median. If we had an even number of items, then there will be *two* middle items. Conventionally, we take the median to be the arithmetic mean of the two middle items. So the median of 4, 9, 13, 17, 30, 32 is $\frac{13+17}{2} = 15$. Now if n is large, the difference between $\frac{(n+1)}{2}$ and $\frac{n}{2}$ is negligible − so take $\frac{n}{2}$ in such cases. Finally, then, we can see that half the items in a distribution will be more than the median, and half the items less than it.

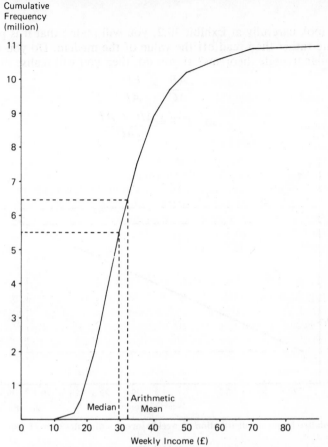

Cumulative frequency distribution of weekly incomes of males over 21 years old 1971

Exhibit 30.1

Look again at the cumulative frequency distribution of weekly incomes. There are 11 million workers, so if we wish to find the median income, this will involve finding the income of the 5.5 millionth worker. Reading off the income of this worker from the ogive, we find that the median income is £29.8, compared with a mean income of £32.16. You would probably find that most people would accept the median as being more representative than the arithmetic mean.

It is often quite difficult to read off the value of the median from the ogive, and to overcome this problem it is useful to magnify that part of the ogive containing the median. From the cumulative frequency distribution, we can see that 5.6 million people earn less than £30 per week, and 4.7 million earn less than £28 per week. So the median lies somewhere between £28 and £30 per week. We can plot these points on a graph and join them with a straight line. Reading off from Exhibit 30.2, we see that the median income is £29.78.

If you look carefully at Exhibit 30.2, you will realise that it is possible to calculate rather than read off the value of the median. Do you remember the similar triangle theorems? If you do, then you will realise that

$$\frac{AB}{AC} = \frac{ED}{AE}$$

so $ED = \frac{AB \times AE}{AC}$

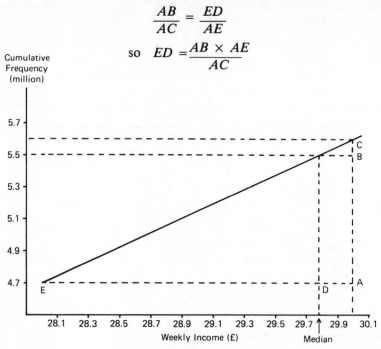

Cumulative
Frequency
(million)

Weekly Income (£)

Median

Cumulative frequency distribution of weekly incomes of males over 21 years old 1971

Exhibit 30.2

Now we can see that *ED* is the amount by which the median exceeds 28, so the median is

$$28 + \frac{AB \times AE}{AC}$$

$$= 28 + \frac{0.8 \times 2}{0.9}$$

$$= 29.78$$

It might be useful to see how we could obtain these figures directly from the cumulative frequency distribution. The relevant parts of this distribution are:

	Cumulative Frequency
Under £28	4.7
Under £30	5.6

so we see that the median is in the group £28—£30, and the median is:

$$28 + \frac{0.8 \times 2}{0.9}$$

Clearly, 28 represents the lower class boundary (LCB) of the median group, and AE represents the class interval of this group. The quantity AC is the frequency of the median group $(5.6 - 4.7)$ and the quantity AB is the median item minus cumulative frequency up to the median group $(5.5 - 4.7)$. So we can calculate the median like this:

$$LCB + \frac{\text{class interval} \times ([\frac{n+1}{2}] - \text{cum. frequency to median group})}{\text{frequency of median group}}$$

Now let us see if we can calculate the median directly, i.e. without reference to graphs.

Size of Companies Acquired 1969

Cost	Frequency	Cumulative Frequency
Not more than £100 thousand	279	279
£100 thou. but under £200 thou.	157	436
£200 thou. but under £500 thou.	166	602
£500 thou. but under £1 mill.	117	719
£1 mill. but under £2 mill.	58	777
£2 mill. but under £5 mill.	66	843
£5 mill. but under £10 mill.	30	873
£10 mill. but under £20 mill.	12	885
£20 mill. but under £50 mill.	5	890
Over £50 million	1	891

Source: *Board of Trade Journal*

We wish to find the median cost of companies acquired, i.e. the cost of the $\frac{891+1}{2} = 446$th company. The median company is in the group £200 thou. – £500 thou., which contains 166 companies. Hence the median is

$$£200,000 + \frac{300,000 \times (446 - 436)}{166}$$

$$= £218,072$$

Notice how difficult it would be to calculate the arithmetic mean of this distribution. It would be extremely difficult to put a lower limit on the first group, or an upper limit on the last group. The median, then, has decided advantages over the arithmetic mean; it can cope with open-ended distributions and is unaffected by extremities at either end of the distribution. Its disadvantage is that it ignores the bulk of the data presented to us, and this disadvantage really is critical! We would like to emphasise again that you should always attempt to use the mean rather than the median, especially if there is not much difference between them. In fact, the difference between them depends on the skewness of the distribution (this is illustrated in Exhibit 30.3). The median splits the area under the frequency curve into two halves. If the distribution is symmetrical, then the mean and median will coincide. With a negatively skewed distribution the median exceeds the mean, and with a positively skewed distribution the mean exceeds the median. The more pronounced is the skew, the greater will be the difference between the mean and median. Let us now attempt to summarise this into a simple rule: if you require a representative measure and the distribution is markedly skew, use the median — otherwise use the mean.

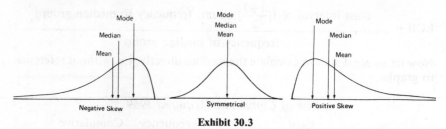

Exhibit 30.3

One final problem concerned with the median is that we cannot pool two medians to find an overall median. If we know that a factory employs 100 women at a median wage of £32 per week and 200 men at a median wage of £43 per week, we cannot calculate the median wage for all workers without consulting the raw data. But this is not the case with the arithmetic mean. Suppose the data referred to mean rather than median wages, then the total wages earned by women would be £32 × 100 = £3200, and the total wages earned by men would be £43 × 200 = £8600. So the labour force of 300 earns £11,800 per week, which gives an average wage of $\frac{11,800}{300}$ = £39.33 per week. This pooling of arithmetic means is extremely useful.

The Mode

The mode is the value or attribute that occurs most often, so is an extremely simple concept. Look again at the incomes of the sales force described earlier and you will realise that the modal income is £2500. Straight away, though, we can see a snag with the mode: if all the numbers in the group are different, then we cannot have a modal value.

With a frequency distribution, the mode is the value with the greatest frequency. Let us examine again the distribution of the number of children of 1000 young married couples.

Number of children	0	1	2	3	4
Number of families	364	362	226	44	4

The mean number of children per family we calculated to be 0.962, and the median number of children is one (i.e. the number of children in the 500th family). But the modal number of children is zero, because more families are childless than have any other number of children.

Finding the mode of a grouped frequency distribution will not be quite so easy. Consider again the distribution of weekly paid adults: the class width is not constant so the modal class cannot be obtained by inspection. Probably the best way to deal with this is to draw the histogram of the distribution. If you examine the distribution carefully, you will see that incomes in excess of £35 are falling off rapidly, so we will concentrate our attention on incomes less than this figure. Consulting exhibit 30.4 we can see that the modal class is £24 – £26 per week, and as the adjacent classes have the same frequency, we might be justified in saying the modal income was £25 per week.

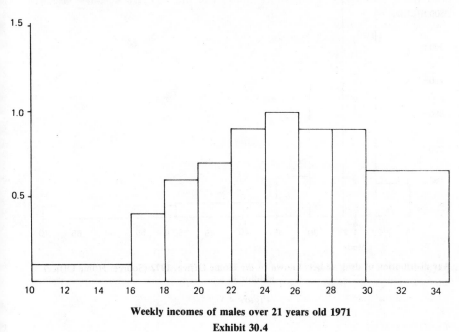

Weekly incomes of males over 21 years old 1971
Exhibit 30.4

Suppose the adjacent classes do not have the same frequencies; then we would estimate the mode by splitting the modal class in the ratio of the frequencies of the adjacent classes. This is often done geometrically as illustrated in Exhibit 30.5.

The mode has the same weaknesses as the median: it ignores the bulk of the data and is not capable of being pooled. We have also seen that in certain groups of numbers, a mode might not be present. Also, in some distributions it is possible to have more than one mode – a distribution like the one in exhibit 30.6 is called bimodal. To quote two modes is just clouding the issue. The strength of the mode is that it is extremely easy both as a concept and as a measure of calculation. It is particularly useful to describe attributes – when we state that the average family cleans their teeth with 'Gritto', we mean more families use Gritto than any other toothpaste. You can readily understand why the mode is so popular with market researchers!

318

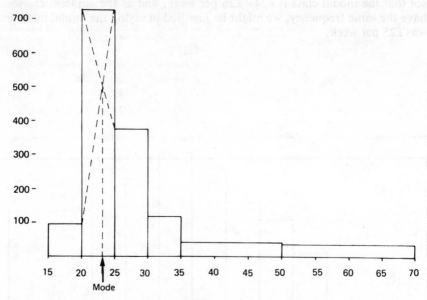

Age distribution of drug addicts known to the Home Office, 1972 (Source: Home Office)
Exhibit 30.5

Figure 4.5

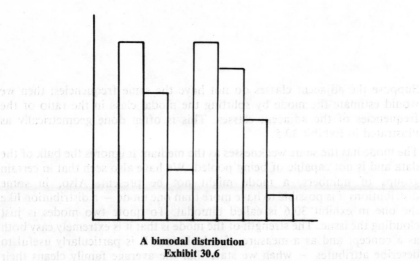

A bimodal distribution
Exhibit 30.6

Assignment Exercises

30.1x Explain why it is frequently necessary to summarise masses of data by using representative or typical values. Describe two such measures and their methods of calculation.　　　　　　　　　　　　　　　　A.C.A.

30.2x If we examine the batting average table for Coalshire we find that Fred Sloggin has an average of 51 runs, and D.E.M. Bones has an average of 39 runs. Would you conclude that Sloggin was the more effective batsman?

Sloggin's average of 51 runs has been obtained in 39 innings. The next innings will be his last of the season. How many runs must he score in the last innings if his final average is to be at least 55 runs?

30.3　　　*No. of children per 1000 families in which couples were married in 1960-4*

No. of children	0	1	2	3	4	5	6+
Frequency (%)	5.3	5.2	55.4	11.4	18.9	1.5	2.3

Source: General Household Survey.

Calculate the median.

Calculate the mean number of children per family for the above data, given that the average size of a family with 6 or more children is 6.5.

30.4x A company employing 60 people found that the number of sick days taken by its employees last year were as follows:

10	5	12	0	2	35	11	12	4	9
12	17	3	7	8	8	8	10	11	29
44	4	9	3	6	6	7	13	18	4
15	25	5	2	7	20	9	16	10	9
5	2	31	6	0	7	10	9	22	1
3	1	23	9	12	18	6	9	31	0

Group the above figures into intervals of five days. Calculate the mean. Draw the cumulative frequency curve of the distribution and comment on the distribution.　　　　　　　　　　　　　　　　O.N.C.

30.5　　　　　　　　　　*Orders Received*

Value of Order (£00)	Number of Orders Received
0 and under 5	20
5 and under 10	51
10 and under 15	139
15 and under 20	116
20 and under 25	31
25 and under 30	14
30 and over	5
	376

(a) From the above table of orders received calculate the mean value of orders received.

(b) Comment briefly on your results for (a)

(c) Suppose the value of the median to be less than the mean. What would this indicate?　　　　　　　　　　　　　　　　O.N.C.

320

30.6x The rateable values of 120 houses were found and the results are shown below.

Rateable Value (£)	Number of Houses
70 – 79.99	3
80 – 89.99	15
90 – 99.99	30
100 – 109.99	36
110 – 119.99	18
120 – 129.99	12
130 – 139.99	6

Calculate the mean of the distribution. O.N.C.

30.7 The table below gives the age distribution of the management of a large company.

Age	Frequency
Under 20	2
20 – 29	12
30 – 39	31
40 – 49	39
50 – 59	26
Over 60	10

Calculate the mean of the distribution. List the assumptions you made in carrying out the calculation and explain why you think you were justified in making them. O.N.C.

30.8x   *Age Distribution of the Members of a Golf Club*

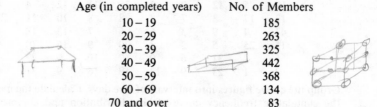

Age (in completed years)	No. of Members
10 – 19	185
20 – 29	263
30 – 39	325
40 – 49	442
50 – 59	368
60 – 69	134
70 and over	83

(a) Calculate the arithmetic mean age for the data. (Use mid-value of Group 40—49 as a working origin.)

(b) Define and distinguish between discrete and continuous variables. O.N.C.

30.9x Distinguish between discrete and continuous data. The data below shows the number of local telephone calls made by 75 subscribers during a certain interval of time.

No. of Calls Made	No. of Subscribers
1—10	9
1⅟—15	12
16—20	24
21—25	16
26—40	14
	75

(a) Draw a histogram to illustrate the data.

(b) Calculate the average number of calls made per subscriber.

(c) Calculate the maximum error in your average due to grouping in the data given. O.N.C.

30.10   *Mileages Recorded by 60 Commercial Travellers in the Course of One Week*

515	611	530	557	586	528
533	516	519	560	572	509
520	543	556	532	512	605
559	549	539	609	589	537
524	521	513	541	581	618
544	545	535	568	583	521
555	552	579	581	558	539
562	578	563	598	594	560
595	507	562	532	590	578
526	533	574	531	584	543

(a) From this data tabulate directly a grouped frequency distribution using equal class intervals and starting with '500-under 520'.

(b) Construct the histogram of this distribution.

(c) What is the direction of skew of this distribution?

(d) Calculate the arithmetic mean of the grouped frequency distribution.

(e) Explain why the arithmetic mean of the ungrouped data would be different from the mean obtained in (d).   O.N.C.

30.11 The following table shows the age distribution of employees in two factories A and B. Estimate the median age in each factory using an appropriate graph and check the results by calculation.

Age of Employees	Number of Employees	
	A	B
15 – 19	79	5
20 – 24	98	23
25 – 29	128	58
30 – 34	83	104
35 – 39	39	141
40 – 44	19	98
45 – 49	11	43
50 – 54	7	19
55 – 59	3	6

O.N.C.

30.12x Explain the difference between a continuous variable and a discrete variable.

The table below gives the earnings (to the nearest £) of 150 employees in a large factory

Income	Frequency	Income	Frequency
£5000 – £5499	1	£2500 – £2999	8
£4500 – £4999	0	£2000 – £2499	34
£4000 – £4499	1	£1500 – £1999	38
£3500 – £3999	2	£1000 – £1499	42
£3000 – £3499	4	£500 – £999	20

(a) What are the class boundaries of the class with frequency 8?

(b) Draw a cumulative frequency curve of the distribution.

(c) What percentage of the group earn less than £2200?

(d) Calculate the median income as accurately as you can.

(e) Under what conditions is the median a better measure of central tendency than the arithmetic mean?   O.N.C.

30.13x   *Distribution of Personal Incomes before Tax in the U.K. 1969-70*

Income Range (£)		Number of Incomes (00,000's)
below	400	7
400 and under	600	26
600 and under	800	27
800 and under	1000	26
1000 and under	1250	32
1250 and under	1500	30
1500 and under	2000	42
2000 and under	3000	19
3000 and over		8
Total		217

Source: Social Trends, 1971 modified.

(a) Obtain the cumulative frequencies.

(b) By calculation or graphically, obtain the median.

(c) Would you expect the arithmetic mean of the distribution to be greater than, equal to, or less than the median?

Explain your answer. (Do not carry out any further calculations.)

O.N.C.

30.14 (a) Define the median, mean, and mode listing the advantages and disadvantages attributable to each.

(b) (i) Calculate the median, mean and mode for the following:

Wage Groups (hourly rate in pence)	Number of Employees
50 and under 60	5
60 and under 70	25
70 and under 80	134
80 and under 90	85
90 and under 100	69
100 and under 110	43
110 and under 120	34

(ii) Illustrate a use for each of the three statistics calculated.

I.C.M.A.

30.15x The marks scored by students in an examination are shown below. (Marking is in whole marks only.)

Marks Scored	10-19	20-29	30-39	40-49	50-59	60-69	70-79	80-89	90-99
No. of Students	4	12	23	37	43	32	19	8	2

(a) Draw a histogram to illustrate the above distribution.

(b) What are the class boundaries of the modal class?

(c) Estimate by calculation the median mark.

(d) If 16⅔% of the pupils are to be given a pass with distinction, what mark will be necessary to achieve this?

(e) What proportion would fail if the pass mark were 48?

O.N.C.

Chapter 31

Index Numbers

Learning Objectives:

At the end of your study of this chapter you should be able to:

1. recognise the need for a weighted average,
2. understand the nature of an index number,
3. construct simple index numbers from given data.

So far, we have explored at some depth the meaning of the word average, and we have been at pains to point out that an average is not necessarily representative of the data it describes. Now we are going to concern ourselves with averages at work. Make no mistake about it, averages do play a very important part in our lives — especially those that try to describe economic data. Now statisticians have constructed a device which attempts to measure the magnitude of changes over time — a device called an *index number*.

Without doubt, an index is an extremely fashionable statistical tool. Open any copy of the Annual Abstract of Statistics and you are sure to be impressed by the number of indexes (or indices, if you prefer this form of the plural) that are calculated by the government statisticians. In fact, no self-respecting government department would fail to produce at least one index! We do not wish you to get the impression that all index numbers are generated by government departments — the Financial Times Ordinary Share Index, and the Economist's Key Indicators are notable indexes generated by the private sector.

What is an Index Number?

One of the commodities which is subject to frequent price fluctuations is gold. The following prices for gold on the London Bullion Market were extracted from the *Financial Times* (prices are approximate as we had to extract them from a graph that was not very easy to read).

	$ per fine ounce
End of	
Aug. 1975	155
Sept.	143
Oct.	144
Nov.	139
Dec.	140
Jan. 1976	131

We notice that the trend in gold prices has been steadily downwards. The price at the end of September was $\frac{143}{155} \times 100 = 92.3\%$ of the previous month's price and the price at the end of October was 92.9% of the price at the end of August. If we call the price at the end of August 100% we can calculate percentages for each of the other months like this:

End of	Price as % of Aug. 1975	
Aug. 1975		100
Sept.	$\frac{143}{155} \times 100$	92.3
Oct.	$\frac{144}{155} \times 100$	92.9
Nov.	$\frac{139}{155} \times 100$	89.7
Dec.	$\frac{140}{155} \times 100$	90.3
Jan. 1976	$\frac{131}{155} \times 100$	84.5

The percentages we have calculated in the final column are index numbers (it is usual to drop the percentage sign). We first decide on a *base* (in this case, August 1975), and calculate the relative change in a price for the following periods. In other words, if we call the price in the base period P_0, and the price in any following period P_n, then the index for that period is

$$\frac{P_n}{P_0} \times 100$$

If this is all that is involved in index numbers you might well wonder what all the controversy surrounding them could possibly be about! Well, for a start, this is a very simple series of index number, and we will soon be examining more complicated ones (and hence more controversial ones). But even with an index as simple as this one, there is a problem involved: the choice of a suitable base period. We wish really to choose a base when the price is as normal as possible, i.e. when the price is not unduly high or unduly low. Otherwise, the index will move away from the base figure too quickly and show very large deviations from it. Suppose, for example, the price of a particular stock at certain periods of time was

April	125p	(takeover rumour)
July	69p	(takeover unsuccessful, poor dividends announced)
Dec.	95p	(quite good dividends forecast)

then the price index for this particular stock could be

	April = 100	July = 100	Dec. = 100
April	100	181.2	131.6
July	55.2	100	72.6
Dec.	76	137.7	100

The best base to choose is probably December, because this minimises the greatest deviation from the base (31.6). Does this matter? Well, there is evidence to show that people are more likely to understand and appreciate smaller percentage changes than larger ones. This is one of the reasons that statisticians tend to update the bases that they use. Another reason is that bases in the not-to-distant past tend to be much more meaningful to the users of the index. It would be much more reasonable to compare prices now with prices in (say) 1970 than it would be to compare them with prices in 1949.

This problem of choosing a suitable base can also be illustrated if we are constructing an index to measure the volume of production. Suppose we wish to measure the increase in motor-vehicle production. If we take as our base a month in which there is a major strike, then the index in the following months would be bound to show a substantial increase and give a misleading impression of the prosperity of the motor industry. If we were constructing an index of motor-car sales, which do you think would be the *worst* month to choose as a base?

This problem of choosing a suitable base can be overcome by using a chain base index where the base used is the previous period. This method has found particular favour in the United States. Let us return to the example of gold prices considered earlier, and calculate chain based index numbers for this data.

Time Period	Price ($)	Price Index, previous month = 100	Price Index Aug. = 100
August	155	100	100
September	143	$\frac{143}{155} \times 100 = 92.3$	92.3
October	144	$\frac{144}{143} \times 100 = 100.7$	92.9
November	139	$\frac{139}{144} \times 100 = 96.5$	89.7
December	140	$\frac{140}{139} \times 100 = 100.7$	90.3
January	131	$\frac{131}{140} \times 100 = 93.6$	84.5

So we can see that in (say) January the price of gold bullion was 6.4% lower than in the previous month.

Chain based index numbers are particularly suited for period by period comparisons, but if we are to compare the movement of prices over time then the fixed base indexes are much easier to interpret.

A Simple Aggregate Index

So far, we have concerned ourselves with measuring the price changes for a single commodity — but suppose we want to measure changes in the cost of living. Our monthly spending is made up of a whole range of goods, and in measuring cost of living changes we will want to take this into account. We could, of course, construct a separate index for each of the goods we buy, but this would be very cumbersome. What we require is a single index that will efficiently measure changes in the cost of living for us. Suppose we wish to construct a price index for gardeners. Typical items that they might buy would be

	Price in 1975	1976
Seeds (per packet)	8p	10p
Onion sets (per lb)	20p	24p
Seed compost (per kilo)	65p	85p
Fertiliser (per kilo)	75p	£1.25p
	£1.68p	£2.44p

So we can see that a bundle of gardening goods costing £1.68 in 1975 would cost £2.44 in 1976. If we take 1975 as our base year, then the price index for 1976 could be calculated like this:

$$\frac{2.44}{1.68} \times 100 = 145.2, \quad 1975 = 100$$

An index constructed like this is called a *simple aggregate index,* and from it we can conclude that the cost of gardening has risen 45.2% between 1975 and 1976. Or can we? Suppose we had quoted the price of fertiliser in 5 kilo units, then the prices would be:

	1975	1976
Seeds (per packet)	8p	10p
Onion sets (per lb)	20p	24p
Seed compost (per kilo)	65p	85p
Fertiliser (per 5 kilo)	£3.75p	£6.25p
	£4.68	£7.44

Again taking 1975 as our base, the price index for 1976 is

$$\frac{7.44}{4.68} \times 100 = 158.9$$

which gives a very different result from the previous one! The trouble with simple aggregate indexes is that the result you get depends on the quantities you choose. If we had quoted the price of onion sets in 3-lb units the result would have been different again. Try it for yourself and see. The problem here is to decide what quantities are appropriate, and for this reason few people would take such indexes seriously (though they are still used). What we require is an index independent of the quantities bought.

Suppose that for each good we divide the 1976 price by the 1975 price. This gives us the *price relatives* with 1975 as base.

	1975	1976	Price Relative
Seeds (per packet)	8p	10p	1.25
Onion sets (per lb)	20p	24p	1.20
Seed compost (per kilo)	65p	85p	1.31
Fertiliser (per kilo)	75p	£1.25p	1.66
			5.42

So the price relative shows the percentage change in price for each of the goods (seeds, for example, cost 25% more in 1976 than in 1975). If we find the arithmetic mean of the price relatives, and multiply by 100, we have the price index for 1976.

$$\frac{5.42}{4} \times 100 = 135.5$$

Suppose we call the price in the base year P_0, and the price in the nth year P_n, then an index of the arithmetic mean of the price relatives can be calculated like this:

$$\frac{\sum \frac{P_n}{P_0}}{x} \times 100$$

where x is the number of goods we are considering.

The great advantage of this index over the simple aggregate index is that it is independent of the quantities used (the price relative for fertiliser is 1.66 whether we measure in kilos or in 5 kilos). In this respect, it is a better index than the simple aggregate index. However, it does have its faults, as it takes no account of the quantities bought. Would it be true to say that a 25% increase in the price of seeds has less significance than a 31% increase in the price of seed compost? On a percentage basis, the answer must without doubt be 'yes', but in fact the significance of price changes depends on the actual price (a 50% increase in petrol prices is more significant than a 50% increase in the price of matches). Also, the significance of a price increase depends on the quantities bought (a 50% increase in the price of tobacco has no significance to the non-smoker). We shall now turn our attention to devising an index that attempts to overcome these problems.

Weighted Averages

Returning to our friend the gardener, suppose we asked him to supply us with details of the quantities of materials he bought in 1975. Suppose he bought the following quantities:

> 20 packets of seeds
> 2 lb of onion sets
> 1 kilo of seed compost
> 3 kilos of fertiliser

Multiplying these quantities by their prices, we can calculate how much he spent on these goods in 1975. Also, we know the prices of these goods in 1976, so we can calculate how much the 1975 quantities would cost if they were bought in 1976.

1975 Quantities (q_0)	1975 Prices (p_0)	1976 Prices (p_n)	$p_0 q_0$	$p_n q_0$
20	8	10	160	200
2	20	24	40	48
1	65	85	65	85
3	75	125	225	375
			490	708

So we can see that the batch of gardening goods bought in 1975 cost £4.90, and if we had bought the same batch in 1976 it would have cost £7.08. So if we say that the goods cost 100 in 1975, their cost in 1976 would be –

$$\frac{708}{490} \times 100 = 144.5$$

that is, a 44.5% increase in price.

Notice that we call the base year quantities q_0, the base year prices p_0, and the prices of the same goods in the nth year p_n. So we can calculate this index by taking

$$\frac{\Sigma p_n q_0}{\Sigma p_0 q_0} \times 100$$

It shows what the cost of goods in the nth year would be, assuming that we bought the same quantities as in the base year, and assuming that we called the base year price 100.

We should, however, note that in practice it is not usually calculated in the way we have done — it is more usual to use price relatives and weights. To understand what is meant by weights, let us examine the total outlay on each good in 1975.

Outlay	Price Relative
£1.60 on seeds	1.25
£0.40 on onion sets	1.20
£0.65 on seed compost	1.31
£2.25 on fertiliser	1.66
£4.90	

The total outlay on each good measures the relative size of each good in our purchases, and we can see that a doubling in the price of, say, fertiliser is more significant than a doubling in the price of onion sets. Alongside the outlays we have written the price relatives. Notice that seed compost has increased in price by a greater percentage than seeds, but as seeds involve a greater total outlay, the increase in the price of seeds is probably more significant. If we multiply price relative by total outlay, then we will be taking into account the fact that expenditure on some items is more significant than expenditure on others. We will be *weighting* the price relatives, and using the expenditures in 1975 as weights. Notice that our suspicions are confirmed: the increase in price of seeds is more significant than the increase in price of seed compost.

Weights (w)	Price Relatives (PR)	$w \times PR$
1.60	1.25	2.0000
0.40	1.20	0.4800
0.65	1.31	0.8515
2.25	1.66	3.7350
4.90		7.0665

An index for 1976 is now obtained like this:

$$\frac{7.0665}{4.90} \times 100 = 144.2, \text{ i.e.}$$

$$\frac{\Sigma \text{ (price relative} \times \text{weight)}}{\Sigma \text{ (weights)}} \times 100$$

This gives an identical index to the previous one (the difference of 0.3 is due to rounding off the price relatives).

More usually, the weights are made to total some convenient figure. Often this figure is one; in the case of the Index of Retail Prices it is 1000. So in the case of seeds, for example, the weights could be expressed as

$$\frac{1.6}{4.9} = 0.3265, \quad \text{in which case the weights would total one}$$

or $1.6 \times \dfrac{1000}{4.9} = 326.5,$ in which case the weights would total 1000.

Whichever way is used, we are considering weights as the outlay on each item relative to total outlay, and the index obtained would be identical to using *actual* outlay on each item. Try it for yourself and see. The reason for using relative outlay is that it is easier to divide by one or a thousand than it is to divide by (say) 4.9 (remember we will be calculating an index for each year). Also, relative outlay makes comparison between items easier than actual outlay.

Both methods that we have used are weighted averages. In the first case, we used prices and quantities — in fact the quantities were acting as weights. So if we wish to use base year quantities as weights, then we must use actual prices to calculate our price index. However, if we use base year expenditures as weights, then we use price relatives to calculate the index. Most statisticians prefer to use expenditure rather than quantities as weights. The reason is quite simply that it is easier to obtain data on expenditure (the cost of living data is obtained by the Survey of Household Expenditure — that is by sampling). Also, we can consider occasions when 'quantities' wouldn't make sense — how can one define 'quantities' of public transport? However, it would be quite possible to obtain details of personal expenditure on public transport.

We have considered weighted averages without considering the problems involved in weighting. Take the example of our gardener: we have included seeds, onion sets, seed compost and fertiliser on his annual shopping list. Clearly, this list cannot be exhaustive: many other items should be included on the list. This is a basic problem of constructing a price index — what should be included and what should be left out. We have not included gardening tools on the assumption that he already has them, but tools wear out and will need replacing. Hence changes in the price of tools will ultimately affect our gardener, and should be included in our index. If we are going to use quantities as weights, then we must take into account the life of tools. It would be much easier to weight tools in our index by taking the money outlay on tools by a number of representative gardeners.

330

Assignment Exercises

31.1x What considerations must be borne in mind when an index number is compiled? You should illustrate your answer by reference to any index number with which you are familiar. O.N.C.

31.2x A company has reached an agreement with representatives of its employees that wages and salaries will in future be tied to a local cost of living index which the company will compile. Advise the company how they should gather information and compile this local cost of living index. What are the problems the company will encounter in completing this exercise? O.N.C.

31.3 (a) Explain briefly the principles of index number construction.

(b) A certain company uses approximately 6, 2, 5, 3 thousand units of raw materials, A, B, C, D respectively. The average price (£) per unit of the raw materials in 1970 and 1973 is given in the following table:

	Average Price in 1970	Average Price in 1973
Raw material A	10	15
B	21	39
C	2	3
D	46	101

Calculate the Simple Aggregative Index for the year 1973 with 1970 as base year. Calculate also a Weighted Aggregative Index for the period 1970-3 and explain why this may be considered preferable to the Simple Aggregate Index.

O.N.C.

31.4x The average prices of four commodities for the years 1969, 1970 and 1971 are shown in the following table:

Commodity	Average Price per Unit (£)		
	1969	1970	1971
A	8	15	14
B	54	70	72
C	15	22	29
D	75	84	78

(i) Calculate the *Simple Aggregative Index* for each of the years 1970 and 1971 with 1969 as base year.

(ii) Write down *two* main disadvantages in the use of the Simple Aggregate Index.

(iii) The number of units used annually by a certain company is approximately 5000, 1000, 3000 and 8000 for commodities A, B, C and D respectively. Calculate a Weighted Aggregative Index for the period 1969-71 and explain to what extent this Index overcomes the disadvantages you mentioned in part (ii) of this question. O.N.C.

31.5 (a) In relation to index numbers explain what is meant by (i) base year, (ii) weights.

(b) Calculate the missing value x, the weighting for housing, and y, the weighted arithmetic mean, the index for all items in the table below.

Index of Retail Prices for 1962 = 100

Group	Weights (1972)	Index (Sept. 1972)
Food	251	172
Alcoholic drink and tobacco	119	153
Housing	x	192
Fuel and light	60	173
Durable household goods	58	141
Clothing and footwear	89	144
Transport and vehicles	139	159
Other	163	177
All items	1000	y

Source: Monthly Digest of Statistics.

O.N.C.

31.6x (a) What is meant by the term 'index number'?

(b) *Index Numbers of Retail Prices in the U.K.*

Group	Index	Weight
Food	104	319
Housing	110	104
Durable household goods	100	64
Miscellaneous goods	108	63

(i) Using a weighted arithmetic mean calculate an index of retail prices for the group combining all four of these items.

(ii) If the index of retail prices for all household items (total weight = 1000) was 104, calculate the index for all items other than those listed above.

O.N.C.

31.7 *Commodity Prices*

Commodity	Relative Quantities	Prices June 1974	Prices June 1975
A	3	27p	29p
B	8	16p	16p
C	14	48p	53p
D	9	47p	42p
E	7	87p	84p

(a) Calculate an all-items price index number for June 1975 based on June 1974 using the data of commodity prices given above.

(b) Explain the difference between an index number and a price relative.

31.8x   *The A.B. Co. Ltd. Indices of Production (1960 = 100)*

		Indices	
Dept.	Weights	1962	1964
A	15	108	116
B	26	122	112
C	4	92	106
D	35	134	130

(a) Calculate for each of the two years 1962 and 1964 an index number of production for the whole firm.

(b) Calculate index numbers for each department and for the whole firm for 1964 taking 1962 as the base year.   O.N.C.

31.9 (a) Explain the difference between a price relative and a price index.

(b) The following data shows the price index numbers of two groups of commodities from 1967 to 1971. Group 1 has been prepared on the fixed-base principle, but Group 2 numbers are chain based and unlinked.

	1967	1968	1969	1970	1971
Group 1	100	106	113	122	128
Group 2	100	102	104	101	103

(i) Convert the Group 2 numbers into a series linked to the index number of 100 for 1967.

(ii) Tabulate the figures for Group 1 and the revised figures for Group 2 and briefly comment on the situation revealed.

     O.N.C.

Assignment Case Problem 1

1.   The following balances have been extracted from the Sales Ledger of Zeon Limited, at 31st December 19-5. Notes have been made of the length of time the debts have been outstanding:-

Sales Ledger Balances at 31st December 19-5

Name	Dr.	Cr.	Notes
	£	£	
Quick Trading Co. Ltd.	15,000		Nov. 6,000 Oct. 9,000
H.D.L. Limited	13,970		Nov.
Basford Limited	31,926		Oct. 8,000 Sept. 23,926
Keen & Sharp Ltd	5,217		Aug. 4,000 July 1,217
Home Counties Ltd	8,300		Dec.
W. T. Limited	7,680		Oct.
Spratt Organisation	750		Sept. 500 Aug. 250
Supply All Stores Ltd.	1,710		Nov. 710 Oct. 1,000
R. Race	350		Sept.
Alpha Discount Co. Ltd.	412		Oct.
A. Brown Ltd.	17,480		Nov. 5,480 Oct. 6,000 Sept. 6,000
B. Jones (Makers) Ltd.	2,720		Dec.
G. Wright	13,460		Dec. 4,000 Oct. 9,460
Glue Enterprises Ltd.	497		Nov.
F. Wellings Ltd.	1,365		Sept. 850 Aug. 515
G. Bacon Ltd.	1,720		Dec. 700 Nov. 1,020
Steverton Ltd.	4,491		June
Queen & Co. Ltd.	11,874		Oct. 6,530 Sept. 5,344
Square Ltd.		230	Oct.
Pegg Corporation	1,720		Nov.
U.R.R. Limited	27,250		Dec. 13,200 Nov. 14,050
A. Black & Co.		1,350	Nov.
CRT Ltd.	2,410		Sept.
J. Crank & Co. Ltd.	380		July.
	170,682	1,580	

You have recently been employed as a credit controller with Zeon Limited, and this is the first time you have been presented with the balances. Draft a new schedule which will analyse the age structure of the debtors using the information given at 31st December.

The normal procedure is to make provision for doubtful debts of 2% on balances two months overdue, and 5% on balances three or more months overdue. The normal credit terms offered to all customers is payment within 30 days.

Draft a letter you would send to debtors more than three months overdue, and to those one month overdue.

Assignment Case Problem 2

2. The Marketing Department of Temic Limited have asked for information which will help them appraise the company's marketing strategy. You have obtained the following data:-

		19x1	19x2
Cash Sales (All Net)		£	£
Direct Industrial (Home)		95,000	105,000
Factors (Home)		48,000	47,000
Retailers (Home)		130,000	135,000
Credit Sales (Gross before Discount)			
(Net after Discount)			
Direct Industrial (Home)	Gross	1,560,000	1,870,000
	Net	1,404,000	1,589,500
Direct Industrial (Export)	Gross	737,000	695,000
	Net	461,700	590,750
Factors (Home)	Gross	553,000	487,000
	Net	442,400	389,600
Factors (Export)	Gross	136,000	153,000
	Net	102,000	114,750
Retailers (Home)	Gross	99,500	112,700
	Net	84,575	98,600
Sales Returns (All Net)			
Direct Industrial (Home)		15,000	19,300
Direct Industrial (Export)		12,500	12,300
Factors (Home)		11,200	4,700
Factors (Export)		4,300	3,900
Retailers (Home)		8,400	10,500

The Gross Price has not changed from 19x1 to 19x2, but some discounts have altered.

The total market in both 19x1 and 19x2 for the company's product was estimated as:

		£'000
Direct Industrial (Home)		160,000
Factors (Home)		32,000
Retailers (Home)		13,000
		205,000

The export markets are very large but cannot be quantified. They are very price competitive.

Summarise and analyse the above data in a form which you think will help the marketing department understand the information.

Assignment Case Problem 3

3. Just over twelve months ago, Harold Partridge finally decided to start business on his own, having been made redundant from his previous job as estimator. Over many years he had been interested in making and mending pottery and had now decided that he could turn his hobby into a profitable business. Basically, he felt that there was a demand for skilful repairs to valuable china and pottery, which had grown with a widespread increase in interest in antiques. If repair work became scarce he felt that he could occupy his time making small novelty items which would sell through gift shops. He already had a small kiln at home and for many years had made gifts for friends at Christmas.

In his previous employment Harold had earned £5,000 a year, and when he finished with the firm had received £7,500 in redundancy pay. This money he had used to open a bank account for his new business. Being an independent person, he had not claimed unemployment benefit, nor had he contacted the Inland Revenue to inform them of his change in occupation. Last week, however, he had received a letter from the local Inspector of Taxes requesting information about his current employment. This had encouraged Harold to approach you whom he knows to be good at accounting. He had drafted some accounts, which he proudly presents to you, and are as follows:-

Results for the year to 30th September		£
Money received from customers for repairs		2,000
Value of novelty items produced (estimated)		4,000
		6,000
Costs		
Materials paid for	600	
Fuel Bills paid	400	1,000
Profit		5,000

In discussion with him you also obtain the following information:-

The novelty items represent 1,000 pieces he has made. He claims to have received verbal orders for these at a price of £4, and they are to be delivered in the next week or two in time for Christmas trade. He reckons they cost him £1 each. He says that customers for repair work owe him £400 for items completed but not yet paid for. He also owes £200 for materials received but not paid for. He holds unused materials worth £100.

His bank account at 30th September contains £1,000. Apart from the old kiln he started with, and which he says was worth £400 with only two years life left, he bought on 31st March, from the bank account, a new kiln costing £3,000, which he says should last him ten years. He intends to keep the old kiln as a standby in case of breakdown. All other items which have come out of his bank account are personal drawings.

He tells you that he hopes to continue working at home which he says does not cost him anything. He says that some of the neighbours have commented on fumes from the new kiln, but he has not had any complaints officially yet.

You are requested to:

1. Restate the Profit and Loss Account in accordance with accepted concepts and conventions.

2. Make notes to explain the concepts and conventions you have used in order to modify his profit statement.

3. Reconstruct his bank account.

4. Prepare Balance Sheets at the beginning and end of the year.

Having prepared this information, make some notes on points which you think Harold Partridge should consider about the future of his business — for example, has it a viable future, or should it become a limited company.

Assignment Case Problem 4

4. You are employed in the accounting department of the Wheatex Company which produces food products. The company is conducting a major review of its activities and your boss is required to make a presentation of accounting information to the board of directors. He presents you with some schedules of accounting information for the past five years and asks you to help him with his task.

Profit & Loss Statement	*19x1* £	*19x2* £	*19x3* £	*19x4* £	*19x5* £
External Sales	700,000	793,000	921,000	1,107,000	1,228,000
Cost of Goods Sold	577,050	639,146	744,099	860,800	950,300
Wages	75,824	87,240	102,584	150,041	158,189
Depreciation	7,329	9,458	12,461	14,852	18,006
Interest paid	2,301	6,582	7,136	11,553	13,897
Other Expenses	21,296	27,433	32,265	35,800	59,204
	683,800	769,859	898,545	1,073,046	1,199,596
	16,200	23,141	22,455	33,954	28,404
Investment Income	1,107	1,532	2,491	2,504	2,717
Profit before Taxation	17,307	24,673	24,946	36,458	31,121
Taxation	6,543	11,202	12,709	18,750	15,813
Net Profit after Taxation	10,764	13,471	12,237	17,708	15,308
Ordinary Share Dividend	5,450	7,280	8,000	8,950	9,330
Balance Sheet					
Ordinary Share Capital	34,102	35,425	44,638	67,379	74,964
Share Premium Account	6,250	8,253	8,253	34,286	34,286
Reserves	135,496	143,507	147,744	156,502	162,480
	175,848	187,185	200,635	258,167	271,730
Loan Capital	109,733	140,177	155,290	170,350	190,267
	285,581	327,362	355,925	428,517	461,997
Fixed Assets	121,824	128,752	143,541	164,155	259,399
Investments	76,700	78,797	81,200	85,130	60,039
Current Assets less Current Liabilities	87,057	119,813	131,184	179,232	142,559
	285,581	327,362	355,925	428,517	461,997

The Accounts expressed in percentage terms are as follows:-

Profit & Loss Statement	19x1 %	19x2 %	19x3 %	19x4 %	19x5 %
External Sales	100	100	100	100	100
Cost of Goods Sold	82.4	80.6	80.8	—	—
Wages	10.8	11.0	11.1	—	—
Depreciation	1.1	1.2	1.4	—	—
Interest paid	0.3	0.8	0.8	—	—
Other Expenses	3.1	3.5	3.5	—	—
	97.7	97.1	97.6		
	2.3	2.9	2.4	—	—
Investment Income	0.2	0.2	0.3	—	—
Profit before Taxation	2.5	3.1	2.7	—	—
Taxation	0.9	1.4	1.4	—	—
Net Profit after Taxation	1.6	1.7	1.3	—	—
Ordinary Share Dividend	0.8	0.9	0.9	—	—

Balance Sheet	%	%	%	%	%
Share Capital	12.0	10.8	12.6	—	—
Share Premium Account	2.2	2.5	2.3	—	—
Reserves	47.4	43.9	41.5	—	—
	61.6	57.2	56.4		
Loan Capital	38.4	42.8	43.6	—	—
	100.0	100.0	100.0		
Fixed Assets	42.7	39.3	40.3	—	—
Investments	26.9	24.1	22.8	—	—
Current Assets less Current Liabilities	30.4	36.6	36.9	—	—
	100.0	100.0	100.0		

You are required to:

1. Complete the accounts expressed in percentage terms for 19x4 and 19x5, by working out the missing figures.

2. Prepare graphs and diagrams which illustrate what you think are the most important features of the Profit and Loss Statement, and which you would suggest for inclusion in the annual report to shareholders.

3. Write a short report on the information contained in the accounts for the benefit of the board of directors. They wish for the most important features of the results to be emphasised in clear, non-technical language.

4. The index of retail prices has been suggested as one way in which the company might convert its sales for the five year period into units of constant purchasing power. Find out what the retail price index has been for the past five years and use it to convert the sales figures for the company into the same units of purchasing power as existed in the last year. Draw a graph to compare your calculated figures with the original sales.

Solutions to selected assignment exercises

1.2   a) stewardship. b) divide. c) limited companies. d) competitors. e) employees, government and the public.

1.3   a) true. b) false. c) false. d) true. e) false. f) false. g) true. h) false.

2.1   a) 14,500. b) 35,200. c) 135,300. d) 62,050. e) 75,000.

2.3   Liabilities; Creditors; Others; Assets.

2.5   a) + Cash: − Debtor. b) + Stock: + Creditor. c) + Debtor: − Stock. d) + Motor Van: − Bank. e) + Bank: − Debtor. f) + Bank: + Loan from Wilson. g) + Bank: + Capital. h) + Stock: − Debtors. i) + Motor Van: + Creditor. j) + Stock: − Cash.

2.7   Capital 23,750 + Creditors 2,450 = 26,200 Total. All others are assets, total 26,200.

2.9   Fixtures 2,000 + Motors 5,000 + Stock 3,500 + Bank 2,800 + Cash 100 = Total Assets 13,400. Loan 3,000 + Creditors 1,400 + Capital (difference) 9,000.

2.11   Fixtures 4,500 + Motor 4,200 + Stock 5,720 + Debtors 3,000 + Bank 4,750 + Cash 320 = Total Assets 22,490. Capital 18,900 + Loan 2,000 + Creditors 1,590.

3.1   i) Dr. Office Equipment: Cr. Bank. ii) Dr. Motor: Cr. Sussex Garages. iii) Dr. Cash: Cr. Loan J. Harwich. iv) Dr. Bank: Cr. P. Redhead. v) Dr. J. Powell: Cr. Cash. vi) Dr. L. Monks: Cr. Bank. viii) Dr. Cash: Cr. Office Equipment.

3.3   Bank Dr. 10,000 + 2,000 Cr. 4,600 + 1,900: Cash Dr. 70: Capital Cr. 10,000: Office Equipment Dr. 1,900 + 740 Cr. 48 + 70: Motor Van Dr. 4,600: F. Kent & Co. Dr. 1,900: Cr. 1,900: J. Surrey Ltd. Dr. 48: Cr. 740: Loan from Cheshire Cr. 2,000: T. Somerset Dr. 70: Cr. 70.

3.5   Cash Dr. 4,000 + 200 + 500 + 70 Cr. 3,700 + 600: W. Machinery Dr. 2,200 Cr. 70: O. Equipment Dr. 280 + 1,200: M. Van Dr. 3,200: Bank Dr. 1,000 + 3,700 Cr. 2,200 + 280 + 200: Capital Cr. 4,000 + 500: K. Devonshire Loan Cr. 1,000: Mini-Computers Dr. 600 Cr. 1,200: J. Hart Dr. 2,200 Cr. 2,200: High Lane Garage Cr. 3,200.

4.1   a) Dr. Barnes: Cr. Sales. b) Dr. Purchases: Cr. Corrigan. c) Dr. Motor Van: Cr. M.C. Ltd. d) Dr. Cash: Cr. Sales. e) Dr. Office Fixtures: Cr. Bank. f) Dr. Purchases: Cr. Bank. g) Dr. Watson: Cr. Cash. h) Dr. P. Power: Cr. Returns Out. i) Dr. Donachie: Cr. Sales. j) Dr. Hartford: Cr. Office Machinery.

4.3   Purchases Dr. 228 + 28 + 190: Sales Cr. 95 + 77 + 63 + 55: Returns Outwards Cr. 14: Kelly Dr. 14 Cr. 228: Murphy Dr. 77: O'Connor Dr. 63: McShane Cr. 190: Brogan Cr. 55. Cash Dr. 95 Cr. 28.

4.5   Bank Dr. 9,000 + 5,000: Cr. 750 + 770: Purchases Dr. 806 + 150 + 420: Returns Inwards Dr. 46 + 30: Lorre Dr. 36 + 770: Cr. 806: Greenstreet Dr. 236: Cr. 46: Fitzgerald Cr. 420: Capital Cr. 9,000 + 500: Cash Dr. 500 + 110: Cr. 150: Sales Cr. 236 + 110 + 308: Returns Outwards Cr. 36: Fixtures Dr. 750 + 306: Cr. 28: Bogart Dr. 308 Cr. 30: Raft Dr. 28 Cr. 306: Redford Loan Cr. 5,000.

5.1   a) Dr. Rent: Cr. Cash. b) Dr. Purchases: Cr. Cash. c) Dr. Bank: Cr. Rates. d) Dr. General Expenses: Cr. Bank. e) Dr. Cash: Cr. Commissions Received. f) Dr. T. Jones: Cr. Returns Out. g) Dr. Cash: Cr. Sales. h) Dr. Office Fixtures: Cr. Bank. i) Dr. Wages: Cr. Cash. j) Dr. Drawings: Cr. Cash.

5.3   Bank Dr. 5,000: Cr. 44 + 330 + 2,160 + 100: Purchases Dr. 1,360: Sales Cr. 280 + 295 + 440: Returns Outwards Cr. 30: Stationery Dr. 44: Wages Dr. 192: Rates Dr. 330: Lighting & Heating Dr. 80: Fixtures Dr. 1,950: Motor Van Dr. 2,160: Cash Dr. 280 + 70: Cr. 192 + 80 + 61: Commission Received Cr. 70: Motor Expenses Dr. 61: Rent Dr. 100: J. Lovis & Son Dr. 30 Cr. 1,360: S. R. Robinson Dr. 295: J. Conte Dr. 440: M. Ali Cr. 1,950: Capital Cr. 5,000.

5.5   Bank Dr. 25,000 + 2,000 + 16: Cr. 500 + 340 + 580 + 590: Purchases Dr. 1,960 + 720 + 190: Returns Outwards Cr. 140: Returns Inwards Dr. 40 + 30: Office Fixtures Dr. 590: Motor Van Dr. 2,350: Capital Cr. 25,000: Eisenhower Cr. 2,000: Travelling Expenses Dr. 48 Cr. 16: Rent Dr. 340: Rent Received Cr. 120: Wages Dr. 220: Cash Dr. 500 + 120 Cr. 190 + 48 + 220 + 50: Sales Cr. 620 + 490 + 70 + 370: H. Hoover Dr. 620 Cr. 40: Wilson Dr. 490 + 70 Cr. 30: Johnson Dr. 370: Roosevelt Cr. 1,960: Coolidge Dr. 140 + 580 Cr. 720: Washington Dr. 590 Cr. 590: Truman Cr. 2,350: Drawings Dr. 50.

6.1   Trial Balance: Drs. Bank 4,058, Cash 20, Purchases 2,060, Insurance 177, Rent 100, Wages 170, Salford 495, Blackpool 424: Crs. Sales 1,479, Capital 5,000, Selby 150, Thirsk 75, York 800. Totals 7,504.

6.3   Trial Balance Drs. Bank 4,849, Cash 270, Fixtures 1,750, Purchases 2,140, Returns Inwards 30, Franklin 220, Whittle 380, Fleming 70, Motor Van 2,950, Rates 310, Insurance 116, Motor Expenses 36, Drawings 100, Postages 28. Crs. Capital 8,000, Sales 1,849, Returns Outwards 51, Bell 1,750, Arkwright 810, Morse 564, Wallis 115, Commission 110. Totals 13,249.

7.1   Trading Dr. Stock 4,080, Purchases 14,305, less Closing Stock 4,960, Cost of Goods Sold 13,425, Gross Profit 13,390, Cr. Sales 26,815: Profit & Loss Dr. Salaries 3,560, Rent & Rates 400, Motor Expenses 735, General Expenses 210, Insurance 392, Net Profit 8,093. Cr. Gross Profit 13,390. Balance Sheet: Assets; Premises 20,000, Motor 2,800, Stock 4,960, Debtors 4,090, Bank 1,375, Cash 25. Capital, Balance 24,347 + Net Profit 8,093 − Drawings 4,350 = 28,090. Creditors 5,160. Totals 33,250.

7.3   a) Motor Expenses: Dr. Paid 744, Accrued c/d 28, Cr. Profit & Loss 772; b) Insurance: Dr. Paid 420, Cr. Profit & Loss 385, Prepaid c/d 35; c) Rent: Dr. Paid 1,800, Accrued c/d 490, Cr. Accrued b/f 250, Profit & Loss 2,040; d) Rates: Dr. Prepaid b/d 220, Paid 950, Cr. Profit & Loss 880, Prepaid c/d 290; e) Rent Received: Dr. owing b/f 180, Profit & Loss 580, Cr. Received 550, Owing c/d 210.

7.5   Trading: Dr. Stock 26,550, Purchases 101,300. Carriage In 404, less Closing Stock 28,480. Cost of Goods Sold 99,774, Gross Profit 22,276; Cr. Sales 122,050; Profit & Loss; Dr. Salaries 6,297, Rent 2,520, Lighting 1,217, Office Expenses 605, Motor Expenses 2,285: Insurance 350, General 745, Net Profit 8,257: Cr. Gross Profit b/d 22,276. Balance Sheet: Capital, Balance 65,697 + Net Profit 8,257 − Drawings 6,300 = 67,654, Creditors 12,253, Expenses Owing 314: Assets: Premises 30,000, Fixtures 3,250, Motors 4,180, Stock 28,480, Debtors 13,100, Prepaid 58, Bank 1,153. Totals 80,221.

7.7   Trading: Dr. Stock 18,160, Purchases 69,185 − Returns 640, Carriage In 420 − Closing Stock 22,390 = Cost of Goods Sold 64,735. Net Profit 27,605; Cr. Sales 92,340: Profit & Loss: Dr. Wages 10,240, Carriage Out 1,570, Rent 3,265, Communication 709, Commissions 240, Insurance 376, Sundries 296, Net Profit 10,909. Cr. Gross Profit 27,605. Balance Sheet: Capital, Balance 40,888 + Net Profit 10,909 − Drawings 7,620 = 44,177, Loan 10,000, Creditors 8,160, Expenses Owing 359. Assets: Buildings 20,000, Fixtures 2,850, Stock 22,390, Debtors 14,320, Prepaid 51, Bank 2,970, Cash 115. Totals 62,696.

9.1 Totals: Cash 791, Bank 5,273, Balances, Cash 216, Bank 4,247.

9.3 Totals: Discounts Allowed 60, Cash 407, Bank 7,403, Discounts Received 41. Balances, Cash 93, Bank 3,518.

9.5 Totals: Discounts Allowed 115, Cash 820, Bank 13,634, Discounts Received 52, Balances: Cash 258, Bank Overdraft 8,141.

9.7 Total Payments 265, Postages 112, Travel 77, Cleaning 10, Sundries 11, Ledger 55.

10.1 Totals: Sales Book 2,213, Purchases 2,996, Returns Outwards 94, Returns Inwards 122, Accounts: Sales Ledger, Nelson Dr. 105, Cr. 12, Frobisher Dr. 306, Raleigh Dr. 208 + 905, Cr. 44, Columbus Dr. 289, Cr. 66. Bruce Dr. 400. Purchases Ledger, Drake Cr. 800, Wellington Dr. 15, Cr. 125, Napoleon Cr. 305 + 609. Hastings Dr. 19, Cr. 201, Gladstone Dr. 60, Cr. 550, Palmerstone Cr. 106, Disraeli Cr. 300. General Ledger: Sales, Cr. 2,213, Purchases Dr. 2,996, Returns Inwards Dr. 122, Returns Outwards Cr. 94.

10.3 Totals: Sales Book 1,570: Purchases Book 2,302: Returns Inwards Book 143: Returns Outwards Book 71. Sales Ledger: Jones Dr. 120, Smythe Dr. 95, Cr. 13, Donaldson Dr. 160, Shaw Dr. 116, Cr. 10, Rossiter Dr. 216, Ramsbottom Dr. 300, Pitt Dr. 390, Cr. 120, McDowell Dr. 64, Lean Dr. 109, Purchases Ledger: Kelly Dr. 15, Cr. 88, Carter Dr. 50, Cr. 550, MacMahon Dr. 6, Cr. 104, Cartwright Cr. 100, Greaves Cr. 200 + 144, Joiner Cr. 72, Johnson Cr. 1,000, Holt Cr. 44: General Ledger. Sales Cr. 1,570, Purchases Dr. 2,302, Returns Outwards Cr. 71, Returns Inwards Dr. 143.

11.1 Machinery: 19-2 Jan. 1 Dr. 2,000, 19-3 Jan. 1 Dr. 3,000, Jul. 1 Dr. 1,800, 19-3 Dec. 31 Cr. Balance c/d 6,800. Provision for Depreciation: 19-2 Dec. 31 Cr. 200, 19-3 Dec. 31 Cr. 590.

11.3 Balance Sheet extracts: Fixtures 31.12.19-1, cost 500 less depreciation 50 = 450, 31.12.19-2 cost 3,700 less depreciation 415 = 3,285. Machinery 31.12.19-1, cost 4,500 less depreciation 900 = 3,600, 31.12.19-2, cost 7,500 less depreciation 2,220 = 5,280.

11.5 Balance Sheet extracts: Motor Vehicles Cost 88,450 less depreciation 43,340 = 45,110: Fixtures Cost 19,500 less depreciation 8,250 = 11,250.

11.7 Motor Lorries: Dr. Bal b/f 25,050, Bank 7,000 + 7,200, Cr. Asset Disposals (B) 5,500, (A) 6,300, Balance c/d 27,450. Provision for Depreciation: Dr. Assets Disposal (B) 2,200, (A) 3,780, Balance c/d 9,290. Cr. Balance b/fwd 9,780, Profit & Loss 5,490. Asset Disposal: Dr. Motors (B) 5,500 (A) 6,300, Cr. Depreciation (B) 2,200 (A) 3,780, Cash (B) 1,350, (A) 2,925, Profit & Loss 1,545. Balance Sheet: Motors at cost 27,450 less depreciation 9,290 = 18,160.

12.1 Bad debts: Dr.: Debts written off 915, Provision c/d 642; Cr. Provision b/d 468, Profit & Loss 1,089.

12.3 19-3 Dr. Debts written off 3,720, Provision c/d 3,180, Cr. Profit & Loss 6,900.
19-4 Dr. Debts written off 3,690, Provision c/d 2,523, Cr. Provision b/d 3,180, Profit & Loss 3,033.
19-5 Dr. Debts, written off 4,862, Provision c/d 2,670, Cr. Provision b/d 2,523, Profit & Loss 5,009.
19-6 Dr. Debts, written off 3,909, Provision c/d 3,200, Cr. Provision b/d 2,670, Profit & Loss 4,439.

12.5 Trading: Dr. Stock 31,630, Purchases 60,800 less Returns Out 1,350, Carriage In 450 less Closing Stock 36,530 = Cost of Goods Sold 55,000, Gross Profit c/d 35,200. Cr. Sales 91,400 less Returns In 1,200. Profit & Loss: Dr. Salaries 5,816, Motor Expenses 1,864, Carriage Out 310. Discounts Allowed 309, Rent

& Rates 810, Insurance 160, Bad Debts 1,516, Provision for Bad Debts 75, Depreciation, Fixtures 2,200 & Motor Vans 1,620, Net Profit 20,730, Cr. Gross Profit b/d 35,200, Discounts Received 210. Balance Sheet: Capital, Balance b/f 47,933 + Net Profit 20,730 less Drawings 7,155 = 61,508, Creditors 11,960, Expenses Owing 506. Assets: Fixtures 11,000 − Depreciation 6,600 = 4,400, Motor Vans 9,400 − Depreciation 3,980 = 5,420, Stock 36,530, Debtors 22,460 − Provision 880 = 21,580, Prepayment 44, bank 5,850, Cash 150. Totals 73,974.

14.1 Profit & Loss Appropriation: Dr. Interest on Capitals, Williams 2,000, Powell 1,500, Howe 900, Salaries, Powell 2000, Howe 3,500, Balance of Profits Williams 10,500, Powell 6,300, Howe 4,200. Cr. Net Profit b/d 30,350, Interest on Drawings, Williams 240, Powell 180, Howe 130. Balance Sheet: Capitals Williams 40,000, Powell 30,000, Howe 18,000. Closing balances on current accounts, Williams 4,920, Powell 3,466, Howe 2,287.

14.3 Trading: Dr. Stock 41,979 add Purchases 85,416, less Closing Stock 56,340 = Cost of Goods Sold 71,055, Gross Profit c/d 52,595, Cr. Sales 123,650. Profit & Loss: Dr. Salaries 19,117, Office Expenses 2,512. Carriage outwards 1,288, Discounts Allowed 115, Bad Debts 503, Loan Interest 4,000 Depreciation 770, Net Profit c/d 24,370, Cr. Gross Profit b/d 52,595, Reduction in provision for bad debts 80. Appropriation: Dr. Interest on Capitals, Melton 3,500, Mowbray 2,950, Salary Melton 800, Balance of Profits, Melton 8,710, Mowbray 8,710, Cr. Net Profit b/d 24,370, Interest on Drawings, Melton 180, Mowbray 120. Balance Sheet: Capitals, Melton 35,000, Mowbray 29,500. Current Accounts, Melton 7,736. Mowbray 6,188. Loan 40,000, Creditors 11,150, Expenses owing 296 = Totals 129,870. Assets, Buildings 50,000, Fixtures 11,000 less depreciation 4,070 = 6,930, Stock 56,340. Debtors less provision 15,923, Bank 677.

14.5 Trading: Dr. Opening Stock 42,850 + Purchases 137,190 + Carriage In 1,500 less Closing Stock 51,060 = Cost of Goods sold 130,480. Gross Profit 73,220. Sales 210,500 − Returns Inwards 6,800. Profit & Loss: Dr. Salaries 18,396, Motor Expenses 3,940, Postages 2,260, Discounts Allowed 110, Rent 2,445, Bad Debts 1,234, B. D. Provision 70, General Expenses 945, Depreciation: M. Vans 1,660, Equipment 1,140. Net Profit c/d 41,020, Cr. Gross Profit 73,220, Appropriation: Dr. Interest on Capital M 3,000, W 1,600, G 1,200, Salaries W 1,200, G 700, Profits M 16,860, W 10,116, G. 6,744. Cr. Net Profit 41,020, Interest on Drawings M 170, W 110, G 120. Balance Sheet: Capitals M 30,000, W 16,000, G 12,000. Current M 8,470, W 4,336, G 4,382, Creditors 24,356. Totals 99,544. Assets: Fixed, Equipment 8,400 less Depreciation 3,840. Motor Vans 12,500 less Depreciation 5,860, Current: Stock 51,060, Debtors less provision 36,308, Prepayments 310, Bank 666.

Because of the complicated provisions of the Companies Act 1981 questions to Chapter 15 have now been deleted.
Your lecturer will supply any appropriate questions which may be needed.

16.1 Gross Profit as % of Sales 19-1 50% 19-2 40% 19-3 60%.
Net Profit as % Sales 19-1 25% 19-2 18.4% 19-3 32.7%.

At Gross Profit comment on wide fluctuations in Stock in Trade levels and Purchases. Also mention possibility of price changes, theft or mistake.

At Net Profit note changes in selling expense levels:-

	19-1 %	19-2 %	19-3 %
Administration	10	10	10
Selling	15	11.6	17.3

16.3 19 × 1 Sales 500,000, Opening Stock in Trade 80,000, Purchases 290,000 less Closing Stock 120,000. Cost of Goods sold 250,000. Gross Profit 250,000. 19 × 2. Sales 600,000 Opening Stock in Trade 120,000 Purchases 360,000, Sub Total 480,000 less Goods destroyed 5000 Closing Stock 130,000. Cost of Goods Sold 345,000 Gross Profit 255,000.

16.5 Using 19-1 as base year 19-2 and 19-3 can be explained as percentages. This shows changes over five years. It may also be useful to split the figures as a percentage of revenue.

	19-1 %	19-2 %	19-3 %	19-1 %	19-2 %	19-3 %
Fees from hire of facilities	100	104	110	83	79	76
Fees from hire of equipment	100	150	217	10	14	18
Receipts from vending machines	100	112	115	7	7	6
	100	109	121	100	100	100
Salaries & Wages	100	110	127	133	134	140
Heating & Lighting	100	115	130	33	35	36
Repairs & Maintenance Buildings	100	80	60	8	6	4
Equipment	100	110	50	2	2	1
Goods for vending	100	75	97	5	3	4
Telephone etc.	100	117	136	12	12	13
Advertising	100	33	17	5	2	1
	100	107	121	198	194	199

Comment on high levels of increase in Salaries and Wages, Heating & Lighting and Telephone etc. over the three years. Also note the very high proportion of costs associated with salaries and wages and also heat and light. These two areas of cost appear crucial.

16.7 Sales divided by:-

		19-1	19-2	19-3
Land and buildings	A	17.5	15.6	15.7
	Q	n/a	n/a	n/a
Plant and Machinery	A	6.8	6.2	5.4
	Q	12.18	14.9	14.8
Motor Vehicles	A	25.2	25.9	25.5
	Q	40.6	39.1	37.8
Fixtures and Fitting	A	117.8	103.9	99.5
	Q	54.1	44.1	68.0
Stock in Trade	A	21.8	20.1	17.7
	Q	12.0	14.2	14.5
Trade Debtors	A	35.3	32.8	30.0
	Q	39.9	34.0	33.0
Cash at Bank	A	147.2	233.7	171.8
	Q	60.9	142.2	226.7
Total Fixed Assets	A	4.0	3.7	3.3
	Q	8.0	8.7	9.2
Total Current Assets	A	12.4	11.8	10.4
	Q	8.0	9.4	9.6
Total Assets	A	3.0	2.8	2.5
	Q	4.0	4.5	4.7

Comment on major importance of fact that Quickbean does not own Land and Buildings, but in addition gets more sales from investment in Plant and Motor Vehicles. However at Current Asset level Agrobeans seems to do better.

17.1 a) -17. c) -504. e) 936. g) 5.

17.3 a) 23. c) -1. e) 8.

17.4 a) 36. c) -2. e) -2.

18.2 a) 5. c) 7. e) 23. g) 14. i) 108.

18.4 a) 16. c) 27. e) 16,384 (i.e. 4^7).

18.5 a) 3.000. c) 2.000. e) 2.000.

19.1 a) 1.23×10^{-4}. c) 1.0×10^{-3}. e) 5.97×10^{-3}.

19.3 a) £3425.65.

19.5 a) 0.069. c) 350.28. e) 15.6864. g) 19.47. i) 30.9.

20.1 a) 1.4972. c) $\bar{2}$ .4972.

20.3 a) 0.5882. c) 1.8184. e) $\bar{1}$ .9461.

20.5 a) 1.859×10^{-3}. c) 3.957. e) 28.18.

20.7 1.099×10^{12}, 5.149×10^8.

21.3 The following can be converted: a), b), d), e).

21.4 a) 0.625. b) 0.6. c) 0.77$\dot{7}$. d) 0.56. e) 0.4.

21.5 a) $\frac{3}{8}$. c) $1\frac{7}{20}$. e) $49\frac{489}{500}$

21.6 a) $1\frac{2}{45}$. c) $\frac{1}{6}$.

21.7 a) $4\frac{5}{6}$. c) 1.

22.1 a) $\frac{1}{9}$. b) $\frac{1}{64}$. c) 4.

22.2 a) 81. b) 31622.776. c) 64.

22.4 a) 0.184. c) 1.18×10^{-2}.

22.5 b) 7.547. d) 0.5338.

23.1 Selling price = £3.55, 20%.

23.3 Tom: £81,672. Dick: £68,060. Harry: £54,448.

23.5 £1,768.93.

23.7 9 years.

24.2 $X - T = N, X = N + T, X - N = T, X - T - N = O.$

24.3 $N = \frac{T}{A}, T = NA.$

24.4 $S = P - R, P = R + S, R = P - S, P - S - R = O.$

25.1 a) $x = 1$. b) $x = 4$. c) $x = 2$.

25.3 3.5 km.

25.5 37.

26.3 Negative coefficient: slopes down from left to right.

26.5 Variable = £1.50 per unit. Fixed costs = £2,350.

27.9

Life (hours)	No. of bulbs
650 and under 660	2
660 –	5
670 –	6
680 –	14
690 –	26
700 –	18
710 –	13
720 –	10
730 –	3
740 –	3
	100

30.3 Median = 2.72, Mean = 2.48.

30.5 Mean = £1,451.50.
assume final group is £30 and under £40
assumed mean = £17.50, c = 5
$\Sigma f = 376$, (hundreds) $\Sigma fd = -224.5$ (hundreds)

30.7 Assuming employment starts at 18, and retirement age is 65 years, $\bar{x} = 43.16$ years.

30.10 Frequencies are 7, 16, 12, 11, 10, 4
$\Sigma f = 60$,
If assumed mean is 549.5 and if C = 20
$\Sigma fd = 13m$ $\bar{x} = 553,83$ miles.

30.11 Factory A, 27.23 years, Factory B, 37.09 years.

30.14 Median = 84p Mode = 76.9p
assumed mean of 75 and C = 10
$\Sigma f = 395$ $\Sigma fd = 453$, $\bar{x} = 86.47$.

31.3 Simple index = 200, weighted index = 194.4.

31.5 $x = 121$, Index = 166.9.

31.7 $\Sigma p_0 q_0 = 1913$ $\Sigma p_1 q_0 = 1923$ Price index (1974 = 100) = 100.5

31.9

	1967	1968	1969	1970	1971
Group 1	100	106	113	122	128
Group 2	100	102	106	107	110

Answers to Revisionary Assignments

17a (a) 11015. (b) 9952. (c) 19390. (d) 28854. (e) 34199.

17c (a) 46.7486. (b) 40.543. (c) 63.7137. (d) 1440.343.

17e (a) 1762.5. (b) 178.56. (c) 2960.2. (d) 2686.5. (e) 2775. (f) 411.68. (g) 2609.65. (h) 5790.9.

17g (a) 1.2. (b) 12.3. (c) 5.2. (d) 37.4. (e) 1.12. (f) 0.21. (g) 1.21. (h) 3.2. (i) 7.8. (j) 80.4. (k) 112. (l) 5.09.

17i (a) $1^1/_{30}$. (b) $1^{11}/_{12}$. (c) $1^{11}/_{12}$. (d) $2\frac{2}{3}$. (e) $3^7/_{12}$. (f) $^7/_{12}$. (g) $3^{11}/_{12}$.

17k Milometer reads 11963.6.
   130 litres of petrol bought
   Journey took 38.4 hrs.
   French car does 35.16 m.p.g.

18a (a) 0.48. (b) 0.28125. (c) 0.859375. (d) 0.785. (e) 0.65625.

18c (a) $^3/_{250}$. (b) $26\frac{3}{8}$. (c) $^{183}/_{50,000}$. (d) $^{21}/_{32}$. (e) $^{113}/_{2,000}$. (f) $\frac{1}{4}$.

18e (a) $^3/_{32}$ 0.09375. (b) $6^1/_{20}$ 6.05. (c) $^{197}/_{200}$ 0.985. (d) $^{50}/_{91}$ 0.5495.

18g Gazette approx. $^1/_{16}$ 0.0657.
   News approx. $^1/_9$ 0.1096.   Times approx. $^3/_{11}$ 0.2849.
   Journal approx. $\frac{1}{8}$ 0.1207.   Express approx. $^4/_{17}$ 0.4191.

18i 0.3353.

19a (a) 35.71%. (b) 36.36%. (c) 30.43%. (d) 20% of profit = 4.1.

19c Debtors as % of turnover
               Smith Ltd 15%   Jones Ltd 8%   Brown Ltd 2.5%

19e (a) 9%. (b) 12%.

20a (a) 3.26×10^5. (b) 4.271×10^6. (c) 3.67×10^{-2}. (d) 1.372×10^1. (e) 2.78×10^{-4}.

20c (a) 5.73×10^2. (b) 5.106×10^4. (c) 1.37×10^3. (d) 4.507×10^4. (e) 1.246×10^6. (f) 1.2×10^0. (g) 1.2×10^{-1}.

20e (a) 1163. (b) 125,000. (c) 3.694. (d) 659.5.

20g (a) 36.85. (b) 385.6. (c) 111.1. (d) 0.1924. (e) 0.05244. (f) 0.004427.

20i (a) 16. (b) $\frac{1}{2}$. (c) 7.477.

21a (a) -3. (b) 40. (c) 4.

21b (a) -6. (b) $^{-39}/_{29}$. (c) $^{-6}/_{25}$.

21d (a) $^1/_{11}$. (b) ∞ (horizontal straight line). (c) -1. (d) $\frac{1}{8}$.

21e $\dfrac{7x}{2} + 4 (1200 - x) = 4{,}400$ (if x invested at $3\frac{1}{2}$%).

                 x = 800
          so £800 invested at $3\frac{1}{2}$%
               £400 invested at 4%.

21g $1.25x + 400 - x = 475$ (x is number of men)
               x = 300

21i If $x > 130$ then to break even
                 $2583 + 16.6x = 300 + 14.1x$
   In which case, x would be negative, so $x < 130$
                 $100 + 19.1x = 300 + 14.1x$
                 x = 40

Index